S0-BZB-272

ZECHARIAH 9–14 AND MALACHI

THE OLD TESTAMENT LIBRARY

Editorial Advisory Board

JAMES L. MAYS
CAROL A. NEWSOM
DAVID L. PETERSEN

David L. Petersen

ZECHARIAH 9–14 AND MALACHI

A Commentary

 Westminster John Knox Press
Louisville, Kentucky

BS
1665.3
.P48
1995

© 1995 David L. Petersen

All rights reserved. No part of this book may be reproduced or transmitted in any form or by any means, electronic or mechanical, including photocopying, recording, or by any information storage or retrieval system, without permission in writing from the publisher. For information, address Westminster John Knox Press, 100 Witherspoon Street, Louisville, Kentucky 40202-1396.

Scripture quotations from the New Revised Standard Version of the Bible are copyright © 1989 by the Division of Christian Education of the National Council of the Churches of Christ in the U.S.A. and are used by permission. (Alterations to NRSV quotations, where used, have been made by the author.)

Book design by Drew Stevens

First edition

Published by Westminster John Knox Press
Louisville, Kentucky

This book is printed on acid-free paper that meets the American National Standards Institute Z39.48 standard. ∞

PRINTED IN THE UNITED STATES OF AMERICA

95 96 97 98 99 00 01 02 03 04—10 9 8 7 6 5 4 3 2 1

Library of Congress Cataloging-in-Publication Data

Petersen, David L.
    Zechariah 9–14 and Malachi : a commentary / David L. Petersen. — 1st ed.
       p.   cm. — (Old Testament library)
    Includes bibliographical references.
    ISBN 0-664-21298-0 (alk. paper)
    1. Bible. O.T. Zechariah IX–XIV—Commentaries. 2. Bible. O.T. Malachi— Commentaries. I. Bible. O.T. Zechariah, IX–XIV. English. 1995. II. Bible. O.T. Malachi. English. 1995. III. Title. IV. Title: Zechariah nine fourteen and Malachi. V. Series.
BS1665.3.P48   1995
224'.9806—dc20   94-43410

CONTENTS

ZECHARIAH 12–14
THE SECOND "ORACLE"

MALACHI
THE THIRD "ORACLE"

PREFACE

This commentary complements an earlier volume that appeared in The Old Testament Library, *Haggai and Zechariah 1–8,* though it must be said that the interpretive problems presented in that former project are considerably different from those posed by Zechariah 9–14 and Malachi.

Commentaries on this literature continue to appear in what might seem to be surprising numbers. After this manuscript had been virtually completed, the Anchor Bible volume on Zechariah 9–14 and the ATD commentary on Zechariah and Malachi appeared. I regret that I have been unable to benefit from this research. One may hope such industry will provide readers with appropriately complementary and diverse resources for biblical study.

Biblical quotations are taken from the NRSV unless they represent my own translations.

I would offer specific thanks to the National Endowment for the Humanities for a fellowship that supported much of this research and writing, to the Iliff School of Theology for various forms of important support, for the collegiality of Kent Richards, particularly regarding Persian-period matters, to Russell Fuller for allowing me to consult a prepublication form of 4QXII^a, and for the considerable help of Susan Brayford and Sandra Smith.

ABBREVIATIONS

BZAW	Beihefte zur Zeitschrift für die alttestamentliche Wissenschaft
CAH	*Cambridge Ancient History*
CAP	A. E. Cowley, *Aramaic Papyri of the Fifth Century B.C.,* Oxford, 1923
CAT	Commentaire de l'Ancien Testament
CBC	Cambridge Bible Commentary on the New English Bible
CBQ	*Catholic Biblical Quarterly*
CTA	A. Herdner, *Corpus des tablettes en cunéiformes alphabétiques*
DTT	*Dansk teologisk tidsskrift*
E	English (where verse enumeration differs from the Hebrew)
Ebib	Etudes bibliques
EI	*Eretz Israel*
ETL	*Ephemerides theologicae lovanienses*
EvT	*Evangelische Theologie*
FTS	Freiburger Theologische Studien
GKC	*Gesenius' Hebrew Grammar,* ed. E. Kautzsch, tr. A. E. Cowley; 2d ed. Oxford, 1910
GNB	Good News Bible
HAR	*Hebrew Annual Review*
HAT	Handbuch zum Alten Testament
HBD	*Harper's Bible Dictionary,* ed. P. Achtemeier et al.
Hebr	Hebrew Text
HSM	Harvard Semitic Monographs
ICC	International Critical Commentary
IDB	*Interpreter's Dictionary of the Bible,* ed. G. A. Buttrick
IEJ	*Israel Exploration Journal*
Int	*Interpretation*
IR	*The Iliff Review*
JANESCU	*Journal of the Ancient Near Eastern Society of Columbia University*
JAOS	*Journal of the American Oriental Society*
JBL	*Journal of Biblical Literature*
JETS	*Journal of the Evangelical Theological Society*
JNES	*Journal of Near Eastern Studies*
JNSL	*Journal of Northwest Semitic Languages*
JPS	Jewish Publication Society (= *Tanakh*)
JSOT	*Journal for the Study of the Old Testament*
JSOTSup	Journal for the Study of the Old Testament Supplement Series
JTS	*Journal of Theological Studies*
KAT	Kommentar zum Alten Testament
LXX	Septuagint
MT	Masoretic Text
NAB	New American Bible

NASB	New American Standard Bible
NEB	New English Bible
NICOT	New International Commentary on the Old Testament
NIV	New International Version
NRSV	New Revised Standard Version
OBO	Orbis biblicus et orientalis
OT	Old Testament
OTL	Old Testament Library
PEQ	*Palestine Exploration Quarterly*
PJ	*Palästina-Jahrbuch*
QMIA	Qedem, Monographs of the Institute of Archaeology, Hebrew University
RB	*Revue biblique,* Paris
RBibIt	*Rivista Biblica Italiania*
REB	Revised English Bible
RefTR	*Reformed Theological Review,* Melbourne
RSV	Revised Standard Version
S	Syriac
SB	Sources bibliques
SBLDS	Society of Biblical Literature Dissertation Series
SBLMS	Society of Biblical Literature Monograph Series
SBT	Studies in Biblical Theology
ST	*Studia Theologica*
SwJT	*Southwestern Journal of Theology*
T	Targum
Tanakh	A New Translation of The Holy Scriptures according to the Traditional Hebrew Text, Jewish Publication Society, 1985
TDOT	*Theological Dictionary of the Old Testament,* ed. G. J. Botterweck and H. Ringgren, Grand Rapids, 1977–
TE	*Theologia Evangelica*
TOTC	Tyndale Old Testament Commentary
TWAT	*Theologisches Wörterbuch zum Alten Testament,* ed. G. J. Botterweck, H. Ringgren, and H. Fabry
TynBul	*Tyndale Bulletin*
UF	*Ugarit-Forschungen*
UT	C. H. Gordon, *Ugaritic Textbook*
V	Vulgate
VT	*Vetus Testamentum*
VTSup	Vetus Testamentum Supplements
WBC	World Bible Commentary
WMANT	Wissenschaftliche Monographien zum Alten und Neuen Testament
ZAW	*Zeitschrift für die alttestamentliche Wissenschaft*

SELECT BIBLIOGRAPHY

I. *Commentaries in Series*

Baldwin, J. *Haggai, Zechariah, Malachi,* TOTC, London, 1972.

Blenkinsopp, J. *Ezra-Nehemiah,* OTL, Philadelphia, 1988.

Chary, T. *Aggée–Zacharie–Malachie,* SB, Paris, 1969.

Elliger, K. *Das Buch der zwölf kleinen Propheten, II,* ATD 25, Göttingen, 1964.

Horst, F. *Die zwölf kleinen Propheten: Nahum bis Maleachi,* HAT 14, Tübingen, 1964.

Lacocque, A. *Zacharie 9–14,* CAT XIc, Neuchâtel, 1981.

Mason, R. *The Books of Haggai, Zechariah, and Malachi,* CBC, Cambridge, 1977.

Meyers, C., and E. Meyers. *Haggai and Zechariah 1–8.* AB 25B, Garden City, 1987.

———. *Zechariah 9–14,* AB 25C, New York, 1993.

Mitchell, H. *A Critical and Exegetical Commentary on Haggai and Zechariah,* ICC, Edinburgh, 1912.

Petersen, D. *Haggai and Zechariah 1–8,* OTL, Philadelphia, 1984.

Reventlow, H. *Die Propheten Haggai, Sacharja, und Maleachi,* ATD 25,2, Göttingen, 1993.

Rudolph, W. *Haggai—Sacharja 1–8—Sacharja 9–14—Maleachi,* KAT XIII 4, Gütersloh, 1976.

Sellin, E. *Das Zwölfprophetenbuch: Nahum–Maleachi,* KAT XII, Leipzig, 1930.

Smith, H. *A Critical and Exegetical Commentary on the Book of Malachi,* ICC, Edinburgh, 1912.

Smith, R. *Micah–Malachi,* WBC 32, Waco, Tex., 1984.

Verhoef, P. *The Books of Haggai and Malachi,* NICOT, Grand Rapids, 1987.

Veuilleumier, R. *Malachie,* CAT XIc, Neuchâtel, 1981.

van der Woude, A. S. *Haggai, Maleachi,* De Prediking van het Oude Testament, Nijkerk, 1982.

———. *Zacharie,* De Prediking van het Oude Testament, Nijkerk, 1984.

II. *Monographs*

Ackroyd, P. *Exile and Restoration: A Study of Hebrew Thought in the Sixth Century B.C.*, OTL, Philadelphia, 1968.

Avigad, N. *Bullae and Seals from a Post-Exilic Judean Archive*, QMIA 4, Jerusalem, 1976.

Avi-Yonah, M. *The Holy Land from the Persian to the Arab Conquests (536 B.C. to A.D. 640): A Historical Geography*, Grand Rapids, 1966.

Bič, M. *Das Buch Sacharja*, Berlin, 1962.

Blake, R. *The Rhetoric of Malachi*, New York, 1988.

Blenkinsopp, J. *A History of Prophecy in Israel*, Philadelphia, 1983.

Bulmerincq, A. von. *Der Ausspruch über Edom im Buche Maleachi*, Dorpat, 1906.

———. *Der Prophet Maleachi*, 2 vols., Dorpat, 1926; Tartu, 1932.

Butterworth, M. *Structure and the Book of Zechariah*, JSOTSup 130, Sheffield, 1992.

The Cambridge History of Iran, vol. 2: *The Median and Achaemenian Periods*, ed. I. Gershevitch, Cambridge, 1985.

Coggins, R. *Haggai, Zechariah, Malachi*, Sheffield, 1987.

Cook, J. *The Persian Empire*, New York, 1983.

Cowley, A. *Aramaic Papyri of the Fifth Century B.C.*, Oxford, 1923.

Davies, P., ed. *Second Temple Studies*, vol. 1: *Persian Period*, JSOTSup 117, Sheffield, 1991.

Eskenazi, T., and K. Richards, eds. *Second Temple Studies*, vol. 2: *Temple and Community in the Persian Period*, JSOTSup 175, Sheffield, 1994.

Galling, K. *Studien zur Geschichte Israels im persischen Zeitalter*, Tübingen, 1964.

———. *Syrien in der Politik der Achaemeniden bis zum Aufstand des Megabyzos 448 v. Chr.*, Leipzig, 1937.

Glazier-McDonald, B. *Malachi: The Divine Messenger*, SBLDS 98, Atlanta, 1987.

Hanson, P. *The Dawn of Apocalyptic*, Philadelphia, 1975.

Hoglund, K. *Achaemenid Imperial Administration in Syria-Palestine and the Missions of Ezra and Nehemiah*, SBLDS 125, Atlanta, 1992.

House, P. *The Unity of the Twelve*, BLS 127, Sheffield, 1990.

Jansma, T. *Inquiry into the Hebrew Text and Ancient Versions of Zechariah IX–XIV*, Leiden, 1949.

Kreissig, H. *Die sozialökonomische Situation in Juda zur Achämenidenzeit*, Berlin, 1973.

Lamarche, P. *Zacharie IX–XIV: Structure litteraire et Messianisme*, Ebib, Paris, 1961.

Lutz, H.-M. *Jahwe, Jerusalem und die Völker: Zur Vorgeschichte von Sach*

12,1–8 und 14,1–5, Neukirchen-Vluyn, 1968.

Mason, R. *Preaching the Tradition: Homily and Hermeneutics after the Exile,* Cambridge, 1990.

———. *The Use of Earlier Biblical Material in Zechariah IX–XIV: A Study in Inner Biblical Exegesis,* London, 1973.

Nogalski, J. *Redactional Layers and Intentions Uniting the Writings of the Book of the Twelve,* Zurich, 1991.

O'Brien, J. *Priest and Levite in Malachi,* SBLDS 121, Atlanta, 1990.

Otzen, B. *Studien über Deuterosacharja,* ATDan 6, Copenhagen, 1964.

Person, R. *Deuteronomic Redaction in the Postexilic Period: A Study of Second Zechariah,* Chapel Hill, N.C., 1991.

Petersen, D. *Late Israelite Prophecy: Studies in Deutero-Prophetic Literature and in Chronicles,* SBLMS 23, Missoula, Mont., 1977.

Plöger, O. *Theocracy and Eschatology,* Richmond, 1968.

Renker, A. *Die Tora bei Maleachi,* FTS 112, Freiburg, 1979.

Reynolds, C. *Malachi and the Priesthood,* New Haven, Conn., 1993.

Saebo, M. *Sacharja 9–14: Untersuchungen von Text und Form,* WMANT 34, Neukirchen-Vluyn, 1969.

Steck, O. *Der Abschluss der Prophetie im Alten Testament: Ein Versuch zur Frage der Vorgeschichte des Kanons,* BTS 17, Neukirchen-Vluyn, 1991.

Stern, E. *Material Culture of the Land of the Bible in the Persian Period 538–332 B.C.,* Warminster, 1982.

Utzschneider, H. *Künder oder Schreiber? Eine These zum Problem der "Schriftprophetie" auf Grund von Maleachi 1,6–2,9,* Frankfurt, 1989.

Willi-Plein, I. *Prophetie am Ende: Untersuchungen zur Sacharja 9–14,* BBB 42, Cologne, 1974.

III. *Articles or Chapters*

Ackroyd, P. "Archaeology, Politics, and Religion: The Persian Period," *IR* 39 (1982): 5–24.

Alt, A. "Die Rolle Samarias bei der Entstehung des Judentums," *Kleine Schriften zur Geschichte des Volkes Israels,* Munich (1964): 316–37.

Althann, R. "Malachy 2:13–14 and UT 125,12–13," *Bib* 58 (1977): 418–21.

Avi-Yonah, M. "The Walls of Nehemiah: A Minimalist View," *IEJ* 4 (1954): 239–48.

Baldwin, J. "Malachi 1:11 and the Worship of the Nations in the Old Testament," *TynBul* 23 (1972): 117–24.

Berquist, J. "The Social Setting of Malachi," *BTB* 19 (1989): 121–26.

Betlyon, J. "The Provincial Government of Persian Period Judea and the Yehud Coins," *JBL* 105 (1986): 633–42.

Blenkinsopp, J. "A Jewish Sect of the Persian Period," *CBQ* 52 (1990): 5–20.

―――. "The Mission of Udjahorresnet and Those of Ezra and Nehemiah," *JBL* 106 (1987): 409–21.

―――. "Temple and Society in Achaemenid Judah," *Second Temple Studies,* vol. 1: *Persian Period,* ed. P. Davies, JSOTSup 117, Sheffield, 1991, 22–53.

Boecker, H.-J., "Bermerkungen zur formgeschichtlichen Terminologie des Buches Maleachi," *ZAW* 78 (1966): 78–80.

Bosshard, E. "Beobachtungen zum Zwölfprophetenbuch," *BN* 40 (1987): 30–62.

Bosshard, E., and Kratz, R. "Maleachi im Zwölfprophetenbuch," *BN* 52 (1990): 27–46.

Botterweck, J. "Ideal und Wirklichkeit der Jerusalemer Priester: Auslegung von Mal 1,6–10; 2:1–9," *BibLeb* 1 (1960): 100–109.

―――. "Jakob habe ich lieb—Esau hasse ich: Auslegung von Malachias 1,2–5," *BibLeb* 1 (1960): 28–38.

―――. "Schelt- und Mahnrede gegen Mischehen und Ehescheidung: Auslegung von Mal 2,10–16," *BibLeb* 1 (1960): 179–85.

―――. "Die Sonne der Gerechtigkeit am Tage Jahwes: Auslegung von Mal 3,13–21," *BibLeb* 1 (1960): 253–60.

Budde, K. "Zum Text der drei letzten kleinen Propheten," *ZAW* 26 (1906): 1–28.

Carter, C. "The Province of Yehud in the Postexilic Period: Soundings in Site Distribution and Demography," *Second Temple Studies,* vol. 2: *Temple and Community in the Persian Period,* ed. T. Eskenazi and K. Richards, JSOTSup 175, Sheffield, 1994, 106–45.

Collins, J. "The Place of Apocalypticism in the Religion of Israel," *Ancient Israelite Religion: Essays in Honor of Frank Moore Cross,* ed. P. Miller et al., Philadelphia, 1987, 539–58.

Cook, S. "The Metamorphosis of a Shepherd: The Tradition History of Zechariah 11:17 + 13:7–9," *CBQ* 55 (1993): 453–66.

Delcor, M. "Deux passages difficiles: Zach XII 11 et XI 13," *VT* 3 (1953): 67–77.

―――. "Les sources du Deutéro-Zacharie et ses precédés d'emprunt," *RB* 59 (1952): 385–411.

―――. "Un problème du critique textuelle et d'exégèse: Zach 12.10 et aspicient ad me quem confixerunt," *RB* 58 (1951): 189–99.

Devescovi, U. "L'alleanza di Jahvé con Levi (Mal 2,1–9)," *BibO* 4 (1962): 205–18.

Dion, P. "The Civic-and-Temple Community of Persian Period Judah: Neglected Insights from Eastern Europe," *JNES* 50 (1991): 281–87.

Duhm, B. "Anmerkungen zu den Zwölf Propheten," *ZAW* 31 (1911): 1–43, 81–110, 161–204.

Dumbrell, W. "Malachi and the Ezra-Nehemiah Reforms," *RefTR* 35 (1976): 42–52.

Eckart, R. "Der Sprachgebrauch von Zach. 9–14," *ZAW* 13 (1893): 76–109.

Elayi, J. "The Phoenician Cities in the Persian Period," *JANESCU* 12 (1980): 13–28.

———. "Studies in Phoenician Geography during the Persian Period," *JNES* 41 (1982): 83–110.

Elliger, K. "Ein Zeugnis aus der jüdischen Gemeinde im Alexanderjahr 332 v. Chr.: Eine territorialgeschichtliche Studie zu Sach 9:1–8," *ZAW* 62 (1950): 63–115.

Eph'al, I. "Syria-Palestine under Achaemenid Rule," *Persia, Greece and the Western Mediterranean c.525–479 B.C.*, *CAH*, vol. 4, Cambridge, 1988, 139–64.

Eybers, I. "Malachi—the Messenger of the Lord," *TE* 3 (1970): 12–20.

Feigin, S. "Some Notes on Zechariah 11:4–17," *JBL* 44 (1925): 203–13.

Finley, T. "The Sheep Merchants of Zechariah 11," *Grace Theological Journal* 3 (1982): 51–65.

Fischer, J. "Notes on the Literary Form and Message of Malachi," *CBQ* 34 (1972): 315–20.

Fishbane, M. "Form and Reformulation of the Biblical Priestly Blessing," *JAOS* 103 (1983): 115–21.

Freedman, D. "An Unnoted Support for a Variant to the MT of Mal 3:5," *JBL* 98 (1979): 405–6.

Fuller, R. "Text-Critical Problems in Malachi 2:10–16," *JBL* 110 (1991): 47–57.

Galling, K. "Denkmäler zur Geschichte Syriens und Palästinas unter Herrschaft der Perser," *PJ* 34 (1938): 59–79.

Gelin, A. "Message aux prêtres," *BVC* 30 (1959): 14–20.

Gese, H. "Nachtrag: Die Deutung der Hirtenallegorie, Sach 11:4ff," *Von Sinai zum Sion: Alttestamentliche Beiträge zur biblischen Theologie*, BEvT 64, Munich, 1974, 231–38.

Glazier-McDonald, B. "Intermarriage, Divorce and the *bat-'ēl nēkār*," *JBL* 106 (1987): 603–11.

———. "Malachi 2:12: *'ēr wĕ'ōneh*—Another Look," *JBL* 105 (1986): 295–98.

———. "*Mal'āk habbĕrît*: the Messenger of the Covenant in Mal 3:1," *HAR* 11 (1987): 93–104.

Gordon, R. "Inscribed Pots and Zechariah 14:20–21," *VT* 42 (1992): 120–23.

Greenberg, M. "Hebrew *sĕgullah*: Akkadian *sikiltu*," *JAOS* 71 (1951): 172–74.

Greenfield, J. "Two Biblical Passages in the Light of Their Near Eastern Background—Ezekiel 16:30 and Malachi 3:17," *EI* (1982): 56–61.

Hanson, P. "Zechariah 9 and the Recapitulation of an Ancient Ritual Pattern," *JBL* 92 (1973): 37–59.

Harrelson, W. "The Celebration of the Feast of Booths according to Zech 14: 16–21," *Religions in Antiquity: Essays in Memory of Erwin Ramsdell Goode-nough*, ed. J. Neusner, Supplements to Numen 14, Leiden, 1968, 88–96.

Hartmann, B. "Mögen die Götter dich behüten und unversehrt bewahren," *Hebräische Wortforschung: Festschrift zum 80. Geburtstag von Walter Baumgartner*, ed. B. Hartmann et al., VTSup 16, Leiden (1967): 102–5.

Hill, A. "Dating Second Zechariah: A Linguistic Reexamination," *HAR* 6 (1982): 105–34.

————. "Dating the Book of Malachi: A Linguistic Reexamination," *The Word of the Lord Shall Go Forth: Essays in Honor of D. N. Freedman in Celebration of His Sixtieth Birthday*, ed. C. Meyers and M. O'Connor, Winona Lake, Ind., 1983, 77–89.

Hoftizer, J. "A propos d'une interprétation récent de deux passages difficiles: Zech 12.11 et Zech 11.13," *VT* 3 (1953): 407–9.

Hoglund, K. "The Achaemenid Context," *Second Temple Studies*, vol. 1: *Persian Period*, ed. P. Davies, JSOTSup 117, Sheffield, 1991, 54–72.

van Hoonacker, A. "Le rapprochement entre le Deutéronome et Malachie," *ETL* 59 (1983): 86–90.

Jones, D. "A Fresh Interpretation of Zechariah 9–14," *VT* 12 (1962): 241–59.

————. "A Note on the LXX of Malachi 2:16," *JBL* 109 (1990): 683–85.

Katzenstein, H. "Gaza in the Persian Period," *Transeuphratene* 1 (1989): 67–87.

————. "Tyre in the Early Persian Period (539–486 B.C.E.)," *BA* 42 (1979): 23–34.

Kruse-Blinkenberg, L. "Joededommen i den persiske tidsalder i lys af Mal-eachis bog," *DTT* 28 (1965): 80–99.

Kuhrt, A. "The Cyrus Cylinder and Achaemenid Imperial Policy," *JSOT* 25 (1983): 83–97.

Lescow, T. "Dialogische Strukturen in den Streitreden des Buches Maleachi," *ZAW* 102 (1990): 194–212.

Lipiński, E. "Recherches sur le livre de Zacharie," *VT* 20 (1970): 25–55.

Locher, C. "Altes und Neues zu Maleachi 2:10–16," *Mélanges Dominique Barthélemy: Etudes bibliques offertes à l'occasion de son 60e anniversaire*, ed. P. Casetti et al., OBO 38, Göttingen, 1981, 241–71.

McEvenue, S. "The Political Structure in Judah from Cyrus to Nehemiah," *CBQ* 43 (1981): 353–64.

McKenzie, S., and H. Wallace. "Covenant Themes in Malachi," *CBQ* 45 (1983): 549–63.

Malchow, B. "The Messenger of the Covenant in Mal. 3:1," *JBL* 103 (1984): 252–55.

Mason, R. "The Relation of Zech. 9–14 to Proto-Zechariah," *ZAW* 88 (1976): 227–39.

―――. "Some Examples of Inner-Biblical Exegesis in Zechariah 9–14," *ST* 7 (1982): 343–54.

Mendecki, N. "Deuterojesajanischer und ezechielischer Einfluss auf Sach 10,8.10," *Kairos* 27 (1985): 340–44.

Meyer, L. "An Allegory concerning the Monarchy: Zech 11:4–17; 13:7–9," *Scripture in History and Theology: Essays in Honor of J. Coert Rylaarsdam,* ed. A. Merrill and T. Overholt, Pittsburgh, 1977, 225–40.

Meyers, E. "The Persian Period and the Judean Restoration: From Zerubbabel to Nehemiah," *Ancient Israelite Religion: Essays in Honor of Frank Moore Cross,* ed. P. Miller et al., Philadelphia, 1987, 509–21.

―――. "Priestly Language in the Book of Malachi," *HAR* 10 (1986): 225–37.

―――. "The Shelomith Seal and the Judean Restoration: Some Additional Considerations," *EI* 18 (1985): 33–38.

Miklik, J. "Textkritische und exegetische Bermerkungen zu Mal 3,6," *BZ* 17 (1925–26): 225–37.

Mildenburg, L. "Yehud: A Preliminary Study of the Provincial Coinage of Judaea," *Greek Numismatics and Archaeology: Essays in Honor of Margaret Thompson,* ed. O. Morkholm and N. Waggoner, Wetteren, 1979, 183–96.

Murray, D. "The Rhetoric of Disputation: Re-examination of a Prophetic Genre," *JSOT* 38 (1987): 95–121.

O'Brien, J. "The Seduction of the Historians: Malachi and the (Re-)Creation of History," unpublished paper.

Ogden, G. "The Use of Figurative Language in Malachi 2:10–16," *BT* 39 (1988): 223–30.

Paul, S. "A Technical Expression from Archery in Zechariah 9:13a," *VT* 39 (1989): 495–97.

Pfeiffer, E. "Die Disputationsworte im Buche Maleachi: Ein Beitrag zur formgeschichtlichen Struktur," *EvT* 19 (1959): 546–68.

Pierce, R. "Literary Connectors and a Haggai/Zechariah/Malachi Corpus," *JETS* 27 (1984): 277–89.

―――. "A Thematic Development of the Haggai/Zechariah/Malachi Corpus," *JETS* 27 (1984): 401–11.

Power, E. "The Shepherd's Two Rods in Modern Palestine and in Some Passages of the Old Testament," *Bib* 9 (1928): 434–42.

Rainey, A. "The Satrapy 'Beyond the River,' " *AJBA* 1 (1969): 51–78.

Redditt, P. "The Book of Malachi in Its Social Setting," *CBQ* 56 (1994): 240–55.

―――. "Israel's Shepherds: Hope and Pessimism in Zechariah 9–14," *CBQ* 51 (1989): 631–42.

———. "Nehemiah's First Mission and the Date of Zechariah 9–14," *CBQ*, forthcoming.

———. "The Two Shepherds in Zechariah 11:4–17," *CBQ* 55 (1993): 676–86.

Rehm, M. "Der Friedensfürst in Zach 9,9–19," *BibLeb* 9 (1968): 164–76.

———. "Die Hirtenallegorie Zach 11,4–14," *BZ* 4 (1960): 186–208.

———. "Das Opfer der Völker nach Maleachi 1,11," *Lex tua veritas: Festschrift für Herbert Junker*, ed. H. Gross and F. Musser, Trier, 1961, 193–208.

Reiner, E. "Thirty Pieces of Silver," *JAOS* 88 (1968): 186–90.

Rudolph, W. "Zu Mal 2:10–16," *ZAW* 83 (1981): 85–90.

Saebo, M. "Die deuterosacharjanische Frage: Eine forschungsgeschichtliche Studie," *ST* 23 (1969): 115–40.

Schottroff, W. "Zur Sozialgeschichte Israels in der Perserzeit," *Verkündigung und Forschung* 27 (1982): 46–68.

Schreinger, S. "Mischehen—Ehebruch—Ehescheidung: Betrachtungen zu Mal 2.10–16," *ZAW* 91 (1979): 207–28.

Seybold, K. "Spätprophetische Hoffnungen auf die Wiederkunft des davidischen Zeitalters in Sach 9–14," *Judaica* 29 (1973): 99–111.

Smith, R. "The Shape of Theology in the Book of Malachi," *SwJT* 30 (1987): 22–27.

Snyman, S. "Antitheses in Malachi 1:2–5," *ZAW* 98 (1986): 436–38.

Stade, B. "Deuterosacharja: Eine kritische Studie," *ZAW* 1 (1881): 1–96; 2 (1882): 151–72, 275–309.

Stern, E. "The Province of Yehud: The Vision and the Reality," *The Jerusalem Cathedra: Studies in the History, Archaeology, Geography, and Ethnology of the Land of Israel*, 1, 1981, 9–21.

Stolper, M. "The Governor of Babylon and Across-the-River in 486 B.C.," *JNES* 48 (1989): 283–305.

Swetnam, J. "Malachi 1:11: An Interpretation," *CBQ* 31 (1969): 200–209.

Torrey, C. "The Prophecy of 'Malachi,' " *JBL* 17 (1898): 1–15.

———. " *'ēr wĕ'ōneh* in Mal 2:12," *JBL* 24 (1905): 176–78.

Tournay, R. "Zacarias 9–11 e a História de Israel," *Atualidades biblicas*, 1972, 331–49.

———. "Zacharie XII–XIV et l'histoire d'Israel," *RB* 81 (1974): 355–75.

Utzschneider, H. "Die Schriftprophetie und die Frage nach dem Ende der Prophetie: Überlegungen anhand von Mal 1,6–2,16," *ZAW* 104 (1992): 337–94.

Vattioni, F. "Malachia 3,20 e l'origine della giustizia in Oriente," *RBiblt* 6 (1958): 353–60.

Vriezen, T. "How to Understand Malachi 1:11," *Grace upon Grace: Essays in Honor of Lester J. Kuyper*, ed. J. Cook, Grand Rapids, 1975, 128–36.

Waldman, N. "Some Notes on Malachi 3:6; 3:13; and Psalm 42:11," *JBL* 93 (1974): 543–49.

Wallis, G. "Wesen und Struktur der Botschaft Maleachis," *Das ferne und nahe Wort: Festschrift Leonhard Rost zur Vollendung seines 70. Lebensjahres am 30. November 1966 gewidmet*, ed. F. Maass, BZAW 105, Berlin, 1967, 229–37.

Watts, J. "Introduction to the Book of Malachi," *Review and Expositor* 84 (1987): 373–81.

Weinberg, J. "Die Agrarverhältnisse in der Bürger-Tempel-Gemeinde der Achämenidenzeit," *AAASH* 22 (1974): 473–86.

————. "Das *beit 'abot* im 6.–4. Jahrhundert," *VT* 23 (1973): 400–14.

————. "Zentral- und Partikulargewalt im achämenidischen Reich," *Klio: Beiträge zur Alten Geschichte* 59 (1977): 25–43.

Wendland, E. "Linear and Concentric Patterns in Malachi," *BT* 36 (1985): 108–21.

Widengren, G. "The Persian Period," *Israelite and Judean History*, ed. J. Hayes and J. Miller, OTL, Philadelphia, 1977, 489–538.

Williamson, H. "The Governors of Judah under the Persians," *TynBul* 39 (1988): 59–82.

Wolff, H. "Der Aufruf zur Volksklage," *ZAW* 76 (1964): 48–56.

van der Woude, A. "Der Engel des Bundes: Bemerkungen zu Maleachi 3:1c und seinem Kontext," *Die Botschaft und die Boten: Festschrift für H. W. Wolff zum 70. Geburtstag*, ed. J. Jeremias and L. Perlitt, Neukirchen-Vluyn, 1981, 289–300.

————. "Die Hirtenallegorie von Sacharja XI," *JNSL* 12 (1984): 139–49.

————. "Malachi's Struggle for a Pure Community: Reflections on Mal 2:10–16," *Tradition and Reinterpretation in Jewish and Christian Literature: Essays in Honor of Jürgen C. H. Lebram*, ed. J. van Henten et al., Leiden, 1986, 65–71.

————. "Sacharja 14,18," *ZAW* 97 (1985): 254–56.

INTRODUCTION

The last nine chapters of the Old Testament (or ten in most Christian English Bible translations, which follow the Septuagint's enumeration) constitute arguably the most difficult texts for the interpreter of the Old Testament. Despite the presence of nations' names (e.g., Zech. 9:1–7), there are no obvious or readily identifiable historical events that lie behind these texts. Moreover, there is no specific individual, like a Haggai or a Zechariah, to whom the literature may be attributed. No prophetic persona glimmers behind the oracles or other rhetorical units that make up these chapters. Finally, the literature itself (e.g., Zech. 11:4–16) is, quite simply, difficult to comprehend. The imagery appears complex, often impenetrable, leaving the reader with the sense that, although the chapters may be read in English translation, they remain incomprehensible. This commentary has as its essential purpose the attempt to make some sense of these ancient canonical texts.

The reader of the Hebrew Bible, whether in its Jewish, Protestant, or Roman Catholic configurations, should be alert to the difference between the traditional ways of labeling this literature and the mode used in this commentary. Medieval Jewish manuscripts as well as modern translations provide titles for the last two books in the canon, namely, the words "Zechariah" and "Malachi" before the chapters in question. As a result, it might seem indefensible to provide a commentary on only a portion of one of those books, especially at a time when sensitivities to the final or canonical form of the text have been raised. My approach might appear even more problematic since this commentary will not treat Malachi as a separate book authored by a prophet named Malachi. However, book titles are not used in the oldest Hebrew manuscripts, such as the Isaiah scroll at Qumran. Without such titles, what we know as Zechariah and Malachi would appear quite differently than they do now, especially if we imagine these chapters to be written together on one scroll, literally, one book of the twelve so-called minor prophets. Put another way, an early form of the minor prophets may not have known a separate book of Malachi. (Sirach 49:10 is the earliest reference to "the Twelve Prophets" and refers to its Septuagint configuration.) A more detailed examination of the literature in question sustains this hypothesis.

1. The Three *maś'ôt*[1]

We must begin with the chapters known as Zechariah. After the two regnal formulae (Zech.1:1; 7:1), which mark Judean chronology with reference to the Persian emperor Darius and which belong to what I have elsewhere described as Zechariah I, the next set of stereotypic formulae that set off or segment the final portion of the minor prophets occurs in Zech. 9:1; 12:1; and Mal. 1:1. These formulae are not identical, for reasons offered below. Nonetheless, a straightforward look at the Hebrew text of these chapters, which have been organized using these formulae, does not make one think of two separate books, namely Zechariah as a book of fourteen chapters and Malachi as a book of three (or four) chapters. Nor does this formulaic organization suggest a twofold structure often presumed by the labels Deutero-Zechariah and Malachi. Rather, the formulae, as well as the material subsumed by them, point to a tripartite collection of prophetic literature.

Zechariah 9:1 through Malachi 3:24 [4:6] comprises three sections—Zech. 9:1–11:17; Zech. 12:1–14:21; and Mal. 1:1–3:24 [1:1–4:6]. Each section includes a roughly similar number of verses: forty-six, forty-four, and fifty-two verses (excluding 3:22–24 [4:4–6], on which see below). They are titled, respectively, "an oracle: the word of the Lord against the land of Hadrach" (Zech. 9:1); "an oracle: the word of the Lord against Israel" (Zech. 12:1); and "an oracle: the word of the Lord to Israel" (Mal. 1:1).[2] Both the number and the content of these formulae, as well as some of the material they subsume, present a structure apparent in other prophetic collections: oracles against the nations, oracles concerning Israel, and oracles on behalf of Israel (e.g., in Amos).[3]

There is more in these chapters than the notion of three *maś'ôt* would suggest. Malachi 3:22–24 [4:4–6] stands outside the tripartite structure I have just adumbrated. These three verses create an epilogue both to the three *maś'ôt* and to the minor prophets as a whole, an epilogue that integrates the minor prophets with the rest of the canon (see commentary). By providing such an epilogue, the author offered a claim that these books may be viewed as one book, similar in scope to the "major" prophet books, namely, Isaiah, Jeremiah, and Ezekiel.

---

[1]*maś'ôt* is the plural form of the singular noun *maśśā'*, "oracle," which appears at the beginning of Zech. 9:1; 12:1; and Mal. 1:1.

[2]See similarly I. Eybers, "Malachi—the Messenger of the Lord," *TE* 3 (1970): 12 n. 2.

[3]Such a judgment necessarily involves reservations about a peculiarly close connection between the first two "oracles," Zechariah 9–11 and 12–14, and Zechariah 1–8. Cf. R. Mason, *The Use of Earlier Biblical Material in Zechariah IX–XIV: A Study in Inner Biblical Exegesis*, London, 1973; and M. Butterworth, *Structure and the Book of Zechariah*, JSOTSup 130, Sheffield, 1992.

The presentation of Zech. 9:1–Mal. 3:24 [4:6] as three *maś'ôt* represents a Persian-period editor's decision to integrate what was originally quite distinct material.[4] There is discourse listed under the first rubric that is not an oracle against a nation (e.g., Zech. 10:1–2). And there are utterances in Malachi or the third *maśśā'* (e.g., Mal. 2:10–16) that are not oracles of weal. Hence, one senses a certain tension between the final redactional structure and the nature of the earlier material.

If this notion of a controlling tripartite structure is apt, then we should think about these concluding chapters to the Hebrew Bible as anonymous collections of divine oracles and prophetic sayings. However, since these collections follow immediately after the book attributed to him, Zechariah ben Berechiah (Zech. 1:1) becomes the "canonical" author of this material. Only later in the formation of the canon did another canonical author, someone "named" Malachi, arise (see below).

2. Historical Context

One hallmark of twentieth-century biblical scholarship has been the attempt to discern the original context in which a text was produced, and with good reason. To know something about the events and conditions that elicited a prophetic oracle enables the reader or hearer to understand something of its rhetorical force (e.g., Amos 4:1–3 and its mid-eighth-century B.C.E. context). However, some biblical literature provides little internal evidence that allows judgments of this sort (e.g., many psalms). Nonetheless, attention to form, redaction, literary features, and religious issues enables the commentator to assist the reader in understanding individual psalms.

The three "oracles" are more like Psalms than they are like Amos to the extent that they provide little internal evidence concerning the date of composition. Moreover, the search for the date of composition for these three *maś'ôt* has produced diverse results. Nonetheless, many scholars now agree that the third *maśśā'*, Malachi, derives from the early-middle Persian period. There is much less of a consensus regarding the origins of Zechariah 9–14. Nonetheless, in my judgment, all three *maś'ôt* date to the Persian period, though the evidence is stronger for Malachi than it is for Zechariah 9–11 or Zechariah 12–14.

Three important studies devoted to Zechariah illustrate the diverse chron-

---

[4]On the formulae as redactional devices, see B. Stade, "Deuterosacharja: Eine kritische Studie," *ZAW* 2 (1882): 308–9; cf. O. Steck, *Der Abschluss der Prophetie im Alten Testament: Ein Versuch zur Frage der Vorgeschichte des Kanons,* BTS 17, Neukirchen-Vluyn, 1991, 128–29, who thinks the second and third formulae were based on the first one.

ological (and literary) judgments concerning these chapters.[5] In an influential article that helped inaugurate *ZAW,* Bernhard Stade maintained that all of Zechariah 9–14 should be dated to the Hellenistic period.[6] He had discerned numerous instances in which these chapters depended on earlier prophetic texts. In addition, he argued that the reference to Greeks (Zech. 9:13) alluded to the period during which Greek control was being exercised in Syria-Palestine. Moreover, he construed nations' names in such a way that Egypt became a way of referring to the Ptolemaic kingdom and Assyria to Seleucid rule. Similarly, he maintained that Zech. 9:1–8 referred to military activity that took place c.306–278 B.C.E. Since Stade's time, attempts to place Zechariah 9–14 in a Hellenistic context have not ceased.[7]

Benedikt Otzen adopted a significantly different tack. He maintained that Zechariah 9–14 is not a literary unity. Moreover, he argued that, on both literary and historical grounds, the constituent units derive from quite different periods: Zechariah 9–10 dates to the Josianic era (c.620 B.C.E.); Zechariah 11 to just before 587 B.C.E.; Zechariah 12–13 to the early exilic period; and Zechariah 14 to the late postexilic period.[8]

Paul Hanson formulated a third line of approach. He reviewed such attempts at establishing a date by means of references outside the literature and found them fundamentally flawed. Instead, he attempted to set up a relative chronology based on formal features of the literature as well as on ideological relations to other Persian-period prophetic literature (e.g., Isaiah 56–66). In addition, Hanson offered a traditio-historical judgment that these texts belong to a transition literature, something between prophetic and apocalyptic literature. In so doing he, like Otzen, postulated different periods of origin for these chapters, but Hanson offered a more compact time frame (roughly 550–425 B.C.E.), the early Persian period.[9] Such a dating in the early to middle Persian period has won some adherents (e.g., Lacocque).[10]

In my judgment, the last of these dating schemes, though not necessarily the

---

[5]For reviews of scholarship on Deutero-Zechariah, see B. Otzen, *Studien über Deuterosacharja,* ATDan 6, Copenhagen, 1964, 11–34; M. Saebo, "Die deuterosacharjanische Frage: Eine forschungsgeschichtliche Studie," *ST* 23 (1969): 115–40; and R. Coggins, *Haggai, Zechariah, Malachi,* Sheffield, 1987.

[6]Stade, "Deuterosacharja: Eine kritische Studie," *ZAW* 1 (1881): 1–96; 2 (1882): 151–72, 275–309. The third section is devoted primarily to the issue of date.

[7]See, e.g., J. Blenkinsopp, who deems Zech. 9:1–8 to reflect Alexander's military ventures or Zech. 10:3–12 to presume Seleucid struggles, *A History of Prophecy in Israel,* Philadelphia, 1983, 260.

[8]Otzen, *Deuterosacharja,* 35–212.

[9]P. Hanson, *The Dawn of Apocalyptic,* Philadelphia, 1975, 280–401.

[10]A. Lacocque, *Zacharie 9–14,* CAT XIc, Neuchâtel, 1981, 139–44.

method, should be sustained. The numerous allusions to sixth-century biblical texts,[11] the character of the language,[12] and allusions to Achaemenid imperial structures (see commentary on Zech. 9:1–8) require dating Zechariah 9–14 to the Persian period. To make this judgment is, however, different from arguing that a particular oracle may be associated with a known event during that period. In no instance is such an identification proposed in this commentary.

Scholars have been much less reluctant to propose a date for Malachi than they have for Zechariah 9–14. However, it must be said that one may read the book and make sense of much of what is said without appeal to a specific historical context (e.g., the critique of Asherah veneration in Mal. 2:10–16). The sole worship of Yahweh was an issue at many times in Israel's history, a fact that makes this pericope intelligible even without specific comment about its date. Nonetheless, considerable evidence allows one to place this third "oracle" in the Persian period.

Many scholars have argued that Malachi most probably postdates the rebuilding of the second temple and predates the activity of Ezra and Nehemiah. A striking number of issues addressed in the third "oracle" are broached in Ezra-Nehemiah as well. For example, concern for proper ritual behavior appears in both Malachi and Ezra-Nehemiah (Neh. 8:13–18; 13:15–18). The need for both a purified priesthood and a recognized place for the Levites is attested in Malachi and in Neh. 13:28–30. And both literatures devote attention to the practice of tithing, Mal. 3:6–12 and Neh. 13:10–14.

There are other forms of evidence as well. The author of Malachi refers to the *pe ḥāh*, "governor" (Mal. 1:8), which was the term used for the ruling regional official during the Persian period. The prominence of Edom in the first diatribe would fit with what we know of the territory known as Edom during the early Persian period (see commentary below).[13] Finally, Hill has argued that the grammar of Malachi stands between classical and late Biblical Hebrew prose, thereby allowing for a date of composition in the late sixth or early fifth century B.C.E.[14] For these sorts of reasons, namely, correlations with Ezra-Nehemiah, apparent rootedness in Persian-period Judah, the character of the language in which the third "oracle" is composed, Malachi has been regularly

[11] See, e.g., N. Mendecki, "Deuterojesajanischer und ezechielischer Einfluss auf Sach 10,8.10," *Kairos* 27 (1985): 340–44.

[12] A. Hill, "Dating Second Zechariah: A Linguistic Reexamination," *HAR* 6 (1982): 105–34, argues for a date c.515–475 B.C.E.

[13] Hoglund has noted that Edom seems to have less habitation evidence after 560 B.C.E. (private communication).

[14] A. Hill, "Dating the Book of Malachi: A Linguistic Reexamination," *The Word of the Lord Shall Go Forth: Essays in Honor of D. N. Freedman in Celebration of His Sixtieth Birthday,* Winona Lake, Ind., 1983, 77–89, who opts for a range between 515 and 458 B.C.E.

dated to the late sixth or early fifth century B.C.E., a judgment with which I concur.[15]

In sum, it is reasonable to hypothesize that all three *maś'ôt* derive from the Persian period. Hence, one must devote some attention to that period and the issues it posed for those who venerated Yahweh as their God.

3. Persian-Period Yahwism

By the mid-sixth century B.C.E., Yahwists were scattered throughout the regions we now describe as the eastern Mediterranean and the ancient Near East. Yahwists lived on Cyprus, in Egypt, in Mesopotamia, in Syro-Palestinian areas other than Judah (so the Tell el-Mazar inscriptions), and, of course, in the subprovince of Judah or Judea. Yahwism or early Judaism was becoming a truly international religion.

To speak about second temple Yahwism or early Judaism risks imposing a monolithic label on what was a very diverse set of communities and practices. Yahwists worshiped in diverse settings and at multiple shrines. Moreover, certain norms of early Judaism, which may be associated with the activities of Ezra and Nehemiah, had not yet developed. There were, of course, those who gathered around the newly built temple in Jerusalem. But even there, Yahwists disagreed among themselves about the nature of the community that had arisen in the Judean subprovince of the Beyond the River satrapy (the river is the Euphrates and "Beyond" means west of that river). There was, for example, conflict about who would be eligible to participate in and officiate at temple rituals. And then, there were other Yahwists in Syria-Palestine, such as those who lived in and worshiped at Samaria and about whom we hear in Ezra-Nehemiah. Even within Syria-Palestine, there was no uniform Yahwism.

Indicative of such variety is the presence of multiple temples devoted to Yahweh. Apart from the newly rebuilt structure in Jerusalem, the best-known temple is the one erected in Elephantine. In addition, there were other temples in Syria-Palestine. Stern reports that three structures have been identified by their excavators as temples.[16] About the one at Jaffa, there is no published material. Another coastal site, Makmish, to the north of Joppa, apparently

---

[15]So the standard commentaries, W. Dumbrell, "Malachi and the Ezra-Nehemiah Reforms," *RefTR* 35 (1976): 42–52, and B. Glazier-McDonald, *Malachi: The Divine Messenger*, SBLDS 98, Atlanta, 1987, 14–18. Cf. J. O'Brien, *Priest and Levite in Malachi*, SBLDS 121, Atlanta, 1990, 113–33, who offers a judicious survey of the arguments and maintains that the book offers little explicit evidence for a date in the Persian period. See also O'Brien's more recent "The Seduction of the Historians: Malachi and the (Re-)Creation of History," unpublished paper.

[16]E. Stern, *Material Culture of the Land of the Bible in the Persian Period 538–332 B.C.*, Warminster, 1982, 61–67. Some have also argued for the existence of temples at Elliachin and at Nebi Yunis (p. 63).

housed a temple of the broad room variety (15 by 5 meters). Inland, there may have been a Persian-period temple at Lachish (Tell ed-Duweir), which would have been located in Idumaea, outside the subprovince of Judah. The excavator thought the orientation of the temple suggested veneration of the sun, hence the phrase "solar shrine." Though such a judgment appears highly speculative, it remains important to note that the shrine was located near and apparently contemporary with the "residency," a rather large structure with atrium and living quarters, which was almost certainly an administrative center and would have been in the hands of local officials.[17] The occupation of the residency has been dated to c.450–350 B.C.E. In fact, at the Lachish shrine, an amulet, probably of Horus, was found along with a limestone altar that had raised carvings.[18] Of course, one may not be certain that any of these ritual sites, apart from the one at Elephantine, was devoted to the veneration of Yahweh. However, an incense altar from Lachish inscribed with the letters *lyh,* part of Deposit 534 and roughly contemporary with the shrine, indicates that Yahweh was probably worshiped there.[19] These various forms of evidence suggest that the very notion of second temple Yahwism—whether in the Levant or beyond—is itself something of a misnomer. "Second temples Yahwism," despite the infelicitous ring, might be better.

The Elephantine texts illumine a community that calls itself *yhwdya,* which is often translated "Jews," but could probably better be rendered "Judeans." At the aforementioned temple, they venerated *yhw,* a shortened form for the name of Yahweh, as well as other deities (Anath, Bethel, Ishum, Herem). On the basis of the recently published Kuntilet Ajrud inscriptions, which apparently refer to Yahweh and "his Asherah," as well as Mal. 2:13–16, which in my judgment is an attack on the veneration of Asherah (see commentary), it is appropriate to view Elephantine practice as consistent with Yahwism as it was known in Syria-Palestine and not as a heterodox development peculiar to the diaspora. Jeremiah 44 suggests that such practice developed almost immediately after a group of refugees had settled in Egypt. They viewed their

---

[17]O. Tufnell, *Lachish III (Tell ed-Duweir): The Iron Age,* Oxford, 1953, 135. Stern summarizes the situation by observing that at many of the Persian-period sites that present major architectural remains (i.e., Hazor, Megiddo, Tel el-Far'ah, Tel Jemmeh, Lachish) "the mound was largely occupied by a palace-fort or other larger building," *Material Culture,* 47.

[18]So Tufnell, *Lachish III,* vol. 1, 143; vol. 2, plate 42, numbers 8–9. For another assessment of this site, see E. Campbell, "Jewish Shrines of the Hellenistic and Persian Periods," *Symposia Celebrating the Seventy-fifth Anniversary of the Founding of the American Schools of Oriental Research (1900–1975),* ed. F. Cross, Cambridge, Mass., 1979, 166.

[19]Tufnell dates the pottery found with the altar in cave 534 to the fifth century, which is consistent with Dupont-Sommer's epigraphic dating of the inscription. Tufnell, *Lachish III,* 226, 358–59.

sacrifices to "the queen of heaven" as consistent with earlier forms of Yahwism (Jer. 44:17).

The Yahwistic mercenaries at Elephantine built a temple even before the temple in Jerusalem had been rebuilt and instituted a round of sacrificial offerings (so *CAP* 30). This last mentioned letter, which dates to the last decade of the fifth century B.C.E., is of particular interest since it was addressed to Bigwahu, governor of Judah. In it the head of the Jewish community, Yedoniah, who was probably both a religious and a civil leader, mentions that he has been in contact with other provincial authorities, namely, those in Samaria, as well as with apparently lesser religious authorities in Jerusalem. The letter reports that the Elephantine temple has been destroyed. This explains why Yedoniah was seeking support for the reconstruction of the temple. It may be that Yedoniah knew that Persian authorities had, at an earlier time, been directed to assist in the reconstruction of the Jerusalem temple, and now he wanted similar forms of help. Bigwahu's response, namely, that those in Egypt should rebuild the temple, is contained in *CAP* 32.

The overall picture presented by the Elephantine materials is important for our purposes since it indicates clearly that Yahwists in Syria-Palestine were in contact with Yahwists elsewhere and did not reject their practices out of hand, even if they worshiped at a temple other than the one in Jerusalem. In his letter, Hananiah advocates certain passover practices and provides evidence of this tacit approval.

It is noteworthy that a poet-prophet living in the Babylonian exile knew about the Yahwists near Elephantine, namely, in a town on the riverbank named Syene (Elephantine is on an island in the middle of the river), and that he looked forward to their return to the land (Isa. 49:12; cf. Ezek. 30:6). Isaiah 19:19–22 provides an interesting counterpoise. Here, in the Isaianic oracles against the nations, we find a prophet saying, "the Lord will make himself known to the Egyptians; and the Egyptians will know the Lord on that day, and will worship with sacrifice and burnt offering, and they will make vows to the Lord and perform them" (Isa. 19:21). One has the impression of a ritual that, if understood as occurring in Egypt and not as part of the "pilgrimage of the nations to Jerusalem" tradition, would require a temple. Would the author of this text have had the Elephantine temple in mind? There is no obvious answer. In any case, the Elephantine evidence points to the international character of Yahwism and suggests the reason why "the family of Egypt" comes in for special mention in Zech. 14:18–19.

During this period when Yahwism became Judaism, prophets were not present in all places. After the rebuilding of the temple in Jerusalem (the second temple was dedicated in 515 B.C.E.), there is no evidence of prophetic literature written outside Syria-Palestine. Moreover, we do not hear about

Yahwistic prophetic activity outside the Levant. Put another way, after the work of Ezekiel and Deutero-Isaiah, Yahwists reported that prophetic interme- diation occurred only in Syria-Palestine. Zechariah 9–14 and Malachi belong to this florescence of prophetic literature written in Persian-period Syria- Palestine. Though there is no strong scholarly consensus on what constitutes the postexilic prophetic corpus, one could add Isaiah 56–66, Joel, and perhaps Jonah to the list. At least this is sure: literature that fits our definition of "prophetic literature" was being composed well into the second temple period.

These exemplars of prophetic literature do not exhaust all evidence of prophetic activity in the early second temple period. Chronicles, also written in the Persian period, attests to another notion of prophetic behavior, that associated with Levitical singers.[20] Some Judahites in the early second temple period thought that the musical activities of Levites could be construed as of a piece with earlier prophetic activity (e.g., 1 Chron. 25:1; 2 Chron. 20:1–30; 2 Chronicles 29). Such claims, no doubt, created the sort of controversy reflected in Zech. 13:2–6. In sum, Persian-period Yahwism was a diverse business; and such diversity played itself out in multiple conceptions of what constituted prophetic activity.

4. The Persian Period

The International Scene

The term "Persian period" is misleading, if it is understood to mean that the only major actors in the eastern Mediterranean region were the Achaemenid Persians.[21] Egypt, though a shadow of its former imperial glory, still had an army and exercised influence over the southern Levant. In addition, the Greek states were increasingly prominent as traders and as a military enterprise on the northern and central Levantine coast. Such Egyptian and Greek presence does not contradict the fact that the Persians had conquered or, perhaps better, dominated those territories that had earlier been under Neo-Babylonian con- trol. But the term "Persian period" recognizes that Syria-Palestine was still very much a crossroads environ and subject to diverse cultural and political influences, as it had been in earlier times.

The fifth century B.C.E. began with the Persian empire, including Egypt,

---

[20]On this see most recently R. Tournay, *Seeing and Hearing God with the Psalms: The Prophetic Liturgy of the Second Temple in Jerusalem,* JSOTSup 118, Sheffield, 1991.

[21]The term "Achaemenid" derives from the name Achaemenes, who was remembered as the first of the Persian dynasts. The period associated with the Achaemenid dynasty, which began with Cyrus the Great and ended with Darius III Codomannus, was roughly 540–330 B.C.E.

under Darius's firm control.[22] However, things were not to continue calmly, particularly in matters that involved Egypt. A pattern well known in earlier ancient Near Eastern history recurred when Darius died in 486: Vassal states at the boundaries of an empire rebelled at the accession of a new king. In this case, Egypt sat on the western imperial perimeter. Though there was no identifiable pharaonic instigator, Egypt revolted, as it had when Darius acceded to the throne. Nonetheless, early in his reign Xerxes was able to reinstitute Persian control over Egypt. To accomplish this feat, he needed to cross through the Levant, the security of which would have been very important for the Persian imperial cause.

The second Egyptian revolt, c.464 B.C.E., which enjoyed the help of the Athenian navy, presented Artaxerxes I Longimanus (464–424) with his first opportunity to confront the emergent Greek threat to the Persian empire.[23] (Earlier, both Darius [at Marathon in 490] and Xerxes [at Thermopylae and Salamis, c.480–479] had also fought the Greeks; but this Egyptian revolt was the first occasion when the Greeks fought on soil that Persia had claimed as part of its empire.) The revolt, led by Inaros and then in a different phase by Amyrtaeus, was put down only after Megabyzos, a Persian military leader, recaptured Memphis, the satrapal seat, and managed to defeat two separate components of the Athenian navy. Portions of this conflict probably extended up the Levantine coast. By 454 the revolt had been put down, but again Syria-Palestine had suffered the march of Persian troops on their way to Egypt. Hoglund has argued that those troops, which had supported the Athenian alliance, would have attacked Dor.[24]

The peace of Callias, 449–448, which was struck between the Athenians and Artaxerxes I (whether or not as a formal treaty remains debated), was supposed to create a thirty-year period of nonintervention by the Greeks in the Persian sphere of influence, including Egypt and Cyprus. This détente was reasonably successful—in part because of the severity of Greek losses in Egypt. One may therefore judge that the first half of the fifth century B.C.E. was considerably more tumultuous for Syria-Palestine than was the second.

Although Egypt was important to the international picture of the Persian period, there is no evidence that Egyptian forces entered Syria-Palestine. Judah, however, felt the effect of Egyptian revolts, since Persians would pass

[22]For a remarkable view, from an Egyptian perspective, on the beginning of Persian rule and its effect on Egypt, see the Udjahorresnet inscription, which is available in M. Lichtheim, *Ancient Egyptian Literature*, vol. 3: *The Late Period*, Berkeley, Calif., 1980, 36–41; see also J. Blenkinsopp, "The Mission of Udjahorresnet and Those of Ezra and Nehemiah," *JBL* 106 (1987): 409–21.

[23]See K. Hoglund, *Achaemenid Imperial Administration in Syria-Palestine and the Missions of Ezra and Nehemiah*, SBLDS 125, Atlanta, 1992, 97–164, for a detailed assessment of this revolt.

[24]Hoglund, *Achaemenid Imperial Administration*, 153.

through its territory on the way to Egypt. One can understand why the Persians wanted stable and secure conditions in the Levant from which to stage campaigns against Egypt and also against the Greeks who would appear on the Palestinian coast.

It would be a significant error to think that the relationship between the Persians and the Greeks was only one of military antagonism. Early on, the Persians welcomed Greeks in their homeland. Achaemenid art and architecture were influenced significantly by "things Greek," that is, by Greek models and craftsmen. The phrase "things Greek" is appropriate in expressing the notion of diversity, since "Greece" itself was no monolithic entity but instead comprised a number of cities that shared certain cultural features. Athens and, later, Sparta were in the lead positions.

Goods imported from various regions of Greece appeared in Syria-Palestine as early as the seventh century.[25] In the Iron Age, most Greek ceramic imports came from the islands of the Aegean. However, early in the Persian period, there was a major change: Imports from Attica, the mainland region around Athens, dominated the import market. Such ware is attested not only in coastal towns but far inland as well. Though some scholars have suggested that these ceramics were imported as containers, more have argued that the pottery itself was the commodity. Such evidence will have to remain indicative; that is, it attests to the important economic interplay between the northern and eastern Mediterranean areas during the Persian period. Greece and Israel were not strangers at the beginning of the Persian period.

To the east, relations between Babylon and its Persian overlords ruptured because of two revolts between 485 and 480 led by Bel-shimanni and Shamash-eriba, respectively.[26] The Persians, again with Megabyzos at the lead, were able to defeat the dissidents, with the result that Babylon was finally separated from "Beyond the River" and treated as a separate satrapy.

In sum, during the early Persian period, military conflict on the western flank of the Achaemenid empire provided strong reasons for its leaders to be interested in secure rule over the diverse peoples of the Levant.

Syria-Palestine

It is a commonplace to begin any discussion of Persian-period Syro-Palestinian literature and history with disclaimers about the lack of evidence

---

[25]For a convenient summary of the evidence, see Stern, *Material Culture,* 137–42.

[26]J. Cook, *The Persian Empire,* New York, 1983, 100.

concerning this era.[27] To a certain extent, this apology remains in order. However, the problem is no more severe than it is for the period of the exodus, and less severe than that for the so-called patriarchal period. The books of Ezra-Nehemiah and Chronicles stem from the Persian period and reflect some of the issues with which Yahwists who were "in the land" grappled. Moreover, extrabiblical evidence, both literary and artifactual, helps us understand the world in which Syro-Palestinian Yahwists lived.[28]

One must first be clear about the way in which Judah, and for that matter Syria-Palestine, fit administratively in the Persian empire. With the inception of Cyrus's reign, Syria-Palestine was part of the huge satrapy that included both Babylonia (*babili*) and Syria-Palestine (*ebir nari*) (their Akkadian names). These subsidiary units corresponded, essentially, to earlier political configurations, namely, the native lands of Babylon and the agglomeration of territories in Syria-Palestine, which had been conquered by the Neo-Assyrians and the Neo-Babylonians in turn. Later, these two quite distinct regions were separated, each becoming a satrapy in its own right. However, there is considerable debate about the date when this division took place.[29] Stolper correctly notes that the extent to which this huge satrapy ever functioned as an integral unit is open to question.

Abar nahara, the Aramaic title for "Beyond the River," was subdivided into a number of provinces (e.g., Samaria).[30] It is difficult to discern one city from

---

[27]One finds similar disclaimers from the classicist side, so H. Bengtson, "Any attempt to present the history of the Greeks and the Persians, from Darius I to Alexander, immediately faces a serious problem: the problem of sources," *The Greeks and the Persians: From the Sixth to the Fourth Centuries*, ed. H. Bengtson, New York, 1968, ix.

[28]The late twentieth century has seen a remarkable surge of interest in and publications devoted to Persian-period Syria. The publication of a new journal *Transeuphratene: Etudes sur la Syrie-Palestine et Chypre à L'Epoque Perse* 1 (1989), sponsored by the Association pour la Recherche sur la Syrie-Palestine à L'Epoque Perse, as well as the existence of an international Achaemenid History Workshop, which published its proceedings through the Nederlands Instituut voor het Nabije Oosten (the first was published in 1987), attests to the burst of interest and information concerning the Persian-period Levant.

[29]See the lucid discussion of the various options in M. Stolper, "The Governor of Babylon and Across-the-River in 486 B.C.," *JNES* 48 (1989): 283–305. If Stolper's analysis is correct, the division could have occurred no earlier than the beginning of Xerxes's reign, namely in 486, and no later than 420, when Gubaru is described as " 'governor of the land of Akkad,' with no mention of Syria" (p. 298). Such a view would suggest that the activities of Ezra and Nehemiah occurred about the same time that significant reorganizations were transpiring in the administrative structure of the Persian empire. I. Eph'al, "Syria-Palestine under Achaemenid Rule," *Persia, Greece and the Western Mediterranean c.525–479 B.C., CAH*, vol. 4, Cambridge, 1988, 153–54, advances a position in agreement with that of Stolper.

[30]See Cook, *The Persian Empire*, 174–75, 204–6, for a brief but excellent description of *abar nahara;* see A. Rainey, "The Satrapy 'Beyond the River,'" *AJBA* 1 (1969): 51–78, for a history of the satrapy in the Persian period; and see C. and E. Meyers, *Haggai-Zechariah 1–8*, AB 25B, Garden City, N.Y., 1987, xxxiii, for a map.

which this *abar nahara* was ruled. Cook suggests that the following cities all had some claim to prominence: Sidon, Tripoli, Damascus, Askalon, Belesys (Eph'al adds Thapsacus to the list).[31] Though our inability to identify the satrapal seat is frustrating, the relative importance of a number of cities may reflect the actual workings of the Persian empire. The lines of administrative communication between the subprovinces and the major centers did not always pass through the bureaucratic structures as one might expect. The network of scribes and other minor officials worked out administrative issues without going through all the provincial channels. For example, a relatively low-level scribe or chancellor could be in direct contact with the imperial authorities.[32]

"Beyond the River" was made up of diverse entities, that is, various religions, ethnic groups, and economies. Eph'al has characterized the political variety as threefold (if one excludes the island Cyprus), namely, "the Phoenician city states, the provinces and the Arabs."[33] The four Phoenician states—Tyre, Sidon, Byblos, and Aradus—remained important as economic centers and gained import as the naval arm of the Persian military establishment, so much so that they exercised considerable independence, both militarily and economically. The provinces, too, though not offering military technology, were important economically to the empire, providing taxes, material goods, and means of communication.[34] Judah belonged in this sphere.

Whether all the Syria-Palestinian satrapy was divided into provinces is a matter of considerable debate. One often reads about certain territories associated with governors' names, Sanballat with Samaria, Nehemiah with Judah, Tobiah with Ammon, Geshem with Kedar. Avi-Yonah represents the standard consensus by arguing for the existence of other provinces, based on the references to the Arabians, Ammonites, and Ashdodites (Neh. 4:7).[35] To this list he adds Idumea, which was south of Judah; Galilee, which lay north of Samaria; territory controlled by either Tyre or Sidon; and two transjordanian provinces north of Ammon: Gilead and Karnaim. Eph'al, however, thinks that the existence of provinces other than Judah and Samaria remains to be demonstrated.[36]

Some provinces in *abar nahara* were created as early as the Neo-Assyrian

[31]Cook, *The Persian Empire,* 174; Eph'al, "Syria-Palestine under Achaemenid Rule," 155.

[32]So Cook, *The Persian Empire,* 175; Stolper, "The Governor of Babylon," 302; S. McEvenue, "The Political Structure in Judah from Cyrus to Nehemiah," *CBQ* 43 (1981): 353–64.

[33]Eph'al, "Syria-Palestine under Achaemenid Rule," 156–64.

[34]So Eph'al, a judgment based on documents from Arad, "Syria-Palestine under Achaemenid Rule," 155.

[35]M. Avi-Yonah, *The Holy Land from the Persian to the Arab Conquests (536 B.C. to A.D. 640): A Historical Geography,* Grand Rapids, 1966, 23.

[36]Eph'al, "Syria-Palestine under Achaemenid Rule," 158.

administration of this same region. However, the status of Judah or Judea in the fifth and fourth centuries remains ambiguous. On the one hand, some scholars (e.g., Alt, Galling, Stern, McEvenue, and apparently Ackroyd) have argued that Nebuchadnezzar joined Judah to the province of Samaria after the defeat of 587 and that the Persians subsequently continued to administer it through the provincial offices of Samaria. Only with Nehemiah, who is titled governor of Judah, is there reason to think about Judah as a separate district, namely, a province. On the other hand, some (M. Smith, Avigad, Rainey, Widengren, Meyers, Eph'al, and most recently Blenkinsopp[37]) have argued that since certain officials titled *peḥāh* predate Nehemiah (Neh. 5:15, "the former governors who were before me," e.g., Zerubbabel or the debated *pḥt* or *pḥr'*, Elnathan, whom Meyers dates to 510–c.490),[38] Judah must have had provincial status in the late sixth century.[39] Even if the just-mentioned seals do read "governor" (*pḥt*), there is considerable debate about their date. Avigad views them as deriving from the sixth century, Stern from the fifth. This is a critical difference, because few would deny that Judah had provincial status by the end of the fifth century, but not all would agree that such is the case c.500. Avigad and Meyers also presume that various references to a "governor" must refer to the same office. However, administrative titles were used with remarkable flexibility in the Persian system. For example, the term "governor," *peḥāh*, was used of both Ushtani and Tattenai, who clearly had different roles.[40] All this suggests that Judah probably became a province separate from Samaria in the mid-fifth century and as a function of the Persian response to the Egyptian revolts during that period.[41]

There were several important cities in Judah during the early Persian

---

[37]J. Blenkinsopp, "Temple and Society in Achaemenid Judah," *Second Temple Studies*, vol. 1: *Persian Period*, ed. P. Davies, JSOTSup 117, Sheffield, 1991, 37, thinks Judah was distinct from at least the time of Darius.

[38]For a nuanced discussion of attempts to create a list of "governors" from Sheshbazzar (c.538 B.C.E.) to Yehezqiyah (c.330 B.C.E.), see P. Ackroyd, "Archaeology, Politics, and Religion," *IR* 39 (1982): 11–13.

[39]The so-called Shelomith seal, which Avigad translates "belonging to Shelomith maidservant of Elnathan the governor," has been viewed by Avigad and Meyers as clear evidence for the existence of the office of governor in the late sixth century (N. Avigad, *Bullae and Seals from a Post-Exilic Judean Archive*, QMIA 4, Jerusalem, 1976; E. Meyers, "The Shelomith Seal and the Judean Restoration: Some Additional Considerations," *EI* 18 [1985]: 33–38). However, this seal is damaged in such a way that the critical letters in question, i.e., the last two letters of the reconstructed *phw'*, are not legible. In addition, Avigad himself states that the paleographic evidence is ambiguous (see plate 7). As a result, the proposed translation rests as much on the presupposition that a potter would not have a maidservant as it does on solid epigraphic evidence.

[40]So McEvenue, "The Political Structure in Judah from Cyrus to Nehemiah," 361–63.

[41]Cf. E. Meyers, "The Persian Period and the Judean Restoration," *Ancient Israelite Religion: Essays in Honor of Frank Moore Cross*, ed. P. Miller et al., Philadelphia, 1987, 516–17.

period.[42] Jerusalem was the ritual center, particularly after the temple had been rebuilt. But, especially prior to the time of Nehemiah, it is not clear that Jerusalem was the most important political site. Interpreters often assume that Jerusalem was the major city or "capital" of Judah, whatever its status or boundaries. Such was not the case, however, immediately after the defeat of Judah in 587. Jeremiah 40–41 reports that Nebuchadnezzar had appointed Gedaliah son of Ahikam "governor over the land" (Jer. 41:18) and "governor of the towns of Judah" (Jer. 40:5), and that Gedaliah exercised authority from Mizpah (Jer. 40:8).[43] (The biblical author uses no specific title to describe that administrative role.) This city, roughly twelve kilometers from Jerusalem, has been identified as Tell en Nasbeh. Excavations at that site reveal evidence of Persian-period occupation. Mizpah continued as a city well into the Persian period, at least until the beginning of the fourth century, though there is no explicit evidence that it retained status as the seat of an official after the Persians assumed control of Syria-Palestine.[44] The excavators reported few significant architectural remains, though there was evidence for some form of city wall.[45]

Mizpah could, therefore, have borne the importance implied by Neh. 3:7, "with the people of Gibeon and of Mizpah—who were under the jurisdiction of the governor of the province Beyond the River." This note, along with the prominence of Mizpah as a district (Neh. 3:15, 19); and the remarkable absence of Mizpah from the village list (Neh. 11:25–36), suggests that this city had special status, first for the Neo-Babylonians and then for Persian authorities, during both the sixth and the fifth centuries.[46] (And 1 Macc. 3:46–56 suggests that it remained important, at least as a religious site, after that.) One would be

---

[42]For a recent review of the archaeological evidence, see C. Carter, "The Province of Yehud in the Postexilic Period: Soundings in Site Distribution and Demography," *Second Temple Studies,* vol. 2: *Temple and Community in the Persian Period,* ed. T. Eskenazi and K. Richards, JSOTSup 175, Sheffield, 1994, 106–45.

[43]J. Blenkinsopp maintains that Mizpah was under the direct jurisdiction of the governor of the Trans-Euphrates satrapy, *Ezra-Nehemiah,* OTL, Philadelphia, 1988, 228.

[44]Blenkinsopp, *Ezra-Nehemiah,* 61, argues that Mizpah "retained its importance after the Persians took over (see Neh. 3:7)."

[45]C. McCown, *Tell en Nasbeh: Archaeological and Historical Results,* Berkeley, 1947, 185. By way of contrast, we know relatively little about the archaeology of Jerusalem in the Persian period. Blenkinsopp has summarized the evidence, *Ezra-Nehemiah,* 239–42, and argued that Jerusalem was reduced to its Solomonic extent, by comparison to its size under Hezekiah and Manasseh. So also Stern, *Material Culture,* 34. Ezra-Nehemiah clearly suggests that the city was underpopulated (Neh. 7:4). See also the brief summary in C. Carter, "The Province of Yehud in the Postexilic Period."

[46]Blenkinsopp has argued convincingly that Neh. 11:25–36 does not record Persian-period settlement patterns but instead represents an important issue present elsewhere in Ezra-Nehemiah, namely, that "history must always conform to ancient patterns" (*Ezra- Nehemiah,* 330), in this case the listing of Judahite and Benjaminite territories in Joshua 15.

hard pressed to defend the note in Neh. 3:7 as a comment about Mizpah's significance if it were important just as the lead city in one of the districts.

Since Judah did eventually become an "independent" province, whether in the sixth or the fifth century, it is appropriate to attempt to discern its boundaries. As Avi-Yonah notes, the most pertinent information relevant to this task is located in Ezra-Nehemiah, namely, in various lists.[47] The most important list details those who helped rebuild Jerusalem's wall (Neh. 3:2–27).[48] This list identifies those who worked by referring to the city (e.g., Tekoa, Neh. 3:5) or region (e.g., "the surrounding area," Neh. 3:22) in which they lived. If one draws a boundary around the cities or regions mentioned there and supplements that listing with the tabulations describing those Judeans who had returned from captivity (Ezra 2:21–34; Neh. 7:26–37), though not the list in Nehemiah 11, then one can create a map of the province known as Judah.[49] However, judging from the archaeological evidence of this region, Judah was, in fact, smaller than these lists would suggest. Carter has argued that the boundaries included the central hill country but not the coastal plain. Moreover, he estimates that the total population would have been less than 20,000 inhabitants, with perhaps 10 percent of that in Jerusalem, after the fortifications of Nehemiah had been erected.[50]

A careful review of the above-mentioned lists in Ezra-Nehemiah indicates that there were divisions internal to this "theoretical" Judah.[51] Nehemiah 11 refers to "the people of Judah" and "the people of Benjamin," language which suggests that even if Judah were the name of a province, it was also the name of a smaller unit, one that could be distinguished from an area such as Benjamin or even from Jerusalem (Neh. 7:6). A hallmark of these lists is the prominence of cities as the critical descriptive category.[52] People in exile traced their heritage to cities (Ezra 2:20–35). And people from exile returned to and lived in cities (Neh. 7:6), even those outside the apparent perimeter of Judah.

Jerusalem is, in contradistinction to other cities, "the holy city" (Neh. 11:1–2). (The Hebrew, unlike the NRSV, does not distinguish city from town.) Cities can "own" other settlements; thus Dibon has its "daughters" or villages

---

[47]Avi-Yonah, *The Holy Land*, 15.

[48]On this see M. Avi-Yonah, "The Walls of Nehemiah: A Minimalist View," *IEJ* 4 (1954): 239–48.

[49]So Avi-Yonah, *The Holy Land*, 15–23, but without internal divisions; H. Kreissig, *Die sozialökonomische Situation in Juda zur Achämenidenzeit*, Berlin, 1973, 33–34; Meyers and Meyers, *Haggai and Zechariah 1–8*, xxxvi.

[50]Carter, "The Province of Yehud in the Postexilic Period."

[51]Cf. the eight "environmental niches" into which Carter divides the province, "The Province of Yehud."

[52]This prominence of city references is especially interesting in light of what K. Hoglund has discerned as a Persian tactic of "ruralization," "The Achaemenid Context," *Second Temple Studies,* 1991, 57–60.

(Neh. 11:25). But Jerusalem is not included in this list of Judah's cities that have villages. It is somehow distinct, set apart or sacred. In this regard it is interesting to note that (according to Ezra 7:20) primarily "holy" people, the priests, the Levites, as well as some of the people, settle in Jerusalem. (The list in Nehemiah 11 is peculiar, as Blenkinsopp notes, since it includes territory under the "control" of Edom and Arabs.) So also in the list in Ezra 2, where those who return are cited by city (vv. 20–35), Jerusalem is not one of the cities named. And Jerusalem was obviously more than just a city, since it could be termed a *pelek* or region.[53]

In addition to the distinctiveness of Jerusalem, the Hebrew Bible also presents a series of hierarchically arranged terms that appear to correspond to regions of various sizes: province=*mĕdînāh* (Neh. 7:6); district=*pelek* (Neh. 3:14–15); city='*îr;* village with field=*hzr* or *bat* (see Neh. 11:25, where these two nouns seem to be interchangeable). The term *mĕdînāh,* typically translated "province," appears only in Ezra 2:1; Neh. 1:3; 7:6; and 11:3; and in Aramaic in Ezra 5:8 ("province of Judah"); 6:2 ("province of Media"); and 7:16 ("province of Babylon").[54] Only in the first-mentioned Aramaic text does the phrase "province of Judah" occur, and McEvenue argues that this phrase does not mean province in the technical sense but, on the basis of the analogy with Neh. 7:16, signifies the region of Judah.[55]

If Judah was not a province in some technical sense, what was it? "Judah" is often used in contradistinction to another geographic description (e.g., Benjamin or Jerusalem). For example, see Ezra 4:1 ("When the adversaries of Judah and Benjamin . . ."; cf. also Ezra 10:9); or Ezra 4:6 ("the inhabitants of Judah and Jerusalem"); or Neh. 11:3 ("These are the leaders of the province who lived in Jerusalem; but in the towns of Judah all lived on their property in their towns"). See also Neh. 13:16 ("and sold them on the sabbath to the people of Judah and in Jerusalem"). This last text implies that to sell something to the people of Judah is to sell something in a place other than in Jerusalem. Judah is, in some consequential way, conceptually distinct from Jerusalem. Nehemiah

[53]Ramat Rahel was surely part of this region in the Persian period. It is also important to adduce the judgment of L. Mildenberg ("Yehud: A Preliminary Study of the Provincial Coinage of Judaea," *Greek Numismatics and Archaeology: Essays in Honor of Margaret Thompson,* ed. O. Morkholm and N. Waggoner, Wetteren, 1979, 183–96), namely, that *yehud* coins may well have been minted to the south and east of Jerusalem. Though none of the coins apparently predates 400 B.C.E., this geographic consideration would be consistent with what we know about other important cities of Judah in earlier periods.

[54]I depend here on the analysis of McEvenue, "The Political Structure in Judah from Cyrus to Nehemiah," 353–64.

[55]Some scholars have understood the Aramaic word *mĕdînāh* to mean province, so Eph'al, though McEvenue would argue that the term is not consistently used in this fashion. Cf. Blenkinsopp, "Temple and Society in Achaemenid Judah," 36 n. 1, on *mĕdînāh.*

11:4 attests: "in Jerusalem lived some of the Judahites and some of the Benjaminites."

The *pelek* was apparently a region over which there was an official (e.g., the *śar,* "ruler," mentioned in Neh. 3:9). Avi-Yonah argues that because three districts were divided into half-districts, we should presume that each subdistrict had a governing city. For example, in the district of Jerusalem, the major city was, of course, Jerusalem, whereas the "other city" was Ramath-Rahel or biblical Bet-hakkerem (though one could argue as well for Anathoth or Bethlehem).[56] That Nehemiah 3 presents a picture of Jerusalem as a region into which subsidiary divisions have been introduced seems clear. Is Judah, then, the entire province, and what is Benjamin? To answer these questions is to recognize that the writers of Ezra-Nehemiah were reusing old titles in new ways as they attempted to describe the new geography of Persian-period Judah. In addition, they were attempting to avoid the provincial labels used from the time of the Neo-Assyrians; thus, Benjamin replaces what might otherwise have been termed Samaria.

In sum, both extrabiblical evidence and canonical texts allow for a complex picture of Persian-period Syria-Palestine. Early in the Persian period, Judah and Jerusalem probably had minimal political importance in contrast to the high status both territory and city had in Yahwistic religious traditions. This situation changed somewhat with the activities of Nehemiah and Ezra. However, the books of Ezra-Nehemiah do not present the expected geographic conceptions. Judah is viewed as something distinct from Jerusalem; thus, Judahites live in Jerusalem. Moreover, Judah and Benjamin provide a way of talking about territory that avoids reference to the apparently odious term Samaria. Jerusalem is itself a complex entity, divided into subdistricts. All this is of direct relevance to understanding texts such as Zech. 12:7, which presuppose that Judah and Jerusalem are distinct in important ways: They are both geographic realities and religious constructions.[57]

Persian Imperial Strategies in the Levant

In standard handbooks the Persians are often viewed as beneficent overlords of this small area known as Judah or Yehud. Such a view has no doubt been influenced by biblical rhetoric, according to which Cyrus was construed as a messiah, "his anointed" (Isa. 45:1), as well as the royal patron of the second temple (Ezra 6:1–6). Moreover, the latter biblical text reports that "the royal

---

[56]See the discussion in Stern, *Material Culture,* 247–49.

[57]One might suggest that, in the late sixth and fifth centuries B.C.E., "Judah" functioned as a label for that territory which was not "Benjamin" and which was not part of the city of Jerusalem, but which may have included part of the "district" of Jerusalem.

treasury" was to subsidize the rebuilding of Yahweh's temple in Jerusalem. Because of such sentiments the Persians, in contrast to the earlier Assyrians or Babylonians, could be viewed as benefactors of Judah. They defeated those who had plundered Jerusalem, they allowed those in exile to return, and they supported the restitution of Yahwistic worship in Jerusalem.

Nonetheless, when one places these texts and judgments within the larger geopolitical context, it is possible to understand them as part of Persian self-interested strategy. The so-called Cyrus inscription serves as a useful case in point. The Persians had a policy of restoring and supporting temples in order to stimulate and control the economy as well as to encourage the loyalty of priests (and at least some of the local population).[58] Such loyalty would have been useful since Judah was proximate to the Mediterranean coast and to Egypt, sources of considerable anti-Persian sentiment and places of combat with Greek forces. Moreover, Cyrus's policy toward Judah was applied to other Syro-Palestinian groups as well—for example, those enfranchised to return to Aleppo and attested in the so-called Neirab texts.[59] Even with this dose of political realism, one may not doubt that Persian policy regarding religious patronage and resettlement of former exiles was welcomed by at least some Judeans who venerated Yahweh, particularly those who had been in exile.

However, not all Persian policies were so readily identifiable with the Judahites' interests. Kenneth Hoglund has identified four imperial tactics that would have influenced significantly those who lived in Judah: militarization, commercialization, ruralization, and ethnic collectivization. Each of these terms requires a brief explication.[60]

First, *militarization*. Throughout Judah, and territory contiguous with it, one may identify a number of relatively small public structures, which a number of scholars have identified as fortresses. Since they are scattered and occur neither on a provincial perimeter nor near cities, they appear designed for regional defense, located as they often are near major roads. Also, since the design of these forts is remarkably similar—square with a large court— Hoglund maintains they are part of a "centralized effort," which he attributes to the Persians. Those who garrisoned these sites would have depended in considerable measure on the local populace for their material support. Judean Yahwists would have had inklings about major conflict, as they observed Persian troop movements and may well have wondered how their God, Yahweh, was related to the ominous interactions between the Persians, Greeks,

---

[58]So A. Kuhrt, "The Cyrus Cylinder and Achaemenid Imperial Policy," *JSOT,* 25 (1983): 83–97.

[59]Hoglund, *Achaemenid Imperial Administration,* 27.

[60]I depend essentially on K. Hoglund, "The Achaemenid Context," 54–72, for this evidence and analysis.

and Egyptians, even though Judahites themselves may not have done the fighting.

Second, *commercialization*. Though Persians wanted to guard Levantine roads from enemy military usage, they were also interested in maintaining the movement of goods through the eastern Mediterranean basin. Such trade not only produced tax revenue but also opened up local communities to the benefits of economic development, which would, in part, have been attributed by those locals to the imperial enterprise. Indicative of the breadth of that trade is the prominence of pottery whose origins may be traced to the Greek mainland. Whether the pottery itself or what it might have contained was the primary object of trade remains unclear. In addition, locally made pottery that was created to contain produce in transit also becomes prominent during the Persian period.

Third, in Judahite territory during the early Persian period, there is an unusual pattern in settlement, namely, a number of new villages. Hoglund takes this to be evidence of a conscious Persian policy, *ruralization*. Those who were returning (or being returned) from exile, were being settled in a particular nonurban mode, one which the Persians hoped would maximize the agricultural productivity of the region. Such a policy is utterly consistent with reports about a depopulated Jerusalem.[61]

Finally, Hoglund reads the Ezra-Nehemiah narratives as consistent with Persian practice attested elsewhere, according to which various ethnic groups were placed in a contiguous relationship and expected to behave in an economically productive manner, *ethnic collectivization*. The practice of inter-marriage would have been a direct extension of this policy. In the eyes of some, such ethnic commingling would have enhanced the viability of newly settled territories; in the eyes of others, it would have threatened the integrity of Yahweh's people.

Of these four manifestations of Persian policy, the third worked against the resettlement of Jerusalem and the first represented a drain on Judahite re-sources. Both are reflected in Zechariah 9–14: militarization—Zech. 9:10; ruralization—14:11 (12:5?). Also, the policy of ethnic collectivization may be reflected in Zech. 14:17, where there is a certain openness to the participation of "the families of the earth" in Yahwistic ritual. However, there is little if any evidence, that the three "oracles" made up a choir of protest against the returnees who had assumed significant status in Persian-period Judah. The texts just cited do suggest that imperial Persian policy would not have been universally appreciated by those who venerated Yahweh. But protest against the authorities who had enabled the reconstitution of a significant Yahwistic

---

[61]See also K. Hoglund, "The Establishment of a Rural Economy in the Judean Hill Country in the Late Sixth Century," unpublished paper.

presence does not occur in these texts. Protest there is, but it is against other Yahwists and regional foes, not against the Persians.

Judahite Social and Religious Structure

Joel Weinberg has, in numerous studies, argued that Persian-period Judah existed in a distinctive form of social and religious organization, a "citizen-temple-community" (*Bürger-Tempel-Gemeinde*), a polity known elsewhere in the ancient Near East, especially Anatolia.[62] In such societies, only landholding individuals were enfranchised to participate in the temple affairs. Moreover, genealogical constructs were used to identify those who could hold power. In the case of Judah, the primary units were "the house of the father" (*bêt 'āb*). Those who belonged to these houses traced their ancestry through genealogies back to those who had been in exile. Since both Yahwists in Babylon (Zech. 6:10) and the Persian empire itself (Ezra 6:4) were instrumental in temple reconstruction, one may surmise that those who had not been in Babylon were peripheral to temple governance and support. The consolidation of power in the "citizen-temple-community" emerged slowly. Weinberg thinks that it did not exist in a strict sense before 460 B.C.E. and that it appeared due to the activities of Ezra. Since the "community" did not include all Yahwists in Judah, the "community" and Judah are not to be viewed as coextensive. (If one substituted "Jerusalem" for "community" in the foregoing sentence, such a distinction may be found in Zechariah 9–14.)

If one postulates such a social and religious structure, it is not difficult to imagine that a significant source of tension occurred between those whose progenitors had remained in the land and those who had been forcibly removed to Babylon. (Ezekiel 11:14–21 demonstrates that such tension occurred in the early sixth century.) Unless one could identify ancestors among those who had been in exile, an individual was not, at least initially, qualified to be part of those people who exercised control over the temple and, more generally, the affairs of Yahweh in Judah.

Though Weinberg's theory has gained considerable favorable response, some scholars (e.g., Blenkinsopp) think that the evidence does not allow one to be so precise about the nature of Persian-period Judah's polity. Blenkinsopp is especially dubious about Weinberg's demographic assessments, which presume a population of 200,000, of whom only 10 percent would have belonged

---

[62]Weinberg's articles are widely scattered. One may recommend three in particular: "Die Agrarverhältnisse in der Bürger-Tempel-Gemeinde der Achämenidenzeit," *AAASH* 22 (1974): 473–86; "Das *beit 'abot* im 6.–4. Jahrhundert," *VT* 23 (1973): 400–14; and "Zentral- und Partikulargewalt im achämenidischen Reich," *Klio: Beiträge zur Alten Geschichte* 59 (1977): 25–43.

to the ancestral houses. Blenkinsopp maintains that the basic population estimate is too high and that the biblical texts have not been assessed with requisite care. Moreover, Blenkinsopp points out that city and temple were routinely codependent throughout the ancient Near East and during many historical periods.

Consequently, Blenkinsopp advances an alternative thesis, namely, that an assembly (*qāhāl*), made up of those whose ancestors had been in exile, was the dominant political and religious group in Persian-period Judah (e.g., Ezra 10:7–8).[63] This group existed in contradistinction to "the people of the land" (*'am hā'āreṣ*). Moreover, according to the narratives that recount the dispute about mixed marriages in Ezra, the "assembly" could confiscate property from those with whom they disagreed. Key in Blenkinsopp's thesis is the notion that those who had not been in exile could at some point join with the assembly (so Ezra 6:21). Nonetheless, the exiles' perspective would have continued to dominate, as is apparent in Neh. 2:16, which limits the term "the Jews" to an apparently small segment of the population. Blenkinsopp concludes by suggesting that the assembly in Judah was basically a form of Yahwistic social and religious life that had been imported by those who had been in exile in Babylon. The only real change from the Mesopotamian context involved the temple as the focus of their religious practices.

What then are the salient points that arise from an overview of the times during which Zechariah 9–14 and Malachi were most probably written? In the fifth century, Judah sat on a critical flank of the Persian empire, namely, its boundary with Egypt. Such a setting meant that Judah would also be affected by the presence of Greeks in the eastern Mediterranean basin (see Zech. 9:13). Persian interactions with Judah would have been heavily influenced by its interests in the security of that area. In the sixth century B.C.E., as a part of this policy, Persia had supported the reconstruction of the temple. In the fifth century, Persia continued to support those Yahwists who could ensure local loyalty toward the Persians and a measure of stability in Judah. One may surmise that those who were politically entitled would normally have been Persian loyalists. Second, those who held power in Judah were those who belonged to the "assembly of the exiles," even though others could join that group. However, some individuals outside "the assembly" venerated Yahweh. Hence, the tone of disputation that one finds in Malachi would be altogether expected. In fact, individuals in Egypt and Babylon, as well as diverse groups in Judah, worshiped this God. Even though the "assembly" governed temple-based affairs in Jerusalem, they were not in a position to administer beliefs and

---

[63]J. Blenkinsopp, "Temple and Society in Achaemenid Judah," 22–53. For a recent and favorable judgment, see P. Dion, "The Civic-and-Temple Community of Persian Period Judah: Neglected Insights from Eastern Europe," *JNES* 50 (1991): 281–87.

practices concerning Yahweh throughout the ancient Near East. Hence, Zechariah 9–14 and Malachi reflect a world of diverse communities who worshiped Yahweh, and yet a world in which one area, Judah, and one city, Jerusalem, claimed special status.

5. Zechariah 9–14

Although this commentary construes Zechariah 9–14 as two "oracles," much of the scholarly discussion has viewed them as an interwoven whole, often known as Deutero-Zechariah. The rubric Deutero-Zechariah even occurs in those studies (e.g., Otzen) that construe Zechariah 9–14 as something other than a seamless literary whole.

The notion that these chapters do not derive from the hand of Zechariah, son of Berechiah, dates to at least the early seventeenth century.[64] Unlike the early arguments about Deutero-Isaiah, which were driven by historical-critical concerns (so Duhm), J. Mede's focus was on the apparent citation of Zech. 11:13 in Matt. 27:9, which attributed that Old Testament citation to the prophet Jeremiah. In the interest of defending the veracity of this New Testament statement about biblical authorship, Mede maintained that Jeremiah was indeed the author of Zechariah 9–11 and that these chapters were distinct from Zechariah 1–8, which he thought were written by the aforementioned Zechariah. This position was later joined with historical and literary observations, such that by the mid-eighteenth century there was something of a consensus that Zechariah 9–14 was separate from Zechariah 1–8 and that these last six chapters of the book, though of diverse origins, were all written prior to the exile.

Near the end of the nineteenth century, B. Stade, in an influential article, argued that these chapters constitute a literary unity. However, he dated them to the Hellenistic period. More recently, the pendulum has swung back to the notion that Zechariah 9–14 is a literary mosaic, with dates of composition in the Persian period (e.g., Hanson). In sum, since the time of Mede there has been considerable diversity of judgment about the dating and literary unity of Zechariah 9–14. However, one constant feature has been the distinction between Zechariah 1–8 and 9–14, a distinction present in this commentary as well.

If Zechariah 9–14 is different from Zechariah 1–8 and if Zechariah 1–8 may be characterized as prophetic literature, how should one construe Zechariah

---

[64]See Otzen, *Deuterosacharja,* 11–34, and M. Saebo, "Die deuterosacharjanische Frage," 115–40, for comprehensive reviews of the history of research on Zechariah 9–14; and for a less technical presentation, see R. Coggins, *Haggai, Zechariah, Malachi,* 60–72.

9–14? I will maintain that Zechariah 9–14 is also best understood as prophetic literature. Despite the discontinuity with Zechariah 1–8, Zechariah 9–14 presents literature formally similar to that which one finds in other prophetic books. There are divine oracles and prophetic sayings. Moreover, typical features of prophetic rhetoric (e.g., the indictment of foreign nations) are present (Zech. 9:1–8). Various literary forms (e.g., the call to communal lament), which were used by other prophets, are also used in this literature. There is language of woe and language of weal, as one finds in the literature attributed to Isaiah ben Amoz. Moreover, literary devices present in Zechariah 9–14 (e.g., the frequent *bayyôm hāhû'*, "on that day") are used prominently elsewhere in the prophetic corpus. Even the use of the term *maśśā'* to introduce a number of discrete sayings (e.g., Isa. 17:1) serves as a strong analogy to the three introductory formulae in Zech. 9:1; 12:1; and Mal. 1:1. More generally, these chapters attest to the work of intermediation, that is, the activity of individuals who communicate the perspective of the divine world to that of human affairs. In sum, Zechariah 9–14 possesses the essential hallmarks of prophetic literature.[65]

The mixture of prophetic sayings and divine utterances that make up Zechariah 9–14 have been framed with the aforementioned formulae, which begin with the Hebrew word *maśśā'*, "oracle." Hence it is appropriate to treat each of these "oracles" in turn. In the first *maśśā'* (Zechariah 9–11), the reader discovers five rhetorical units, the interrelationships of which are complex. The discourse is formulated primarily as poetry. The first section (9:1–8) begins with a formula that also serves as the formulaic introduction to the entire *maśśā'*. In rhetoric familiar from other and earlier prophetic literature, we are told that certain foreign nations are subject to Yahweh's control and predation (9:1–8).[66] With Zion and the temple as motifs that link the first two poems in this "oracle," the next poem (9:9–17) offers weal for God's people. Militarization will cease, peace will ensue. Then, in dialectical fashion, God's people will become weaponry ("I have filled Ephraim, my bow," 9:13). Moreover, the people outside Jerusalem are admonished to fill the city (9:12); those in diaspora are admonished to return. The next poem,

---

[65]Cf. P. Hanson, *The Dawn of Apocalyptic,* who views Zechariah 9–14 as an early form of apocalyptic literature. More recently, J. Collins, among others, has recommended greater precision in identifying certain literature as apocalyptic, suggesting that apocalyptic literature includes a transcendent judgment and a vision interpreted by an angelic intermediary ("The Place of Apocalypticism in the Religion of Ancient Israel," *Ancient Israelite Religion,* ed. P. Miller et al., Philadelphia, 1987, 539–58). If one uses such criteria, it is difficult to construe any portion of Zechariah 9–14 as apocalyptic literature. In fact, using Collins's criteria, one might have a stronger case for arguing that Zechariah's visions (in Zechariah 1–6) tend toward the apocalyptic.

[66]Blenkinsopp, *A History of Prophecy,* 260–61, maintains that the tensions between Jerusalem and the Samaritans lie behind much in Zechariah 9–11.

Zechariah 10:1–12, while indicting Israel for improper forms of intermediation, reiterates the theme of return from among the nations—a theme struck in
the previous poem. In elaborately symbolic language, the poet envisions a
military role for God's people ("war bow will come from them," 10:4). The
briefest discourse, Zech. 11:1–3, provides a taunt to Israel's neighbors, but
alludes to disaster that will reach Israel, up to "the verdant banks of the Jordan"
(11:3). Finally, Zech. 11:4–17 concludes the first "oracle" with a dismaying
tone. In a complex symbolic action report, the prophet conveys a message that
God has given over dominion in Syria-Palestine to leaders who will not act
effectively on behalf of the people. A curse on an important leader ends the
first of the three oracles.

In the second *maśśā'* (Zechariah 12–14) there are two long discourses
and one short one, as opposed to the five smaller units in the first oracle. The
entire "oracle" is introduced by a prologue, Zech. 12:1. Then each of the two
major units (12:2–13:6 and 14:1–21) is introduced by a *hinnēh* ("behold")
clause in which a masculine singular participle occurs (12:2, "Truly I am
making . . ."; 14:1, "Truly Yahweh has a day . . ."). These initial elements
comprise the prologues for their respective units, namely, 12:2 and 14:1–3. In
between the long compositions sits a short poem, 13:7–9, which provides a
transition between the two long montages.[67]

The second "oracle" is different from the first one not only by dint of its
structure but also because of a shift in focus. The authors now address the
"domestic" setting of Yahweh's work, particularly as that involves Judah and
Jerusalem. Further, in its rhetoric the passage is different from the foregoing
one. In the first "oracle," divine speech predominated, whereas in the second,
prophetic speech appears more prominently, though each of the two major
sections includes both types. Also, the second "oracle" includes literature that
is more like prose, especially chap. 14, than the poetry in Zechariah 9–11.
Finally, the phrase "on that day" (12:3, 4, 6, 8 [twice], 9, 11; 13:1, 2, 4; 14:4, 6,
8, 9, 13, 20), whether it serves as a suture that links originally distinct material,
or whether it provides a literary motif that highlights the importance of
Yahweh's future action, is a hallmark of this second "oracle." This formulaic
phrase serves two quite distinct though complementary functions: it both
separates and integrates diverse sayings.[68] It separates distinct utterances and
integrates them into larger, meaningful montages, which provide a comprehensive picture of the nations, Judah and Jerusalem "on that day." "On that day"
stylizes the second "oracle," giving it a more integrated feel than Zechariah

---

[67]On 13:7–9 as transitional and therefore integral, see O. Plöger, *Theocracy and Eschatology*,
Richmond, 1968, 88–89.

[68]Blenkinsopp, *A History of Prophecy*, 261–62, has suggested that a particular form of literature,
a kind of interpretation or *pesher*, normally follows this formula.

9–11 possesses. Moreover, this phrase focuses temporally on the notion that God will act sometime in the future. Although Zechariah 9-11 expresses the hope that the deity will act with and on behalf of Israel (e.g., 9:11), Zechariah 12–14 affirms that the critical moment, "on that day," lies in the future.

It is difficult to characterize the relationship between the two major literary pieces (12:1–13:6; 14:1–21) in the second oracle. Stade described them as doublets; Lacocque as parallel collections.[69] Some scholars think they represent similar traditions; others argue that they have different origins. Lutz, who represents the latter position, thought the differences, especially perspectives on the defeat of Jerusalem, derive from diverse religious traditions.[70]

By way of preliminary comment about 12:2–13:6 and 14:1–21, I would offer the following comparisons between these two sections, though without attempting to theorize about the reasons for these differences. The first montage is concerned with Judah and Jerusalem, whereas the second focuses almost exclusively on Jerusalem. The first montage speaks of an attack on Jerusalem in which, apparently, the enemies will be rebuffed, even though Judah will incur losses; whereas according to the second, Jerusalem will suffer significant military casualties. In the first, there is concern for Yahwistic leaders and troops, even prophets; these concerns are not present in the second discourse. In both montages, the authors have presented dialectical elements. In the first, though Jerusalem is defended and the foreign troops defeated, the remainder of the chapter is filled with language of lamentation and punishment. In the second, though the opening scene conveys the sense of vicious destruction, all the remaining vignettes present a fundamentally positive viewpoint. In the first montage, divine discourse predominates; in the second, prophetic sayings. In the first, concrete military action and social existence function as the backdrop; whereas in the second, a reconfigured cosmos, Judah, and Jerusalem provide the setting for weal. Zechariah 14 is more radical; it envisions greater disruption for Jerusalem, but it also depicts greater change on the positive side. The author of the second montage appears to think that if real change is to occur, the world as stage will need to be restructured in fundamental ways. Then—perhaps only then—Judah and Jerusalem can exist peacefully with "the nations" and, as well, together provide the basis for an appropriate ritual life.

Scholars have normally attributed the differences between the first and second montages either to diverse authorial hands or to different periods of

---

[69]Stade, "Deuterosacharja" (1881), 36; Lacocque, *Zacharie 9–14*, 1981, 198.

[70]H. Lutz, *Jahwe, Jerusalem und die Völker: Zur Vorgeschichte von Sach 12,1–8 und 14,1–5*, Neukirchen-Vluyn, 1968; cf. R. Mason, *The Use of Earlier Biblical Material in Zechariah IX–XIV*, 293–98.

composition.[71] Both views are reasonable. However, if one may press the artistic analogy, these two montages work like a Cubist painting in which the same artist, on one canvas, presents diverse views of a human face or figure. To show something at the same time but from different angles helps the viewer or reader to see and comprehend something more fully. The basic problem confronting those who reflected on the day of the Lord was a dialectical one, continuity versus discontinuity, good times versus wicked times. These montages highlight one and then another element in these fundamental dichotomies. Accordingly, the second "oracle" presents a complex perspective concerning "Yahweh's day." For example, if Amos could speak of that day as a time of darkness (Amos 8:9), Zechariah 12–14 holds that it is to be a time of liminal light (Zech. 14:7).

The previous artistic analogies aside (montage, Cubist painting), many scholars continue to theorize about the composition history of Zechariah 9–14. For the purposes of this survey, one may identify two distinct approaches, driven by form-critical and redaction-critical concerns respectively, and also a third perspective that decries these concerns. The form-critical perspective highlights a discrete rhetorical unit (e.g., Zech. 9:1–17), with its formal features, and may postulate a date for its composition. Though their dating schemes and their divisions of the text are radically different, both Rudolph and Hanson represent such an approach.[72] A primary emphasis here is on identifying the points of origin for the elements that make up these chapters. Less emphasis is devoted to hypothesizing about the ways in which the distinct units were brought together to create the larger "oracles." On the other hand, Saebo, who also pursues essentially a form-critical approach, does broach the means by which the larger complexes (e.g., 12:2–13:6) were created.[73] However, the further question, that is, how these units were configured into the *maś'ôt,* lies beyond the scope of his analysis.

What I have termed the redaction-critical approach is less concerned with the origins of discrete sections—though the issue may be addressed—and more concerned about the way in which Zechariah 9–14 evolved. The work of Steck and Person exemplifies this approach. Steck maintains that Zechariah 9–14 (and Malachi) developed in a series of redactional stages. He identifies four primary levels in the composition of Zechariah 9–14: first, Zech. 9:1–10:2; second, 10:3–11:3; third, 11:4–13:9; and finally, Zechariah 14, which was inserted into an already extant composition that continued from Zech. 13:9 into Mal. 1:2. Steck thinks these stages grew out of and were responses to

[71]So R. Tournay, "Zacharie XII–XIV et l'histoire d'Israel," *RB* 81 (1974): 355–75.

[72]W. Rudolph, *Sacharja 9–14,* Gütersloh, 1976; Hanson, *The Dawn of Apocalyptic.*

[73]M. Saebo, *Sacharja 9–14: Untersuchungen von Text und Form,* WMANT 34, Neukirchen-Vluyn, 1969.

earlier texts.[74] For Steck, the various components of Zechariah 9–14 are far more interrelated than the form-critical approach of Hanson or Rudolph would suggest.

Person, by contrast, advocates a prominent role for the deuteronomic redactor. He maintains that, apart from Zechariah 9, Zechariah 10–14 has been heavily influenced by deuteronomic phraseology and ideas. As a corollary, Person deems Zechariah 10–14 to be cut from the same basic cloth.[75] And in the work of Bosshard and Nogalski, among others, discussion about the origins of Zechariah 9–14 has now become embedded in theories about the origins of the Book of the XII (and for Steck, the formation of Zechariah and the Book of the XII is related to the formation of the book of Isaiah).[76] And since this latter topic has appeared only recently on the agenda of many scholars, it is one about which no scholarly consensus has emerged.

A third approach eschews discussion of this literature's formation and points instead to the coherence or cogency of the final form of the text. Lamarche, Baldwin, and, to a lesser extent, House, fall into this camp.[77] Even before the recent spate of literary studies devoted to biblical literature, Lamarche claimed to have discerned a number of elaborate chiastic and other literary structures in Zechariah 9–14.[78] The literary configurations of these chapters were so intertwined that Lamarche felt constrained to argue they must represent the work of one hand. However, the very detail of his theses has struck many as unconvincing, more a tour de force than a compelling explanation of this literature. Lamarche's hypothesis was based on the notion that a messianic royal figure was central to the message of Zechariah 9–14. Few scholars today hold this to be the case.

This commentary does not present a systematic hypothesis about the formation of Zechariah 9–14. Nonetheless, it seems clear that these chapters have grown out of originally diverse material. This commentary attempts to use various methods to assess the meaning of the respective basic literary units

---

[74]See the convenient chart in Steck, *Der Abschluss der Prophetie,* 197–99.

[75]R. Person, *Deuteronomic Redaction in the Postexilic Period: A Study of Second Zechariah,* Chapel Hill, N.C., 1991.

[76]E. Bosshard, "Beobachtungen zum Zwölfprophetenbuch," *BN* 40 (1987): 30–62; J. Nogalski, *Redactional Layers and Intentions Uniting the Writings of the Book of the Twelve,* Zurich, 1991, forthcoming in BZAW. See also R. Pierce, "Literary Connectors and a Haggai/Zechariah/Malachi Corpus," *JETS* 27 (1984): 277–89; "A Thematic Development of the Haggai/Zechariah/Malachi Corpus," *JETS* 27 (1984): 401–11.

[77]P. House, *The Unity of the Twelve,* BLS 127, Sheffield, 1990.

[78]P. Lamarche, *Zacharie IX–XIV: Structure littéraire et messianisme,* Paris, 1961, whose judgments were essentially accepted by J. Baldwin, *Haggai, Zechariah, Malachi,* TOTC, London, 1972, and to a lesser extent by Lacocque. For a critical discussion of Lamarche, see Otzen, *Studien,* 214–22, and M. Butterworth, *Structure and the Book of Zechariah,* 166–68.

and to point to the significance of these units as they have been configured secondarily into the first two *maś'ôt*.

6. Malachi

This biblical book commences with a title that might lead one to expect literature similar to Zechariah 9–11 and 12–14. However, we enter a new world in the chapters known as "Malachi." The third "oracle" is decidedly different from the foregoing ones. It is longer, 52 verses (with another three verses for the epilogue) versus 46 verses for the first oracle and 44 for the second. Literary style, though, rather than amount of text, constitutes the major difference. This third "oracle" is made up of brief dialogues between the deity and the people. Instead of a persistent eschatological emphasis, immediate verbal encounter between the deity and other parties characterizes this final "oracle" with which the "Prophets" concludes.

Many scholars have assessed the literary characteristics of Malachi from a form-critical perspective. Since the influential article of Egon Pfeiffer, there has been a strong consensus that Malachi comprises six primary units or speeches. Pfeiffer argued that these six speeches shared a common structure, which could be classified as a disputation.[79] Such disputations are normally made up of three elements: an established proposition (*eine hingestellte Behauptung*), the respondent's objection (*die Einreden des Partners*), and the key and concluding element, which may itself be made up of smaller elements, that is, oracle of salvation, threat, or admonition. Some have thought such disputations (elsewhere attested in Micah 2:6–11; Isa. 40:27–31) were rooted in legal proceedings. However, Pfeiffer, following Gunkel, argued that they had their origins in typical human differences of opinion (*der Alltag*).

Hans-Jochen Boecker offered a refinement of Pfeiffer's proposal by suggesting that these units be understood as "discussions" (*Diskussionsworte*) or "controversies" (*Streitgespräche*), and that the initial element be labeled the "opening element of the discussion" (e.g., Mal. 3:13a).[80] Boecker's judgments underlined Pfeiffer's point, namely, that these units reflected normal patterns of human communication. Building on the aforementioned two studies, G. Wallis focused on the identity of the discussants.[81] He observed that they were

---

[79]E. Pfeiffer, "Die Disputationsworte im Buche Maleachi: Ein Beitrag zur formgeschichtlichen Struktur," *EvT* 19 (1959): 546–68.

[80]H.-J. Boecker, "Bemerkungen zur formgeschichtlichen Terminologie des Buches Maleachi," *ZAW* 78 (1966): 78–80. Glazier-McDonald, *Malachi*, 20, thinks Boecker's refinements were unwarranted.

[81]G. Wallis, "Wesen und Struktur der Botschaft Maleachis," *Das ferne und nahe Wort: Festschrift Leonhard Rost zur Vollendung seines 70. Lebensjahres am 30. November 1966 gewidmet*, ed. F. Maass, 1967, 229–37.

not always the same. Sometimes the deity addressed the priests (e.g., 1:6–2:9); sometimes Yahweh spoke to the people as a whole (e.g., 3:6–7). Wallis then analyzed the units on the basis of the various issues taken up by the various respondents. He too offered a new term: *Streitreden*, "argumentative speeches," which he thought reflected the formalized and literary character of the texts.[82] Most recently, Lescow has attempted to refine the form-critical terminology. He maintains that the basic units may be characterized as prophetic instructional discussions (*prophetische Lehrgespräche*).[83] These are tripartite, made up of an opening speech, torah, and concluding word (*Redeeröffnung/Einrede, Torah, Schlusswort*). These basic units, which have been expanded (e.g., Lescow deems portions of 1:6, 7, 10; and 2:3, 9 to be the original elements in 1:6–2:9), focus on the importance of torah as an answer to questions germane to the Persian-period Judean community.

Other scholars have noted the prominence of a question-answer pattern in these six rhetorical units, particularly in the respondent's objection.[84] However, two things must be said. First, a question-and-answer pattern is not identical to Pfeiffer's idea of a tripartite structure. For example, in Mal. 1:6–2:9, the deity's initial speech includes questions, which themselves initiate a series: question-response (6b-7a), question-response (7b–c). Second, though questions occur in each of the six units, as Fischer correctly notes, they do not all occur in the mouth of humans, so Mal. 1:6.[85] Hence, the conclusion that a consistent question-answer pattern is present seems unwarranted.[86]

---

[82]On the basis of this form-critical work, Renker (*Die Tora bei Maleachi*, FTS 112, Freiburg, 1979, 67–84) has identified elements traceable to another hand, someone with a concern for reform of the priesthood and who worked using keyword connections, e.g., *ḥālal* in Mal. 2:10–11.

[83]T. Lescow, "Dialogische Strukturen in den Streitreden des Buches Maleachi," *ZAW* 102 (1990): 194–212. See also the brief discussion in D. Murray, "The Rhetoric of Disputation: Re-examination of a Prophetic Genre," *JSOT* 38 (1987): 110–14, which treats Malachi.

[84]For example, Glazier-McDonald, *Malachi*, 19, 21, seems to equate the question and the answer. One of the two disputations used to define the form, Amos 5:18–20, offers no answer to the questions.

[85]J. Fischer, "Notes on the Literary Form and Message of Malachi," *CBQ* 34 (1972): 315–20.

[86]Cf. J. Watts, "Introduction to the Book of Malachi," *Review and Expositor* 84 (1987): 376–79, on Malachi as "a series of speech acts," and R. Blake, *The Rhetoric of Malachi*, New York, 1988, 25, who disavows a form-critical approach: "From our own literary analysis we will go beyond any one genre for Malachi; it is a mixture of forms which, taken as a whole, produce a rhetoric—a persuasive address." Blake (p. 58) does, however, posit five basic speech types—audience questions, divine questions, audience contrary statements, deity's identification of speaker, deity's statements. Blake's "paragraph structure" is, however, problematic.He identifies (p. 73) eleven literary units (1:1–5; 1:6–11; 1:12–14; 2:1–3; 2:4–7; 2:8–9; 2:10–17; 3:1–4; 3:5–12; 3:13–18; 3:19–24). Blake posits a basic generic character of paraenesis, or sermon, for the rhetoric of the book, which does not seem to fit the acerbic character of the book (see my discussion of diatribe below).

I propose to advance the analysis of this third *maśśā'* in the following way. Some of the basic units of discourse in Malachi (e.g., 1:6–2:9 or 3:13–4:3) do not have a straightforward structure of three parts. Nor do they all have a regular pattern of question and answer. Instead of a simple tripartite structure or a question-answer format, two parties engage in direct discourse, which is focused on a particular topic. However, the dialogues are stylized; they do not appear as verbatim transcripts of human speech (so, similarly, Fischer and Wallis). Moreover, they have been enhanced, though not in the fulsome way Lescow suggests (see below).[87] One of the two dialogue partners is quoted. That party often asks questions; sometimes the questions are rhetorical, more often they are not. One could label this discourse as dialogue, but there is an even more fitting category: diatribe.[88] And it is this term—diatribe or, better, "diatribe-like"—that best describes these six literary units.

In Hellenistic Greece, the diatribe was similar to a dialogue, except that only one party spoke.[89] The other party was quoted or referred to in imaginative ways by the primary speaker. Questions were prominent, used as a way to allow the speaker to make a point. Hyperbolic claims were often put into the mouth of the persons presumably being quoted. The dialogue was often stylized, hence creating a literature that was at least one step removed from ordinary human discussion. The discourse was brief, the language vivid, and the intention often didactic. All these features appear in the third "oracle."[90]

The diatribe-like discourses in Malachi enable this literature to explore a number of ritual and theological issues. For example, in Mal. 1:2–5, God and Israel contend over the extent to which Yahweh is committed to his people. Or in Mal. 1:6–2:9, Yahweh argues with the priests about what constitutes appropriate worship. However, such discourse between Yahweh and all Israel is ultimately abandoned. In the final diatribe (Mal. 3:13–21 [3:13–4:3]),

---

[87]Cf. E. Wendland, "Linear and Concentric Patterns in Malachi," *BT* 36 (1985): 112–14, for a depiction of discourse according to the categories of assertion, objection, and response. Wendland observes triads of elements but does not find it necessary to equate one dialogue with one triad.

[88]I am indebted to Dennis R. MacDonald for introducing me to the literature on diatribe. Verhoef, *The Books of Haggai and Malachi*, NICOT, Grand Rapids, 1987, 165–66, notes general similarities between the style of Malachi and that of later Jewish authors and that of Greek authors.

[89]For brief discussion of the diatribe, see A. Lesky, *A History of Greek Literature*, New York, 1966, 670–71; D. Aune, *The New Testament in Its Literary Environment*, Philadelphia, 1987, 200–202. I am indebted to Dennis R. MacDonald for these references.

[90]I do not claim that Persian-period Judeans invented the diatribe. Moreover, I am uninterested in attempting to demonstrate a lineal connection between Yahwistic and Greek cynic diatribes. Rather, the claim is one of generic similarity. Two societies in the eastern Mediterranean region used similar forms of literature to address important topics.

conversation between Yahweh and "all Israel" ends. Only the "fearers" are now addressed. And Yahweh alone speaks; the "fearers" remain silent.[91]

If it is licit to argue that the primary unit of the book is diatribe-like discourse, then one is constrained to ask, both on redaction-critical and literary-structural grounds, whether these units have been ordered in a meaningful way. The last major unit (3:13–21 [3:13–4:3]) must be the concluding one, since it spells the end to a conversation between Yahweh and all Israel. Moreover, if one were to pick a diatribe with which to begin the book, Mal. 1:2–5 would have been most appropriate. It addresses all Israel and affirms the presence of the deity as a potential dialogue partner. However, one can imagine that the third diatribe (2:10–16) could occur between 1:2–5 and 1:6–2:9. One searches in vain for compelling architectonic scheme, whether driven by redaction-critical, literary-critical, or canonical-critical perspectives, to explain the order of all the diatribes.[92]

The prominence of diatribe-like discourse in Malachi may provide a clue about the social location of its author. The diatribe was, in other cultural settings, rooted in schools and/or pedagogical discourse. Since it now seems virtually certain that schools existed in Israel even before the exile, one may theorize that these diatribe-like discourses may reflect the activity of schools in Persian-period Judah.[93] Moreover, Levitical instruction may be preserved in these speeches (e.g., 2:6–9).

A writer composing diatribe-like discourse in the first century of the Persian period would have been informed by manifold elements of Israel's religious heritage. Biblical scholars have normally explored this issue from a traditio-historical perspective. Put more simply, they have asked: Have any texts or traditions influenced the book of Malachi? Though there has been no comprehensive effort on Malachi similar to those of Saebo and Mason devoted to Zechariah 9–14, several studies have identified important perspectives that appear in Malachi. There is a relatively strong consensus that Deuteronomistic traditions (e.g., language of covenant, vocabulary frequent in Deuteronomy)

---

[91]Those who write diatribes often invent audiences to make their point. Hence the various dialogue partners or objects in Malachi may not reflect true audiences. Cf. J. Berquist, "The Social Setting of Malachi," *BTB* 19 (1989): 124, who argues that Malachi is in dialogue with three distinct groups: "the pious orthodox, the skeptics or free thinkers, and the ungodly of Israel," though he too admits that "it is not possible to say unreservedly that these three groups actually existed in the early post-exilic society."

[92]Cf. the attempt of Blake, *The Rhetoric of Malachi.*

[93]A. Lemaire, *Les écoles et la formation de la Bible dans l'ancien Israël,* Göttingen, 1981.

are prominent in Malachi.[94] This observation became embedded in various arguments involving the relative priority of the various pentateuchal sources (JEDP). Some (e.g., Coggins; see above note) thought Malachi reflected D more than P, and in so doing advanced a late date for P. Eric Meyers and J. O'Brien have argued that so-called priestly perspectives inform Malachi, though whether such perspectives reflect specific tetrateuchal priestly material is open to question.[95]

The key issue in assessing the conceptual world of this third *maśśā'* is not whether the tetrateuchal priestly material had achieved fixity by the time of Malachi, or even whether Malachi knew certain priestly or ritual details or principles. Rather, one must recognize that the author of Malachi uses numerous and diverse elements from Israel's religious heritage. The author refers to the so-called patriarchal era (Jacob and Esau), to the Mosaic period (Horeb and Levi), and to the monarchy (with the epilogue and its reference to Elijah). The author of these fifty-some verses brings to bear numerous motifs from the history of Israel's experience with Yahweh in order to engage and confront the people.

Despite the breadth of historical allusion, the subject of Malachi's diatribes is more focused than the expansive discourse that makes up the first two "oracles." There, Judah's place in Yahweh's international plan stands as the subject for reflection. In Malachi, the religious life of the community in Judah, and especially Jerusalem, exists as the primary concern. The first two "oracles" foresaw significant destruction, whereas Malachi provides a means by which at least some Judeans might survive. To this extent, Malachi remains a hopeful book, as one might expect of literature rooted in the discourse of instruction. Both the final diatribe and the epilogue conclude on a positive note.

Just as diatribes in the Hellenistic world addressed diverse topics, so too the discourses in Malachi, though concerned with life in Judah, are manifold in topic: the permanence of Yahweh's care for Israel, the need to venerate Yahweh alone, the justice of Yahweh, the importance of tithing, justice and hope for those who fear Yahweh. Some of the topics are "theological," some involve human behavior. One important leitmotiv is the international scope of Yahweh's activity, even as he devotes special attention to Judah and Jerusa-

---

[94]The point has been made by many scholars, e.g., A. van Hoonacker, "Le rapprochement entre le Deutéronome et Malachie: une notice inédite de A. van Hoonacker (1908)," *ETL* 59 (1983): 86–90; Blenkinsopp, *Ezra-Nehemiah*, 242; R. Coggins, *Haggai, Zechariah, Malachi*, 75–76. See also the discussion of Deuteronomistic and Priestly tradition in Malachi by C. Reynolds, *Malachi and the Priesthood*, New Haven, Conn., 1993, 27–92.

[95]E. Meyers, "Priestly Language in the Book of Malachi," *HAR* 10 (1986): 225–37; O'Brien, *Priest and Levite in Malachi*.

lem. Though proper behavior at the ritual center—the temple—remains constitutive for Yahwism, the implications of such behavior and of Yahweh's own claims extend beyond Judah's provincial boundaries. Such breadth of vision seems especially important in a time when those who venerated Yahweh were located throughout the eastern Mediterranean basin and in Mesopotamia.

This collection of six diatribe-like discourses (Mal. 1:2–43) is framed by a formulaic introduction and an epilogue. The introductory formula defines Malachi as a *maśśā'* and links it with the two foregoing *maś'ôt*. The preposition *'el*, "to," in Mal. 1:1 suggests that this third oracle promises weal to Israel. In contrast, the epilogue (Mal. 3:22–24 [4:4–6]) integrates this "oracle" with both the pentateuch and former prophets (see below). Moreover, the epilogue was composed with specific linkages to the book of Malachi; thus, it would not work well at the end of Zechariah. The epilogue presupposes a collection of the latter prophets with Malachi at the end and with a collection of torah and former prophets preceding it.

7. The Text

Our ability to speak about the condition of the text of Zechariah 9–14 and Malachi has been enhanced by the discovery of the Dead Sea Scrolls.[96] Cave 4 included a series of twenty-one fragments known as 4QXII[a,c] which have been identified as a version of the minor prophets. Though in fragmentary condition and not yet officially published, they present some of the oldest extant texts of this biblical literature, more particularly of Mal. 2:10–14; 2:15–3:4; 3:5–14; and 3:15–24 [3:15–4:6].[97] They provide readings that agree some of the time, though not uniformly, with ancient Greek versions.[98] Apart from these ancient Hebrew manuscripts and though it is difficult to generalize, the LXX tends to expand on the earlier (and shorter) Hebrew text.[99]

The text of Malachi is in decidedly better shape than Zechariah 9–14, which is not to presume that the two sections had a separate textual history. In Malachi, I have found it necessary to formulate a reading other than the MT in

---

[96]A number of studies have focused on text-critical issues., e.g., K. Budde, "Zum Text der drei letzten kleinen Propheten," *ZAW* 26 (1906): 1–28; L. Kruse-Blinkenberg, "The Pesitta of the Book of Malachi," *ST* 20 (1966): 95–119; "The Book of Malachi according to Codex Syro-Hexaplaris Ambrosianus," *ST* 21 (1967): 62–82, as well as the monographs of Otzen and Saebo.

[97]See Russell Fuller, "76. 4QXII[a]," forthcoming in the Discoveries in the Judean Desert volume devoted to 4QXII. The same text includes fragments of Jonah, which poses interesting questions about the canonical order of these biblical books.

[98]For example, LXX and 4QXII[a] agree against MT in Mal. 2:12; see R. Fuller, "Text-Critical Problems in Malachi 2:10–16," *JBL* 110 (1991): 51.

[99]Verhoef, *The Books of Haggai and Malachi,* 169, lists 1:1, 7; 2:2, 4; 3:2, 5, 8, 19 [4:1] as obvious instances of such Septuagintal expansion.

the following verses: Mal. 1:1, 9, 11, 12; 2:2, 3, 11, 12, 13, 16, 17; 3:5, 13. Some of my construals follow ancient readings (e.g., 1:1; 2:2); others involve accepted text-critical principles such as dittography (1:12) or incorrect word division (2:3). The list is longer for Zechariah 9–14, the ancient versions of which diverge more from MT, in part because of the complex imagery that forced ancient translators to become interpreters.

Until the Qumran material has been published and assessed, it would be premature to speak definitively about the textual character of these nine chapters. However, it does appear that the order of these chapters is regular in most ancient manuscripts—that is, the order within the respective *maś'ôt* and the sequence of the *maś'ôt* themselves. The noteworthy exception is the presence in LXX of Mal. 3:2 after vv. 23–24; 4QXII[a] agrees with MT in this regard.

ZECHARIAH 9–11
THE FIRST "ORACLE"

Zechariah 9:1–8

God's word of oversight concerning "Beyond the River"

9:1 An oracle, the word of Yahweh against the land of Hadrak,
  and against[a] Damascus, its secure place.[b]
 Yahweh truly has a view of all humanity,[c]
  as well as of all the tribes of Israel;
2 And also (against) Hamath, which borders it;[d]
  even (against) Tyre and Sidon,
  though they are very wise.[e]
3 Tyre has built fortifications[f] for herself.
  She has piled up silver like dust,
  and gold like mud in the streets.
4 Nonetheless, Yahweh will dispossess her;
  he will hurl her riches into the sea,
  and she will be devoured by fire.
5 Ashkelon will see this and fear,
  Gaza will tremble violently.
 So too Ekron, her hope will wither;
  the king will be carried off from Gaza.
 Ashkelon will be uninhabited,
6 whereas an incestuous[g] population will inhabit Ashdod.
 "I will destroy the Philistine arrogance,
7 I will remove the blood from its mouth,[h]
  the detestable things from between its teeth."
 That which remains will belong to our God.
  It shall be like a clan[i] in Judah,
  Ekron like the Jebusite.
8 "I will encamp at my house[j]
  against any army.[k]
 No such oppressor will ever again pass through them,
  for now I look after (them) with my own eyes."[l]

a. I construe the preposition *b* to serve double duty, modifying both "land of Hadrak" and "Damascus."

b. *mĕnuḥātô* is difficult to translate. LXX (*thysia*), which derives the noun from the Hebrew word *minḥāh,* "sacrifice," offers little help. It is surely a fem. sing. noun, *menuḥāh,* with a third masc. sing. pronominal suffix. What is the antecedent of the pronoun? Some (e.g., Hanson, *The Dawn of Apocalyptic,* 297) have suggested Yahweh, from the expression "the word of Yahweh." However, one would normally take the first noun, i.e., the *status constructus*—in this case "word," as the referent. The author, though mistaken geographically, views Damascus as the capital of Hadrak.

c. Literally, either "Yahweh has a human eye" or "Yahweh has an eye for/on humanity." LXX follows this latter sense. Many have emended conjecturally to read Aram instead of Adam; see, e.g., NRSV; Rudolph, *Sacharja 9–14,* 167–68. This judgment, however, presupposes that Aram is the object of discussion, which, as the rest of the oracle makes clear, is palpably not the case. The more difficult reading supplies the appropriate notion, namely, that Yahweh's oracle has international implications.

d. Again, it is difficult to identify the antecedent of the pronoun "it," which is a fem. sing. suffix. I opt for the land of Hadrak, which was probably contiguous, though to the north of Hamath, which was also the name of both a city and a province.

e. Literally, "it/she is wise." Some have suggested that this singular adjective calls for the deletion of one of the aforementioned cities. Thus Hanson, *The Dawn of Apocalyptic,* 298, removes Tyre. However, as Otzen has argued, *Deuterosacharja,* 237, Tyre and Sidon occur elsewhere with a singular verb.

f. The term *māṣôr* is commonly used to describe siegeworks against a city. However, in postexilic texts (e.g., 2 Chron. 8:5, "fortified cities with walls, gates, and bars") the term refers to defenses of a city. Cf. the use of the cognate noun *mĕṣûrāh* in 2 Chron. 11:10, "fortified cities."

g. The noun *mamzēr* is difficult, occurring in only one other place, Deut. 23:2. One does wonder whether, in both Zech. 9:6 and Deuteronomy, the noun might refer to a child of mixed ethnic background, since Deut. 23:3 treats the "full-blooded" Ammonite or Moabite.

h. Literally, "its blood," in which case the pronominal suffix serves to make the noun definite. One senses double entendre, since the author may be referring either to people or to blood sacrifice; see Lev. 5:9.

i. Reading *kĕ'elep,* "a clan," instead of MT *kĕ'allup,* "a chieftain."

j. The verb *ḥnh* with the preposition *l* means "to camp at," so Num. 2:34.

k. One can translate either with MT, "against an army," or with LXX, "against a garrison." One may read MT *miṣṣābāh,* "against an army," with the preposition *min* prefixed to the noun *ṣābāh* from the root *ṣbh* instead of the expected root *ṣb'* (the *aleph* has quiesced). One can repoint and read *maṣṣābāh* and derive the word from the noun *maṣṣāb,* which has been prefixed by the preposition *min,* and translate "as a garrison," so LXX. See Rudolph, *Sacharja 9–14,* 169, and Saebo, *Sacharja 9–14,* 49–51, 151, for a discussion of these options. Though the semantic fields of the two proposed nouns are quite different, the purport is not radically different: Yahweh will act against military forces.

mē'ōber ûmiššāb appears to be a dittographic expansion based on *ya'ăbōr,* which occurs in the next colon. Cf. Saebo, *Sacharja 9–14,* 151, who argues that these two words represent an early alternate reading.

l. The nuance of the clause is difficult. Does the author intend something neutral, as in RSV "for now I see with my own eyes"? The phrase *r'h b* can signify dative of agency, "see with eyes," as in Deut. 3:27, in which case the object of the gaze is not specified. I supply it on the basis of context; it is the group signified by the pronominal suffix in the previous clause, the Yahwists. But it is also possible to translate the final clause, "for now I see with my own eyes," with the emphasis on Yahweh's seeing directly and not through some intermediary, which might be the Persian authorities.

There is no scholarly consensus about the extent of the first pericope in Zechariah 9. On the one hand, P. Hanson has argued that the first poem comprises Zech. 9:1–17 and may be characterized as "a divine warrior hymn."[1] More typical is a delimitation of a unit comprising the first eight verses, a view that may be sustained on both form- and literary-critical grounds.[2]

This first poem includes a title that presents a claim about the extent of Yahweh's purview (9:1–2); a prophetic oracle involving the destruction of four coastal cities (9:3–6a); and a divine oracle (9:6b–7a, 8) that includes a snippet concerning Judah (9:7b). To proceed with such a division and to presume standard form-critical perspectives would involve the assumption that these eight verses are a combination of originally disparate elements. One must recognize the tension between first- and third-person language concerning Yahweh, and that there is both language of woe toward foreign nations and weal toward Yahweh's house. However, there is little evidence that these aforementioned elements ever existed independently of their juxtaposition in this divine oracle against foreign nations.[3] This oracle against the nations attests to the international sway of Yahweh's powerful word. The deity's purposes extend beyond the borders of Judah. Nonetheless, the prophet focuses on Syro-Palestinian territory, not all of the Persian empire.

[9:1–2] The word *maśśā'* does not occur in isolation, as is suggested in both Hebrew *(BHS)* and English (NRSV) editions. Rather, this word provides a structuring device here and in Zech. 12:1 and Mal. 1:1 to introduce three separate collections. In each case, the noun *maśśā'*, or "oracle," is part of a phrase, "an oracle, the word of the Lord," which is then followed by a preposition (*b* in Zech. 9:1; *'al* in 12:1; and *'el* in Mal. 1:1), a toponym or name of an ethnic community, and then material of varying sorts. Since the object of the preposition *b* in 9:1 (which may be translated in an adversative sense, "against") is directed, at least initially, against non-Israelite territory, one may infer that an author construed this first collection to be something like oracles

---

[1]Hanson, *The Dawn of Apocalyptic,* 315–24.

[2]So, e.g., Lacocque, Saebo, Rudolph, Otzen, van der Woude, Willi-Plein.

[3]Hence I disagree with Saebo, who argues that vv. 1–2, 3–6a, 6b-7, and 8 were originally separate and only reached their present form as the result of a long and complicated process of development, *Sacharja 9–14,* 136–74. The history of the use of *děbar yahweh* language in the Hebrew Bible is different from the history of the composition of this particular text.

against foreign nations (cf. Isa. 14:28–17:6; Jeremiah 47–49; Amos 1). And, as is the case with several other prophetic books that contain oracles against the nations (e.g., the Septuagint version of Jeremiah), a basic tripartite division occurs: oracles against the nations, oracles against Israel, and oracles on behalf of Israel. This tripartite division represents more of an ideal type than a definitive report about the actual contents of each section.

The syntax and semantics of the first two verses are extremely complex. At first glance it appears that there is a separate, brief, formulaic introduction, "an oracle, the word of the Lord." But any attempt to discern a break between these and the ensuing Hebrew words fails. Rather, formulaic language has been included in a complicated sentence that affirms the international and inclusive character of Yahweh's word.

The author conveys the international scope of this saying by listing specific areas, which we may compare with those in the oracles against the nations in the book of Amos. There, as in Zechariah 9, a collection of prophetic materials begins with oracles against the nations and is directed only toward "nations" in Syria-Palestine. In each, Syria is the first region named. Moreover, just as with oracles against the nations in the book of Amos, Zech. 9:1–8 presents difficult problems for the interpreter, particularly regarding historical background. Scholars have long noted that the events which seem to be presupposed in Amos' oracle against Damascus predate his own time. Haza'el, referred to in Amos 1:4, reigned from 842–806 B.C.E.; whereas Amos uttered his oracles during the middle of the eighth century. Some scholars (e.g., Otzen) have maintained that Zech. 9:1–8, too, alludes to historical events before the putative time that the oracle was written. Few "historical" occasions of a sort attested in Amos 1 seem to lie behind Zech. 9:1–8.[4] Instead of "events," there are toponyms, which do not, in the very nature of the case, involve particular events. Rather, the text presents specificity, that is, names of certain Syro-Palestinian city-states.[5] As a result, the question of background must be nuanced. One might ask: When did all these place-names cohere (e.g., as a political unit), to such a degree that one can postulate a time at which the text

[4]The use of these northern Syria toponyms in the prophetic corpus is not new with Zechariah 9–14. Although Hadrak occurs only here in the OT, Damascus and Hamath appear in Jeremiah's oracle against Damascus (Jer. 49:23–27). Moreover, both cities figure prominently in the description of restored Israel (Ezek. 47:16–48:1). In addition, Amos 5:27 attests the notion of exile in an area like Hamath and beyond Damascus (Isa. 11:11); see D. Jones, "A Fresh Interpretation of Zechariah 9–14," *VT* 12 (1962): 241–59, and Mason, *The Use of Earlier Biblical Material in Zechariah IX–XIV,* 8–17.

[5]Otzen has argued that the most cogent context in which to set these verses is that of the Neo-Assyrian empire. Others, however, have maintained that the context is considerably later, namely, that of Alexander's conquest of Syria-Palestine, e.g., Elliger. This debate is, of course, critically important for a proper understanding of this oracle.

was written? Or one might ask: What holds these names together so that they, and not other names, make a sensible whole? The latter question clearly focuses on literary sensibilities and not on a specific historical rootage.[6]

The first toponym is the most difficult. Although the term "Hadrak" does not appear elsewhere in the OT, this toponym is well attested in Neo-Assyrian texts during Tiglath Pileser III's reign (745–727 B.C.E.) as *Hatarikka,* and in the Aramaic Zakir inscription (c.780 B.C.E.) as *hzrk.* In these extrabiblical materials, the noun apparently refers both to a city, the capital of La'ash, and the region in northern Syria associated with it. Since Zech. 9:1 uses the language of *'ereṣ,* "land," one may infer that the latter sense is conveyed here. It would be useful to know how long this name was in use. Was the term used by the native population or by later imperial authorities (e.g., Babylonians or Persians)? And if so, for how long after the late eighth century B.C.E.? The latest clear attestation of the Akkadian word occurs in an eponym list, "Gihilu, (governor) of Hatarika," c.689 B.C.E.[7] However, toponyms are regularly conservative, that is, local traditions typically preserve such names for centuries, if not millennia.

Whatever Hadrak might have meant in the eighth or early seventh century B.C.E., the author of Zech. 9:1–2 now uses it in a creative way, mirroring what we know of the provincial government of northern Syria in the Persian period. In Zech. 9:1, Hadrak appears to signify a region. And, as we shall see, this initial poem has as one of its hallmarks the interplay between regional and urban toponyms (this feature occurs elsewhere in Zechariah 9–14; cf. Judah and Jerusalem in Zechariah 12–14).

By contrast, Damascus, though that name could also signify a region, denotes here a specific city against which Yahweh's word could alight. We know little about Damascus in the Persian period. It presumably remained a provincial capital, as it had been under the Assyrians and Babylonians. Whether it was the satrapal residence of "Beyond the River" is a matter of debate (see Introduction).[8] And if such were the case, we would have an obvious explanation for the prominence of northern Syria at the beginning of this poem. That territory, which could be described either as Hadrak or as Damascus, may well have been the satrapal headquarters of which Judah and Jerusalem were part.

The ensuing two lines add three more toponyms, all three of which involve cities with attendant territories: Hamath, Tyre, and Sidon. On the basis of the

---

[6]Hanson correctly avoids the attempt to discern one historical moment that lies behind the text. However, he argues that a mythic pattern explains the toponyms.

[7]D. Luckenbill, *Ancient Records of Assyria and Babylonia,* vol. II: *Historical Records of Assyria from Sargon to the End,* Chicago, 1927, 438.

[8]I. Eph'al, "Syria-Palestine under Achaemenid Rule," 155–56.

Aramaic Zakir inscription mentioned above, we know that King Zakir ruled territory that could be described as Hamath and La'ash (Hadrak). Zakir was king of a "dual kingdom" known as Hamath-La'ash.[9] This early political history of northern Syria could explain why Hadrach, Damascus, and Hamath belong together at the inception of the poem. However, it is the political realities of the Persian empire, namely, the "Beyond the River" satrapy, with its headquarters likely in Damascus, that make northern Syria so important for Judah and Jerusalem. The initial lines of this first "oracle" offer toponymic specificity, which orients the reader to the northern part of the satrapy and its capital. Moreover, such orientation introduces Yahweh's negative intent toward this area. Though the author is aware of the larger Persian imperial context, this region receives pride of place, since it is there that the imperial policies are working themselves out (e.g., the militarization mentioned in the Introduction).

Things change with Tyre and Sidon.[10] Instead of inland Syria, the poet moves south and to the coast. (The author could have moved directly west and to the coast by citing Aradus and Byblos.) During the Persian period, Tyre and Sidon, as well as Byblos and Aradus, were the important Phoenician city-states, the ones that held considerable territory and exercised significant economic and political influence.[11] Whether they functioned like provinces is a matter of much debate.[12] Some scholars have proposed to delete Sidon from v. 2.[13] However, since the author seems interested in multiplying toponyms, such an excision would work against the rhetorical strategy of this poem. A second striking feature of this material devoted to Tyre and Sidon is the presence of personification. They are described as a "wise" people, and then later, Tyre alone as someone who builds and piles up (vv. 2–3). (Personification continues with the other cities in the passage: Ashkelon sees and fears, Gaza trembles violently.) The tone of specificity introduced by the place-names becomes humanized.

In order to gain a sense of what Tyre and Sidon might have signified to Yahwists in Judah during the Persian period, we must note that at least two

[9]So M. Unger, *Israel and the Arameans of Damascus,* Grand Rapids, 1957, 85–89. I am indebted to T. Bagley for this reference.

[10]On these sites, see J. Elayi, "The Phoenician Cities in the Persian Period," *JANESCU* 12 (1980): 13–28.

[11]The inscription on the sarcophagus of Eshmun'azar, which probably dates to the fourth century B.C.E., reports that Sidon "owned" Dor and Joppa, by dint of their having been given to Sidon's king because of his work on behalf of the Persian emperor.

[12]See J. Elayi, "Studies in Phoenician Geography during the Persian Period," *JNES* 41 (1982): 83–110.

[13]Hanson, *The Dawn of Apocalyptic,* 298.

elements contributed to this process of signification: earlier traditions and contemporary political realities.[14] As for the first, the mention of these two cities could serve as a shorthand reference to the Phoenician coast. For example, in Isaiah 23, which is titled "*maśśā'* Tyre," Sidon figures prominently (Isa. 23:2, 4, 12), so that one can affirm with Isa. 23:2 that the poem is addressed to the "inhabitants of the coast," who can be described using the toponyms of Tyre and Sidon. Further, as regards Tyre alone, Hanson has noted that there are a number of threads that continue from the cloth of earlier prophetic discourse concerning Tyre: references to Tyre's wealth and power, predictions that Yahweh would remove her goods and throw them into the sea, and that Tyre would suffer conflagration.[15]

However, Zech. 9:1–2 presents no simple recapitulation of earlier traditions.[16] Tyre was the paradigmatically wise city; so Ezek. 28:3–4: "You are indeed wiser than Daniel; no secret is hidden from you, by your wisdom [the same word used in Zech. 9:2] and your understanding you have gotten wealth for yourself. . . ."[17] Now both Tyre and Sidon have received the appellation "wise." This poet is interested in broader strokes than was the penetrating analyst of Ezekiel 28.

Second, this Persian-period author surely knew something about the geopolitical realities of the time. Ezra-Nehemiah refers to the Tyrians and Sidonians as the sources of raw materials (Ezra 3:7). Moreover, the Tyrians represented the sort of presence in Jerusalem that they held in other cities, that is, a colony engaged in trade (Neh. 13:16). However, it is the extrabiblical materials that compel us to recognize the special importance of Tyre and Sidon in the Persian period. These cities provided naval support for the Persians in several critical wars with the Greeks during the first half of the fifth century, before the peace of Callias in 449 B.C.E. Moreover, kings, not governors, ruled these cities, suggesting that they were not administered in the same ways as were other cities and territories of the Levant (compare, e.g., the administration of Samaria or Jerusalem under a governor). Thus, Phoenician prominence in trade, raw materials, and military power were known to any author writing in Jerusalem during the Persian period, though such realia were surely read

---

[14]Mason, *The Use of Earlier Biblical Material in Zechariah IX–XIV*, while illumining the earlier traditions that might inform Zechariah 9–14, does not integrate these data with Persian-period political and religious realia.

[15]Hanson, *The Dawn of Apocalyptic*, 318.

[16]See similarly, I. Willi-Plein, *Prophetie am Ende: Untersuchungen zur Sacharja 9–14*, BBB 42, Cologne, 1974, 68, who maintains, against Stade, that Zechariah 9 is not a direct "parallel" to Ezek. 28:3–4.

[17]In the brief Ezekielian oracle directed against Sidon, 28:20–23, there is no such characterization.

through the lens of earlier Israelite discourse about and experience with Phoenicia and, more particularly, Tyre and Sidon.[18]

What, then, has the author accomplished in the first two verses of this poem? First, a simple geographic half-arc, created by the five toponyms, sets the context for Yahweh's active word. That word is against something; though we cannot be clear whether it is against local constituents of "Beyond the River," or against "Beyond the River" as an expression of the Persian empire, though the former is more likely. If the author had intended the latter, the oracle would have been directed solely at Damascus, or some other entity that signified the Persians. Second, no reason is offered for this dangerous judgment. Yahweh will act despite, but not because of, the wisdom of Tyre and Sidon. Third, in the parenthetic statement of v. 1b, the author provides a virtual statement of theme, namely, that Yahweh's purview is international, not focused simply on the "tribes of Israel," whether they are construed as located in the land or dispersed through the eastern Mediterranean and Mesopotamian regions.

[3–4] The author continues providing toponyms, though now moving down the Mediterranean coast. First, however, the author pauses to focus on Tyre, vv. 3–4, the city that captures more attention than any other in vv. 1–9. Here our approach must be diverse, including attention to form-critical structure, traditio-historical issues, and historical background.

When reading vv. 3–4, one is initially struck by the similarity between the apparent "judgment oracle" and the surrounding materials. It appears that there is a situation, v. 3, to which Yahweh responds in a punitive way, v. 4, with vv. 5–6a spelling out the implications of this action in other geographic areas.[19] However, v. 3 does not function as a reason for Yahweh's action. It is, as was 2b, concessive; in spite of all these things (ramparts, silver, gold), Yahweh will act against Tyre. Why, then, might this author let Tyre figure so prominently? The answer derives from attention to historical background and to the prominence of Tyre in earlier prophetic literature, particularly Ezekiel.

If Sidon's fleet was truly preeminent, if Sidon was the earliest city to strike coins,[20] in sum, if it was (as Elayi claims) "the leading Phoenician city in the

---

[18]Phoenician inscriptions, which may be traced to the Persian-period Levant, attested to the inland extent of Phoenician trade, e.g., the Tell el-Kheleifeh inscription (ostracon 2070) that includes a list of Phoenician names, found near Elat (N. Glueck, "Tell el-Kheleifeh Inscriptions," *Near Eastern Studies in Honor of William Foxwell Albright*, ed. H. Goedicke, Baltimore, 1971, 229–31); and more generally on Persian-period Phoenician inscriptions, see A. Lemaire, "Les inscriptions palestiniennes d'époque perse: un bilan provisoire," *Transeuphratene* 1, 1989, 92–93.

[19]Saebo holds that such a judgment oracle pattern is present, *Sacharja 9–14*, 147–48.

[20]On this see Eph'al, "Syria-Palestine under Achaemenid Rule," 156–57.

Persian period,"[21] then why does Tyre have pride of place in this poem? The reasons are surely complex. Tyre was, in fact, closer to Jerusalem, especially because there were more roads leading from Tyre to the inland than there were from Sidon. And one of these roads headed south, toward Jerusalem. As a result, one may presume that, for Judah and Jerusalem, Tyre was a better known trading partner.[22] In addition, the Tyrians had refused to serve with Cambyses in campaigns against northern Africa, which would have involved attacks against Carthage. Hence, Cambyses and his Persian imperial successors acted more favorably toward Sidon than they did toward Tyre.[23] Third, Tyre was, unlike its physical setting today, an island, which gave it excellent protection from attack but also made it a less efficient port since goods transported from elsewhere in the Mediterranean had to be moved to the mainland before shipment throughout the Levant. Nonetheless, such insular status afforded it a certain preeminence due to geographic remove from the more vulnerable coastal cities. Fourth, the Tyrian colony in Memphis provides evidence of well-known abilities, as exemplified in the silver bowls discovered there.[24] All these elements explain why Tyre might have been viewed as *the* Phoenician city that deserves special mention in an oracle written during the Persian period.

However, a fuller response to the question about the prominent place of Tyre in Zechariah 9 derives from the attention to the place Tyre receives in earlier prophetic literature. Although Tyre appears in a rather stock manner in Amos 1:9–10 (though Tyrian influence is understood to affect Edom, cf. Ezek. 27:16), this city is prominent in the oracles against the nations of Isaiah and especially Ezekiel (there is no separate oracle against Tyre in Jeremiah). Isaiah 23, which includes several oracles concerning Tyre, treats it as one with Sidon[25] and even, in vv. 15–18, speaks about restoration for Tyre after military defeat and about increased trade that will benefit Yahweh and those who

---

[21]J. Elayi, "Studies in Phoenician Geography during the Persian Period," 93–95. H. Katzenstein, "Tyre in the Early Persian Period (539–486 B.C.E.)," *BA* 42 (1979): 23–34, maintains that Tyre's loss of Carthage, "the greatest Tyrian colony," and the related increase in Sidon's status were the signal issues in this period.

[22]This judgment should not be taken to deny the importance of Joppa as the closest port to Jerusalem.

[23]See Katzenstein, "Tyre in the Early Persian Period," 27–28.

[24]Katzenstein, "Tyre in the Early Persian Period," 29–31.

[25]Kaiser, *Isaiah 13–39*, OTL, Philadelphia, 1974, 159–72, views it as originally directed against Sidon; with only 23:15–18 related to Tyre, and all dating to the third and second centuries B.C.E. Compare the nuanced discussion of H. Wildberger, *Jesaja 13–27*, BK X/2, Neukirchen-Vluyn, 1989, 853–84, who views vv. 1–14 (except vv. 5 and 13) as directed to Tyre, with vv. 15–16 and 17–18 attributed to a later hand. Wildberger dates the original oracle to the late Assyrian period.

venerate him. However, nothing in Isaiah seems to have influenced directly that which is said in Zechariah 9. The case is different with Ezekiel.

In v. 3, the poet uses various literary techniques to focus our attention on Tyre. The phrase "Tyre . . . fortifications" involves a case of paronomasia, *ṣōr māṣōr,* and alliteration, particularly the consonant *ṣade* in the first three cola. And, as noted earlier, personification is present. The poet construes Tyre as a woman who built fortifications and who has "piled up" silver and gold. Then two similes explore the immensity of the treasure but also cast it in a pejorative light. The treasure is immense, but also common, as are dirt and streets. And then, in chiastic order, we hear that Yahweh will dispossess Tyre, presumably of its silver and gold, by throwing its riches into the sea, just over the city wall, and then Tyre will be destroyed by fire.

How, then, has this brief section devoted to Tyre been influenced by earlier traditions? The notion that Tyre will be burned is surely "traditional" (Amos 1:10). However, the mention of silver and gold, as was the case with wisdom in Zech. 9:2, occurs elsewhere only in Ezekiel (Ezek. 27:12, 22; 28:4), thereby suggesting that Ezek. 28:4 is in some way a "source" for Zechariah 9. In addition, Zech. 9:3–4 is consistent with the feminine personification in Ezekiel (e.g., Ezek. 26:4). Furthermore, the notion of other kings and countries being affected by Tyre's demise in Zech. 9:5 is similar to that of the coastal kings being dismayed, Ezek. 27:35. Moreover, the language of human architecture, whether fortifications, *māṣōr,* or a semantic equivalent (e.g., *'armĕnôt* in Amos 1:10) also appears in the extensive Ezekiel material devoted to Tyre (gates, Ezek. 26:10; walls, Ezek. 26:4, 9, 10, 12; pillars, 26:11; towers, Ezek. 26:4, 9).[26] Finally, the specific character of the punishment has a precursor in Ezek. 26:12 (following the T V, so Zimmerli), "throw x into the sea," though there it is the rubble rather than riches as in Zech. 9:4.[27] However, appeal to Ezek. 26:12 as a source is not wholly satisfactory, since the notion of Tyre's having gold and silver in abundance is present in another late prophetic text, namely, Joel 3:5, though that author claims the gold and silver came from Yahweh and has been taken into coastal temples. In addition, key features of the Ezekiel "Tyre" material (e.g., the pride of Tyre, Ezek. 28:2–5) are not present in Zechariah 9.[28] In sum, there are noteworthy similarities between

---

[26]W. Zimmerli, *Ezekiel 2,* Hermeneia, Philadelphia, 1983, 24, attributes Tyre's prominence in Ezekiel to the theological problem that unconquered Tyre's (and Egypt's) rebellion against Babylon presented, that is, an affront to Yahweh's plan for these nations. The last oracle in the Tyrian assemblage (Ezek. 29:17–20) retrofits the earlier projections of Tyre's destruction with the predictions of Egyptian defeat.

[27]According to Ezek. 26:12, the Babylonians will steal the treasure; whereas according to Ezek. 27:27, Tyre's treasures will sink into the sea.

[28]Contra Mason, *The Use of Earlier Biblical Material in Zechariah IX–XIV,* 21–22.

Ezekiel 26–28 and Zech. 9:2–5.[29] Nonetheless, there are such important differences as well that it is inappropriate to contend that the author of Zechariah 9 is simply reusing a "tradition" that he has inherited from Ezekiel. Tyre was known to Yahwists living in the Levant in such a way that their knowledge surely informed their use of earlier notions about Tyre. Further, one important motif in the Ezekiel Tyrian material, Tyre's pride, is absent from vv. 3–4, whereas the basic point of Zechariah 9 involves the demise of a major Phoenician port for no apparent reason.

[5–6a] Personification continues: Ashkelon sees and fears, Gaza trembles violently, Ekron loses hope, and then the rhetoric moves back into more neutral language of a king's being removed from Gaza, and population problems: depopulation of Ashkelon and improper repopulation of Ashdod. This change in the character of the language highlights two issues, what some have called two lists: Ashkelon-Gaza-Ekron and Gaza-Ashkelon-Ashdod.[30] These parallel lines of toponyms do not reflect political or geographic reality. Rather, they provide a way of referring to "traditional" Philistine sites and depict two forms of disaster, that indicated in the "personification" section and that conveyed in the political section. The "incomplete" parallelism includes a number of alliterative elements, whether explicit, the connection of "fire," *'ēš* to *'ašqĕlôn,* or implicit, a wordplay on two homophones *'azzāh,* "strength," and *'azzāh,* "Gaza."[31] Clearly, aesthetic considerations, rather than direct concern with political reality, undergird this section of the poem.

These verses, which mention several coastal cities, present various questions for the interpreter: Why are they to be destroyed, and what is the significance of this collection of cities? As for the first, just as with Tyre, the author presents no rationale for the confusion and destruction of these southern coastal cities mentioned in vv. 5–6a, though such an effect was surely expected.[32] The toponymic specificity of Zechariah 9 sets it apart from the mercantile particularity of Ezekiel (Ezek. 27:12–24).

Second, it is no accident that so-called Philistine cities occur next, since other Persian-period prophetic literature views Phoenician and Philistine cities as one unit, so Joel 3:5. And during the Persian period, there were no

---

[29]Stade, "Deuterosacharja," 46–52, and Saebo, *Sacharja 9–14,* 148–49, attribute the similarities almost exclusively to the influence of traditional material on Zechariah 9. Mason, *The Use of Earlier Biblical Material in Zechariah IX–XIV,* 19, speaks about Zechariah 9 echoing and evoking the Ezekiel material.

[30]Rudolph, *Sacharja 9–14,* 173.

[31]On this see Rudolph, *Sacharja 9–14,* 173–74.

[32]So Ezek. 27:35, though in Ezekiel the effect is on the coastland generally; no specific cities are named.

fundamental cultural differences between the central and southern coast.[33] With these names, the poet has expanded his treatment of cities in the province of "Beyond the River," and in so doing, he has moved as far south on the coast as is possible to refer to earlier major cities.

The extent to which the Phoenicians dominated these and other cities on the southern Levantine coast is a matter of considerable debate. Elayi maintains that Phoenician control extended no farther south than Ashkelon and that since no coinage from Ashkelon had been discovered, one may infer that it was under Tyrian rule.[34] As Joel 3:4 (see also Ps. 83:7) and ancient literary and archaeological evidence suggests, Phoenicians either controlled or were significantly present in most coastal Levantine cities, even down as far as Memphis (though no Phoenician presence has been discovered at Ashdod).[35] Elayi notes that only Tyrians and Sidonians "seemed to have exerted control in southern Phoenicia. . . . It seems that the Sidonian presence in this area increased through the Persian period at the expense of the Tyrians."[36] All this suggests, as with Tyre, that instead of being "traditions," these coastal cities represented important political and economic realities for those living in Judah.

But again, as was the case with Tyre, the cities of Ashkelon, Gaza, Ekron, and Ashdod were attested in earlier Israelite traditions. Along with Gath, which does not occur here presumably because it was not a coastal site, these cities constituted the earlier and Philistine pentapolis. Though references to the Philistines occur in historical narratives, the oracles against the nations have special importance for an understanding of Zech. 9:5-6a. It is precisely these four cities that suffer punishment according to Amos 1:6–8 (even though only Gaza is indicted; and again, as with Tyre, contact with Edom was important). Just as Zech. 9:6b summarizes these cities as Philistia, so too does Amos 1:8. The issue of depopulation is shared, as it is with Zeph. 2:4, 6. There is no oracle against Philistia in Isaiah. In Jeremiah, the same four cities appear as representative of the "Philistine" territory, Jer. 25:20; and there is, as well, an oracle in Jer. 47:1–6, in which only Gaza and Ashkelon are mentioned by name. Ezekiel 25:15–17 provides only a briefer poem.

Just as Tyre's wealth will be destroyed, the Philistine population will be decimated. Each area suffers a different form of destruction. The ordering of sites reflects political reality in the Persian period. Tyre and Sidon controlled or

---

[33]The distinctive material culture of the Philistines was no longer in evidence. Many of these cities were conquered by the Neo-Babylonians and were later under Egyptian control.

[34]See Eph'al, "Syria-Palestine under Achaemenid Rule," 150, on alternating settlement patterns. Such a perspective should keep us from using earlier and anachronistic notions concerning the disparate character of Phoenicia and Philistia.

[35]Elayi, "Studies in Phoenician Geography during the Persian Period," 103.

[36]Elayi, "Studies in Phoenician Geography during the Persian Period," 104. The situation would be the reverse of that which lies behind Ezek. 27:8.

influenced significantly southern coastal cities, to such an extent that if Tyre were to fall, it would have an impact on those cities.

[6b–7a] Yahweh appears vigorously in first-person rhetoric. The last explicit reference to Yahweh occurred in v. 4, in which case Yahweh's treatment of Tyre was foretold. Now Yahweh himself reports what will happen. The reader must ask: Is this something different from that which has just been described in vv. 5b–6a? In my judgment, the answer is yes—the prior verses indicate the impact of the destruction of Tyre on the "Philistine" cities and then their depopulation by an unknown agent. The acts of Yahweh are here of a qualitatively different sort from those narrated earlier. First, we hear about Philistia the region, as opposed to individual cities. Second, Yahweh will destroy the arrogance of the Philistines, a notion that suggests the reason for the destruction (note that, unlike Tyre, Philistine arrogance is not mentioned in earlier oracles against the nations). However, the author has made a subtle claim, since it is their arrogance, rather than the Philistines themselves, that will be destroyed. Third, in this divine speech the tone runs counter to that expressed in Jer. 47:4, a text that anticipates the destruction of all Philistines, and is more like that of Jer. 25:20, which refers to a remnant of Ashdod.

The next two lines are ambiguous, which is unfortunate, since they are integral to the interpretation of the entire poem. All of Philistia is personified as one person or animal (since human personification occurred earlier, I prefer the former option). The key question is: Does Yahweh act toward Philistia beneficently or punitively? The text presents an image of the deity's removing bloody, impure things from someone's mouth. Since there was blood in his mouth, we presume that the author thought the "Philistine" must have eaten something impure; otherwise the blood would have been drained. However, the logical force of the deity's action is, in some odd way (odd because explicit language of ritual and purification is not used), to cleanse this Philistine person. The noun, translated here as "detestable things," is used elsewhere to describe that which is ritually impure (Lev. 7:21; 11:10–12), something—regularly food, hence the imagery of having food in one's mouth in Zech. 9:7—that serves to cut a person off from the temple.[37] The image appears to be of a Philistine who has eaten unclean food and who is now having the remnant or a portion of that meal removed from its mouth. The picture is graphic (and resonates with the notion of the impure ethnic background stated in v. 6).

[7b] Such radical rhetoric seems to force the poet back to third-person, namely, more impersonal, language about the deity. At this point, one senses a sequence of events lying just beneath the surface of the poem. After the destruction of Syria, Phoenicia, and Philistia, and after the removal of impurity

---

[37]Cf. Num. 11:33, "while the meat was yet between their teeth," as a figurative way of indicating that food was in someone's mouth.

from the "Philistine," something will remain, and that something will belong to Israel's deity. The poet chooses two similes to express this almost inexpressible notion, namely, how it is that something which is related to Philistia can be acceptable. "It" will be like a "clan" in Judah. One must wonder to what the "it" refers. Is it that which was in the Philistine maw, or is it the Philistine himself? The poet provides the answer with the toponym Ekron in the very next line. Ekron, the only inland site among the "Philistine" cities mentioned in these verses, will be like the Jebusite. The similes continue the radical tone but help the reader understand, on the one hand by allusion to contemporary reality, and on the other by allusion to the past, how such an integration is possible. The first simile indicates that the remnant will be like a Judahite clan, a notion that picks up semantically, if not lexically, Zech. 9:1, in its reference to all the tribes of Israel.[38] Just as Bethlehem Ephrathah (Micah 5:2), another urban toponym, may be called one of the clans of Judah, here it is possible to construe a non-Israelite entity as one of these Judahite clans. The second simile alludes to the Jebusites, the Canaanite population of Jerusalem, which were absorbed into Israel after David conquered Jerusalem. Just as that Jebusite city became Yahweh's home, and by extension a ritually acceptable place, and just as the Jebusites came to have a place within Israel, so too the Philistine remnant can be accepted. That which remains (it is useful to think of a text like Jer. 25:20, which refers to "the remnant of Ashdod") will belong to Yahweh, not to some other God. The key notion here is Yahweh's surprising claim to benevolent sovereignty over a Philistine remnant. He will purify and possess something utterly foreign.

The area known as Philistia in this poem was densely occupied during the Persian period.[39] However, none of the cities in Zech. 9:1–8 appear in the lists of Ezra-Nehemiah as cities in which Judeans dwelled. Hence one may infer that this "Philistia" was truly "foreign" (see also Neh. 13:23). Nonetheless, since the territory was contiguous with Judah, it was reasonable for an author to think about having a remnant of Philistia associated with Judah.

[8] Again, the poet changes voice and tone; Yahweh now speaks in the first person, as in vv. 6b–7a. Moreover, Yahweh no longer addresses peaceable relations with the Philistines but military relations with an unnamed "oppressor."[40] With such a shift in tone, it is difficult to think about the Philistine as the oppressor. Rather, the notion of an eye, which had occurred earlier in Zech. 9:1

---

[38]Not the phrase "clans of Judah" in Zech. 12:6. The term *'elep* is not prominent in the description of Persian-period social realities. Though this term refers to the same social unit as the *mišpāḥāh*, it carries different social connotations, namely, military and other relationships.

[39]Stern, *Material Culture of the Land of the Bible in the Persian Period,* 243–44.

[40]See Isa. 14:1–2, which, since it envisions aliens joining Israel and oppressors no longer exerting power over them, is similar in tone to Zech. 9:8. Cf. Zech. 10:4, in which the term *nōgēś,* is used for "ruler" without apparent negative connotations.

and which creates a semantic and lexical inclusio, drives one to conclude that the geographic sweep of the toponyms throughout the poem has created a picture in which the "oppressor" could be viewed as any tormentor—whether Philistine overlord or local Syro-Palestinian tormentor (perhaps regional Persian authorities)—within the Levant.

The previous verses had provided a transition whereby the poet could address the place of Yahweh's dwelling, namely, by referring to the Jebusites, pre-Israelite inhabitants of Jerusalem. In v. 8 the author adopts the language of military encampment to describe the way in which Yahweh will be present at Jerusalem and against any enemy forces. This final verse offers a promissory note, namely, that Yahweh will not allow anyone to devastate militarily his people. The verse emphasizes Yahweh's protective oversight, not actual conflict and not, for that matter, the place. The emphasis falls instead on the parties—no one shall march, no one shall overrun them—presumably those who dwell in Jerusalem.

In sum, one may think of Zech. 9:1–8 as a complex mosaic, the key tesserae of which are toponyms. Consistent with these multiple elements, the poet addresses a number of important issues rather than offering a poem with singular theme. The poet selected these place-names for a variety of reasons: historical memory, traditions attested elsewhere in the oracles against the nations, and the contemporary geopolitical reality. The text is the product of a creative poet and does not express a fixed set of motifs or a mythic pattern. Informed by earlier prophetic traditions, particularly as exemplified in the oracles against the nations, the author attests to the power of Yahweh's word against prominent sites in the "Beyond the River" satrapy, sites that comprise something of a rim on the north, northwest, and west of the satrapy. The changes in divine voice, third and first person, do not represent originally distinct segments of the text, but involve a difference in the sort of action directed toward the Philistine territory. The author is interested in places and people, using toponyms to create a field of vision in which the relations of Judahites to non-Yahwists is explored within the particular purview of "Beyond the River." That region, and not a putative province of Judah, provides the key political frame of reference. For this poet, Judah is a collection of tribes, to which a Philistine remnant can be joined. The region, which some neutral political observer might think is under the political sway of the Persians, is, according to this poet, properly Yahweh's possession.

Zechariah 9:9–17

God's *shalom* at home and abroad

9:9   Rejoice greatly, O Daughter Zion!
        Shout aloud, O Daughter Jerusalem!
        Your king is coming to you!
           Righteous and victorious is he![a]
        Humble, riding on a donkey,
           on an ass, born of a she-ass.

10   I[b] will remove chariots from Ephraim,
        horses from Jerusalem.
        The warrior's bow will be removed.
           He will offer peace[c] to the nations.
        His rule will extend from sea to sea,
           from the river to the ends of the earth.

11   As for you[d], because of the blood of your covenant,
        I have set free your prisoners from the pit
           in which there was no water.

12   Return[e] to the stronghold,[f]
        O prisoners of hope!
        Indeed, this is a day for proclamation:
        I will return again to you.

13   Truly, I myself have drawn Judah,
        I have filled Ephraim, my bow.[g]
        I will arouse your sons, O Zion,
           against the sons of Yawan.[h]
        I will use you as a warrior's sword.

14   Yahweh will appear against them,
        his arrow will strike like lightning.
        Yahweh of Hosts will trumpet with a horn,
        he will proceed in a wind-driven sandstorm.[i]

15   Yahweh of Hosts will protect them.
        They will devour and crush the stone slingers.
        They will drink their blood as wine.[j]
        They will be full like a bowl,
        like the corners of an altar.

16   Yahweh their God will save them on that day,
        his people, like a flock,
        Like[k] crown jewels
        glistening[l] on his land.

17 How fair! How beautiful![m]
Fine grain for vigorous men,
effervescent wine to make the young women flourish.[n]

a. The word *nōšāʿ*, translated here "victorious," is a niphal participle, which normally has a medio-passive meaning (cf. Ps. 33:16). LXX translates with an active verb, i.e., "saving," which seems to be the required sense.

b. LXX provides a third-person form, which would make consistent the actor in these verses, namely, the king. MT provides the more difficult, and therefore preferable, reading. See similarly Saebo, *Sacharja 9–14,* 53.

c. Literally, *dibbēr šālôm,* "he speaks peace." Cf. Deut. 20:10, for a similar idiom, *qr' lšlm.*

d. The pronoun is feminine in gender. Hence one should understand the referent to be the personified Zion/Jerusalem of v. 9.

e. Here the imperative is masc. plur., i.e., Zion is no longer addressed.

f. Various conjectural emendations have been proposed to make sense of this colon. MT reads *šûbû lĕbiṣṣārôn,* literally, "return to the fortress," which provides an alliterative play on the noun Zion, *ṣiyyôn,* thereby indicating that the fortress is Zion.

g. So Otzen, *Deuterosacharja,* 242, and most recently, S. Paul, "A Technical Expression from Archery in Zechariah 9:13a," *VT* 39 (1989): 495–97.

h. Since the *Vorlagen* of T and LXX probably read *bĕnê yāwān* (so Saebo, *Sacharja 9–14,* 58; cf. Otzen, *Deuterosacharja,* 242), and since the prior *bānayik* could have contaminated *bene*,* I read "the sons of Yawan" instead of MT "your sons, O Yawan." This reading accords with the sense of the poem, in which Yahweh addresses Yahwists, not non-Israelites.

i. Much depends on whether one sees *têmān* as a geographic reference, either a place-name or "south" (e.g., NRSV), or (with JPS) a reference to wind (Job 9:9; 39:26). LXX provides an interpretive reading based on the previous colon.

j. LXX W B S and the Ethiopic and Arabic translations preserve a form of the tradition that reads "They will drink them like wine" (reading a pronoun *autous* instead of the verb). Other LXX manuscripts, which would include A Q and Tertullian's Latin, read "They drank blood like wine," a reading that can be understood in one of two ways. Either the LXX translator read a Hebrew manuscript that had a consonantal text *dmm,* "blood," instead of MT *hmw,* "be tumultuous," or it is possible that these LXX readings represent a phonetic error, reading *haima* for MT *hāmû,* which is not a particularly common Hebrew verb (I am indebted to Dennis R. MacDonald for this suggestion). Put another way, all the LXX evidence can be understood if the Hebrew text were *hāmû.* Moreover, the principle of the more difficult reading would support *hāmû,* since with that form the text does not specify what they are to drink. On purely text-critical grounds, one could sustain MT's reading. However, since the technical text-critical arguments are inclusive, Saebo, in defense of A Q et al., points in the correct direction by appealing to a tradition concerning the consumption of blood in military contexts. See below in commentary on v. 15.

k. I read *kĕ'abnê* instead of *kî 'abnê.* The particle that introduces v. 17 may have "contaminated" the last colon of v. 16 by vertical dittography.

l. MT *mitnôsĕsôt* can be parsed as a hithpolel participle from *nws*, "to flee," which offers little sense. I follow Köhler and Keil, as cited by Rudolph, *Sacharja 9–14*, 185, in suggesting a phonological misreading of the verb *nṣṣ*, "to sparkle."

m. The third masc. sing. pronominal suffixes on "fair" and "beautiful" are ambiguous; see commentary.

n. The syntax is difficult because there is no verb in the first of the last two lines. The NRSV, among others, solves the problem by introducing the verb into the penultimate line. I prefer to preserve the Hebrew style since it drives one to finish the last line before one can understand the previous one. For the verb *nwb* in the qal conjugation, see Pss. 62:11; 92:14; Prov. 10:31.

Attempts to specify the extent of this poem, as well as its internal structure, have occasioned much debate, and for good reason. Some (e.g., Hanson) have argued for a literary unit as large as 9:1–17; others (e.g., Saebo) have discerned a number of small oracles and/or speeches: 9:9–10, 11–12, 13–16a, 16b–17. The driving force for the former position is the conviction that a mythic pattern undergirds these (and prior) verses, whereas the primary methodological underpinning for the latter view are form-critical judgments. The interplay between prophetic utterance and divine oracle further complicates this poem. In my view, this literature demands that the interpreter integrate various critical perspectives in order to address its complexities. Only then is it possible to discover in these verses one complex poem, which has as its primary theme the manner in which Yahweh's peaceful imperium for his people will be created. This poem stands as a complement to the former one, which focused on the international extent of Yahweh's sovereignty. Here two themes are present, the role of the deity in establishing this order and the place of a king, a role that is remarkably understated. The role of God's people is manifold—they will be freed, they will return to Jerusalem, they will be used as weapons, they will be vigorous and beautiful.

[9:9] In Zech. 9:1–8, the poet used the indicative mood to describe the power and scope of Yahweh's word. At the beginning of the next poem, and again in v. 12, the prophet speaks in the imperative mood. The poet seems to presume something like that which was described in Zech. 9:1–8 as the basis for the imperative call to action. Since Yahweh's word of oversight offered assurance to "them" (v. 8), the author thinks it now appropriate to challenge those individuals to respond. However, rather than using a straightforward plural imperative of the verb "to rejoice," as we typically find in Israelite hymnic rhetoric (Ps. 32:11; Isa 65:18; 66:10), the author personifies those addressed as Daughter Zion/Daughter Jerusalem and, in so doing, calls this individual to act.[41] The same may be said for the verb "to shout aloud" (cf. Pss.

---

[41]In both cases in which the plural imperative of *gyl* is used in Isaiah, Yahweh acts with regard to Jerusalem (so Isa. 66:10, "Rejoice with Jerusalem").

47:1; 66:1; 81:1; 98:4; 98:6; 100:1). Both forms of action involve the ritual service of song. One may, therefore, presume that Daughter Zion will respond at the place mentioned in v. 8, namely, "my house" or, more neutrally, the temple, which provides something of a link between these two poems.[42]

The first two lines of v. 9 echo earlier prophetic rhetoric, as a number of scholars have argued. But what are the critically important allusions? It is one thing to say that the text contains a number of allusions (Willi-Plein);[43] and it is quite another to argue that there are one (or several) textual forerunners (Fishbane, who points to Gen. 49:10–11).[44] Is one simply to note the closest grammatical parallels or should one link that sort of observation with traditio-historical concerns? I opt for the latter and maintain that the critically important textual forerunners are Zeph. 3:14 and Zech. 2:13 [10], while at the same time not wanting to deny the highly allusive character of the composition, namely, of v. 11 to a text like Gen. 37:24.[45] Put another way, there may be texts that belong to a tradition or theological stream and there may be texts to which an author alluded in order to create a certain tone or perception. Obviously allusions of the first sort work quite differently than do allusions of the second sort. These echoes provide significant evidence for the major interpretive problem that this verse presents, namely, what is the character of this king, who is presumably different from Yahweh, the divine king?

Zephaniah 3:14–15 and Zech. 2:13 [10] address Daughter Zion in the imperative mood in much the same way that she is addressed in 9:9: Zephaniah: sing aloud, shout, rejoice, exult; Zechariah: sing, rejoice. And the reason is fundamentally the same in both cases. Zephaniah: "the king of Israel, the Lord is in your midst"; Zechariah: "I come and I will dwell in the midst of you." Yahweh's immediate presence provides the ultimate ground for the imperative rhetoric in these two prophetic texts, and Zephaniah especially makes it clear that the king is Yahweh, not a Davidide.[46] By connotation through allusion, the author indicated that the arrival of this king should be

---

[42]Saebo, *Sacharja 9–14*, 176–81, argues convincingly that this rhetoric, rooted in ritual discourse, is most prominent in the book of Isaiah and preserves military connotations.

[43]Willi-Plein, *Prophetie am Ende*, 93, includes in her catalog of references Gen. 37:24; Ex. 24:3–8; Isa. 31:1–3; 42:6–7; 61:1, 7; Jer. 31:10–20; Hos. 2:20–25; Micah 4:10; 5:10; Zech. 2:14.

[44]M. Fishbane, *Biblical Interpretation in Ancient Israel*, New York, 1985, 501–2, maintains that the author of Zech. 9:9–10 is recasting the blessing of Jacob (Gen. 49:10) into a royal-messianic oracle. However, if one begins the analysis with Zechariah 9, this singular connection is not so evident.

[45]Mason, *The Use of Earlier Biblical Material in Zechariah IX–XIV*, 39–41, has correctly discerned the importance of these two texts for a proper understanding of Zech. 9:9–10.

[46]Most scholars argue that the king described in Zech. 9:9b is a human, e.g., Saebo, *Sacharja 9–14*, 184; Mason, *The Use of Earlier Biblical Material in Zechariah IX–XIV*, 88; Baldwin, *Haggai, Zechariah, Malachi*, 165; Rudolph, *Sacharja 9–14*, 168; Hanson, *The Dawn of Apocalyptic*, 320.

celebrated in much the same way that Yahweh's presence as king deserves accolade. Moreover, the logic of the poems in Zechariah 9 suggests that the presence of the king depends on the prior presence of the deity in Jerusalem (Zech. 9:8).

The remaining lines in v. 9 depict, in surprising order, the manner in which the king will arrive, as well as his attributes. We might expect the poet to write "Humble, riding upon a donkey" immediately after the report that the king is coming. Instead, the poet offers two adjectives to define the salient features of this king. He, like other idealized earthly kings, will be righteous (so 2 Sam. 23:3) and victorious. This king shares these attributes with the deity.[47] The imagery of just ruler and military savior are pivotal to the author's understanding of the king.

Just as the author of the previous poem used surprisingly vivid imagery to describe Yahweh's presence in Jerusalem, namely, camping at his house, so too the author of this second poem uses vivid language to depict the king's arrival in Jerusalem. To think of a king riding on a donkey may strike one as farfetched. However, we know that human kings in the ancient Near East, particularly as attested in second millennium B.C.E. texts, rode donkeys.[48] Genesis 49:10–11 also clearly demonstrates that these animals are mentioned in references to royalty (cf. 2 Sam. 16:2).[49] The sole exception to this pervasively royal imagery is the term "humble," which is used here to redefine the character of the divine king.

Zephaniah 3:12 uses the term "humble" to describe a group: "For I will leave in the midst of you a people humble and lowly." This corporate character of the humble is informed by Deutero-Isaiah (so Isa. 49:13; 51:21; 54:11; and similarly Isa. 53:4). The author of Isaiah 40–55 used the technique of personification in subtle ways, namely, in the figures of Jacob, Zion, the servant, all of which signify the fate and identity of groups of people. The same tactic seems to be at work in Zech. 9:9–10, both with Daughter Zion referring to those in Jerusalem and with the king as a cipher referring to those who exercise rule in the community. Just as certain Yahwists could be viewed as humble or afflicted (so the above-mentioned texts in Deutero-Isaiah), the king could also

---

[47]It is well known that such language can be applied to human kings. However, ancient Israelite writers could, as well, define Yahweh as righteous (Pss. 119:137; 129:4) and as one who is victorious (Deut. 33:29; Isa. 64:3).

[48]See E. Lipiński, "Recherches sur le livre de Zacharie," *VT* 20 (1970): 51–52, for a brief overview of the ancient Near Eastern evidence.

[49]Though there seems to be a tradition of the king—in Israel, David—riding on a donkey, I do not think the poet is quoting another biblical text, contra K. Seybold, "Spätprophetische Hoffnungen auf die Wiederkunft des davidischen Zeitalters in Sach 9–14," *Judaica* 29 (1973): 104–5. Though there is clear allusion to royal traditions, I do not think that Zech. 9:9–10 presents a specific allusion to a *Vorbild* in the Davidic period.

be so described in Zech. 9:9b. One should note that this "corporate" character of kingship is implied in Deutero-Isaiah as well, as in Isa. 55:1–5, which refers to the ratification of David's covenant with all the people.[50]

The author of Zech. 9:9 is presenting a highly nuanced form of political expectation. This is no standard royal or messianic expectation, namely, the return of a real or ideal Davidide. This expectation has little in common with the hope for a prince (Ezekiel 40–48), a crowned Zerubbabel (Hag. 2:23); a Davidide à la the oracles of Zechariah (Zech. 4:6–10). Instead, the poet focuses on collectivities, addressed through the technique of personification.[51]

[10] One may characterize the state of affairs envisioned by this poet as a kind of demilitarized dominion that would provide a decided change from Persian-period Judah.[52] This verse contains, on the one hand, the vocabulary of political units—city (Jerusalem), state (Ephraim), nations—and on the other hand, the language of military enterprise—chariots, (war) horses, and warrior's bow. The poem allows the deity to speak in the first person and to state that activity of two different sorts will occur. First, the native soil of Yahwism, though one would expect Judah rather than Ephraim, will have chariots and horses removed from it.[53] Mention of Ephraim probably involves an expression of hope for the "reunification" of territory that had been one under the Davidic imperium but now involved different provincial statuses.[54] Then, using the same verb but without the same geographic limitation, the author tells us that the warrior's bow will be removed. Is this additional weaponry to be removed from Judah/Israel or is it weaponry to be removed from the nations? We do not know if the nations will have their weapons removed before the king offers peace. The commitment to peace on Yahweh's side, via explicit disarmament, appears to be the critical first step.[55]

In v. 10b, the poem returns to the activity of the king. Once the disarmament has occurred, the king will offer peace. We are not told explicitly what the

[50]My approach here is similar to that of Mason, *The Use of Earlier Biblical Material in Zechariah IX–XIV*, 36–63, to the extent that I agree the royal figure has been revalued, though I would make a stronger claim for the corporate character of the figure.

[51]Seybold, "Spätprophetische Hoffnungen auf die Wiederkunft des davidischen Zeitalters in Sach 9–14," 99–111, does not recognize the corporate character of the Davidic figure in Zech. 9:9.

[52]Hoglund has argued that the Persian empire used the tactic of militarization, that is, the construction of numerous garrisons throughout the Levant, as one way to impose imperial control over this territory. Hence, concerns for demilitarization would fit well within this period. See discussion in the Introduction.

[53]One does wonder whether the author mentioned Ephraim in order to introduce consideration of Samaria and its role as provincial headquarters.

[54]See the restoration vision of Ezekiel (especially Ezekiel 47–48) for a similar expression of hope.

[55]To be sure, Isa. 2:1–4 involves the expression of hope for peace among the nations. However, it would be inappropriate to suggest that Zech. 9:10 draws on that pericope in a direct way.

response of the nations will be. However, since the poet anticipates dominion from sea to sea, one may infer that the offer is accepted, with the result that "the king" will assume rule of the extent described in this verse. Some have suggested that this description mirrors the extent of the territory held by the united monarchy. The details are impressionistic. What, for example, are the two seas—the Mediterranean and what else? And the river—is it the Euphrates (probably) or the Nile?[56] Since virtually identical language is used in Ps. 72:8 to describe the rule of a Davidide ("May he have dominion from sea to sea, and from the River to the ends of the earth"), one may suggest that what is at stake is the general rule rather than readily identifiable borders.

These two verses present an implicit understanding for the governance of the community. Unlike the editorial framework of Haggai and unlike the visionary rhetoric of Zechariah, there is no place for a high priest. Instead, two kings—divine and human—acting in complementary fashion, are the pivotal characters. The role of "internal" governance is not addressed. International issues (such as the geographic extent of the human king's rule or the role of king to offer peace) rather than domestic issues are at stake.

[11] By way of a grammatical inclusio, the author returns to the gender initiated in v. 9 with the feminine singular pronoun "you" and, in so doing, signifies that Daughter Zion is being addressed again. The verse functions as commentary; it interprets present reality by alluding to earlier Israelite traditions. More particularly, this commentary explains why Yahweh acts beneficently toward Israel and offers figurative language to describe the fate from which Israel was rescued. "Through the blood of your covenant" almost certainly alludes to Ex. 24:8, namely, the blood rite that ratified the covenant between Yahweh and Israel at Sinai. The poet offers this text as a reason for Yahweh's action on behalf of Daughter Zion. Such allusion demonstrates that Yahwists believed even though the covenant curses had been enacted, the constitutive covenant between Yahweh and his people was still in force. Moreover, it suggests that during the time this text was written, the originally distinct Zion and Sinai traditions had been fully melded. Zion can be comforted using then-current notions about the significance of the Sinai events.

In addition, Yahweh reports that his actions may be construed as releasing prisoners from a dungeon. The particular vocabulary for the place of bondage, *bôr*, allows the poet to adduce a phrase from Gen. 37:24, though the last two words occur in reverse order from the form of that verse. The point of this allusion is not altogether clear. Does it mean that the exilic bondage could have been worse, that is, the pit could have contained threatening water? Does it mean that the pit, which marked one of the low points in the Joseph story before his ultimate ascendance, prefigures movement for Israel beyond its

---

[56]See Rudolph, *Sacharja 9–14,* 182, for a discussion of the possible geographic candidates.

current degradation? Perhaps both notions are implied. Even more, Yahweh, not the king, is the one who has taken the initiative for freedom.

[12] If v. 11 served as a gender-specific parallel to v. 9, v. 12 serves as a verb mood parallel to that opening verse. As did v. 9, v. 12 opens with an imperative verb, though now masculine plural in gender and number. The difference in gender suggests that the audience is now different. Daughter Zion was addressed in v. 9. The imperative verb also indicates that the audience is different, a notion reinforced by the meaning of the verse. Those commanded to return are told to return to a specific place, "the stronghold," which, as I have suggested in the note above, is to be understood as Zion. The wordplay suggests that the stronghold is not to be construed as some structure in Jerusalem, but as Zion itself.

The language of "return" played an important part in the rhetoric of exilic and postexilic prophetic literature. Yahwists were called to leave Babylon and return to Syria-Palestine (Isa. 52:11; Zech. 2:6–7 [2–3]). With Zech. 9:12, one senses a different meaning, namely, that those being addressed are already in Syria-Palestine. The Ezra-Nehemiah narratives are important here because they depict a situation in which those who rebuilt the walls of Jerusalem came from areas other than Jerusalem, and a situation in which the city needed to be repopulated (Neh. 7:4). In the fifth century B.C.E., the call to return was no longer directed only to those in Mesopotamia. Many of those who had their origins in the diaspora had returned to the land. But the repopulation of Jerusalem, whether in a straightforward demographic sense or in more limited terms, namely, to provide sufficient people to participate in temple ritual, was still an issue.

The language of return functioned in another way. Zechariah 1:3 states: "Return to me, says the Lord of Hosts, and I will return to you, says the Lord of Hosts." Here the language of return works in a figurative sense, that of repentance rather than that of physical movement. The author of Zech. 9:12 seems to have taken a formulation like that of Zech. 1:3 and made it literal. The "returns" of Zechariah 9 are palpable, involving both Yahwists' and Yahweh's presence in Jerusalem.

This verse develops the imagery of v. 11 since it, too, uses the language of prison, though now in a figurative sense. Whereas v. 11 referred to prisoners in a dungeon, v. 12 points to prisoners of hope, which borders on being an oxymoron. Prisoner of doom or despair seems a more natural expression than does prisoner of hope. How can hope imprison or how can one be bound to hope? The text offers no obvious answer. However, Israel's beliefs about the significance of Zion provide the hint of an answer, namely, that those who are in fortress Zion are heir to the security offered by it, *when* Yahweh resides there.

The key promise offered in this verse is Yahweh's return. Such a promise elicits the notion that the day on which this promise has been made is "a day for proclamation." This phrase, ambiguous in Hebrew, picks up on the use of the verbal adjective *maggîd,* as that term is used in Deutero-Isaiah to refer to the sort of proclamation that distinguished Yahweh from other gods (e.g., Isa. 45:19; 46:10). However, unlike the usage in Deutero-Isaiah, the proclamation now refers to a much more discrete activity than asserting "my purpose will stand." Rather, the day of proclamation involves very specific images of Yahweh's activity.

The poem takes a surprising turn in vv. 13–15. Instead of using the language of disarmament and peace (v. 10), the author envisions Yahweh as divine military hero with Yahwists as his weaponry (but not his army). This imagery seems, on the face of it, inconsistent with that present earlier in the poem, namely, the disarmament of v. 10a, and the peace of v. 10b. However, at least two elements distinguish vv. 9–11 from vv. 12–16: the nature of the Yahwistic audiences and the nature of the "enemy." In the first section of the poem, the critical players were Zion and the nations; in the second, Yahwists outside Jerusalem and the "sons of Yawan." Further, in the first section, the name "Yahweh" never appears, whereas in the second, Yahweh as proper name appears four times (vv. 14–16). As a result, the inconsistency may not be as absolute as it might initially appear. Further, the disarmament of v. 10a is entirely domestic. The nations still possess their implements of war. Hence, if conflict occurs, Yahweh will perforce have to fight on Israel's behalf, since they no longer possess the requisite weaponry. Verses 9–11 display what will happen when the two kings work conjointly; vv. 12–16 focus on that which Yahweh as warrior will do with and for his people, with no mention of the earthly king.

[13] The poet continues to describe the activity of Yahweh in first-person language, which stops at the end of this verse. The presence of four first-person verbs provides various forms of repetition that help create a unified vignette of Yahweh in action. The verbal sketch concerns the preparations for battle, which belong essentially to the future but which have already begun. The bow has been drawn. The figurative language—Judah//Ephraim, a metaphor for bow, Zion as a war sword—offers no reason to translate this sketch into notions of political reunification of the northern and southern kingdoms. Instead, we find a poet meeting the demands of reinforcing parallelism, namely, providing three toponyms to describe Yahwists. Judah, Ephraim, and Zion are not intended to refer to different entities here, as they are elsewhere in these chapters. They are diverse only as weapons for war are diverse: bow, arrows, and swords.

In the middle of this vignette, we may discover the enemy's identity, "the sons of Yawan." The word *yāwān,* which is the Hebrew form of the Greek word *'Iaones,* or Ionians, may be understood here simply as "Greeks." The term occurs elsewhere in the OT (Gen. 10:2, 4; 1 Chron. 1:5, 7; Isa. 66:19; Ezek. 27:13; Dan. 8:21; 10:20; 11:2; Joel 3:6) and in all cases may be translated as "Greeks." It has been a commonplace to suggest that the term in Zechariah 9, and elsewhere, should be excised as a late addition, since the Greeks controlled Syria-Palestine only after the conquests of Alexander. However, such a position ignores the prominence of Greek military and economic activity in much earlier periods, namely, at least as early as the sixth century (see Introduction). As a result, there is no prima facie reason to omit references to the Greeks in any of the above-mentioned texts.

When one reviews the occurrences of *yāwān* in the OT (and apart from the much later texts in Daniel), one discovers that two texts, written during the early postexilic period, refer to the Greeks in a similar way. In Ezek. 27:13, *yāwān* (and Tubal and Meshech) sell slaves and bronze vessels for Syro-Palestinian merchandise. Joel 4:6 also refers to trade in slaves, but this time trade in "the people of Judah and Jerusalem," whom they have purchased from Phoenicians. However, only Zech. 9:13 presents the Greeks as an object of judgment, and here there is no reference to the slave trade. The OT itself provides no particular reason for *yāwān* to be the target of Yahweh's wrath.

Hence one must appeal to what we know about the history of Syria-Palestine during the early Persian period, and here we find the answer. Three times during the first half of the fifth century B.C.E. (490 at Marathon, 480–479 at Thermopylae and Salamis, 460–the second Egyptian revolt), the Persians had engaged the Greeks in battle. There is strong evidence to suggest that these encounters affected those in Syria-Palestine, namely, through the creation of garrisons and the general militarization of the region. There is no reason to think that this program involving Persian security would have been viewed favorably by Yahwists.[57] As a result, one may infer that the Greeks were, from the perspective of those living in "Beyond the River," properly viewed as "the" enemy. The Greeks become the Yahwists' enemies because the Greeks have become enemies of the Persians.

As a result, one may read a text like Zech. 9:13 as consistent with the interests of the Persian empire, just as it is possible to read Isa. 44:28 in such fashion. The interests of Yahwists coincided at various times with the health of the Persian empire, particularly regarding its control of the Levant. However, the text is Yahwistic, not Persian, and uses the imagery of native, Northwest Semitic religion to pursue its claim concerning military action against the Greeks (just as does Daniel seven centuries later).

[14] With this verse, the poem moves to third-person language about Yahweh, rhetoric that is consistent with other third-person formulations about Yahweh the warrior in early Israelite texts, such as Exodus 15 (cf. Deut. 32:42 for early poems that provide such descriptions in the first person). Although

---

[57]Of course, some Yahwists benefited from this policy, namely, Nehemiah and those affected positively by his policies.

the "real" military conflict is between the Greeks and the Persians, the Yahwistic writer emphasizes the nature of the conflict as one in which Yahweh is a cosmic actor and one that may be described using traditional language. Verses 14–16, which initially appear stereotypic, are in fact creative formulations. These lines provide Yahwists with a way of understanding military conflict and ensuing prosperity within their own symbol system—not in the language of neutral political description and not in the symbolic language of the Persians.

What then are the salient symbols used by this poet? Verse 14 includes three elements, two typical and one unusual. Typical is the description of Yahweh as warrior, as one who shoots arrows. It is this motif, Yahweh as archer, that explicitly links v. 14 with v. 13. However, in v. 14, the motif is articulated differently, namely, with one simile instead of a series of parallel metaphors. This simile employs the traditional comparison of lightning as the arrow or weapon of the deity ("at the light of your arrows," Hab. 3:11; cf. Deut. 32:41 for the sword as lightning), a comparison that has its roots in Canaanite culture (cf. the many Baal statues with lightning in the hand of the deity). The careful reader notes, however, that unlike the multiple lightning strokes of the thunderstorm (Hab. 3:11), the poet has focused on a singular arrow, which will strike like lightning. It is as if the poet were emphasizing the singularity of the deity's act by this use of the arrow-lightning simile. So even here, with this standard motif, one may discern a creative formulation consistent with the larger perspective of the poem.

The second and unusual element, related to the first, involves the claim that Yahweh trumpets with a horn. No other OT text includes this image. However, it is surely reasonable to think that this line involves a musical military version of the claim that Yahweh's voice as thunder accompanies lightning (Psalm 29), which, of course, complements the image of Yahweh's lightning-like arrows. The final element, again typical, the sandstorm, allows us to claim that this military imagery is couched within the context of a divine theophany, since the storm is one vehicle by means of which Yahweh may appear in the natural order. Early Israelite literature preserved a tradition about Yahweh's coming from the South (*têmān*), which may well be implied in this verse, though I have chosen, as with JPS, to translate *têmān* "wind-driven." Judges 5:4, which attests this tradition, notes that Yahweh came from Seir//Edom with an attendant disturbance of the natural order: earth trembling, mountains quaking, with language of the thunderstorm, heavens dropping, clouds dropping water (cf. Deut. 33:2; Hab. 3:3–4, which also cites *têmān*). In sum, through the creative collocation and formulation of traditional language about the appearance of Yahweh as warrior, the prophet has proclaimed that this God, and not one of the competing world powers, namely, the Greeks or the Persians, will be the preeminent actor on Judean Yahwists' behalf.

[15] Verse 15 participates in the standard logic of Israel's holy war traditions. Yahweh will act definitively to win the war (see the "classic" confrontations, such as Joshua at Jericho or Gideon vs. the Amalekites). Israel's troops do not wage war; they witness Yahweh's glorious victory and then engage in skirmishes. Yahweh will protect his people and not use them as frontline troops. His heavenly hosts are normally the critical military actors (cf. Judg. 5:20, "From heaven fought the stars, from their courses they fought Sisera"). For this reason the language of eating and drinking, and not fighting, is paramount in this poem.

The poetic logic of v. 15 requires the reader to remember that which has been established earlier (in v. 13), namely, that, using the language of metaphor, Yahwists could be thought of as Yahweh's weapons. Saebo has noted that texts such as Deut. 32:42; Isa. 34:5; Jer. 46:10; and Ezek. 39:17–19 suggest there was a tradition lying behind this text, but he neither defines the tradition nor indicates how it is used in Zech. 9:15.[58] The first three texts speak of Yahweh's weaponry—arrows or sword—drinking its fill, the last text refers to a sacrificial banquet in which the beasts of the field will consume flesh and blood of horses and warriors whom Yahweh has defeated. If Yahwists are now Yahweh's weaponry, so Zech. 9:13, then they, like his weapons in the above-mentioned three texts, could consume the blood of the enemies. The image is not literal as it is in Ezekiel 39; rather, "they" in Zech. 9:15 are at one and the same time Yahweh's people and Yahweh's weapons. The imagery is not that of a banquet, eschatological or otherwise, but of devouring sword, bow, and arrow.

They—people as sword—will devour the stone slingers. Hurling stones, though it may sound primitive when compared with metallic weaponry (Stone versus Iron Age), remained an important military image into the Persian period (2 Chron. 26:14). The actual destructive force involves people as sword against those who hurl stones, that is, sword against flesh. As a result, the next line can refer to drinking; the sword-people will drink the blood of the stone slingers as if it were wine, that is, in copious amounts. The final two lines emphasize the vast amounts of blood that will be spilled in the conflict with the sons of Yawan. In both cases, the prophet creates similes drawn from the world of ritual activity. The sword-people will be full like a bowl. Here the bowl is not that of the dining table but that of ritual receptacle in which blood from an animal that has been sacrificed will be collected (Ex. 27:3; 38:3; Num. 4:14). There will be so much blood from the slain victims that these bowls will be filled, not simply half full. Then, in a second simile, the corners of the altar, which were smeared with blood (Lev. 1:5), will run red with blood.

[16] After three verses devoted to military rhetoric, the final two verses of the poem move to pastoral imagery involving agricultural fertility. As with the

[58]Saebo, *Sacharja 9–14*, 59–61.

previous verses, the emphasis is on "them," Yahweh's people. And just as in v. 15, this verse opens with a general declaration, which the prophet elucidates with a number of graphic images. The declaration includes the notion that Yahweh is "their God," a claim that invokes the covenant relationship and explains why Yahweh will act on their behalf. Further, the prophet uses the same word as in v. 9b, *yš'*, "victorious," to describe the deity's future action. That which could be personified by the figure of the king as victorious figure will be shared by the people as a whole—through the action of the deity. Just as neutral as that pronouncement is the temporal phrase, "on that day," namely, the day of Yahweh. This phrase, which occurs with insistent regularity in the second "oracle," Zechariah 12–14, introduces here the similes that articulate the initial statement of weal.

The syntax of the Hebrew text appears odd and, as a result, the final lines have been the subject of much emendation. However, as they stand, these lines provide two complementary similes, the latter of which serves to interpret the former. The first simile likens "his people," a phrase that again attests to the covenant relationship, to a flock. This notion is hardly original; compare the claim that Yahweh acts like a shepherd toward his flock (Pss. 77:20; 78:52; 80:1; Ezek. 34:12). It is striking, however, that in each of the aforementioned texts, the notion of the people as flock is couched as a simile. With Yahweh as shepherd, people as sheep populate the Old Testament figurative world of reality. In this world, as in the four above-mentioned texts, Yahweh leads his people as a flock and in so doing, according to the logic of Zech. 9:16, "saves" them. Once the subject—people—has been conveyed with the vehicle in the simile—flock—the poet proceeds with a second simile to elucidate further the nature of the subject, but in an unusual way. The motif of crown jewels elaborates the notion of sheep as flock.[59] The imagery is complex, now two steps removed from the "real world": people are like a flock; the flock can in turn be viewed as numerous jewels on a crown, jewels that bedeck the landscape. The emphasis here is less on Yahweh the shepherd and more on the splendor of the sheep themselves, a notion consistent with an emphasis on the people as a group, and not on their leader. This complex pastiche of images drawn from successful animal husbandry remains bound to the land—with Yahweh as shepherd and owner of the land.

[17] Vocative discourse both provides a response to the aforementioned scene and introduces the concluding metaphors, which serve more powerfully to depict this time of bliss. If there is ambiguity, it involves the pronominal suffixes on "fair" and "beautiful." The suffixes are singular. Hence they could

---

[59]Cf., e.g., Mason, *The Use of Earlier Biblical Material in Zechariah IX–XIV*, 94–95, who understands the two images as unrelated. H. Mitchell, by contrast, views them as related, *A Critical and Exegetical Commentary on Haggai and Zechariah*, ICC, Edinburgh, 1912, 281.

refer to the day, describing how fair and beautiful it—the day of Yahweh—will be. Or, alternatively, they could serve as collective suffixes and refer to the people mentioned either in v. 16—particularly as jewels—or v. 17. It is most likely that this vocative clause points forward, but to what aspect of the imagery? There is no verb in the first clause, and the verb "flourish" in the second clause could mean that either the wine causes the women to flourish or the women will flourish like effervescent wine. The former is preferable on grammatical grounds, because the noun "wine" and the verb are singular, whereas the noun "women" is plural. Further, this particular conjugation of the verb can serve as a causative (i.e., wine causes people to become ebullient). One may also argue that the verb does double duty. It is present by implication in the first line; that is to say, fine grain will invigorate young men just as new wine empowers young women.

What does this imagery convey? It relates to the former verse by addressing now the character of the "sheep" or people. And it is related in another way. Just as sheep represent fertility in fauna, grain and wine are traditional symbols of fertility in the realm of flora. Together, they represent the full agricultural yield of the promised land. "His land" (v. 16) produces grain and grape that strengthen the sheep (staying with the imagery of v. 16) or the people (who are mentioned in both vv. 16 and 17). These two verses present intricate imagery of agricultural bounty, which would be appealing to those suffering drought (cf. Neh. 5:3). The unstated claim at the beginning of v. 16 undergirds this imagery. Yahweh will save his people as a shepherd saves his flock.

The final four verses of this poem highlight Yahweh's actions: He will appear, trumpet, protect, and save. And the poem concludes on the note of Yahweh's beneficent actions toward his people. One senses that these strong promises serve as reasons for the people to follow the admonition offered in v. 12, "Return to the stronghold." If they do not return, Yahweh will not return—with the result that the momentous acts described in the ensuing verses will not take place.

What might these claims have meant to a Yahwist living in Syria-Palestine during the Persian period? There is no obvious answer. Clearly there is reference to a royal figure, descriptions of whom derive from earlier Israelite traditions. Some scholars have suggested that the presence of this material hints at an expectation for the reappearance of monarchy. However, this view cuts against the overall character of the text. The king is not the preeminent actor; rather Yahweh fills that role—as military hero and as shepherd for Israel. The text offers hope set within standard Israelite traditions, but addresses a situation radically different from that during which those traditions originally came to expression.

Zechariah 10:1–12

Yahweh, the militant shepherd

10:1 They asked Yahweh for rain,[a]
  the spring rain in its season!
Yahweh who makes the thundercloud
  that yields rain,[b]
he [who] makes for each of them
  plants in the field.[c]

2 But the teraphim spoke deceitfully;
  the diviners envisioned falsehood.
They uttered meaningless dreams;
  they provided consolation that was not real.
In sum, they [the people] set out like a flock;
  but they were afflicted because there was no shepherd.

3 "I am angry about the shepherds;
  I will punish the he-goats."
Truly, Yahweh has mustered[d] his flock,
  the house of Judah.
He will deploy them
  like his magnificent steeds[e] in battle.

4 Leader[f] and tent peg
  (will come) out of them;[g]
War bow will come from them;
  every general will come from them.

5 All together[h] they will be as warriors,
  marching in the mire of streets.[i]
They will fight because Yahweh is with them.
  They will embarrass horsemen.

6 "I will make great the house of Judah,
  I will save the house of Joseph.
I will make them dwell[j] (in the land),
  because I have had compassion on them;
  they will be as though I had not rejected them.
Truly, I am Yahweh their God;
  I will respond to them."

7 Ephraim will become a warrior.[k]
  They [their heart] will rejoice as with wine.
Their children will see and rejoice;
  they [their heart] will celebrate because of Yahweh.

8   "I will call out[l] to them and gather them.
        Truly, I will free them;
        they will be as numerous as before.
9   Although I scattered them among the nations,
        in distant lands they will remember me.
        Their children will remain alive and return.
10   I will return them from the land of Egypt;
        I will gather them from Assyria.
     I will bring them to the land of Gilead and Lebanon,
        but it will not be enough for them."
11   He will pass through the hostile sea,[m]
        he will strike the sea waves;
        then, all the depths of the sea will dry up.
     The pride of Assyria will be brought down,
        the scepter of Egypt will depart.
12   "I will make them great through the Lord;
        they will march in his name,"
                    says Yahweh.

a. Reading *šā'ălû* (perfect) instead of MT *ša'ălû* (imperative). I follow Otzen's line of argument, *Deuterosacharja*, 247.

b. The clause contains no verb. It is possible to amend MT *ûmĕṭar*, with the support of the LXX *cheimerinon*, to *yimṭar*, to provide the appropriate verb. See similarly Rudolph, *Sacharja 9–14*, 190 n. 1 c.

c. The stichometry of this verse is complex. Cf. Hanson, *The Dawn of Apocalyptic*, 324–25. In addition, the sense is not clear. To whom does the pronoun refer?

d. The verb *pqd* is notoriously ambiguous. The author has just used it to refer to punishing action in v. 3a. Here, however, in v. 3b, the sense could be of either "punishing," "considering" (so *Tanakh*), "caring for" (so Hanson, 324), or "mustering," as proposed here. The decision rests less on the meaning of *pqd* itself and more on the context; i.e., has a new rhetorical unit begun with v. 3b? I think the *kî*, both here and at the beginning of v. 2, introduces a new section. And since the verses that follow provide weal for Israel, a translation of *pqd* that involves action other than punishment is called for.

e. A reasonable case could be made for a translation of *sûs* as a singular noun (so Rudolph, *Sacharja 9–14*, 192; Hanson, *The Dawn of Apocalyptic*, 324; NRSV). However, the descriptions of Yahweh as divine warrior never include reference to Yahweh mounted on horse. Hence, the collective or plural translation, i.e., horses as part of his battle array, is preferable. In addition, Zechariah I clearly attests to the knowledge of several horses that belong to the deity, Zech. 1:8–10; 6:2–5.

f. The noun *pinnāh*, which may be derived from *pnh*, is often translated woodenly as "corner" or "cornerstone." However, this noun occurs in Judg. 20:2; 1 Sam. 14:38; and Isa. 19:13 and clearly means "human leader"; and in the first of these cases, the leadership role is exercised in a military context.

g. The suffix is singular, a collective referring to the singular collective noun, Judah.

h. The word *yaḥdāw*, "together," concludes v. 4 in the Hebrew text.

i. I omit *bammilḥāmāh* as a dittographic expansion based on the next word *wĕnilḥāmû*.

j. MT *wĕhôšĕbôtîm* does not parse readily. I adopt *wăhašîbôtîm* (so Otzen, *Deuterosacharja,* 249), a hiphil from *sûb,* supported by T V Pesh, as opposed to the other option, supported by LXX, *wĕhôšabtîm.* See Saebo, *Sacharja 9–14,* 66–67. The former reading is consistent with v. 10.

k. The idiom *wĕhāyāh k* . . . may be translated "to become" instead of the more wooden "be like," cf. *Tanakh.*

l. On Yahweh's "calling out," see Isa. 5:26 and 7:18. In both these texts, Yahweh calls out an enemy against Israel.

m. LXX reads "They will pass through," which is surely the easier and therefore later reading. The notion of Yahweh's passing through and striking the sea is unusual and surely original to the poem.

MT reads *bayyam ṣārāh,* which is normally translated "the sea of distress." Mitchell, *Haggai and Zechariah,* 301, among others, amends to *bĕyam miṣrayim,* which mirrors the language of v. 10. (Cf. Otzen, *Deuterosacharja,* 251–52, who reads *ṣārāh* as a verbal form, though one would expect the form to be prefixed by a *waw.* Otzen has correctly discerned that Yahweh is the subject of the verbs in the first two lines of v. 11.) However, MT, as it stands, provides a phonological parallel to v. 10, without the conjectural emendation. And this phonological play, as well as the semantic content, helps create an allusion to the earlier Reed Sea events. To amend the text to "the Egyptian sea" is to make wooden the intended poetic effect of recalling, but not specifying, the earlier occasion.

The extent of this poem has occasioned considerable debate. It is not uncommon to find judgments that 10:1–2 and 10:3–12 are two separate pieces, e.g., Rudolph, Mason, Saebo (though Saebo discerns two distinct forms in vv. 3–12, a divine speech and a prophetic speech). Alternately, some think that 10:1–12 comprises a unit (Hanson), and a few have suggested that the poem comprises 10:1–11:3 (Lacocque). In my judgment, 11:1–3 is distinct, both because these verses seem to be an entire poem and because they may be identified clearly with one genre, the taunt (see below). Moreover, Zech. 10:1–12 also makes up one poem that includes elements of reprise and indictment (vv. 1–3a), help for Israel (vv. 3b–7), and return from various diaspora settings (vv. 8–12).[60] This poem offers both critique and solace to its readers. Even though Israel had consulted diviners in time of drought, God will lead the people to fertility and prosperity. In so doing, the deity will seek the

[61]Though visions and dreams could provide insight to an Israelite prophet, this text denigrates them by linking these sources with a diviner, *qsm,* and not with a prophet, *nābî'.* Moreover, there are Israelite texts that present a preference for the word of Yahweh over visionary experience, whether waking or sleeping (dream) vision, e.g., Jer. 23:23–32.

return of those Yahwists who remain outside the promised land. As in Zech. 9:9–17, the people have a "military" role (v. 5).

[10:1] The poem opens with a report about past behavior. It is vague because we are not told who asked Yahweh for rain. Since "they" reappear in v. 2, where it seems clear that those referred to are the people of Israel, or to use the diction found later in this poem, "the house of Judah," and since it makes sense to think about the general population making a request for rain, one may assume that a request by Yahwists occasions this reprise. The text alludes to some moment when drought prompted the people to petition the deity for rain.

The character of their past behavior is not as straightforwardly clear as the translation would suggest. In antiquity inquiring of the deity could take a variety of forms. We sometimes assume, anachronistically, that to ask something of the deity occurs through the medium of petitionary prayer. And such is, of course, attested in the OT. However, other forms of inquiry existed, namely, various forms of divination. The word š'l, is used on occasion to describe "mechanical" divination (e.g., Num. 27:21, which refers to Israelite oracular inquiry through the medium of the Urim). This same word may also allude to improper inquiry, at least from an Israelite perspective, as in Hos. 4:12 (inquiring of a "thing of wood"); Ezek. 21:26 (probably inquiring with teraphim); or 1 Chron. 10:13 (inquiring of a medium). Since v. 2 introduces explicitly a range of improper forms of intermediation, and since the verb š'l refers to these sorts of activity, Zech. 10:1 probably involves the claim that in a time of duress people were seeking help through improper divinatory practices.

The word *malqôš* signifies the rain that normally falls in the spring months and is of critical importance for the proper early development of crops. Such rain ensures agricultural fertility (see especially Deut. 11:13–17). The use of this term in other OT texts demonstrates that Israel understood Yahweh to be the author of rain. However, as Deut. 11:13–17 demonstrates, Yahweh does not guarantee the presence of such rain. Yahweh threatens to shut up the heavens if Israel does not obey his commandments. Jeremiah 5:24 underlines the same point, namely, that people run the risk of ruination if they do not fear Yahweh, "who gives the rain in its season, the autumn rain and the spring rain."

In almost catechetical formulation, Zech. 10:1 affirms Yahweh's role in providing verdure for humanity. One senses that the questions asked in Jer. 14:22 ("Can any idols of the nations bring rain? Or can the heavens give showers?") have become pressing questions, and that Zech. 10:1 offers an answer that is colored by the use of the phrase "plants of the field" (Gen. 3:18). Zechariah 10:1b emphasizes the orders of creation that Yahweh has established and intended for human bounty.

[2] Reprise continues as the author describes several forms of intermediation and reports that none were successful. Teraphim, physical objects (Gen.

31:19, 34–35; 1 Sam. 19:13, 16), were polemicized in some OT texts (2 Kings 23:24; Ezek. 22:3) though not all (Hos. 3:4). Whatever they were understood to utter provided no solution. Diviners, which appeared on the list of divination proscribed in Deut. 18:10, effected no viable solution because their visions and dreams were of no account.[61] Those whom the people consulted were unable to present Yahweh's true response to the situation; hence, one may presume that the fertility engendered by the spring rain did not occur.

In the final lines of v. 2, the poet presents a summary version of the foregoing material in figurative language. The people set out *like* a flock, which symbolizes their search for the deity in a time of distress.[62] However, the journey was fruitless because, as in the case with a flock without guidance, their difficulties were compounded. Since these lines derive from the world of simile, it would be pointless to attempt to identify the notion of a single shepherd in the "real" world of Yahwists living in Judah during the Persian period. The key correlation between the simile and the real world is that between sheep and people. In the simile, the author claims that the people suffer because they have sought out inappropriate means for discerning an answer to their problems.

Considerable attention has been devoted to the question of what the shepherd symbolizes in this and other verses (cf. 11:4–17). The figure of the shepherd could, throughout the ancient Near East, refer to the king, whether human or divine.[63] On the former option, see the prologue to Hammurabi's law code, "Hammurabi, the shepherd, called by Enlil, am I," (*ANET,* 164) or Isa. 44:28 on Cyrus as a shepherd. On the latter, the deity, as divine king, could be construed as shepherd and his people as flock (Ps. 23:1; Gen. 49:24; Isa. 40:11). However, a nonroyal leader could also be viewed as a shepherd (Num. 27:17; cf. Micah 5:5E). Mason identified a number of texts in which he thought the shepherd symbol referred to nonroyal leaders, quite possibly priests (Jer. 2:8; 3:15; 10:21; 12:10; 22:22; 25:36–38; Ezekiel 34).[64] There are even Jeremianic texts in which the term "shepherd" refers to leaders of foreign armies (Jer. 6:3; 12:10). Holladay argues that virtually all the references to

---

[61]Though visions and dreams could provide insight to an Israelite prophet, this text denigrates them by linking these sources with a diviner, *qsm,* and not with a prophet, *nābî'*. Moreover, there are Israelite texts that present a preference for the word of Yahweh over visionary experience, whether waking or sleeping (dream) vision, e.g., Jer. 23:23–32.

[62]The claim is, therefore, much different from that in Jer. 50:6–7, where shepherds led people astray. In Zech. 10:1–2, the people have let themselves suffer by accepting inappropriate leadership.

[63]So also Akkadian *re'um, AHW* II, 977. See also V. Hamp, "Das Hirtenmotiv im Alten Testament," *Festschrift Kardinal Faulhaber zum achtzigsten Geburtstag, dargebracht vom Professorenkollegium der Philosophisch-theologischen Hochschule Freising,* Munich, 1949, 7–20; Otzen, *Deuterosacharja,* 150–51.

[64]Mason, *The Use of Earlier Biblical Material in Zechariah IX–XIV,* 102–9.

shepherds point to the civil or political leaders of Judah.[65] In a similar vein, Isa. 56:11 uses the term "shepherds" without any royal connotation. In sum, the symbol of shepherd was multivalent, available for Israelite and non-Israelite kings (or apparently princes, Nahum 3:18), Israelite and non-Israelite deities, and for human leaders other than kings.

It is altogether likely that the author of this poem knew and appropriated earlier prophetic texts and traditions that used this shepherd image. In a negative and plural sense, the image is especially prominent in Jeremiah (Jer. 23:1–4; 25:34–38) and Ezekiel (Ezekiel 34). In these texts, one does not sense that shepherds signify royal figures, but, instead, they refer to various leaders—political, religious, economic—of the people, who may be indicted for their faulty leadership.

[3] The rhetoric of the first section of the poem shifts from third- to first-person address as it moves toward a conclusion. Verse 3a may well be material of different origin and yet be now included because of a linking word connection—"shepherd." What continues from the foregoing material is the tone of indictment, but the object of the indictment has changed. Whereas in 10:1–2a the people had erred by seeking help from unproductive forms of intermediation, the deity here promises judgment on shepherds//he-goats. Moreover, the object is plural, as opposed to the singular shepherd in v. 2. Further, the figurative language is not consistent with the earlier simile; the deity now offers judgment regarding shepherds and animals, whereas the earlier simile focused on the plight of the people, that is, their self-induced suffering. Finally, whereas vv. 1–2 offer a retrospective view on the effects of improper intermediation, v. 3a is concerned with the future. In sum, though one may argue readily that v. 3a stems from a different hand and represents different interests than vv. 1–2, it concludes this section by linking past and future and by making explicit Yahweh's view of both people and leader, goats and shepherd.

Zechariah 10:3b–7 makes up the second section of the poem. With the shift back to third-person language (though first-person language does reappear in v. 6), the poet highlights the deity's work on the errant people's behalf. The people are still depicted as Yahweh's flock. But, in contrast to their directionless wandering and suffering, Yahweh now provides initiative and direction. The character of his action jars us, since the notion of mustering sheep borders on the outlandish. Also unusual is the presence of "real world" political language, namely, "the house of Judah." This phrase, which also occurs in v. 6, pushes the reader to think about the meaning of Yahweh as one who musters

---

[65]W. Holladay, *Jeremiah 1: A Commentary on the Book of the Prophet Jeremiah, Chapters 1–25,* Hermeneia, Philadelphia, 1986, 89, 206.

his flock in Syria-Palestine, and not throughout the diaspora. Put another way, martial imagery is localized to the homeland.

The prophet introduces a new simile that seems better suited to the topic at hand. The house of Judah will be like glorious horses, arrayed for battle. The strength and speed of the horse had by this time become part of that which was expected of a victorious army. Nahum 3:2–3 presents imagery of the horse-driven chariot, whereas Jer. 50:42 conveys the notion of cavalry. That we cannot tell which of these military modes is involved in Zechariah 10 testifies to the evocative nature of the discourse. In physical vigor and magnificence, the house of Judah will be like Yahweh's steeds.

[4] The poet leaves the world of explicit simile and introduces various entities that attest to the richness of Judah as a resource for military activity. The resources are described subtly, involving both physical objects and humans. Of the four nouns, "leader" (or more literally, "corner") and "general" refer to human resources. The "tent peg" is more difficult to understand. Though Sisera was killed by a tent peg (Judg. 5:26, hence one might view it as a weapon), I think it more likely that the noun functions here in a less literal way, as it does in Isa. 33:20, a text in which Zion is likened to a tent. Here its tent pegs are simply bases for support; whether human or structural, the poem does not allow us to specify. In any case, the tent peg and the leader/"corner" share one essential feature, namely, each is an obvious and structurally significant feature in a physical structure. And both appear here to symbolize human strength. The final element, the war bow, appears in a straightforward sense, as it did in Zech. 9:10. However, the use to which these elements are put in v. 5 suggests that even the war bow can symbolize a person.

[5] The biblical author links all four of the objects cited in v. 4—leader/corner, tent peg, war bow, and general—by the word "together" (v. 5). These resources, which are devoted to the martial arena, are then explored by means of a simile, "as warriors." The tendency toward personification evident in v. 4 is here made explicit. The picture, elicited by the continuing simile, is that of heroes marching in the streets of a city (cf. Nahum 2:4, "the chariots race madly through the streets," not out in the fields); and heroes in combat with cavalry. The simile also contains an element typical of Israel's holy war traditions, namely, the notion that Yahweh accompanies his people. This element provides the reason for the battle. It is something impelled by the deity. We know nothing specific about the enemy, where it is coming from or what nation it represents. These issues seem unimportant for the prophet. What remains important is the role of Yahweh in mustering his flock to the end described in the final section of the poem.

[6] The poem moves again from prophetic speech to divine oracle and, in so doing, provides a change in perspective. No longer do we hear about explicit military imagery. Rather, the reader is presented with Yahweh's larger plan,

which involves "making great" Judah//Joseph and a resettling of Yahwists in the land. The verse focuses more on the reasons for Yahweh's action than it does on the particularities of what Yahweh will do. Those reasons are both explicit and implicit. Yahweh states explicitly that his compassion explains his behavior. Further, the final lines of the verse formulate the claim of the house of Judah that Yahweh is their God, a phrase that echoes Sinai covenant formulations, "I will be their God, and they will be my people." Despite the changes in political circumstance, namely, Judah as a minor part of the Persian empire, the prophet-poet argues that the formative traditions—here of covenant and, in the foregoing verse, of holy war—still inform Yahweh's commitment to and interaction with his people.

Within the larger context of the entire poem, v. 6 addresses an issue raised in the first two verses, namely, the people inquiring of the deity. Here, at least, Yahweh offers a promissory note: namely, if the people petition him in an appropriate way, that is, not through teraphim, he will answer them.

[7] In what has almost become a pattern of alternation, the poet returns to prophetic speech, referring to the deity in the third person. This section concludes by introducing new language to describe Israel in the poem, i.e., Ephraim, and also by repeating earlier language, i.e., warrior (from v. 5). Here Israel—a "warrior"—is personified using the vocabulary of the battlefield, though martial imagery does not continue. In lines that share vocabulary, "their heart rejoices," the poet defines the response of the people, who are now in a position to garner a response from the deity. They will rejoice as does someone "with wine." This simile is ambiguous: It could refer to the joy one has at receiving or drinking wine or it could refer to the effect that wine, in proper amounts, has on the one who drinks it. Many of the texts that speak positively about the consumption of wine in the OT do link it to the heart, so Eccl. 9:7, "drink your wine with a merry heart"; or Ps. 104:15, "wine to gladden the human heart." These texts, along with those that do not mention the heart explicitly, such as Eccl. 10:19 ("wine gladdens life"), suggest that Zech. 10:7 refers to the effect of wine that has been consumed. One should note that the simile fits the larger perspective of the poem, since the request with which the poem began, the request for rain, would, if answered, provide the agricultural fertility appropriate for the production of wine.

The joy of the people is explored first using the simile regarding wine. But then, outside that world of agricultural imagery, the poet provides the "real" reason for the people's joy, namely, the one who responds to requests, the one who provides wine (cf. Hos. 2:8), Yahweh.

[8–10] The third section of the poem commences with a new theme, the return of the Yahwists to the land, though that notion had been foreshadowed in v. 6, "I will make them dwell." In a divine oracle, Yahweh proclaims what he is about to do. Using diction otherwise attested only in Isaiah, the prophet envisions Yahweh's calling out to those in diaspora.[66] The notion of Yahweh's summoning those in diaspora is attested in a number of exilic and postexilic prophetic texts (e.g., Isa. 51:9–11; Zech. 2:10).[67] Verse 8 is filled with first-person verbs, which emphasize the initiative and activity of the deity on behalf of his people. The first two verbs require little comment. The third, "redeem," is rooted in the legal realm. See Ex. 21:8, 30, concerning instances in which legal release (e.g., of a slave) is at stake.[68] However, early on, some Israelites claimed that Yahweh could free or liberate individuals as well as groups, a notion that occurs in late prophetic texts as well (e.g., Isa. 35:10; 50:2; 51:11), with specific reference to a freeing from exile that would allow Yahwists to return to the land. In v. 9, the poet continues with first-person language but moves to retrospective considerations that explain how Yahweh might free Israel. He was the one who drove them out in the first place, and therefore he has the right to act again. Having made this point about the past and future roles of the deity, the author considers the response of the people, that is, they will "remember" the deity. The notion of "remembering" is a complex one, which here involves not only remembering in some cognitive sense but also responding on the basis of certain recollected knowledge.[69] In this instance the act of remembering is described in the very next line. The people—more particularly, the children of those who had been taken into exile—will return to the land.

In this oracle, the prophet emphasizes the truly international scope of Yahweh's activity. Whereas Deutero-Isaiah envisioned a return from Babylon to Israel, Zechariah 10 refers to exile among "the nations" and means by this not just multiple national entities in Mesopotamia, such as Babylonia, Assyria, Persia, but a nation on the other side of the ancient Near East: Egypt (v. 10).[70] Not only is this accurate history (see the Introduction regarding the extent of the Yahwistic diaspora), but it emphasizes the extent of Yahweh's ability to act on behalf of those who venerate him.

Like Zech. 9:1–8, Zech. 10:10 is replete with toponyms. Yahweh's folk will leave Egypt//Assyria and return to the land of Gilead//Lebanon. Whereas the

---

[66]The idiom of Yahweh calling out is attested in Isa. 5:26; 7:18. Both texts involve Yahweh whistling to (i.e., calling out), an enemy against Israel. Presumably in the former and clearly in the latter, the whistling is perceptible at great distance, i.e., in Egypt or in Mesopotamia.

[67]See N. Mendecki, "Deuterojesajanischer und ezechielischer Einfluss auf Sach 10,8.10," *Kairos* 27 (1985): 340–44, who points as well to Ezek. 36:10, 11 and Isa. 11:11, which may have influenced the author of Zechariah 10.

[68]See for a brief but excellent discussion, "*pdh,*" *TWAT* 6:514–22.

[69]See the classic study, B. Childs, *Memory and Tradition in Israel,* SBT 37, London, 1962, 69.

[70]Assyria serves here as a general reference to Mesopotamia, see, e.g., Micah 7:12, which defines in a similar way the extent of a return to Syria-Palestine. It does not specify the exile of certain Israelites in 721 B.C.E. by the Neo-Assyrian empire (2 Kings 17:6).

first two names refer to two classic (and now moribund) powers in the ancient Near East, the last two place-names refer to regions in Syria-Palestine. Lebanon, of course, refers to the mountain range, which begins north of the Leontes River, north of territory normally controlled by Israel. Gilead refers to the hill country immediately east of the Jordan River and bounded on the north by the Yarmuk and on the south by the Arnon Rivers. Lebanon and Gilead share several features: They are defined by river cuts, they are rugged, and they are Syro-Palestinian territories neither heretofore controlled by Israel nor part of Persian-period Judah. These toponyms function importantly to make the point with which this verse concludes. Even the breadth of land conveyed by the territory extending from Gilead and Lebanon will not hold all the people who will be returning, a hyperbolic notion of resettlement.

When set within the political context of the Persian period, the prophet's point is stronger than it would have been during an earlier period, such as the time of Solomon. Even non-Judahite Syro-Palestinian territory will not suffice to contain the number of Yahwists who will be returning from both east and west.

At this point, one must draw back and ask why a topic one normally associates with middle and late sixth-century B.C.E. prophetic literature continues in the fifth century? Why is there a continuing concern for return to the land? The answer to these questions surely lies in the inextricable link between concern for return and repopulation, especially of certain critical areas. First, it is a commonplace to observe that many Yahwists did not return from their various places of exile, and for a variety of reasons. The important Jewish communities in Egypt and Mesopotamia during the Greco-Roman period bear ample testimony to this reality. Second, the actual population pattern in Judah appears designed to serve the interests of the Persian empire, not traditional Yahwistic ideology.[71] In this regard, Ezra-Nehemiah attests to the apparent problems that Yahwists confronted in restoring and repopulating Jerusalem. To rebuild the temple was one thing, to re-create a city was another. Given the prominence of Jerusalem in Zechariah 9–14, sometimes in tension with Judah, one may infer that the repopulation of Zion was a critical issue for this prophet, even though the city itself does not appear by name in this oracle.

[11] What might appear to be a separate oracle is, in fact, a powerful poetic statement that interprets the return of Yahwists and the fate of those where they currently dwell. Other prophets had understood the return to the land by relating this event to other signal moments in Israelite tradition. For example, Isaiah 35 and 41:17–19 invoke the wilderness tradition to explore the ways in which Yahweh will lead and assist his people on their way back to the land. In

---

[71]I depend here on K. Hoglund's argument that the Persians adopted a policy of ruralization in Judah; see Introduction.

addition, Deutero-Isaiah attests the Reed Sea tradition to explore how it is that Yahweh will assist his people.

Crossing through the waters (Isa. 43:2) is one way in which the events associated with the return may be construed. And it was none other than Yahweh who assisted Israel when they crossed through the waters. The author of Zech. 10:11 uses language associated with this event but in a way that echoes earlier Canaanite mythology. Just as Ba'al struggled with the sea god, Yam, so Yahweh, though his name does not appear here, will attack the sea and defeat it. This allusion is complex because it points not only to the Reed Sea tradition but to earlier Northwest Semitic notions as well. Moreover, it is a historicized allusion, since the concluding lines include the same toponyms that occur in v. 10, Egypt and Assyria.[72] In that earlier verse Egypt and Assyria functioned essentially as regions. In v. 11, they clearly signify imperial powers—hence the language of "pride" and "scepter." One may infer that this poet thought the release of Yahweh's people would involve conflict, just as it had when Israel left Egypt many centuries earlier. Verse 11, therefore, functions rather like a commentary on v. 10, emphasizing that returning and gathering will involve strife with those in the places where Yahwists dwell. However, as with the earlier release from Egypt, the conflict is not between Israelites and foreign rulers but between Yahweh and those in power.

[12] The final verse of this poem may strike the reader as odd. Is it possible that the deity would refer to himself in the third person while speaking in the first person? Some have suggested that we hear the voice of the prophet here.[73] However, such an interpretation cuts against the grain of what has just been established in the poem, namely, that Yahweh will act on Yahwists' behalf throughout the world. As a result, it is preferable to recognize that such peculiar syntax is at home in earlier prophetic literature, for example, in Hos. 1:7, "I will deliver them by the Lord their God," a text in which the deity is clearly speaking. These unusual formulations highlight the role of the deity and the right relationship that the deity will have with his people. This situation stands in marked contrast to the one with which the poem began, in which the people, through various forms of divination, are asking the deity for rain. Now the people, not just their crops, will be great as a direct result of the deity's intervention on their behalf.

---

[72]Cf. the similar imagery in a Jeremianic oracle against Babylon, "I will dry up her sea and make her fountain dry," Jer. 51:36.

[73]So Rudolph, *Sacharja 9–14*, 197.

Zechariah 11:1–3

Destruction in Syria-Palestine

11:1 Open, O Lebanon, your doors,
    so that fire may consume your cedars!
2   Wail, O Cypress[a], because the cedar has fallen,
    since the majestic ones are devastated!
    Wail, oaks of Bashan,
    for an impenetrable forest has fallen!
3   Listen![b] the wailing of shepherds,
    truly their glory has been ruined.
    Listen! the roaring of lions,
    truly the verdant banks[c] of the Jordan are destroyed.

a. As with many plants referred to in the OT, the precise species is debated. Some have argued that the tree in question is a fir; others say a juniper, which is a shrub.

b. On this use of the noun *qôl,* see GKC, 146b.

c. The Hebrew noun *gě'ôn* may be translated literally "majesty" or "pride." However, the phrase *gě'ôn hayyardēn,* e.g., Jer. 12:5; 49:19; 50:44, indicates that the noun, when it occurs in construct with "Jordan," refers to the thick foliage that lined the river Jordan's banks and served as cover for animals. The last two Jeremianic texts refer to lions coming up from the *gě'ôn hayyardēn.*

Most of the discourses that make up Zechariah 9–14 are long, extending ten verses or more. Nonetheless, here we find a poem much shorter than any of the others. Brevity is not the only hallmark. Striking imagery and the pervasive presence of personification in the first two verses also set this oracle apart. Moreover, different parties are addressed—the region of Lebanon in v. 1 and cypress//oaks of Bashan in v. 2. As a result, few would deny that Zech. 11:1–3 is a distinct and carefully crafted rhetorical unit.[74]

Also, unlike many of the poems in Zechariah 9–14, many of which appear to be made up of a pastiche of formally distinct elements, Zech. 11:1–3 has often been described using a single genre label, the taunt. The matter is, however, more complex.[75] It is well known that nations or local communities engaged in communal lamentation, whether in time of military peril or natural disaster. Wolff has argued that the OT contains a number of texts that preserve

[74]At a minimum, one may argue that 11:1–3 is an identifiable unit, so, e.g., Rudolph, *Sacharja 9–14,* 199; M. Bič, *Das Buch Sacharja,* Berlin, 1962, 131–33. Stade, "Deuterosacharja," 25 n. 1, 68–70, had argued that 11:1–3 belonged inextricably to the remainder of chap. 11.

[75]See Saebo, *Sacharja 9–14,* 230, for a description of the text's structure.

or derive from "the call to communal lament" (*Aufruf zur Volksklage*), one of
which is Zech. 11:2.[76] He further maintains that this call to lament includes
three essential elements: an order in the imperative mood, naming of the party
specified in the vocative, and the occasion for the lament introduced by the
Hebrew particle *kî*. All these elements occur in Zech. 11:2, and, as a result, it is
licit to think of v. 2 as a call to lament. However, such a judgment does not help
explain the nature of vv. 1 and 3. As a result, one should think that a call to
lament has been included in this three-verse poem, but not that the poem is
itself a call to lamentation.

The other prophetic texts Wolff identified as calls to lament do help us
understand Zech. 11:1–3. Of the nine compelling examples, five are directed to
foreign nations: Isa. 14:31—Philistia; 23:1–14—Tyre; Jer. 25:34—foreign
rulers ("shepherds"); 49:3—Moab and Ammon; Zech. 11:2—foreign rulers.
Further, and apart from Zechariah 11, two of the calls directed to foreign
nations utilize the technique of personification to compose the second element
of the genre: "O Gate" (Isa. 14:31) and "O ships of Tarshish" (Isa. 23:1).
Zechariah 11:2 is similar, "O Cypress." In sum, these prophetic texts suggest
that Zech. 11:2 includes rhetoric typical of the call-to-lament formulations,
especially as these are directed to foreign nations.

However, to note this similarity is not to address the issue of the form of vv.
1–3. On formal grounds, v. 1 appears similar to v. 2, that is, it shares the same
threefold structure with the typical call to lament. However, there are differences. The first involves syntax. The final clause in v. 1 is a result clause,
whereas in v. 2, as in most calls to lament, the clause provides a reason.
Second, and more important, there are fundamental semantic differences.
Instead of the vocabulary associated with the call to lament (e.g., "wail"), the
imperative verb "open" involves a call to surrender and destruction, not a call
to surrender and capitulation.[77] None of the other calls to lament directed to
foreign nations include such unusual language. Hence, though some elements
of the taunt appear in these verses, the entire poem should not be construed as
a taunt.

Though empires (Egypt and Assyria) are addressed in 10:1–12, the fate of
foreign nations is here symbolized by local entities, Lebanon and Bashan. The
poem envisions the fate of these non-Israelite areas but also demonstrates that
the fate of those in Judah is intertwined with others in the Levant. At this time
all those in Syria-Palestine were subject to the same imperial rulers.

---

[76]H. W. Wolff, "Der Aufruf zur Volksklage," *ZAW* 76 (1964): 48–56. Other texts include Isa.
14:31; 23:14; 32:11–14; Jer. 6:26; 25:34; 49:3; Ezek. 21:12; Joel 1:5–14; Zeph. 1:11. Since Ezek.
21:17 is directed to Ezekiel and not to Israel, it is not really an exemplar of the call to communal
lament.

[77]Contra Saebo, *Sacharja 9–14*, 232.

[11:1] The prophet addresses a region, not a city, not a country. Lebanon serves, especially in the prophetic literature, as a complex symbol.[78] It is a region made famous by its primary natural resource—its timber (Isa. 2:13; 14:8; 40:16; Ezek. 27:5).[79] Moreover, Lebanon as a mountain range can symbolize pride, as in Jer. 22:6–7 and even more clearly Isa. 2:12–17. In Zech. 11:2, though, Lebanon is personified as a city, something with doors that might be opened. However, it would be improper to treat the poem as an allegory, namely, to think that the prophet has identified one particular city in Syria. Rather, the entire region of Lebanon is personified as a city, and in an ironic manner, since it is commanded to allow fire to consume its critical commodity. The prophet thinks that the destruction of Lebanon's cedars will be like the conflagration that destroys a city. With its cedars burned, Lebanon might present an image of previously forested hills and mountains that have suffered a forest fire—a ravaged landscape. However, v. 1 urbanizes this image of rural destruction. In addition, v. 1 conveys the connotation of stupidity. A city would only open its gates to surrender if those inside had reason to think they might survive. Here they are only promised death. The verse derogates the vague foreigner symbolized at the beginning of this poem.

[2] Although v. 2 parallels the syntax of v. 1, the meaning is much different. The verse commences with a typical call to lamentation, though here to an individual personified as a tree. Whether the tree in question, *bĕrôs*, is a cypress or fir remains difficult to decide. Nonetheless, a number of OT texts view the cedar and cypress as similar; they are large and significant enough to be mentioned in parallel lines (e.g., Isa. 14:8). Moreover, cypress and cedar could grow together in a single grove. Only by noting this integral connection between cedar and cypress can one understand the force of this verse. The cypress, which might grow together with the cedar, is called to lament the destruction of that latter tree, the destruction of which is commanded in v. 1. Verse 2, therefore, depends logically on v. 1. The cypress would only be subjected to a call for lament after the cedar has been destroyed. The cedars are the "majestic ones" mentioned in the second line of v. 2. Though the word *'addîr* can refer to human leaders (e.g., Jer. 14:3), the term can also be applied to flora (e.g., Ezek. 17:23, where it serves as an adjective modifying cedar).

In the second half of v. 2, the morphology of the verb more closely mirrors

---

[78]Otzen, *Deuterosacharja,* 163, argued that Lebanon is a symbol for the Jerusalem temple, which is a judgment that belongs to the history of the text's interpretation, influenced possibly by Jer. 22:6, and not to its earliest meaning.

[79]It is inappropriate to focus on the *māšāl,* Ezekiel 17 or Ezekiel 31, as a "source" for this poem, since in both cases the "cedar" refers to one specific nation, the royal line of Judah in the first and Egypt in the second. On the cedars of Lebanon, see F. Stolz, "Die Bäume des Gottesgartens auf dem Libanon," *ZAW* 84 (1972): 141–56, and the response of Willi-Plein, *Prophetie am Ende,* 73–74, n. 17.

the call to lament, which is addressed to a human audience. The verb is plural, as befits one addressing not an oak but oaks. And just as the form of the verb is closer to one suited for a human audience, the location, Bashan, in southern Syria, is closer to Israel. Bashan served as a vague toponym, which in this case included an association with a particular fauna. Just as cedars were associated with Lebanon, oaks were associated with Bashan (Isa. 2:13; Ezek. 27:3).[80] Both oaks and cypresses are called to lament the destruction of the cedars of Lebanon. The loss of one form of mighty fauna is the occasion for lament by those who remain. It is important to note that the prophet continues the same motif initiated in v. 1, namely, that of using urban vocabulary to describe the destruction of a forest. The word *habbāṣîr* often describes a city as fortified and therefore well defended (e.g., Deut. 1:28). Again, therefore, the prophet makes the point that the decimation of trees will be like the destruction of a city. In sum, in vv. 1–2 the prophet has sardonically called for the destruction of the cedars of Lebanon and then offered a call for lamentation over their fate. Urban imagery and personification are hallmark features of these lines.

[3] If vv. 1–2 present the voice of the prophet calling for destruction and attendant lamentation, v. 3 presents the response. That someone should respond to the call for lamentation is not surprising. But why the shepherd and lion? This question may be answered on a variety of levels. The first answer stems from the world of the poem. The destruction of a stand of trees impacts the ecology in various ways. Both humans and animals suffer. This ancient poem recognizes such ecological reality.

There has been a tendency to view the shepherd and lion as quasi-allegorical elements, namely, as referring to political leaders.[81] Elsewhere in Zechariah 9–14, the symbol of the shepherd does seem to function in this way; in Zech. 10:2–3 and 11:4–17 the shepherd seems to refer to a domestic leader. However, Zech. 11:1–3 addresses all of Syria-Palestine, not simply Persian-period Judah. Moreover, the lion would seem to move the poem away from language of concrete political reality. Though Judah could be viewed as a lion (e.g., Gen. 49:9), and an Israelite leader could be described in an allegory using the image of the lion (Ezek. 19:6)—and though the image of the shepherd was elsewhere used to describe political leaders (Jer. 25:34–37), whether Israelite or not—no

---

[80]Both texts refer to cedars of Lebanon and oaks of Bashan in related verses.

[81]I think it impossible, given the broader Syro-Palestinian context in this poem, to maintain that the shepherds refer to Judahite leaders, whether political, religious, or a combination thereof (contra Hanson, *The Dawn of Apocalyptic,* 335). To lump the trees together and think that together they suggest "pride" does not recognize the lack of indictment language in the poem. In addition, Lebanon, not the cedar, is addressed directly. Baldwin (*Haggai, Zechariah, Malachi,* 177), Rudolph (*Sacharja 9–14,* 200), and Saebo (*Sacharja 9–14,* 231, primarily on form-critical grounds) correctly note that the poem belongs to the international idiom. Rudolph as well correctly discerns that the toponyms are not meant in some strict geographic sense.

Hebrew poet mixed metaphors by construing the lion's leadership as shepherds, or more simply, by viewing lions as similar to shepherds.

That the shepherds wail as a response to the call for lamentation should provoke no surprise. However, the reason offered in the poem itself is peculiar, "their glory has been ruined." What is "their glory"? The pronoun must refer to the shepherds. One would not normally think that the shepherds had a particular investment in the timber mentioned earlier in the poem. Ehrlich may not be off the mark by suggesting that the term "glory" ('*adderet*) refers to the flocks of the majestic ones ('*addirîm*).[82] However, it is also possible to suggest that the glory does refer to the trees and that the shepherds possess an agricultural portfolio like that of Amos (Amos 7:14), namely, trees and livestock. And wild animals, too, take up the lament. Lions, who were known to inhabit the dense foliage that lined the Jordan, roared by way of response to the destruction of their habitat.

I have attempted to make the case that this poem may be read as meaningful literature—without viewing it as an allegory and without arguing that it is a transformation of earlier prophetic themes or texts. Now these issues must be addressed, since many scholars, especially Delcor, Mason, Saebo, and Willi-Plein, have argued that these lines derive, in some way, from earlier prophetic literature.[83] When one reads Jer. 25:34–38, one is struck by the presence of language and imagery quite similar to that in Zech. 11:1–3. Mason, who, like others, has noted this similarity, proceeds to set the context by assessing those texts, particularly in Jeremiah and Ezekiel, that mention shepherds. However, in so doing, he is unable to take fully into account the larger literary contexts that establish the meaning of the words in the other texts. In addition, he, like Willi-Plein, assumes that if one text alludes to another, both have essentially the same meaning. Hence there is a leveling, which does not help much in determining the significance of "shepherd" in 11:1–3.[84] If, on literary and form-critical grounds, Zech. 11:1–3 may be construed as separate from 10:1–12, then we need not think that "shepherds" mean the same thing in these two texts. Mason's conclusion, that Jeremiah influences Zech. 10:3–11:3, becomes far too general and treats Jer. 25:34–38 as no more significant than Jer. 2:8, another text that mentions shepherds.[85] The issue of allusion must be addressed

---

[82] So also Rudolph, *Sacharja 9–14*, 199–200. The same root ('*dr*) had, of course, been used in Zech. 11:2, there to refer to the destroyed trees.

[83]M. Delcor, "Les sources du Deutéro-Zacharie et ses precédés d'emprunt," *RB* 59 (1952): 385–411; Mason, *The Use of Earlier Biblical Material in Zechariah IX–XIV*, 101–34; Saebo, *Sacharja 9–14*, 229–33; Willi-Plein, *Prophetie am Ende*, 73–76.

[84]Mason, *The Use of Earlier Biblical Material in Zechariah IX–XIV*, 129–30.

[85]Mason, *The Use of Earlier Biblical Material in Zechariah IX–XIV*, 102–8, maintains that Zech. 10:3–12; 11:1–3 depends on Jer. 2:8; 3:15; 10:21; 12:10; 22:20–23; 23:1–6; 25:34–38; 31:10; and Ezekiel 34.

much more carefully. And individual poems or rhetorical units must be treated as meaningful wholes.

The criteria for arguing that an author has alluded to a text are difficult to identify and involve a different claim than does a traditio-historical argument. Nonetheless, it is possible to make the case that Zech. 11:1–3 alludes to Jer. 25:34–38. Jeremiah 25:34 includes the call to lamentation. Jeremiah 25:36a is identical in syntax with Zech. 11:3a, the only difference is that of root, namely, two different words for "cry." The two texts share similar vocabulary: *šdd, 'dr, yll, npl, r'h*. However, even after noting these similarities, it is important to highlight differences. Trees and their destruction do not appear in Jeremiah 25, nor do toponyms. In Jeremiah, Yahweh is, like a lion, a punishing agent; whereas Yahweh is not mentioned in Zech. 11:1–3, fire is the punishing agent.[86] In Zechariah the lion laments, as do the shepherds; whereas in Jeremiah the lion is an enemy. In Jeremiah the shepherds appear to be culpable, as they are in Zech. 10:3; whereas in Zech. 11:3, the shepherds, like the lions, simply suffer the effects of the destruction. In sum, though there may be an allusion, the poem that includes the allusion may mean something quite different from the poem or elements in a poem to which it alludes. Jeremiah 25:34–38 means something quite different from Zech. 11:1–3, especially because the shepherd is used quite differently in these two texts.

If this poem is not to be read as an allegory, nor as of a piece with the foregoing verses, what would it have meant to a Judahite city-dweller (so the urban imagery earlier in the poem) in the Persian period? Quite simply this: Any destruction, here conveyed by the symbol of destroyed timber, will have far-reaching effect. For Yahwists to hope for the destruction of any element of Syria-Palestine, or for an end to Persian hegemony over this territory, is to risk radical and violent dislocation. If the cedars of Lebanon are destroyed, the banks of the Jordan River will feel the effect. As a result, the poem seems to encourage acceptance of the status quo.[87]

One may at this point offer a suggestion about this oracle's current place in Zechariah 9–14 by pointing to the presence of the toponym Lebanon and noting that this same noun occurs near the end of the previous poem. "Lebanon" links these two units.[88] In addition, Zech. 10:1–12 alludes to the fate of other nations.

---

[86]Contra Rudolph, *Sacharja 9–14*, 200, who presumes Yahweh must be behind what is going on.

[87]There have, of course, been attempts to locate the meaning of the poem in other ways. For example, Bič and, to a certain extent, Hanson have argued for a ritual background. Others push for a historical-political interpretation, e.g., Willi-Plein.

[88]Rudolph, *Sacharja 9–14*, 200, maintains that Zech. 11:1–3 serves properly as a conclusion to chap. 10. Cf. Otzen, *Deuterosacharja*, 162–64, 226. Hanson, *The Dawn of Apocalyptic*, 334, 337, thinks it serves as an introduction to that which follows. I argue that the poem is of a piece with neither but has been introduced redactionally. The notion of shepherd is different in each of the three poems in which it occurs: 10:3; 11:3; and 11:4–17.

Hence both discrete diction as well as larger theme bind this three-verse unit to that which precedes it. Moreover, the word "shepherd," with which Zech. 11:3 concludes, links that poem with the one that follows, Zech. 11:4–17.

Zechariah 11:1–3 does more than provide a mechanical linkage between 10:1–12 and 11:4–17. The tone of these three verses softens the militaristic blare of the previous poem. The reader should not hope for fire in Lebanon, because of its ultimate impact on those in Israel. Hence, even though Yahweh promises restoration to Israel in 10:6–12, the traumatic character of the birth pangs may prove overpowering (Zech. 10:3–5).

Zechariah 11:4–17

Shepherding a flock

11:4 Thus says Yahweh, my God,
"Tend the flock that is to be slaughtered,
5 whose owners[a] will slaughter it—
they will not be held guilty;
whose sellers will say:[b]
'Blessed be Yahweh,
because I have become wealthy';
and whose shepherds will not spare them.
6 Indeed, I will no longer spare
those who inhabit the earth,"
says Yahweh.
"I am placing each human group under the authority of its shepherd,[c]
under the authority of its ruler;
they [the ones in power] will crush the earth;
I will not rescue it from their power."
7 Hence, I tended the flock, which was as good as dead,
the flock that belonged to the sheep dealers.[d]
I took for myself two crooks:
one I called Pleasure,
the other I called Agreement.[e]
8 Whereupon I removed[f] three shepherds in one month.
I became impatient with them,
and they disdained me.
9 Then I said:
"I will not act as a shepherd toward you;
the one who is dying, let her die,
the one who is being destroyed, let her be destroyed.

> As for those who remain,
>> let each consume the flesh of the other."g

10   Then I took my crook Pleasure and broke it,
>> so as to break the covenant of Yahweh,h
>> which he had made with all the peoples.

11   When it was broken on that day,
>> the sheep dealersi, the ones who were watching me,
>> understood that this was a message from Yahweh.

12   Then I said to them,
> "If it seems well done in your judgment, give me my wages.
>> If not, desist."
> Then they paid me my wages,
>> thirty pieces of silver.

13   Yahweh said to me,
> "Hurl it toward the treasury!"—j
>> that precious amount with which I had been honored by them.
> So I took the thirty pieces of silver,
>> and I threw them toward the temple treasury.

14   Then I broke the second crook, Agreement,
>> so as to fracture the brotherhood
>> between Judah and Israel.k

15   Yahweh spoke to me again:l
> "Take the gear of an ineffective shepherd!

16   For I am raising up a shepherd in the land,
>> but he will not search for the missing ones,
>> he will not seek the one who cries out.m
> He will not heal the injured one,
>> he will not care for the exhausted one.n
> Rather, he will consume the flesh of the fat,
>> he will even break open their hooves.

17   Woe, O worthless shepherd,
>> who abandons the flock.
> May a sword attack his arm,
>> also his right eye,
> so that his arm is paralyzed
>> and his right eye blinded."o

a. *qnh* does not mean "purchase" here, but "own," as it does in Isa. 1:3.

b. The verbs "will say" and "I have become wealthy" are set in the singular, whereas one might expect plural forms. One may, however, argue that the sellers have been treated grammatically as a collective noun. *yaḥmôl*, "pity," may refer to the sheep by way of the collective noun "flock," *ṣō'n*. There is tension between the gender of the pronominal suffixes: feminine—"their purchasers," "their sellers" vs. masculine—"their shepherds." But the feminine suffixes can be explained by the gender of *ṣō'n*, which is feminine. Hanson is probably correct in thinking that the reference of the masculine suffix is the sellers and/or dealers. For a full discussion of these issues, see Otzen, *Deuterosacharja*, 253–55; Saebo, *Sacharja 9–14*, 72–75; and Hanson, *The Dawn of Apocalyptic*, 340. Duhm, followed by Otzen, makes a strong case for reading singular nouns and verbs, "their seller, their purchaser," a proposal that would require emendation of *ye'šāmû* to a plural form but that allows *yō'mar* to stand (Duhm, "Anmerkungen zu den Zwölf Propheten," *ZAW* 31 [1911]: 193). However, if one were to adopt this proposal, there would be problems in understanding the coherence of the poem since there are multiple shepherds (v. 8) and multiple sheep dealers (vv. 7, 11) later on. Saebo, *Sacharja 9–14*, 74, reconstructs the text to allow consistently for plural forms.

c. Instead of MT *rē'ēhû*, "its colleague," I revocalize and read *rō'ēhû*, "its shepherd."

d. MT *lākēn 'ăniyyê*, which makes little sense, should be reconstructed as one word, *likna'ăniyyê*, on the basis of the LXX, *eis tēn Chanaanitin*, so Stade ("Deuterosacharja," 26). The most thorough defense of this view is T. Finley, "The Sheep Merchants of Zechariah 11," *Grace Theological Journal* 3 (1982): 51–65. The Qumran evidence, 4QpIsa^c 21, l. 7 attests the MT reading, which demonstrates that the corruption in the MT tradition postdates at least one LXX tradition. The term "Canaan" or "Canaanite" is used many times in the OT to describe mercantile behavior (Job 41:6; Prov. 31:24; Ezek. 17:4; Hos. 12:7; Zeph. 1:11; Zech. 14:21).

e. There are several Hebrew roots *ḥbl*. Ancient versions and modern translators uniformly translate with *ḥbl* I, "to bind together." The masc. plur. form of this noun allows it to function as an abstract noun, so GKC, 124d–e.

f. It is difficult to discern the precise nuance of *kḥd*; so Otzen, *Deuterosacharja*, 255. Though the verb can mean "destroy" (1 Kings 13:34), it more typically means "to disappear, hide, efface."

g. The gender of those addressed in this verse is uniformly feminine, for reasons that are not altogether clear.

h. I read *bĕrît yhwh 'ăšer kārat* instead of MT *bĕrîtî 'ašer kārattî*, a proposal which is consistent with T.

i. See the note on v. 7 regarding "sheep dealers."

j. I read *hā'ôṣār*, "the treasury," with Syriac, instead of MT *hayyôṣēr*, "the potter." See Mitchell, *Zechariah*, 313; Saebo, *Sacharja 9–14*, 78–83; and Rudolph, *Sacharja 9–14*, 202–3, for discussion of this problem. Rudolph follows MT and translates "smelter." This view would be consistent with the proposal of C. C. Torrey, "The Foundry at the Second Temple at Jerusalem," *JBL* 55 (1936): 156. Cf. G. Ahlstrom, "'*ēder*," *VT* 17 (1967): 3–5, who thinks *hā'ôṣār* signifies "some kind of a vessel."

k. LXX 1 I–86 and Ethiopic manuscripts read Jerusalem instead of Israel, on which see Saebo, *Sacharja 9–14*, 83–84; Otzen, *Deuterosacharja*, 257. This reading has probably been influenced by Zechariah 12 and 14, texts in which the ambiguous relationship between Jerusalem and Judah is of key importance.

l. I construe *'ôd* to modify *wayyōmer*, not *qaḥ*; so Ehrlich, *Randglossen* 5, 349. Cf. Otzen, *Deuterosacharja*, 258.

m. So Otzen, *Deuterosacharja,* 258–59, and Rudolph, *Sacharja 9–14,* 203, who read *hannō'ărāh,* on the basis of *n'r* II, "to lament." (See Jer. 51:38 for another OT text in which this root is attested.)

n. So W. Holladay, *A Concise Hebrew and Aramaic Lexicon of the Old Testament,* on *nṣb* II.

o. The semantics and syntax of the curse are complex. The essential question is whether there is one curse or two. One should note the repetition of infinitives absolute to create alliteration.

The first problem these verses pose is the correct delimitation of the unit. Following Ewald, Stade maintained that Zech. 13:7–9 belonged with 11:4–17 because both sections dealt with the role of a shepherd and his impact on the flock, and because 11:4–17 seems to lack a conclusion.[89] Many scholars agreed with this judgment.[90] However, despite the similarity in imagery, others have raised significant questions about the proposal.[91] The debate has swirled essentially around three issues: whether 11:4–17 makes a coherent whole, whether 13:7–9 makes sense in its current literary setting, and whether the "shepherd" in chap. 13 is identical with the ineffective or worthless shepherd of Zech. 11:15–17.[92] Form-critical insights, which one would think might help resolve the matter, have been included all too rarely in the discussion. And there are good, though perhaps not sufficient, reasons for such an omission. The key questions are twofold: What is the literary genre of Zech. 11:4–17, and is it possible to construe 13:7–9 as a distinct literary unit? I will argue that the answer to the first question is a combination and elaboration of two symbolic action reports, and my answer to the second is affirmative.[93]

[89]Stade, "Deuterosacharja," 29.

[90]So, e.g., T. Chary, *Aggée–Zacharie–Malachie,* SB, Paris, 1969; P. Hanson, *The Dawn of Apocalyptic;* Mason, *The Books of Haggai, Zechariah, and Malachi,* CBC, Cambridge, 1977; and W. Rudolph, *Sacharja 9–14.*

[91]Some demur, e.g., Willi-Plein, *Prophetie am Ende,* 59; K. Elliger, *Das Buch der zwölf kleinen Propheten, II,* ATD 25, Göttingen, 1964, 165–67; Otzen, *Deuterosacharja,* 162–63, 192–94; Plöger, *Theocracy and Eschatology,* 88–89; Jones, "A Fresh Interpretation of Zechariah 9–14," 251; Saebo, *Sacharja 9–14,* 276–82. Most of these scholars maintain that 13:7–9 makes sense in its current textual setting. For example, Plöger thinks it is "a divine announcement of what is depicted in chap. 14." See most recently S. Cook, "The Metamorphosis of a Shepherd: The Tradition History of Zechariah 11:17 + 13:7–9," *CBQ* 55 (1993): 454–56.

[92]Because one may view Zech. 11:4–17 as a coherent genre, I find it unnecessary to identify a core text to which additions have been added. Cf. Mason, *The Use of Earlier Biblical Material in Zechariah IX–XIV,* 160–65, who thinks vv. 11–13 are secondary; Rudolph, *Sacharja 9–14,* 206, who deems v. 6 an addition; or Elliger, *Das Buch,* 151, who allocates vv. 15–16 to a redactor. Saebo maintains that, though there is an identifiable genre at the heart of the text, it has grown over time; so v. 5 and other more subtle changes, e.g., MT of vv. 7, 11 or LXX of v. 14.

[93]Elliger, *Das Buch,* 165; Otzen, *Deuterosacharja,* 193; and Saebo, *Sacharja 9–14,* 276–82, also agree that Zech. 13:7–9 is not of a piece with 11:4–17.

Scholars have answered the question about genre in myriad ways: shepherd allegory,[94] sign narrative (*Zeichenerzählung*),[95] shepherd vision that includes the report of two symbolic acts,[96] two unrelated sign acts (*Zeichenhandlungen*),[97] commissioning narrative,[98] symbolic act report,[99] and parable.[100] This plethora of proposals is problematic. Some are so topic specific (that is, they include the term "shepherd") that they are not legitimate form-critical designations.[101] Other proposals (e.g., vision, commissioning narrative) simply do not present genres with which Zech. 11:4–17 may readily be identified.[102]

When one reviews these proposals, several things become apparent. Most scholars who focus on the literary and structural characteristics of Zech. 11:4–17 argue that 11:4–17 is a meaningful unit without 13:7–9 (so Otzen, Elliger, Saebo). Second, all these proposals emphasize that most of 11:4–17 involves prose elements that report action. When one focuses on these features, only two genre labels remain: allegory and report(s) of symbolic action. Since an allegory is less a form than a figure of speech, I will maintain that it is best to construe these verses as reports of a symbolic action.[103] The issue of whether

[94]See M. Rehm, "Die Hirtenallegorie Zach 11,4–14," *BZ* 4 (1960): 186–208; Otzen, *Deuterosacharja,* 226 [11:1–17]; Plöger, *Theocracy and Eschatology,* 81–82; H. Gese, "Nachtrag: Die Deutung der Hirtenallegorie, Sach 11,4ff," *Von Sinai zum Zion: Alttestamentliche Beiträge zur biblischen Theologie,* BEvT 64, Munich, 1974, 231–38. See also L. Meyer, "An Allegory concerning the Monarchy: Zech. 11:4–17; 13:7–9," *Scripture in History and Theology: Essays in Honor of J. Coert Rylaarsdam,* ed. A. Merrill and T. Overholt, Pittsburgh, 1977, 225–40 (argues for a three-part allegory); P. Redditt, "Israel's Shepherds: Hope and Pessimism in Zechariah 9–14," *CBQ* 51 (1989): 634 ("a lengthy allegory"); A. van der Woude, "Die Hirtenallegorie von Sacharja XI," *JNSL* 12 (1984): 139–49.

[95]Elliger, *Das Buch,* 150–51.

[96]Rudolph, *Sacharja 9–14,* 204.

[97]Willi-Plein, *Prophetie am Ende,* 52–56.

[98]So Hanson, *The Dawn of Apocalyptic,* 343, 431, though he does suggest that vv. 7–14 contain "striking resemblances to the prophetic sign-act."

[99]Saebo, *Sacharja 9–14,* 234–52, and for a nuanced version, Lacocque, *Zacharie 9–14,* 174.

[100]Mitchell, *A Critical and Exegetical Commentary on Haggai and Zechariah,* 303.

[101]As Willi-Plein, *Prophetie am Ende,* 52, rightly points out.

[102]Of the six elements that N. Habel, "The Form and Significance of the Call Narratives," *ZAW* 77 (1965): 297–323, identified as characteristic of the call or commissioning narrative, Hanson, *The Dawn of Apocalyptic,* 341, identifies only one, the imperative commission (vv. 4, 15a), in Zech. 11:4–17 and 13:7–9.

[103]The question of allegory or allegorical elements is a vexing one. Even Fohrer argued that Zech. 11:4–14 constituted an allegorical version of a symbolic-action report. My own position is this: The rubrics of the symbolic-action report seem to explain the formal features of Zech. 11:4–17. Second, allegory as such does not offer perspective about structure; allegory is more a figure of speech than a structuring device. In theory, a prophet might present either an allegorical symbolic-action report or a nonallegorical symbolic-action report. Further, even if these verses include allegorical features, scholars have been unable to identify symbols outside the text that would correspond to the important details inside the text, e.g., the three shepherds or the thirty pieces of silver. Cf. van der Woude, "Die Hirtenallegorie von Sacharja XI," 143.

vv. 4–17 are a literary appropriation of the genre does not affect the basic form-critical judgment.[104]

G. Fohrer, in a classic monograph, identified the "report of a symbolic act" in several OT prose prophetic texts (e.g., Isa. 8:1–4; Jer. 13:1–11; Ezek. 5:1–17; Hos. 1:2–9; Zech. 6:9–15).[105] The key elements were the command to perform a task, a report of the performance, and a statement about the meaning of the task. It is possible to discern two such reports in Zech. 11:4–17. Saebo identifies the two primary commands in vv. 4b and 15, only one performance report in vv. 7–12, and two interpretations, v. 6 and v. 16.[106] In each case, the commands and the interpretations are speeches of the deity, whereas the report is human (Saebo would say prophetic) speech.[107] This analytical vocabulary presents us with a way to move through and make sense of this difficult text.

Having argued that Zech. 11:4–17 presents two reports of symbolic actions, it is then possible to infer that Zech. 13:7–9 need not be viewed as a part of these reports. In fact, one cannot view these verses as part of a symbolic-action report. Hence, one should, on prima facie grounds, address these latter verses, which I view as a coherent poem, within their canonical context, that is, within the second "oracle," Zechariah 12–14.

In addition, to claim that the controlling notion is the symbolic-action report and to highlight those verses that are central to this genre, leads one to downplay the significance of vv. 13–14 as subsidiary (so Saebo). In addition, such form-critical considerations encourage the reader to focus on vv. 6 and 16, since it is there that the internal "interpretations" are to be found. This symbolic-action report presents dire news. The prophet proclaims that God will not function as divine king and announces a world in which Yahweh cedes power to malevolent human rulers.

[11:4] A form of address familiar in prophetic literature initiates this twofold report of symbolic acts. Oracles often begin with the formula "thus says the Lord." However, the inclusion of "my God" (*'ĕlōhāy*) is unusual. On the basis of vv. 13 and 15, which include a word (*'ēlay*) similar in Hebrew consonants to "my God," some scholars have proposed reading "to me." However, it is not unusual to find a prophet referring to Yahweh as "my God"

---

[104]Cf. Saebo, *Sacharja 9–14*, 243–47.

[105] G. Fohrer, *Die symbolischen Handlungen der Propheten*, ATANT 54, Zurich, 1968. See p. 18 for a basic sketch of the form. Fohrer views Zech. 11:4–14 as an allegory, p. 73.

[106]Fohrer and W. Zimmerli, *Ezekiel 1*, Hermeneia, Philadelphia, 1979, 28, note that the report of the act being performed is not always present. Hence one may still construe Zech. 11:15–17 as a second report of a symbolic act. Cf. D. Jones, "A Fresh Interpretation of Zechariah 9–14," 253, who maintains that there are "four prophetic signs."

[107]Saebo views vv. 13–14 as a secondary command and report. In addition, he deems some of the text to be later expansion, e.g., v. 5.

(Isa. 7:13; 57:21; Hos. 9:8, 17; Joel 1:13; Micah 7:7; Zech. 14:5) when not addressing the deity directly. In fact, one might even expect such a personalization of the formula since the deity has called the prophet to enact God's word.[108]

The command to perform an act occurs in v. 4b. The command contains two elements: the act and that which will be affected. The person addressed is commanded to act as a shepherd toward a particular kind of flock.[109] The flock is intended for slaughter. The image is, of course, violent, but it is the fate to which many sheep and goats were always intended. So, on the one hand, there is nothing unusual in thinking about slaughter for these animals.[110] On the other hand, normally only part of a flock was harvested for food; some animals were kept for breeding, some for milk, others for wool. So the picture here is decidedly negative. The entire flock, not just one portion, is destined to be killed. Hence, the act of shepherding becomes strikingly futile, since the shepherd normally did not have all of the flock slaughtered.[111]

This poem uses the image of the shepherd, which is also present in the preceding poem, Zech. 10:1–12 (see commentary there on multiple uses of that image). Here, as there, we find no easy or simple allegorical correspondence to a single role in the ancient religious or political world.[112] Moreover, any attempt to identify a particular historical figure with the shepherd fundamentally misunderstands the nature of this literature, especially since the prophet is asked to act like a shepherd. Because the symbol of the shepherd could be used in various ways, it is inappropriate to proceed with a disquisition about what the shepherd might signify without first observing what sort of interpretation is placed on that role in the symbolic-action report. However, before moving directly to the explicit "interpretation" provided by the text itself, it is important to set the stage with several observations. First, as Rudolph notes, this symbolic-action report involves the notion of multiple shepherds, so v. 8.[113] This notion of multiple shepherds is fully consistent with the use of the shepherd image in Jeremiah and in Isaiah 56. Second, the same individual—

---

[108]Cf. R. Mason, *The Use of Earlier Biblical Material in Zechariah IX–XIV*, 139–40, who maintains that the prophet is setting himself over against his audience by the use of "my God."

[109]Shepherd imagery is prevalent in Zechariah 9–11, e.g., Zech. 9:16; 10:2–3.

[110]Cf. Baldwin, *Haggai, Zechariah, Malachi*, 180, who argues that the feminine suffix refers to the ewes of the flock, which should not have been slaughtered.

[111]Attention to Jer. 12:3 might seem to complicate the issue. There Jeremiah calls for God to separate them like sheep for slaughter. The same Hebrew word (*ṣ'n*, "sheep") that occurs in Zech. 11:4 there refers to part of, but not an entire, flock. Cf. Mason, *The Use of Earlier Biblical Material in Zechariah IX–XIV*, 144. See also Ps. 44:11, 22, according to which Yahweh is, by implication, the shepherd-like figure.

[112]It is, however, difficult to think that the prophet is called to enact the role of Yahweh as shepherd. Cf. Otzen, *Deuterosacharja*, 156, who thinks the shepherd figure refers to Yahweh.

[113]Rudolph, *Sacharja 9–14*, 206.

the prophetic "I"—is called to "tend the flock" (v. 4) and to "take the gear of an ineffective shepherd" (v. 15). In both cases, the prophet enacts the role of shepherd, though obviously in diverse ways.

[5] Verse 5 elaborates the description of the flock for which the prophet as shepherd has responsibility. In so doing, these verses provide perspective on this action, but not an explanation of why it must be performed. This verse indicates that the shepherd does not own the flock. The role of shepherd in ancient Israel was, and is in this symbolic action, not necessarily identical with that of the flock owner. A shepherd could work in the employ of others (e.g., 1 Sam. 25:7. Moreover, in the world of this symbolic action, those who own the flock are those who will slaughter or, at a minimum, make a decision about slaughtering the flock. And they will not be judged negatively for their actions. Indeed, these owners, in a position to sell the flock, will be able to attribute their prosperity to Yahweh. The terse expression, "Blessed be Yahweh, because I have become wealthy," which in Hebrew encompasses only three words, might lead the reader to view negatively those who benefit from the slaughter of the flock. According to Hos. 12:7–9, those who are engaged in mercantile activity, those who say "I have gained wealth for myself," are subject to Yahweh's punitive action.[114] However, the deity can grant wealth, as in Gen. 31:16 (cf. more generally Deut. 7:12—16). Hence for someone to garner wealth does not necessarily authorize indictment. In addition, the formulation "Blessed be Yahweh . . ." is fully consistent with psalmic (and other biblical) language in which the deity is praised for providing concrete forms of weal (e.g., Ps. 31:21; Gen. 24:27) and, more generally, for being beneficent (e.g., Pss. 41:13; 66:20). Such language belongs in a world of agricultural and mercantile bounty, one in which those who benefit praise the deity.[115]

If there is one phrase that complicates the picture, it is "their shepherds will not spare them." Why is there mention of shepherds when the prophet has already been asked to discharge the duty of shepherd? One can only infer that the task of acting as prophet involves enacting that role within a context in which other shepherds are active as well. Such a notion is fully consistent with multiple shepherds working conjointly in the real world as well as the multiple shepherds that populate this symbolic-action report. One may appeal to the shepherds who are dismissed and who disdain the recently designated shepherd as of the sort who will undertake the task of total slaughter.

In sum, Zech. 11:5 does not offer indictment, either of the sheep or of those

---

[114]The term "Canaanite" occurs in both Hos. 12:7 and Zech. 11:7; in both cases, it refers to mercantile activity.

[115]Since this text is not an allegory, it is inappropriate to presume that the act of selling (v. 5) involves slave trade.

who own the sheep. Rather, it anticipates total slaughter of the flock. In addition, the task of the shepherd, which has been conferred on the prophet, appears futile, given the plans that the owners have for their flock.

[6] Initially, one is jolted by the presence of first-person language in v. 6, and as a result, a number of scholars have deemed this verse to be secondary.[116] However, if these verses constitute a symbolic-action report, then v. 6 may be understood readily as the interpretation, which is essential to the report. Since the interpretation that occurs in the symbolic-action report appears regularly in the form of divine speech, first-person language is hardly an unusual element.

The deity interprets that which has been commanded—and since, surprisingly, the interpretation precedes the report of the action (vv. 7–12), one may say provisionally that the order of these elements highlights the importance of the act's meaning as well as the complexity of the sign act's performance. The meaning of the act involves not only the activity of the shepherd but the performance of the other actors as well. Yahweh states that he will no longer spare humans—from what he will spare them is left unstated. Rather the deity is placing various human groups, including Israel, under the control of individual "shepherds," a role which is here explicated as "king" or "ruler." These rulers, who will act without interference from the deity, will beat or crush the earth. In Ps. 89:23, Yahweh states, "I will crush his foes before him. . . ." Zechariah 11:6 reports that such activity of Yahweh on behalf of any human community will no longer be the norm. He is abdicating his role as king and allowing human rulers to exercise power over humanity, power that bears the promise of their annihilation (vv. 4–5). This view of the political order may reflect Judahite dismay at their lack of power in the Persian-period Levant.

This truly pessimistic reading of political reality appears as a decision of Yahweh. Moreover, this interpretation of political reality places whatever might transpire in Syria-Palestine within cosmic perspective. What Yahweh does involves all humanity. This prophet's activity, like that of Jeremiah, reflected more than just the deity's interaction with his own people. Just as Jeremiah was "set over kingdoms and nations," and just as his task involved "plucking up and pulling down; destroying and overthrowing," so too the prophet addressed in Zech. 11:4–17 is charged with the task of enacting a message of woe for "each human group" that inhabits the earth.

[7] Someone speaks in the first person, but it is no longer the deity. With v. 7, we move from divine speech to prophetic speech, just as we move from the interpretation of the symbolic-action report to the report of the act's performance. The first line of v. 7 mirrors the deity's command to the prophet in v. 4. And the second line offers new vocabulary concerning those responsible for the flock, the sheep dealers. However, truly new, even innovative, is the way in

---

[116]See, e.g., Rudolph, *Sacharja 9–14*, 205.

which the prophet-shepherd chooses to tend the flock. He takes two crooks—implements of a shepherd, the bent stave used for manipulating the individual sheep—and names them. At this point in the report, we know that the individual is narrating something other than standard pastoral activity. First, it is unusual for a shepherd to carry two staves.[117] Further, there is little reason to think that pastoralists named their staves. Rather, the naming of something, more often individuals, occurs in earlier prophetic symbolic-action reports (e.g., Isa. 8:1–4; Ezek. 37:13–23; Hos. 1:4–11). However, in those cases, the naming was itself mandated by the deity, which may or may not be the case in Zech. 11:7. Like the names proffered in the symbolic act of Hosea 1, the names here carry meaning—"Pleasure" and "Agreement." It is better to use the vocabulary of labeling rather than naming, since there is little reason to think that the author of Zech. 11:4–17 employs personification. In any case, v. 7 presents symbolic preparation, the shepherd selecting and labeling the tools of his trade so that he will be able to work with the flock.[118] The full meaning of these names is revealed only when the staves are destroyed (vv. 10, 14).

[8] Verse 8 is, at first glance, surprising. The reader expects the shepherd to tend the flock. Instead, we discover that the shepherd has been active with other shepherds, but not with sheep. Since the flock and its care often involved the activity of more than one shepherd, such an eventuality might not seem surprising.[119] Moreover, the shepherd and the flock may be construed as one entity. Hence, to affect a shepherd is to affect the flock. In any case, the prophet-shepherd's dismissal of other shepherds creates problems: the prophet-shepherd's impatience with the other shepherds (the reasons for such impatience are not specified) and the disdain of the prophet-shepherd by the other shepherds (presumably because of their dismissal). One may infer that Yahweh works like this shepherd, that is, by dismissing or rejecting certain leaders, prior to his final decision to adopt a hands-off policy (see vv. 6, 9).

[9] Within the world of symbolic action, the prophet-shepherd speaks directly to the flock, which is personified at least to the extent that the sheep can be addressed by human speech. The shepherd explains that he will not

---

[117]Cf. E. Power, "The Shepherd's Two Rods in Modern Palestine and in Some Passages of the Old Testament," *Bib* 9 (1928): 434–42, who maintains that the two rods referred to are two different implements, a club and a staff, like those of "the modern Palestinian shepherd."

[118]The extent to which Zech. 11:4–17 has been influenced by and/or is a response to Ezek. 37:15–23 or 37:15–28 is a matter for considerable debate. Mason, *The Use of Earlier Biblical Material in Zechariah IX–XIV*, 150–53, and Hanson, *The Dawn of Apocalyptic*, 343–45, both maintain that Zech. 11:4–17 presents a reversal of Ezekiel's perspective. However, this claim has been developed by assessing the way in which the symbolic-action report works in Zechariah 11 before moving to the question of one text's influence on another.

[119]For evidence of shepherds working together, see S. Feigin, "Some Notes on Zechariah 11:4–17," *JBL* 44 (1925): 207.

function as their shepherd, and in so doing he continues to act out Yahweh's command. This statement is not a rejection of the deity's mandate. Instead, it is a further working out of the shepherd's task, which has already included the removal of several shepherds from their position. The laissez-faire attitude of the shepherd is underlined by the three parallel jussive formulations, each of which begins with a capsule description of the flock's status. It is dying, being destroyed, and involves a remnant (cf. Isa. 6). By way of response to these respective statuses, the prophet-shepherd says, using impersonal formulations, that he will let the flock die//be destroyed//devour itself. This willingness to allow destruction conveys the message that had been presented earlier. Yahweh will, like this shepherd, let the flock of humanity be destroyed. As v. 10 makes clear, this is a message addressed to all humans, not just to Judeans or Yahwists.

[10] As if to emphasize, or formally certify the utterance of v. 9, the prophet-shepherd begins a series of actions that involve tending a flock destined for slaughter. The shepherd takes one of the crooks, "Pleasure," and breaks it. This is, in itself, not a symbolic action. The breaking of this staff is not designed to communicate a message; rather, the act of breaking "Pleasure" is intended to do something—to break a covenant. Just as certain actions, whether the manipulation of blood or the eating of a ceremonial meal (Genesis 15; 17; Exodus 24), can ratify a covenant, so other actions, here the breaking of a shepherd's crook, can fracture an agreement.

It is impossible to read this verse and not ask, to what covenant is the author referring?[120] One might suggest the Noachic covenant, a covenant clearly made between Yahweh and all humanity, which is the sort of relationship at stake in Zech. 11:4–17. This suggestion may, however, be too quick, since there are more general allusions to "covenants," which involve more than just Israel and Yahweh, so the "covenant of brotherhood" mentioned in Amos 1:9. Nonetheless, the decimation of all humanity is an issue both in Genesis 9 and in Zech. 11:4–17. Hence, the breaking of "Pleasure" may be understood as the revision, if not termination, of the divine promise regarding the protection of humanity from destruction.[121]

There is a subtle difference between the covenant in Genesis 9 and the issue

---

[120]The issue of covenant per se is not important in Ezek. 37:15–23; cf. Mason, *The Use of Earlier Biblical Material in Zechariah IX–XIV*, 153. H. Gese, "Nachtrag," 233, suggests that the covenant refers to the Persian imperium. Cf. M. Rehm, "Die Hirtenallegorie Zach 11,4–14," 203–4, who focuses on the retrospective features of vv. 4–14, a position that A. van der Woude, "Die Hirtenallegorie von Sacharja XI," *JNSL* 12 (1984): 139–49, challenges.

[121]Cf. Otzen, *Deuterosacharja*, 154–56, for the argument that this covenant involves only Israel, and Elliger, *Das Buch,* who holds that it is an addition to the text and refers to a universal eschatological judgment. Mason, *The Use of Earlier Biblical Material in Zechariah IX–XIV,* 155–56, thinks the text is related to Abrahamic covenant formulations.

addressed in Zechariah 11. In Genesis 9, Yahweh appears to promise that he will not act as enemy agent against all humanity, whereas in Zechariah 11, Yahweh indicates that he will let earthly powers operate without control. As a result, though cataclysmic destruction might occur, it may not be attributed to Yahweh but to human or, better, inhuman rulers. The word *'ammîm*, "peoples," frequently refers to human groupings of the sort we might call a state or a nation. Therefore, it is appropriate to think that Yahweh is turning over sovereignty to those beneath him, to those in charge of various nations.

[11] Although *bayyôm hahû'* often occurs as an editorial phrase with eschatological purport, linking elements that were earlier distinct (Zechariah 14), in Zech. 11:11 it both serves a straightforward adverbial function and colors that temporality with an eschatological connotation. The act of breaking "Pleasure" did not go unobserved. The owners-merchants were watching. When they saw what happened, they deemed, correctly, that Yahweh was communicating a message: that the deity was ceding ultimate political authority to those in charge of earthly kingdoms. These merchant–flock-owners are hearing a message that emphasizes their control over the flock.

[12] Verses 12–14 depict an episode in which the prophet-shepherd interacts directly with the sheep-dealer–merchants and, then, in which the deity intervenes to provide instructions. Those whom the prophet-shepherd addresses are the ones who owned, sold, and slaughtered sheep, those who garnered wealth from this form of economic activity. The prophet-shepherd initiates this interchange with the merchants. With the task at an end (vv. 9–10), this individual seeks recompense for the work of shepherding that he had undertaken, which includes a qualitative judgment, namely, whether or not the merchants perceive that he had performed his task effectively.

The interpretation of the remainder of this poem depends on an assessment of his payment. Were "the thirty pieces of silver," as some commentators suggest, "no mean sum," that is, an appropriate payment?[122] Or was it an insultingly low sum? Two biblical texts are regularly cited in search of an answer. Exodus 21:32 stipulates that thirty shekels of silver are an appropriate sum to pay to the owner of a male or female slave if that slave has been gored, that is, killed, by an ox. Nehemiah 5:15 notes that forty shekels of silver were taken by certain governors of Judah (whether as taxes is unclear). Both these texts use the noun *šekel*. Not so in Zech. 11:12, though the verb *škl*, "to weigh out," is present. Put another way, Zech. 11:12 does not specify the exact denomination of payment.

Erica Reiner has argued that early on in the ancient Near East the phrase

---

[122]See, e.g., Baldwin, *Haggai, Zechariah, Malachi*, 184.

"thirty shekels" occurs as an expression for a minimal or trifling amount.[123] In the Sumerian poem "Gilgamesh and the Huluppu tree," Gilgamesh "put on armor weighing fifty minas (about 50 lbs.), he *considered* the fifty minas as (a mere) thirty shekels." Moreover, Lipiński has identified this same expression in Akkadian, in one of the texts from Tell el Amarna (Knudtzon, #292).[124] In sum, the expression "thirty pieces of silver" should be understood as an insultingly low wage.[125] One may, therefore, infer that the sheep dealers thought the prophet-shepherd had not done an effective job, which is hardly a surprising judgment. He had broken one of the tools of his trade and had stated flatly that he would not act as a shepherd (v. 9).

[13] We are not told at first how the prophet-shepherd views this trifling payment of thirty pieces of silver. However, it did affect Yahweh. He speaks immediately to the prophet-shepherd and orders him to toss the amount toward the treasury, which we learn later in the verse was located at the temple. However, as soon as the deity has mandated this action, the prophet-shepherd breaks in with a sarcastic aside that describes those thirty pieces of silver as "that precious amount with which I had been honored by them." Those thirty pieces were not a precious amount, and as a result, the prophet-shepherd has not been honored but rather insulted by the sheep dealers. Hence, especially since he agrees with the deity's judgment, he hurls the silver toward the temple's treasury.

[14] The prophet-shepherd continues with the symbolic action, which had been interrupted by the negative response of the sheep dealers. He broke the second crook, "Agreement." This act is both similar to and different from the earlier act of breakage. On the one hand, it is different: The earlier one deals with all people, whereas v. 14 involves the two entities that comprise Yahweh's people, Judah and Israel.[126] On the other hand, the similarity involves the notion of breaking a contract or covenant. Verse 10 addressed the abrogation of something like the Noachic covenant. Verse 14 relies on that agreement which unified the peoples of Yahweh, the national unity created by David. (The extent to which the Sinaitic covenant underlies this text could be debated. Obviously, this covenant was remembered as "creating" the people, but not,

---

[123]E. Reiner, "Thirty Pieces of Silver," *JAOS* 88 (1968): 186–90; see similarly Lipiński, "Recherches sur le livre de Zacharie," 53–55.

[124]Lipiński, "Recherches sur le livre de Zacharie," 54–55, and see J. A. Knutzon, *Die El-Amarna Tafeln, mit Einleitung und Erläuterungen,* Leipzig, 1907–15.

[125]So also Rudolph, *Sacharja 9–14,* 209.

[126]Some commentators have argued too quickly for a relationship, namely, one of challenge, between Ezek. 37:16 and Zechariah 11. In Ezekiel 37, both Judah and Joseph are construed as part of Israel, which is a quite different way of setting up the relationships than that found in Zechariah 11.

however, the operative categories of Judah and Israel.) The language of brotherhood and being brothers was one way of expressing the covenant relationship.[127] Hence, the issue is not that of the reunification of the two separate Iron Age nations but is, instead, that of the very existence of Yahweh's people, using the diction of national entities.

[15] Verse 15 introduces a new symbolic-action report, obviously related to the preceding one. In fact, it responds to the foregoing report. Yahweh commands the prophet to enact again the role of shepherd.[128] The command in v. 4 had included a certain negative quality, that of the entire flock being destined for slaughter. The second command has an even stronger negative quality. Whereas earlier the flock was doomed, here, quite apart from any explicit description of the flock, the shepherd himself will perform inadequately because he is mandated to take faulty equipment—"the gear of an ineffective shepherd." Given the actions reported in vv. 10 and 14, it might not be too much to suggest that broken crooks would count as such inadequate gear. In any case, the mandate indicates clearly that the shepherd's inadequacy is linked directly to inappropriate gear—whether that involves implements for the care of the flock (e.g., crook) or implements for the defense of the flock (e.g., sling and stone).

Before proceeding further, it is necessary to comment on the form of this symbolic-action report. As did the earlier one, it includes a command (v. 15) and an interpretation (v. 16). However, there is no report about the performance. Instead, we find, by way of a conclusion, a lament over the shepherd who performs inadequately. As a result, the text ends in an open-ended manner. It announces what Yahweh now intends but does not report that it has happened. Perhaps the prophet refuses to perform the act; we are simply not told.

[16] Just as in v. 6, Yahweh interprets the action that has been commanded. The interpretation complements that which had been proffered earlier. In v. 6, we learned that Yahweh would not stop earthly rulers from oppressing those under their rule. Verse 16 reports that Yahweh will still be active, though in an invidious manner. Whereas the first symbolic action conveyed the image of a "hands off" posture by the deity, the second symbolic action reports that the deity is authorizing "a shepherd in the land." Verse 6 sets the international context, while v. 16 reports what will happen in one situation.

In contrast to the previous report, this symbolic act emphasizes the singularity of the shepherd. There is no reference to other shepherds. Rather, the

[127]J. Priest, "The Covenant of Brothers," *JBL* 84 (1965): 400–406.

[128]I find unconvincing those attempts made to suggest that someone other than the prophet, e.g., "a type of forerunner for the Antichrist," e.g., Rudolph, *Sacharja 9–14,* 211, is intended here. Such a claim does not accommodate the genre of the literature as symbolic-action report.

interpretation focuses on the negative interaction between the sole shepherd and flock. The writer has created a powerful picture by presenting four clauses, each of which begins with the negative particle *lō'*. The similarity of syntax emphasizes the semantic similarity, namely, that the shepherd will not do certain things that a shepherd would normally do: search, seek, heal, and care for. There are certain ones in the flock who require attention, the ones who are missing, cry out, are injured, and are exhausted. In no case will the shepherd attend to these who deserve his ministrations.

Using a different form of syntax, disjunctive clauses without negative particles, the author reports that which this ineffective shepherd will do. He will devour the flock. This would seem to be the particular case that defines and illustrates the sort of oppression foreseen in v. 6. The word order in Hebrew, in which the objects of the verbs occur first, emphasizes that which the shepherd will consume. We are here presented with a case of merismus, the use of two poles to indicate a totality. The author is not interested in claiming that the shepherd will consume just the choice portions and the small amount of flesh in the hoof. Instead, these examples of edible meat function meristically, the two extremes which symbolize that all edible flesh will be eaten. The flock will be slaughtered, so the first report, and consumed totally, the point of the second vision report.

As I have just suggested, there is a certain consistency in the imagery of the two reports, namely, both use the language of flock and shepherd. However, the second report does not include the mercantile diction, and for a reason. Material gain, whether for the prophet-shepherd or for the sheep dealers, is important in the world of the first symbolic action. In the second, neither the shepherd (nor by inference the owner//seller) will benefit materially. Instead, the shepherd will devour the flesh to satiate his own hunger. The flock no longer functions economically as it should, but instead becomes the private preserve for personal oppression. The flock is perverted by the inaction and then improper action of this one shepherd.

[17] Though it may seem surprising to find the language of a woe oracle here, such an oracle seems an appropriate response to this perverse profanation of such an important economic resource.[129] One may even suggest that the woe oracle replaces the expected report of the act's performance. Just as there is a certain ambiguity about the place of this woe statement in a symbolic-action report, there is, as well, ambiguity about who is speaking. Saebo suggests that it is the prophet, probably the most cogent suggestion.[130] If such is the case,

---

[129]Cf. Mason, *The Use of Earlier Biblical Material in Zechariah IX–XIV*, who notes that woe statements (vv. 6 and 9) occur in the symbolic-action report of Ezek. 24:1–14; and Elliger, *Das Buch*, 155–56, who argues that 11:17 is an independent poem.

[130]Saebo, *Sacharja 9–14*, 239.

then we are presented with a picture of a prophet inveighing against the role that he has been commanded to perform in a symbolic act. This suggestion may explain why we find no report of the act being performed. The prophet himself has provided a negative perspective on the action mandated by the deity. In complex fashion, the prophet addresses in direct discourse the very person whose task he was to perform.

The woe formula appears to be typologically of an early sort;[131] there is no preposition prefixing the person addressed by the woe. In addition, the word "worthless," *'elîl*, is linked by assonance, if not by triconsonantal root (a complicated question), to the word "ineffective," *'ewilî* (v. 15). The author describes the shepherd in a relative clause, which highlights the acts of omission specified in v. 16. The woe is uttered on a shepherd who abandons, not devours, the flock.

A curse or imprecation follows hard upon the woe statement, again presumably offered by the prophetic voice. The diction is martial. Rather than simply call for blindness and paralysis, the prophet invokes a sword to disable the shepherd.[132] Verse 17 offers a human response to that which Yahweh is doing. The prophet utters both a statement of woe and of curse. Yahweh has given over control of human affairs to shepherds and sheep dealers. And the consequences are dire. However, such abdication has elicited a human response. One of the most powerful forms of human utterance, the curse, concludes this action. Whether or not Yahweh had intended such to occur, the human voice begins to assert itself as a response to the plight of the flock and the dismal performance of the shepherd. The curse does not solve the former problem, for the flock is still in disarray, but it does address the ineffective, even malevolent shepherd. If the curse is effective, then the shepherd will only be ineffective; that is to say, by dint of the intended blindness and paralysis the shepherd will no longer be able to plunder the flock.

In sum, Zech. 11:4–17 presents two symbolic actions in which Yahweh eschews direct control, gives over control to others, and raises up a shepherd, one who will not provide appropriate leadership. The first *maśśā'*, or oracle, ends on a radically negative note, one of a flock abandoned and an ineffective shepherd under curse.

It has been a commonplace to treat these symbolic actions as allegories and to view the author of this text as in some way attacking specific leadership roles in Persian-period Judah, in particular the priests. Such a move, however, absolutizes what is obviously highly picturesque discourse, constrained by the

---

[131]R. Clifford, "The Use of *HOY* in the Prophets," *CBQ* 28 (1966): 458–64.

[132]Jeremiah 50:35–38 presents a call for the sword against the Babylonians. Here too the curse is formulated *ḥereb 'al . . .*, "a sword against [name]." (Curses or imprecations include formulations that do not commence with "Cursed . . . / *'ārûr*.)

form of the symbolic-action report. Hence, one senses that the texts are perspectival rather than particular. They report Yahweh's general response to and perspective on the international scene (as in the first report) and the Judean scene (the second report).[133] The present situation stands ready for divine response, which comes at the beginning of the second *maśśā'*.

[133]Those comments that focus on the dependence of Zech. 11:4–17 upon Ezekiel 38 assume the prominence of the second act over the first one.

ZECHARIAH 12–14
THE SECOND "ORACLE"

Zechariah 12:1–13:6

Yahweh speaks concerning the place of a purified Judah and Jerusalem among the nations

12:1 An oracle, the word of Yahweh concerning Israel, a saying of Yahweh,
who stretched out the heavens,
who founded the earth,
who formed the vital impulse within humanity:[a]

2 "Truly, I am making Jerusalem a shaking foundation[b]
for all the peoples who surround (it).[c]
The siege against Jerusalem will also involve Judah.[d]

3 On that day I will set Jerusalem as a heavy stone against all the peoples;
all who lift it will injure themselves;
(when) all the nations of the earth gather against her."

4 "On that day,"
        says Yahweh,
"I will strike every horse with terror,
every rider with despair.
When I open my eyes over the house of Judah,
I will strike every horse of the peoples with blindness.

5 The leaders[e] of Judah will say to themselves,
'My strength resides in the inhabitants of Jerusalem,[f]
in Yahweh of Hosts, their God.'

6 On that day I will place the leaders of Judah
like a fire pot amid trees,
like a fiery torch in harvested grain.
They will consume, on the right and on the left, all the surrounding
    peoples;
Jerusalem will continue to exist where it is in peace.[g]

7 At first Yahweh will give victory to the tents of Judah,
so that the pride of the house of David
and the pride of the inhabitants of Jerusalem
may not overwhelm Judah.

8 On that day Yahweh will shield them,
the inhabitants of Jerusalem.
Whoever on that day is weak
will be like David,

and the house of David will be like a deity,
>   like the messenger of Yahweh before them.

9   On that day I intend to destroy[h] all the nations
>   who come up against Jerusalem.

10   I will pour out upon the house of David
>   and upon the inhabitants of Jerusalem,
a favorable spirit, in answer to (their) supplications.[i]
>   They will look upon him[j] whom they stabbed.
They will lament over him,
>   as one laments an only son.
They will grieve over him,
>   as one grieves over one's firstborn.

11   On that day, the lamentation over Jerusalem will be as great
>   as the mourning over Hadad-rimmon,
>   in the valley of Megiddon.[k]

12   The land will lament,
>   each family by itself,
the family of the house of David by itself,
>   their women by themselves;
the family of the house of Nathan by itself,
>   their women by themselves;

13   the family of the house of Levi by itself,
>   their women by themselves;
the family of the Shimeites by itself,
>   their women by themselves;

14   and all the remaining families,
>   each family by itself,
>   their women by themselves.

13:1   On that day there will be a fountain
>   that will open forth for the house of David
and for the inhabitants of Jerusalem
>   for (removal of) sin and impurity.[l]

2   On that day," saying of Yahweh of Hosts,
>   "I will cut off the names of the idols from the land.
>   They shall be remembered no more.
Also, I will remove the prophets
>   and the unclean spirit from the land.

3   If anyone again attempts to prophesy,
>   his father and his mother who bore him will say to him,
'You shall not live,
>   because you have spoken falsely in Yahweh's name.'

His father and his mother who bore him
   will stab him when he prophesies.
4   On that day, every prophet will be ashamed of his visions
       when he prophesies.
   He will not wear a hairy cloak,
       a cloak made out of skins in order to deceive.
5   He will say,
       'I was no prophet,
   I was a tiller of the ground,
       but a man seduced me from my youth.'ᵐ
6   When someone asks,
       'What are these wounds between your shoulders?'ⁿ
   He will respond,
       'I was beaten in the house of (illicit) love.' "ᵒ

   a. The three relative clauses contain participles, which seem to require a translation in the past tense. See *GKC*, 116d and, e.g., Ps. 136:4–7 for such use of participles to describe Yahweh's primeval acts of creation.

   b. There are two nouns, *sap*, in classical Hebrew: I—bowl or goblet, and II—threshold. Either noun could make sense here. The notion of a shaking foundation or threshold is prominent in prophetic rhetoric, e.g., Isa. 6:4 and Amos 9:1. And in the latter, the notion of shaking foundation is a symbol for Yahweh's destruction. LXX understood *sap* to signify threshold, as do I. So also Rudolph, *Sacharja 9–14*, 217; cf. Saebo, *Sacharja 9–14*, 88–89.

   c. The word *sābîb* can denote something that surrounds something else (Zech. 2:9 [5]), the wall of fire that surrounds the city. In Zech. 12:2, the image is of Jerusalem surrounded by peoples, presumably in a military confrontation.

   d. MT reads literally, "and even against Judah, there shall be in the siege against Jerusalem." (The noun here translated "siege" occurs in Zech. 9:3, with the meaning "fortification," of the sort that is to withstand a siege.) LXX and S read "and there will be a siege against Jerusalem in Judah," whereas T and V read "and even Judah will be in the siege against Jerusalem." V could mean that Judah will suffer in the siege of Jerusalem, whereas T suggests that Judah will be engaged with other enemies in laying siege to Jerusalem, so Otzen, *Deuterosacharja*, 261, who thinks both T and V involve the sense of Judah against Jerusalem. Hanson takes both traditions seriously, *The Dawn of Apocalyptic*, 357, 361–62, but opts for the LXX and S as likely to be original. Most solutions involve deletions of prepositions, either *b* prefixing "siege," which allows one to follow LXX; or *'al* standing before "Judah," which allows one to follow T and V. Lutz, *Jahwe, Jerusalem und die Völker*, 11, is more radical, depending essentially on excisions, "and Judah will also be under threat." Ehrlich, *Randglossen*, vol. 5, 349–50, offers a conjectural emendation, which Otzen, *Deuterosacharja*, 262, adopts, reading *'ārê*, "cities" (and a plural verb), instead of *'al*, thereby allowing one to translate "cities of Judah." However, the two primary reasons that Ehrlich offers, namely, the text cannot mean what it says and a land cannot be construed in this way, are contradicted by Zech. 14:14. Saebo, *Sacharja 9–14*, 90, rightly rejects this way of approaching the text since one should prefer precisely the sort of reading that seems "impossible." He thinks the text has been "demilitarized" in most of the textual traditions. Saebo, *Sacharja 9–14*, 91, reconstructs as original "and Judah shall be in the siege against Jerusalem" but does not think that, though Judah is the grammatical subject, it will actually take part in the siege (cf. Ezek. 4:1–7). Rudolph, *Sacharja 9–14*, 217, suggests reading *māṣôr* with the meaning of "affliction."

The issue is an important one since it involves the relation of Judah, that is, those people living in towns other than Jerusalem, to the regional center—Jerusalem—a relation that appears prominent in v. 5, but cf. v. 7; and one that is clearly negative in tone, at least in Zech. 14:14. The evidence is complex, and it finds a reflex in certain textual traditions of Zech. 11:14 (see Hanson, *The Dawn of Apocalyptic*, 361–62).

I have proposed a translation that is intentionally ambiguous, allowing either the notion that Judah could be attacked or that Judah might be involved in the attack. In either case, I deem v. 2a to be a comment, similar in tone to Zech. 14:14, on the earlier tradition that has at its core statements by Yahweh about how he will use Jerusalem against the nations, as in vv. 2a and 3a.

e. MT *'allupê*, "chiefs," is often emended (e.g., Ehrlich, *Randglossen*, vol. 5, 350) to *'alpê*, "clans," a change without good warrant. Zechariah 9:7 provides no clear guide to the reading here.

f. LXX and T read "we shall find for ourselves the inhabitants of Jerusalem." These textual traditions clearly and mistakenly understood MT *'amṣāh* to derive from the root *mṣ'*, instead of being a noun from *'mṣ* which makes excellent sense here.

g. Reading *bĕšālôm* instead of *bîrûšālāim*, so Ehrlich, *Randglossen*, vol. 5, 350.

h. Cf. *Tanakh*, "I will all but annihilate."

i. Literally, "a favorable and supplicant spirit," which involves a case of alliteration, since both nouns stem from the root *ḥnn*.

j. Reading *'ēlô* instead of MT *'ēlay*. MT could be translated, "they will look to me concerning the one whom they stabbed," or "they will look to me, the one whom they have insulted," the latter is supported by Delcor, "Un problème du critique textuelle et d'exégèse: Zach 12.10 et aspicient ad me quem confixerunt," *RB* 58 (1951): 189–99.

k. MT reads *mĕgiddôn*, which may be analogous to the paragogic *nun*, or as Otzen, *Deuterosacharja*, 265, suggests, for purposes of alliteration with *rimmôn*. LXX avoids reference either to a deity's name or to a toponym, "as the mourning for the pomegranate grove hewed down in the plain."

l. The LXX evidence is complex. Many manuscripts omit the last two lines, others omit only the last one, which may suggest that an early form of this tradition did not offer a comment about the function of the fountain. See Saebo, *Sacharja 9–14*, 103, for a brief discussion.

m. So Otzen, *Deuterosacharja*, 265–66, who follows S and construes the verb to derive from *qn'*. Cf. Ehrlich, *Randglossen*, vol. 5, 351 et al., who argues that the *he* of the original *'ădāmāh* has been joined to the verb, MT *hiqnanî* (the only time *qnh* would have occurred in the hiphil), and therefore read *'ădāmāh qinyānî*, "ground possessed me."

n. Cf. 2 Kings 9:24 on this meaning of *yad*.

o. So Otzen, *Deuterosacharja*, 197; Ehrlich, *Randglossen*, vol. 5, 351; Lacocque, *Zacharie 9–14*, 195–96; cf. Rudolph, *Sacharja 9–14*, 227.

No one has argued convincingly that Zech. 12:1–13:6 (or 12:1–13:9) presents a sole literary genre.[1] This remains true, in part, because these verses are of diverse origin. I will maintain that Zech. 13:2–6 and 13:7–9 have been appended to Zech. 12:2–13:1. Moreover, there is a prologue, Zech. 12:1, which introduces the entire second "oracle." And the core unit, Zech. 12:2–13:1, is itself thematically diverse, with strands of the Zion, Davidic, and holy war traditions intertwined within it. These verses are structurally complex. Hence, traditional form-critical labels are of little use. However, Zech. 12:2–13:1 does have structural integrity, a shape that gives meaning to the divine and human words that occur here.

Scholars use various and general terms to describe 12:1–13:6 (and for that matter also chap. 14), terms such as "composition" (Hanson) or "*Komposition*," "*Abschnitt*" (Saebo).[2] These labels have the benefit of not straitjacketing the discussion. However, they also offer the reader little preliminary guidance about the specific character of these chapters. Hence, I would offer the term, "montage," which is borrowed from the world of pictorial art, to describe the two major sections that make up the second "oracle." The boundary of the individual literary elements are almost always created by the presence of the formula "on that day." The extent to which the smaller vignettes are of diverse origin is a matter of considerable debate.[3] However, for the viewer or interpreter of the montage, the origins of the individual pieces are of less impor-

[1]Scholars do construe this material differently. For example, Saebo views the units to be 12:1; 12:2–13:6; 13:7–9 (*Sacharja 9–14*, 252–82); Hanson, 12:1–13:6 (he places 13:7–9 with chap. 11; *The Dawn of Apocalyptic*, 354–68); Rudolph, 12:1–14; 13:1–6; 13:7–9 with chap. 11. (*Sacharja 9–14*, 218–29); Otzen, 12:1; 12:2–7; 12:8–13:1; 13:2–6; 13:7–9 (*Deuterosacharja*, 173–94).

[2]Hanson, *The Dawn of Apocalyptic*, 354; Saebo, *Sacharja 9–14*, 254, 266). Saebo argues that the texts are structured in tripartite fashion: A 12:3–8; B 12:9–13:1; C 13:2–6 (*Sacharja 9–14*, chart on p. 261). This structure, which depends on the presence of the long "on that day" formulae, fails to account for the presence of these longer formulae in vv. 3 and 4. Moreover, there does not seem to be a fundamental shift in topic between A and B, as there is with what Saebo identifies as C. In sum, the claim for a tripartite structure founders on grounds of both form and content. Saebo is correct that the longer formula consistently introduces a divine and not a prophetic saying. However, his reconstruction of the text's formation, e.g., the three-stage process in 12:2–6, does not materially help the interpretive process.

[3]Saebo exemplifies an approach that plumbs the origins of the individual elements. Elliger maintains that there was a basic text (12:2a, 3a, 4abb, 5, 6b), which has been revised by the addition of sayings dealing with Judah (12:2b, 3b, 4ba, 6a, 7f), *Das Buch der zwölf kleinen Propheten*, 157–64. Lutz thinks there is greater diversity in the secondary material, namely, pro-Jerusalem and pro-dynastic (5, 6b, 8), pro-Judahite (2b, 4ba, 6a,7); *Jahwe, Jerusalem, und die Völker*, 12–21.

tance than the overall configuration and effect of the final piece. In sum, I will be concerned to identify the individual elements and to suggest their meaning, but within the larger context of the entire montage.

[12:1] Zechariah 12:1 constitutes the prologue for Zechariah 12–14.[4] Like Zech. 9:1 and Mal. 1:1, the prologue begins with the phrase, "an oracle, the word of Yahweh. . . ." However, in each instance the preposition that follows is different; in this case *'al,* which is normally translated "concerning" or "against." And unlike the formula in Zech. 9:1, Israel, and not "the land of Hadrak . . . ," is now the subject of Yahweh's oracle, a notion that is born out by what follows: Israel, or perhaps better Judah, interacts with "the nations." The formulaic prologue, though editorial in origin, is a reasonable guide to what it introduces.

This prologue is not as long as the first one, Zech. 9:1–2, but it is longer than the last one, Mal. 1:1. Moreover, after the initial phrase "an oracle, the word of Yahweh concerning Israel," the prologue in Zech. 12:1 is much different syntactically than are either of the other prologues. Following immediately upon the phrase that designates the object of the oracle, the prologue includes the stereotypic "saying of Yahweh," which is followed by three parallel participial clauses. The phrase "saying of Yahweh" is used loosely in this "oracle." It marks intermediate transitions, but not in the classical way.[5]

The phrase "saying of Yahweh" introduces distinctive language. Though the ensuing lines resonate with the doxologies that occur in the book of Amos (e.g., 4:13) and formulations in Isaiah 40–55, it seems most at home in the Psalter.[6] These three lines include what some scholars have termed "hymnic" participles, since participial clauses provide the reason for praise of the deity.[7] Various topics or themes occur in these participial clauses, one of which is reference to the deity as creator, as in the Deutero-Isaianic corpus (40:22, 28; 42:5; 45:18). Certain songs of praise treat the theme of creation, e.g., Pss. 8; 19:1–6; 33; 104; 136.[8] Of these psalms, Ps. 104:2–4, 5–6 includes participles that depict Yahweh as creator. There are, in addition, other types of psalms that include such participial constructions that refer to Yahweh as creator (e.g., Ps. 146:6).

Zechariah 12:1 belongs to this participial, doxological world of discourse,

---

[4]So, e.g., Plöger, *Theocracy and Eschatology,* 82; Saebø, *Sacharja 9–14,* 252–54; cf. Rudolph, *Sacharja 9–14,* 219–20.

[5]On which, see F. Baumgärtel, "Die Formel *ne'um jahwe,*" *ZAW* 73 (1961): 277–90; and more recently, Saebø, *Sacharja 9–14,* 253.

[6]F. Crüsemann, *Studien zur Formgeschichte von Hymnus und Danklied in Israel,* Neukirchen-Vluyn, 1969, 152, has argued convincingly that they do not occur solely or predominantly in one genre.

[7]See Crüsemann, *Studien,* 83–154; and H.-J. Kraus, *Psalms 1–59,* Minneapolis, 1987, 43–47.

[8]Kraus, *Psalms 1–59,* 45.

particularly the one in which a series of related formulations occurs (e.g., Job 5:9–16; 9:5–10).[9] The notion of Yahweh as creator mirrors earlier language, particularly Isa. 42:5, which also refers to a deity who stretched out the heavens, who spread forth earth (as opposed to "founded" in Zechariah), and who gives "spirit" to people.[10] Hence, one may infer that the general claims presented in the prologue are traditional. However, one must recognize to what use such traditional claims have been put in Isaiah 42. In Isa. 42:5–9, v. 5 serves as a prologue, namely, to that which follows. Moreover, the rest of the unit, vv. 6–9, presents claims about what the deity has done and is about to do. The appeal to primordial creative acts provides the reason that those who are addressed should believe the prophet. In a similar manner, Zech. 12:1 provides the rationale for the "believability" of this "oracle." The deity who creates heaven, earth, and human life can do anything which involves that created order. Life throughout that created order—including even fundamental disruptions within that created order—is the subject of this oracle, Zechariah 12–14.

[2] This divine speech presents a prologue to the "on that day" montage, Zech. 12:3–13:9. Yahweh proclaims that which he will do, namely, wield Jerusalem against the surrounding peoples. The author uses an image which had appeared in earlier prophetic literature, namely, that of the shaking foundation. In Amos 9:1, the deity commands his minions to attack the capitals of the temple's columns so that the foundations (*sippîm*) shake. Clearly, the imagery here is architectural, as in Isa. 6:4, where the foundations of the thresholds shake as they resound with the impact of speech in the divine council. In both cases, the foundations are those of a building, the temple in Jerusalem. Zechariah 12:2 is, by contrast, more imagistic. Yahweh will make Jerusalem—a city, not a building—a shaking foundation. But for the imagery truly to make sense, one must ask: for what building or artifice does Jerusalem serve as the foundation? In this regard, the larger context makes clear that Jerusalem is under attack by the nations; the notion of siege is itself proffered in the same verse. Hence, one may infer that the prophet imagines a situation in which siegeworks have been erected against the city wall and that the city itself, which serves as the prop or "foundations" of the enemies' constructions, will shake and in so doing wreck their siegeworks. That Yahweh would annihilate those who came up against Jerusalem inheres in the Zion tradition. That Yahweh would manipulate Jerusalem, as a foundation for enemy siegeworks, is a highly innovative claim, one that emphasizes Yahweh's willingness to work through and with all that Jerusalem represents. Just as with Zech.

[9]Crüsemann, *Studien*, 115–18.

[10]Some of these descriptions are obviously formulaic, e.g., "stretching out the heavens." See Isa. 40:22; Ps. 104:2; Job 9:8.

9:1–8, the diction of toponyms is important, but in this case, it is a Judahite site that dominates, not other Syro-Palestinian places.

The final line in v. 2, as I indicated in the philological note, presents ambiguity of at least two sorts. First, there is ambiguity about literary integrity. One has good reason to view this line as an addition to the astounding image of Jerusalem's shaking like a threshold.[11] This last line explicates the earlier discourse. It states that there will be a siege, something that the reader would have discovered earlier in the verse. The second element of ambiguity involves the place of Judah in this siege. Will the siege be against Judah as well as against Jerusalem, or will Judah be involved in the siege against Jerusalem? Unfortunately, the manuscript evidence is so ambiguous as to disallow an answer. Other texts in the second "oracle" provide evidence that Judah and Jerusalem might be construed as diverse, even antagonistic entities (Zech. 12:4–5, 6–7; 14:14). However, since the range of the relationships between province and city is so potentially broad, it is impossible to be precise about the nature of that relationship in v. 2.

[3] With v. 3, the first in a series of "on that day" sayings occurs. The formula that introduces v. 3, *wĕhāyāh bayyôm hahû'*, also occurs in 12:9 and 13:2, 4. This formula is different from the simpler *bayyôm hahû'* in 12:4, 6, 8, 11. Saebo maintains that the longer formula introduces three different sections, but this thesis does not account for the presence of the longer formula in 13:4.[12] As a result, it is probably best to suggest that the longer formula provides minimal variety in what otherwise might be a wooden series of formulaic expressions.

The imagery of v. 3 is deceptively puzzling. One might think that the author intended the reader to imagine several people struggling to move a heavy stone and, in so doing, suffering muscle strain or hernia.[13] However, the Hebrew verb, *śrṭ*, which occurs in only one other place, Lev. 21:5, means, apparently, to cut or incise human flesh. Hence, the form of injury must be a gash rather than a strain.[14] Jerusalem as a rock positioned by Yahweh will injure and defeat the enemy.

Though the rhetoric of v. 3 may seem similar to that of the prologue in v. 2, there are important differences.[15] The grammar of the verbs changes from

---

[11]So, e.g., Elliger, *Das Buch der zwölf kleinen Propheten,* 158–64; Lutz, *Jahwe, Jerusalem und die Völker,* 13.

[12]Saebo, *Sacharja 9–14,* 260–76.

[13]So, e.g., Rudolph, *Sacharja 9–14,* 221, who appeals to the sport of lifting heavy stones.

[14]So Mitchell, "as one, handling a heavy stone, tears one's hands on its rugged surface . . . ," *A Critical and Exegetical Commentary,* 322.

[15]Cf. Lutz, *Jahwe, Jerusalem und die Völker,* 18, for a discussion of the similarities and differences between vv. 2 and 3. He emphasizes their parallel structure, whereas Saebo, *Sacharja 9–14,* 268, points to the differences and argues v. 2 is an addition.

participle to the imperfect, which signifies something akin to the future tense. Moreover, the language of what is surely a military attack is much more personal in this first saying than it is in the prologue. Such differences, however, should not prevent the reader from discerning the obvious similarities. The same verb, *śym*, is used to describe the action of the deity. In both cases, Yahweh is using Jerusalem against "the peoples." In both cases, the nations will be gathered around Jerusalem. Hence, the same basic tradition seems to underlie both the prologue and the first vignette.

It would be difficult to deny that something like the so-called Zion tradition—as it is found, for example, in Pss. 46, 48, 76 as well as Isa. 17:12–14—undergirds these verses.[16] There was, apparently, a standard expectation that nations would come up against Jerusalem and that Yahweh would protect his city from defeat. However, the vivid images—of shaking foundations, of siegeworks, and of hurtful rock—provide truly innovative modes for expressing this tradition. These images are not present elsewhere in the Hebrew Bible. This portion of the second "oracle" is no hackneyed version of the Zion tradition. Rather, moving beyond the formulaic rubrics present in vv. 1 and 3, the prophet-poet has vividly and memorably highlighted the nature of Yahweh's use of Jerusalem in the defense of that city.

Not only do the prologue and the first saying reflect the Zion tradition, they represent a development of it. In postexilic Judah it was no longer possible to think about a Jerusalem that could be undefeated and unsullied. Jerusalem had been shaken, lifted as a rock by the Babylonians. Hence, the claims of the earlier Zion texts (e.g., Ps. 46:5, "she shall not be moved") were no longer possible. Nations had built siegeworks against Jerusalem, they had lifted up its population and exiled significant portions thereof. The imagery in Zech. 12:2–3 reflects a postexilic understanding of the Zion tradition, namely, that Jerusalem will shake, will be lifted, but that, finally, Yahweh will assist his city during military encounter. One specific element in these two verses, the word "all," which involves an element of hyperbole, is indicative of this postexilic setting. To be sure, the earlier form of the Zion tradition involved nations, peoples, or kingdoms; now all such entities will be involved in the attack against Yahweh's city.

[4] The second saying is longer than the first one and involves more overt martial discourse. Moreover, the geographic venue widens; Judah as well as Jerusalem is under attack. If the prologue and first saying focus on Jerusalem and the nations, the second two sayings, vv. 4–5 and vv. 6–7, have the larger entity Judah as a leading motif. This concern with the larger territory, rather

---

[16]Lutz, *Jahwe, Jerusalem und die Völker*, discerns three basic components in this tradition: the battle of the peoples against Jerusalem, Yahweh's battle against the peoples, and Yahweh's battle against Jerusalem.

than just the divine dwelling, is consistent with the imagery of this saying since it involves the use of ancient traditions that relate to all of Israel, not just Jerusalem. Unlike the foregoing verse, the prophet uses here a common notion drawn from Israel's holy war traditions. Yahweh rather than the Israelite army will engage the enemy's forces. Further, to describe the enemy in terms of horse and rider is attested in earlier poetic literature such as Ex. 15:1. Moreover, the deity's onslaught can be effected by terror or despair (which in Hebrew provides something of a rhyme in the form of assonance, *timmāhôn* and *šiggā'ôn*), rather than sword or siegework. The diction of "striking" is preserved elsewhere in the Hebrew Bible in Deut. 28:28, which contains traditional curse language directed against those Israelites who violate Yahweh's covenant. Nonetheless, in both cases, Yahweh is the one who uses terror and despair as weapons; thus the verb *nkh* with Yahweh as the subject occurs both in Zech. 12:4 and Deut. 28:28.

The connection between Deuteronomy 28 and Zech. 12:4 continues since Deut. 28:29 introduces the imagery of blindness as a malediction ("and you shall grope at noonday, as the blind grope in darkness"), a notion that also occurs in Zech. 12:4. It would appear that standard imprecation formulations could include the language of terror/despair and the language of blindness, and in that order. Zechariah 12:4 is, however, different from Deut. 28:29. Whereas the latter text includes a simile to elucidate the image of the blind, who are helpless even in bright light, Zech. 12:4 uses irony to explain how it is that blindness will be engendered. Yahweh will open his eyes, whereupon the horses will become blind.[17] The notion of Yahweh opening his eyes, though attested elsewhere in the OT (Isa. 37:17//2 Kings 19:16; Jer. 32:19), is not used in this way to describe something akin to military assault. In sum, Zech. 12:4 provides a renovated form of holy war traditions to speak of Yahweh's intervention on behalf of Judah.

[5] Although many scholars think the author has referred to "clans" in vv. 5 and 6, I follow MT in reading "leaders" (see note e). In either case, whether the reference is to a group or to a leader of a group, the terminology involves large tribelike groupings in Judah. Instead of the large social grouping referred to in Ezra-Nehemiah (the house of fathers, *bêt 'ābôt*), the vocabulary in Zechariah 12 archaizes, referring to postexilic realities but with language that comes from a much earlier period and social reality (cf. Ex. 15:15). The term most often refers to leaders of a territorial state, particularly of Edom (Genesis 36; Ex. 15:15; 1 Chron. 1:51). Zechariah 12:5 provides the only instance in which the OT refers to the *'allupê* ("leaders") of Judah. The text mentions the leaders, and not clans, because the leaders would have been those called on to

---

[17]It is inappropriate to view the last line of v. 4 as a gloss. Cf. Otzen, *Deuterosacharja*, 186; Lutz, *Jahwe, Jerusalem und die Völker*, 15; Hanson, *The Dawn of Apocalyptic*, 355–57.

create whatever military defenses might have been possible. However, Zech. 12:5 does not report them to be engaged in battle. Consistent with holy war language, these individuals note that Yahweh provides them strength. But there is an astounding claim, which occurs in the penultimate line of the verse. The leaders speak as with one voice, "My strength resides in the inhabitants of Jerusalem."[18] The leaders of Judah attest to the weal Yahweh is able to effect for their territory (v. 4). However, they claim that the inhabitants of Jerusalem, as well as the deity, are a source of strength. If there is a sociopolitical reality lying behind this distinction, it is no longer readily discernible. On traditio-historical grounds, the holy war tradition seems bound here to the Zion tradition. Yahweh, who acts on behalf of Judah, is related intimately to the inhabitants of Jerusalem, so much so that the latter provide strength for the former. Moreover, Yahweh can even be referred to as "their" (that is, the Jerusalemites') God.

Is the special status of Jerusalem to be explained solely by reference to the Zion tradition? Probably not. Nehemiah 11:1 records that the leaders of the people, namely, Judean Jews, lived in Jerusalem whereas the rest of the people lived "in other towns." Place of residence and power are clearly related according to Ezra-Nehemiah. Not surprisingly, Yahweh is associated with those who exercise power, namely, those who live in Jerusalem. Those who live "in other towns" benefit from the deity's military largesse, and yet they testify that Jerusalem is the source of their connection to the deity's power. This saying does not suggest tension between the capital and the hinterlands, but it does demonstrate that the source of power and military strength reside clearly in the hands of Jerusalemites.

[6–7] The third saying continues the focus on Jerusalem that was established in the previous one. It also repeats the vocabulary used to depict Yahweh's actions in the prologue and in the first saying: the verb *śym*—in v. 2 "make," in v. 3 "set." This third saying develops thematically what has come before—the conflict between Judah and the nations, the relationship between Judah and Jerusalem, and the notion of the "leaders" of Judah. This third saying emphasizes that "leaders" perform at the command of Yahweh, they are like a torch in his hand rather than independent actors or thinkers, as seems to be the case in v. 5.

Verse 6, like the prologue and the first two sayings, involves the conflict between Judah/Jerusalem and foreign peoples. In v. 6, however, the conflict is more "humanized." Instead of language about terror or heavy stones, one has the sense of direct military conflict. Yet the writer chooses similes involving

---

[18]It is such an astounding claim that many scholars emend the verse conjecturally, e.g., Hanson, "If only the inhabitants of Jerusalem would raise a shout for Yahweh of Hosts, their God." *The Dawn of Apocalyptic,* 356–57.

fire imagery in the first several lines rather than straightforward martial diction to describe human military encounter. Again, it is the leaders that are so described, rather than the entire army itself. The poet views their effects on the enemy to be like that of a conflagration in two different agricultural settings: field and grove (the conflagration in Judg. 15:5 makes clear that orchards as well as grainfields could be destroyed in this manner). One is reminded of Samson's destruction of Philistine wheatfields by similar means (Judg. 15:1–8). Perhaps such a background explains why the leaders are the subject of the saying, rather than an entire army. Not many torches are needed to burn off a field.

The imagery changes subtly with the verb *'kl,* "consume, devour," which in Hebrew can have fire or a human as subject. The leaders/fire will consume "all the surrounding peoples," a classic case of hyperbole. This object of Yahweh's enmity had already been articulated using the same word, *'am,* in vv. 2 and 4. The imagery is graphic and suited to the location of Persian-period Judah. It was surrounded by peoples and nations, which would burn if Judah—or its leaders—were ignited. Judah was embedded in the Persian empire and was able, because of its position, to affect directly the lives of those who surrounded it, in ways almost the opposite of that which one might expect. A neutral observer might have thought that Judah had been swallowed up by the Persian empire; this poet, by contrast, viewed the situation as one in which Judah would consume those on its borders.

The final line of v. 6 sounds like an afterthought. However, it would have been altogether legitimate to wonder if anything in Judah might survive such a conflagration. This final line certifies that Jerusalem will remain secure, in spite of the destruction that encircles it. (Zechariah 14 presents a picture that is not so sanguine about Jerusalem's ability to survive unscathed.)

The concluding lines (v. 7) of this saying almost sound as if they belonged to the previous utterance. The relation between Judah and Jerusalem reappears as an important issue; but there is also a constant, namely, Yahweh's initiative in this military event. These lines are of a piece with v. 6 since they explain why it is that the leaders of Judah, and not all Yahweh's people, will be the destructive agent. Yahweh acts through nonroyal, non-Jerusalemite leaders so that they may not be overwhelmed by the pride, even the arrogance of those associated with the regional capital and the old dynastic line. (See also Isa. 10:12; 13:11 for *tip'eret,* meaning arrogant pride instead of splendor or glory.)

This verse raises a very important issue, namely, the extent to which it refers to the role of Davidides in the fifth-century polity of Judah. It would be inappropriate at the outset to assume that actual Davidides are in purview, the more so since in this saying, and in 12:10 and 13:1, the phrase "house of

David" stands in a construction parallel with the phrase "inhabitants of Jerusalem."[19]

The poet is using phrases, not single nouns: "tents of Judah," "house of David," "inhabitants of Jerusalem." These "Israelite" entities are understood, from the context provided by v. 6, to be surrounded by "the peoples." The phrase "tents of Judah" occurs nowhere else in the Old Testament, though the phrase "tents of [place-name]" is attested in Ps. 83:6 (Edom); Ps. 120:5 (Kedar); Jer. 30:18 (Jacob); Hab. 3:7 (Cushan). These texts demonstrate that the phrase in no way refers literally to tents or to nonurban existence (so Jer. 30:18) but instead provides figurative language, such as tents like curtains trembling (Hab. 3:7), by which means an author could refer to an ethnic or national entity. In addition, one should note that the phrase refers to physical objects, not humans. Put another way, the phrase in Zech. 12:7 enables the author to speak of victory given to Judah without being given explicitly to people. The poetic diction disallows an immediate inference that there is tension between two groups of people, since one of the two poles does not even speak literally of people.

The entity "Judah" can be viewed as either different from Jerusalem or including Jerusalem. Most interpretations of this verse presume the former; I prefer the latter. That is to say, Judah will be victorious, not simply Jerusalem. Yahweh is associated not just with a city but with a region and a people, as he was in earlier days. Yahwists lived not only in Jerusalem but in a region— Judah (Ezra 4:4, "the people of Judah"), which fits into the imperial structure and which had identifiable boundaries.[20]

The phrase "house of David," though present in the following sayings, is remarkably infrequent in postexilic texts. For example, it does not occur in Ezra-Nehemiah, Trito-Isaiah, Joel, or Malachi. Despite the absence of this phrase from postexilic literature, there is some evidence for identifiable members of David's lineage in the postexilic period. First Chronicles 3 presents a genealogy stemming from David, one that continues for at least six generations beyond Zerubbabel, who was active in 520 B.C.E.[21] One of these names appears in the books of Ezra-Nehemiah (Neh. 3:29), Shemaiah son of Shekaniah (1 Chron. 3:22), though there is no reason to think that the

---

[19]The phrase, "house of David," occurs without the parallel phrase in Zech. 12:8, 12.

[20]On the notion of the land in the Persian period, see S. Japhet, "People and Land in the Restoration Period," 103–25, and R. Hanhart, "Das Land in der spätnachexilischen Prophetie," 126–40, both of which appear in *Das Land Israel in biblischer Zeit,* ed. G. Strecker, Göttingen, 1983.

[21]On the difficulties of these verses, see W. Rudolph, *Chronikbücher,* Tübingen, 1955, 29–31, and R. Braun, *1 Chronicles,* Waco, Tex., 1986, 47–55. If one follows the LXX, there are ten generations; if MT, then six.

individual so named in Nehemiah 3 has any sort of privileged status. In addition, Anani (1 Chron. 3:24) may be the individual alluded to in Elephantine papyrus #30, line 19, who in that letter is listed as a brother of Ostanes. The only thing certain is that the Anani attested in Elephantine #30 lived in Jerusalem. To be sure, Zerubbabel, a Davidide, exercised some sort of role in the provincial government and was designated "governor." Though "governors" exercised an administrative role after the time of Zerubbabel (Neh. 5:15), there is no reason to assume that they were Davidides.[22] Moreover, of the Davidides mentioned after Zerubbabel in the genealogy of 1 Chronicles 3, none are remembered as having exercised a political role. In sum, for several reasons, it is inappropriate to think that the "house of David" signifies members of the Davidic lineage or aspirations for a renaissance of kingship associated with them.

Of the three phrases under discussion, only "inhabitants of Jerusalem" is reasonably straightforward. It allows us to judge that not just those in Jerusalem (whether regional administrators, priests, merchants or aristocracy, and the urban lower class) but all those in Judah, including Jerusalemites, will benefit from Yahweh's action. Moreover, the *tip'eret*—pride or glory—of the house of David and of the inhabitants of Jerusalem is the subject of reflection, not simply the status of those in Jerusalem.

This third saying attests to the power, the catalytic role, that Judah and its leaders will have in effecting Yahweh's destructive work. Judah, and not simply Jerusalem, remains Yahweh's concern. The third saying provides something of a response or corrective to the prologue and the first saying, which place so much emphasis on the role of Jerusalem.

[8] The fourth saying is shorter than the previous two utterances and is couched in the rhetoric of a prophetic (not a divine) saying. In it the prophet returns to language that expresses a specific concern for Jerusalem. The house of David will protect those who live in Jerusalem.[23]

The first line includes a promissory note, Yahweh's promise of protection, which is then developed in the rest of the verse. The promise, though addressed presumably to all Jerusalemites, is elucidated as of primary importance to those who are weak, those likely to fall when under attack.

The author of this saying, like someone in the previous saying, addresses

[22]See E. Meyers, "The Shelomith Seal and the Judean Restoration: Some Additional Considerations," *EI* 18 (1985): 33–38, for a discussion of the governorship in Judah between 520 B.C.E. and the time of Ezra-Nehemiah. Meyers suggests that Elnathan, governor after Zerubbabel, married Shelomith, member of the Davidic lineage, in order to enhance his status. However, the other governors that Avigad postulated, Yeho'ezer and Ahzai, do not appear related to the lineage of David.

[23]Cf. Mason, *The Use of Earlier Biblical Material in Zechariah IX–XIV,* 229, who argues for a distinction between the house of David and the inhabitants of Jerusalem in vv. 8 and 10.

the issue with figurative language, similes. However, the structure of the similes in the two sayings is different. The similes in v. 6 are strictly parallel, whereas in v. 8 the second simile builds on the first one. The formula "on that day," which occurs both at the inception and within this saying, provides a temporal reference; someone who may not otherwise be weak will become weak on a day of military onslaught. However, because of Yahweh's protective action, that person will be like David. This phrase, *kĕdāwîd*, is used in this sense only here in the Hebrew Bible. (Elsewhere the phrase "like David" refers to something that David had done, e.g., 1 Sam. 22:14; 1 Kings 11:33, and not something that Yahweh had done on David's behalf.) The notion of Yahweh helping David in a time of duress is attested in psalm titles (such as that which prefaces Psalm 18). This world, which is reflected in the psalm titles and which Jerusalemites would know through their participation in temple ritual, seems to inform Zech. 12:8.

The final two lines also present similes that offer a promise. But the promise seems new, directed more at the house of David than at the inhabitants of Jerusalem. However, as the previous and following sayings suggest, the notions ("inhabitants of Jerusalem" and "house of David") are inextricably linked. Hence, it would be inappropriate to suggest, simply on the basis of the apparent focus on "the house of David," that these lines are secondary or of subsidiary importance, the more so since their claims are so extraordinary.

What might it mean to suggest that the house of David will be like a deity? The claim must derive from the universe of discourse attested elsewhere in the Hebrew Bible. The king, exemplified by David, had held a theologically elevated position in ancient Israel—he was an adopted son of the deity (so Ps. 2:7) and could therefore be addressed using language befitting a deity (thus 2 Sam. 14:17, which refers to the king using the phrase "messenger of God," which itself can be a circumlocution for the deity; cf. Genesis 16 for the ambiguous relation between the deity and his messenger).[24]

If one attempts to "decode" the similes, the author is suggesting that the inhabitants of Jerusalem, who may be symbolized by David or the house of David, will achieve the sort of divine status associated with the king in Israelite royal ideology. Though feeling weak in the face of military attack, they will be as secure as an offspring of the deity. The author continues to democratize the Davidic covenant, as the author of Isa. 55:3 had done. The people, who according to that latter author were the recipients of the "everlasting covenant, my steadfast, sure love for David," are, according to the author of Zech. 12:8, to be viewed as having the same semidivine status as the royal house. It is

---

[24]Mason, *The Use of Earlier Biblical Material in Zechariah IX–XIV,* 227, notes that the phrase "like God" (Ex. 4:16) is used to describe Moses' status vis-à-vis Aaron. However, it is difficult to imagine the way in which this verse might have influenced Zechariah 12.

difficult to imagine a more elevated notion of urban-dweller status than that expressed in this fourth saying.

One problem remains: who is the "them"? There is no obvious answer. A strict grammatical answer would be "the inhabitants of Jerusalem." However, that interpretation presents difficulties if the entities—David//house of David// messenger of Yahweh—also refer to the inhabitants. Perhaps the "them" refers to Judahites or to "the peoples" of the previous saying, or, proleptically, to "the nations" of the ensuing saying. Or perhaps the "difficult" interpretation is to be preferred, namely, the people witness to one another as they express their special status as divinely protected folk.

[9–10] The fifth saying is introduced by a form of the "on that day" formula, which is identical to the one that introduced the first saying in v. 3, *wĕhāyāh bayyôm hahû'* (versus *bayyôm hahû'* in vv. 4, 6, 8). The occurrence of this formula here has led some interpreters to speak of Zechariah 12 as being created in two halves. However, such a judgment does not explain well the presence of this longer formula in 13:2 and 13:4 (the latter occurrence definitely does not mark a major break in the text). Hence, I view this longer formulation as simply a stylistic variant that enables the author to avoid a monotonous repetition of "on that day" formulations. On purely formal grounds, these longer formulae divide this "oracle" into major sections.[25] However, there appears to be no basic change in content when one moves from the fourth to the fifth saying.

The subject matter of this saying is remarkably similar to the prior one, so much so that some have claimed that one is a variant of the other. Both begin with reference to Yahweh, Jerusalem, and then David. Though similar, they do make different points and are formulated using different rhetorical strategies. First, the fifth saying is a divine and not a prophetic speech. Yahweh is immediately present. Second, this speech focuses on Yahweh's action against the nations rather than toward Jerusalem, as it had in v. 8. Third, the phrase "all the nations coming up against Jerusalem" appears to be a more standard expression of the Zion tradition than did the previous verse. In sum, the fifth saying has its own raison d'être and integrity.

If v. 9 is stereotypic, v. 10 presents particularity and has frustrated commentators for centuries. (The latter lines of v. 10, though written in the past tense, have been construed by Christian commentators to reflect the death of Jesus of Nazareth.) The verse treats two quite distinct issues: the response of Yahweh to a request, and the lamentation over some unknown figure. According to the first two lines of the verse, Yahweh will respond positively—in the form of a favorable spirit—toward those who have sought help from him. The notion of Yahweh "pouring out spirit"—so Ezek. 39:29 and Joel 2:28—is attested in

[25]See Saebo, *Sacharja 9–14*, 261–76.

other late prophetic texts. In those two instances, Yahweh pours out his own enlivening spirit, whereas the spirit is not so defined in Zech. 12:10. Moreover, in the other texts, all Israel, even all flesh, will receive this spirit, whereas in Zech. 12:10 that bounty is reserved for the inhabitants of Jerusalem//house of David. So, despite the similar rhetoric involving a pouring out of spirit, the saying in Zechariah 12 involves an exclusivism, a focus on Jerusalem, that is not present in the other prophetic texts. In addition, this spirit is the result of a request, presumably in a ritual setting, that differentiates it from the Joel and Ezekiel texts. This outpouring of spirit seems to respond to the "event" alluded to in the final part of v. 10, the death of someone and the resulting lamentation.[26] Plöger is surely correct in eschewing attempts to identify this individual.[27] However, one should doubt Plöger's suggestion that the suffering servant figure in Isaiah 53 provides an earlier form of this tradition. The differences remain important. In Isaiah 53, the suffering of an individual results from Yahweh's intent. Moreover, the suffering and death have some sort of vicarious effect on the people. In Zechariah, the people have killed the individual, and the effect is one of lamentation—which is not present in Isaiah 53—and then, there is an outpouring of divine spirit.

If neither an identifiable event nor a particular tradition lies behind Zech. 12:10, how are we to understand this reference to the death of an unknown individual? I suggest, tentatively, that this verse be read within the context of the attack on Jerusalem referred to at the beginning of the fifth saying. It may be that the text alludes to a military confrontation and a ritual response, namely, child sacrifice. Second Kings 3:27 recounts the sacrifice of Mesha's oldest son at a time of military duress. Since child sacrifice was known in Israel as well (2 Kings 16:3; 17:31; 23:10), the death referred to in Zech. 12:10, which was effected by the people and involved lamentation as one grieves for an only son (cf. Jer. 6:26), was a sacrificial and not murderous act.

In sum, the fifth saying provides material stemming from the normative Zion tradition and a promissory note that Yahweh will act beneficently toward those in Jerusalem after they have made supplication and, possibly, engaged in human sacrifice as a way of averting attack.

[11–14] On form-critical grounds, vv. 11–14 appear to be a new saying, the sixth one in this "oracle." However, some scholars have viewed these verses as a continuation of the lamentation described in v. 10.[28] To be sure the vocabulary of lamentation, that is, the word *spd*, occurs in vv. 10, 11, and 12. However, one may maintain that two originally separate sayings were linked

---

[26]See Mason, *The Use of Earlier Biblical Material in Zechariah IX–XIV*, 234–36; Delcor, "Les sources du Deutéro-Zacharie et ses precédés d'emprunt," 398.

[27]Plöger, *Theocracy and Eschatology*, 84–85.

[28]So Plöger, *Theocracy and Eschatology*, 84; Rudolph, *Sacharja 9–14*, 224.

by this catchword connection, a judgment that enables one to account for the presence of a formula in v. 11 that otherwise might introduce a new rhetorical unit. The lamentation is no longer over an unidentified individual, but over Jerusalem itself.

This saying is long; the length, as such, underlines the extraordinary extent of the mourning that will occur over Jerusalem, presumably when it is under attack and some of its inhabitants have died. What follows, the comparison and the list of families, should be read from this perspective; that is to say, the details in vv. 11b–14 emphasize the incredible scope of the lamentation. To make the point initially, the poet offers a comparison:[29] the mourning over Jerusalem will be as great as that associated with Hadad-rimmon. What or who is Hadad-rimmon? Some have suggested that it is a place-name, others take it to be a form of Ba'al Hadad's name.[30] If the former, then the lamentation may well have been that referred to in 2 Chron. 35:20–25, over Josiah, who fell in battle at Megiddo. In this case, the lamentation would have been current in the time of the Chronicler ("all the singing men and singing women have spoken of Josiah in their laments to this day," 2 Chron. 35:25). This option seems more consistent with the overall unit—namely, an important lamentation that lasts a long time after the event it commemorates—than does a reference to lamentation rites over a dying and rising deity such as Ba'al.

The list makes a similar point, but now by identifying the numerous parties to the lament. The repetition of words (e.g., "the family of") and phrases ("their women by themselves") creates an aura of redundance, which reinforces the author's claim that widespread lamentation is taking place. The author provides a list of those families that will participate in the lamentation. The key claim is presented in v. 12a: that the entire earth will be involved. Verses 12b–14 spell out who will comprise this choir of lamenters. Four names occur: David, Nathan, Levi, and Shimei. Since the names are those of males, the author provides a sort of gender balance by stating that women of each family will lament by themselves.

Two elements require comment: the character of the four names and the role of women in ancient Israelite lamentation. First, the names: It is possible to maintain that they make up two pairs. The first pair is associated with the royal house, the second with a priestly house. David, the dynast, begot a son, Nathan (1 Chron. 14:4), whereas Shimei was a grandson of Levi, through the line of

---

[29]Not a simile; cf. Baldwin, *Haggai, Zechariah, Malachi,* 192.

[30]See, for a review of these positions, Delcor, "Deux passages difficiles: Zach xii 11 et xi 13," *VT* 33 (1953): 67–77; Mason, *The Use of Earlier Biblical Material in Zechariah IX–XIV,* 242–44; J. Hoftizer, "A propos d'une interprétation récent de deux passages difficiles: Zech. 12.11 et Zech. 11.13," *VT* 3 (1953): 407–9. Rudolph (*Sacharja 9–14*) defends the place-name; Mason defends the deity's name. Delcor thinks that the Aramaic version provides evidence for the place-name by discerning the name Amon, Josiah's father.

Gershom (1 Chron. 6:16–17). The poet's claim seems to be a straightforward one, the lineages in ancient Israel that symbolize political and religious power will be related to the lament. However, the lament will be universal; all remaining families will be involved as well. "The earth" and "all the remaining families" provide an inclusio to the specific names and are couched in general terms. The elements that make up the inclusio, vv. 12a and 14, are pivotal in suggesting the vast extent of the lamentation.[31]

Second, the mention of women as separate practitioners of lamentation may reflect gender-specific behavior in ancient Israel (2 Chron. 35:25; Jer. 9:17, 20). However, the author's point by identifying differentiation according to both lineage and gender highlights the universality of the lamentation that will occur over Jerusalem at some point in the future. By mentioning specific elements that make up Israelite society, the poet creates a picture of the total society.

The sixth saying makes a point different from the fifth one. The former saying identified Yahweh's response to lamentation over a corpse in the form of "a favorable spirit," whereas vv. 11–14 focus on the universal character of the lamentation over Jerusalem. To be sure, "lamentation" is a word common to both sayings, but the two lamentations are quite distinct.

[13:1] Introduced by a brief form of the *bayyôm hahû'* formula, the seventh saying presents what might be construed as the divine response to the forego-ing lament. If a response, it provides an answer outside of the saying itself, unlike the situation in the fifth saying. The house of David and the inhabitants of Jerusalem reappear, as they had in the third, fourth, and fifth sayings. The divine response to these now-familiar parties occurs in the form of a cleansing fountain.

The waters will remove sin and impurity, but of what sort and to what effect? Water was used in ancient Israelite ritual to effect purification of various sorts (e.g., Lev. 15:5; Ezek. 36:25). However, the concern articulated in the previous sayings in Zechariah 12 was that of lamentation and death. As a result, one must ask if purification of corpse-engendered uncleanness may be effected by water. The salient rituals, outlined in Numbers 19, indicate that water is, in fact, the appropriate purificatory agent (Num. 19:11–12). Hence, it becomes appropriate to postulate that this saying is, in some measure, a response to the foregoing cosmic lament. Yahweh will cause flowing water to remove sin and impurity. Since the motif of flowing water may be associated with the temple (e.g., Ezek. 47:1 and esp. Joel 3:18, though a different Hebrew word for fountain occurs there), one may assume that the fountain mentioned

---

[31]So similarly Mason, *The Use of Earlier Biblical Material in Zechariah IX–XIV*, 245, though the universality is of lamentation, not "divine renewal."

in Zech. 13:1 was thought to be located at the temple.[32] In this case, the flowing water would purify those in Jerusalem who are explicitly mentioned in this saying. The sin and impurity in and of Jerusalem will be removed by the presence of this new, divinely authored fountain.

There is a subtle undercurrent in this saying, namely, that water appropriate for this task of purification is not now present. One could push this inference in one of two directions: either none of the water available at the temple was pure, which would involve a severe critique of the temple cultus, or the task of purification was beyond that of normal ablutions available at the temple. In either case, the author thought a new source of water was necessary, one that, presumably, Yahweh would provide and that would allow for ritual cleanness. With this purification, the various forms of impurity that were created in Jerusalem when it was under military attack would have been removed. Stasis was achieved. As a result, it seems altogether likely that this montage ended with the seventh saying. This rhetorical unit had as its primary subject matter the fate of Jerusalem when it was under attack and the manner in which Yahweh would rescue and reclaim it.

[13:2–6] Scholars have offered widely divergent answers to the question: In what way is Zech. 13:2–9 integral to the foregoing seven sayings that make up the first montage? Rudolph suggests 13:1–6 is an addition but links vv. 7–9 with chapter 11.[33] Saebo argues that 13:1–6 is the third element ("C") in a long, redactional composition, Zech. 12:2–13:6. (For Saebo, 13:7–9 is simply a different unit, a position with which I agree.) Plöger judges 13:1–6 not to be "the direct continuation of chap. 12" and deems vv. 7–9 to be a development and yet transitional to chap. 14.[34]

The issues are complex. The topic of intra-Israelite religious practice now rises to the fore, an issue that was foreign to Zech. 12:1–13:1.[35] But, despite the new topics, formulae that had occurred earlier recur here, as in the long "on that day" clauses in vv. 2 and 4. These formulae make it appear as if 13:2–3 and 4–6 are simply an eighth and a ninth saying. However, this appearance may be the result of an editor woodenly using two of the longer formulae, one right after the other. The other occurrences of the long "on that day" formulae placed them quite far apart and for the purposes of providing variety in a long collection of seven sayings. In sum, there is good reason to think that 13:2–3 and 4–6 are additions to the seven-saying structure. And 13:7–9 is simply a

---

[32]The fountain, according to Joel 3:18, will "water the valley of Shittim"; that is to say, fertility rather than purification is the issue in Joel; so too Ezek. 47:9, 12.

[33]Rudolph, *Sacharja 9–14*, 227–29.

[34]Plöger, *Theocracy and Eschatology*, 87.

[35]Cf. Hanson, *The Dawn of Apocalyptic*, 367, who would argue that much involves a critique of the cult.

new saying, without benefit of introductory formulae, as was the case with 11:1–3, which also began with imperative rhetoric.

[2–3] Zechariah 13:2–3 and 4–6 involve similar topics: veneration of false deities and inappropriate intermediation. It is, therefore, not difficult to understand why they are conjoined. However, one struggles to understand their relationship to the foregoing material. The answer probably lies in the fact that vv. 2–3 pick up certain elements of the vocabulary used in the fifth saying (namely, "spirit" and "stab" in v. 10) and the semantic, though not lexical, parallel between one word in the seventh saying, "impurity," and "unclean" in 13:2.[36] It would, therefore, appear that the two sayings, 13:2–3 and 4–6, were known to an editor, who thought their inclusion would help articulate the general theme, "on that day." From this person's perspective, it was important for Judeans to know not only how Yahweh would save Jerusalem on that momentous day, but also that the religious practice of Yahwists, namely, venerating Yahweh alone and not engaging in a prophetic style of behavior, was also important and therefore belonged with this montage of divine and prophetic utterances.

Verse 2 begins with the longest of the long formulae since it includes not only the verb, *wĕhāyāh,* but also the phrase "saying of Yahweh of Hosts," which occurs nowhere else in the second "oracle," Zechariah 12–14. The length and singular character of this formula creates a major disjunction in the text, a judgment that on formal grounds is corroborated by the content of what follows. After that introduction, the saying develops in two different, though complementary directions. Verse 2 is a divine oracle in which Yahweh reports how he will act toward various forms of religious impropriety. Then v. 3, in a manner that mirrors the Decalogue (Ex. 20:8–12) by moving from God to human parents, indicates how humans will deal with one form of such impropriety, namely, prophetic activity.

Yahweh claims that he will cut off the names of the idols so that they will not be remembered. But what does that mean? At least two things. First, the issue of the veneration of deities other than Yahweh was still very much alive in the Persian period (see commentary on Mal. 2:13–16). The Syro-Palestinian deities against which Hosea and Jeremiah had inveighed remained compellingly attractive to some Judean Yahwists. Hence, as had been the case with preexilic prophets, prophets in the Persian period were compelled to address the sole veneration of Yahweh. Second, the phrase "the names of the idols" is a sophisticated formulation, one that occurs nowhere else in the Hebrew Bible. One had to have a name in order to be "remembered." For example, a human must have offspring in order to have a name and to be remembered over time

---

[36]Cf. Rudolph, *Sacharja 9–14,* 228, who describes the similarity in meaning as *Stichwortanordnung.*

(Deut. 25:5–10). Moreover, a deity, like humans, could have a name (e.g., Deut. 18:5, 7, 20, 22). In fact, the name of Yahweh was virtually reified in ancient Israel. The name of Yahweh became the form of the deity as he was venerated in Jerusalem (Deut. 12:5, 11; 1 Kings 8:29; Isa. 18:7). The author of Zech. 13:2 has placed an attack on idol veneration in this sophisticated context. Even though those who use idols might construe them theologically, by using the notion of "name," such idols, like other improper forms of religious behavior, will be "cut off." The vocabulary of "cutting off" is often used to describe the punishment associated with improper religious practice (e.g., Mal. 2:12). In this first verse, the focus is on the idols themselves, not those who act in a heterodox manner, as is the case in Malachi 2.

Yahweh will act against individuals as well as against the unclean spirit (cf. Deuteronomic formulations that require humans to remove "the evil," Deut. 17:7; 21:21). The first of these claims might strike one as unusual. Why would prophets be included in a saying that debunks idols and an unclean spirit? Some have answered this question by suggesting that the prophets represent a deity other than Yahweh. However, there is no hint of such a situation in the text. Further, "the unclean spirit" provides little help in addressing this issue since that phrase occurs nowhere else in the Hebrew Bible. However, the noun *tum'āh* apparently never refers to uncleanness caused by contact with foreign gods or religious practices.

The source of punishment in v. 3 moves from the divine to the human, but apparently for the same infraction, namely, humans acting as prophets. This verse is carefully crafted so as to denigrate in several ways those who attempt to prophesy. First, they are to be viewed as immature, still subject to parental authority. Second, as with Deut. 21:18–21 (the law concerning the stubborn and rebellious son), the prophet is to be killed. Third, unlike the stipulation in Deuteronomy 21, the one who prophesies is to be killed immediately by his parents, without even being sent before the elders' legal assembly. Fourth, according to this author the act of prophecy may be compared to a violation of one element in the Decalogue, that of speaking falsely in Yahweh's name (Ex. 20:7). This author apparently thinks that someone who says, "Thus says the Lord," is speaking lies in Yahweh's name, an even stronger formulation than occurs in the Decalogue. It is difficult to imagine a more negative construal of prophetic activity.

Although this saying begins by offering a critique of several forms of religious activity, veneration of idols and prophetic behavior, the latter topic becomes the focal point in v. 3, wherein the author not only creates a polemic against prophetic behavior but also calls for a death sentence on those who have acted as prophets.

[4–6] The polemic against those who prophesy continues, though now from a different tack. There is no divine utterance as part of this saying; hence, one may claim that it is a prophetic speech. Furthermore, whereas Yahweh or a parent would punish the prophet in the prior saying, here the prophet will condemn himself or express guilt of some sort. The saying presumes that prophetic activity will, in fact, continue.

In language that alludes even more fully than did the last saying to earlier Israelite texts and traditions, this author creates a picture in which there is a tone of confession and contrition expressed by the prophet. First, those who see visions will be embarrassed. The author has linked the unfavorable view of visions (Jer. 23:16) with the notion of prophets of peace being embarrassed when Yahweh provides them with no oracles to offer (Micah 3:5–8). Second, the prophet will no longer wear garments to deceive his audience. The garments in question are probably not the mantle passed from Elijah to Elisha (1 Kings 19:19; 2 Kings 2:13). Rather, the author is probably referring to a different cloak that was used for the purposes of deception, namely, the cloak worn by Jacob when he tricked Isaac out of his birthright (Gen. 25:25). In any case, prophets will no longer deceive those whom they serve "on that day."

The subject of the verb with which v. 5 begins is surely one of the prophets who has been described in the previous verse. This prophet continues as the subject throughout the remainder of the saying. He speaks in something of a parody, recasting the words of Amos 7:14 and instead of offering a defense of his prophetic role, he creates a confession of earlier error. Unlike Amos, who was no prophet and then became a prophet, this individual was no prophet and then was seduced by a man—and not by God, as was the case with Jeremiah (Jer. 20:7). Moreover, he was seduced into behavior inappropriate for an intermediary. When someone asks about the marks on his back, he reports that they were the result of some illicit sexual activity (cf. the reports of Ba'al prophets inflicting wounds on themselves; 1 Kings 18:28). Here too, there is a note of self-recognition and contrition on the part of the intermediary who has been seduced and wounded.

How are we to understand such a thoroughgoing critique of things prophetic?[37] As the second saying suggests, even more strongly than the first, intermediaries continued to be active in the Persian period. Nehemiah 6:10–14 attests to the activity of Shemaiah, Noadiah, and "the rest of the prophets." Furthermore, the books of Chronicles, which allude to ritual behavior of the second temple period, describe the Levitical singers as "prophets" (1 Chron. 25:1, 5; 2 Chron. 20:14; 29:30). For some in the restoration period, participation in the service of song could count as prophetic behavior. However, other texts suggest that some Israelites thought prophecy, at least as it had been

---

[37]Cf. my earlier treatment question, D. Petersen, *Late Israelite Prophecy*, Missoula, Mont., 1977, 33–38, and more recently, R. Tournay, *Seeing and Hearing God in the Psalms: The Prophetic Liturgy of the Second Temple in Jerusalem*, Sheffield, 1991.

manifest in the monarchic and exilic periods, was a thing of the past and was only to return in the future (Joel 2:28–29 and Mal. 4:5). Moreover, since the prophetic literature was gaining authority, perhaps one might even say proto-canonical status, it is likely that a notion of the closed character of the canon, along with the corollary notion of no more holy speakers, namely, prophets, was evolving as well. It would, therefore, appear that there were diverse judgments about the status of prophecy in the post-Haggai and Zechariah I period. Some held that it was to be impugned; others continued to act as prophets and in diverse ways. The two sayings that make up Zech. 13:2–6 suggest that this conflict would only be resolved "on that day." Moreover, the sayings present two different ways by means of which the conflict might be resolved.

By the end of this large montage, the focus has shifted from Jerusalem under attack by the peoples to matters within Judah and Jerusalem. There is still conflict, but it is of a sort in which Yahweh will not be the only major actor. Those with authority over the prophets, and even the prophets themselves, will address the problematic that prophecy in the Persian period presents.

Zechariah 13:7–9

Death, destruction, and renewal by refining

13:7 "O Sword, awake against my shepherd!
   and against each of his compatriots!"[a]
      says Yahweh of Hosts.
   "Strike the shepherd!
      so that the flock is scattered.
   I will turn my hand against the little ones[b]
8   throughout all the land,"
         says Yahweh of Hosts.
   "Two-thirds shall be cut off in/from it,
      and they will perish;
      but one-third will remain in it.
9   Then I will bring the one-third into the fire.
      I will refine them as one refines silver.
      I will test them as one tests gold.
   He will call on my name,
      and I will respond to him.
   I will say,[c] 'He is my people';
      and he will say, 'Yahweh is my God.' "

a. The Hebrew here is difficult. There are two nouns, *geber,* "man," and *'amîtî,* literally, "my compatriot," which seem to be the object of the preposition. Some have suggested *'amîtô* (so Lev. 19:11; 24:19) as a reflexive noun, though the forms in Leviticus are prefixed with *b.* Rudolph, *Sacharja 9–14,* 212, construes the final *i* vowel to be the sign of an abstract noun and translates the phrase, "and against my companion." Saebo, *Sacharja 9–14,* 106–7, thinks LXX, though ambiguous, and the *Damascus Document,* which preserves the *i* vowel, sustain MT, though he does not suggest how the phrase might be translated. I solve the problem by reconstructing a plural form of *'āmît.* The phrase read originally *'al geber 'amîtaw,* "against each of his compatriots." The terminal *waw* was lost by haplography. *geber* can, like *'îš,* function denominatively.

b. One could, as well, translate Zoarites, which, though a proper name, can have a more general semantic force, so Gen. 19:20.

c. So Otzen, *Deuterosacharja,* 266; Rudolph, *Sacharja 9–14,* 212–13, who, following LXX, argue the *waw* was lost by haplography.

As noted above, some scholars have argued these verses should be linked with 11:4–17, since both sections focus on shepherds. This argument is, however, not compelling and for a variety of reasons, as I indicated earlier.[38] The earlier verses make up two symbolic-action reports that focus on the figure of a shepherd, whereas 13:7–9, though mentioning a shepherd in the first verse, makes up a different genre and soon moves beyond the figure of the shepherd.

This saying begins without any introductory formulae. It is positioned between two "on that day" montages, 12:1–13:6 and 14:1–21. However, this transitional piece is not marked by that phrase. The imperative rhetoric with which this brief poem begins will initiate the events that will eventuate in the appearance of Yahweh's day. It serves as a proleptic—and a mildly sanguine—summary of the events that are described in greater detail in chap. 14.[39]

If these verses are indeed a separate unit, are they coherent and may they be characterized using form-critical nomenclature? Those scholars who have argued that they are separate regularly maintain that these verses are made up of diverse elements.[40] As a result, they do not offer an overarching label for all three verses, though Saebo does think v. 7 may be described as a *Schwertspruch* (sword saying). One does well to keep these issues separate. Even if these verses were composed of poetic fragments, it might be possible to characterize them with a title or theme. And even if these verses constitute a single poem, they might be difficult to label. Since I do not find compelling the argument that these verses are of diverse origin, the latter approach, namely,

---

[38] So also Elliger, *Das Buch der zwölf kleinen Propheten,* 165; Saebo, *Sacharja 9–14,* 276–77; Willi-Plein, *Prophetie am Ende,* 59.

[39] Cf. Saebo, *Sacharja 9–14,* 282, 313, who argues that 13:7–9 is redactional and attributable to the same hand as 12:1a.

[40] So Saebo, *Sacharja 9–14,* 277; Willi-Plein, *Prophetie am Ende,* 58–59.

the difficulty of providing a label for the form of this poem, becomes the most pressing matter.

Set between two much longer sections, these verses are uniformly accorded the status of poetry. What makes analysis of this poem so difficult is the juxtaposition of a number of figures of speech, for example, the personification of a sword along with an incipient narrative. Saebo noted that there were three distinct elements, "a three-beat theological main theme."[41] However, it is appropriate to observe that these three elements—destruction, refining, restitution—make up something of a sequence, a protonarrative that includes a plot driven by the question, will anyone survive? Just as with major airplane accidents today, when newscasts typically focus on the question of how many died and whether anyone survived, so too this epigram is interested in numbers. But it is interested in more: how will the process start and what will be the eventual outcome? These were the truly important questions for this author.

[13:7] The poet proceeds in a series of brilliant moves, which often baffle the casual reader. The poem begins with a noun, "sword," though in the vocative mood and personified. The Hebrew Bible elsewhere includes texts in which someone addresses a weapon. In Jer. 47:6 someone says, "Woe, O sword of Yahweh! How long till you are quiet?" However, unlike Zech. 13:7, Yahweh is not the speaker. In Ezek. 21:16, Yahweh does address a weapon, though without naming the sword as he does in v. 7, "Cut sharply to right and left where your edge is directed." Moreover, in both Ezek. 21:16 and Zech. 13:7b the deity commands the weapon.

The sword is to strike the shepherd and his compatriots. As with 10:2–3 and 11:4–17, such a reference to a shepherd immediately raises the question, to what does this image refer? At the outset, one need not think that the notion of shepherd functions identically in these various texts. Second, the image of the shepherd can describe a number of different roles (see commentary on 11:4–17). Third, as was the case with Zech. 10:2–3, though a text might refer to a shepherd, the primary focus may well be on the flock and not on the shepherd. This appears to be true for Zech. 13:7–9. In the second line of the poem, the author moves from the figure of the shepherd to his compatriots, which indicates that a sole shepherd is not the primary focus of attention.

After the *incipit,* which is set off by the formulaic expression "says Yahweh of Hosts," the poem continues the same dynamic established in the first two lines. Another imperative verb is directed toward the shepherd, but again attention moves to another and plural entity. Now, however, this second concern occurs in a result clause, so that we know the attack on the shepherd is

[41]Saebo, *Sacharja 9–14,* 279.

designed to effect something other than his death or demise. Yahweh is essentially interested in scattering the flock, "the little ones."[42]

[8] The poet proceeds to delimit the conflict, both geographically and numerically. The phrase "throughout all the land"[43] localizes the conflict in the homeland, Syria-Palestine.[44] This conflict will not take place on diaspora soil. Moreover, it will not involve total decimation. Though a stereotypic two-thirds will die, one-third will remain in the land.[45]

The critical question here is whether the image conveyed of a one-third that remains in the land is essentially positive or negative. Rudolph and others affirm the latter option. However, if one compares the fractional imagery in Ezekiel 5, in which all three-thirds are destroyed (though Ezek. 5:3–4 allows for the possibility that a few will survive only to be destroyed, so "all the house of Israel"), the situation described in Zech. 13:8 is palpably more favorable. Moreover, that third remains in the land. It is not, as was the last third in Ezek. 5:2, 12, "scattered to the wind."

[9] Verse 9 introduces a new image, that of fire, which is consistent with the mode of destruction included in Ezek. 5:2. However, the poet takes this motif of punishment by fire and explores it using two parallel similes that allow, as did the previous verse, for a more positive outcome than one might have imagined. The key concept that lies behind these similes is refining or testing, which is a prominent symbol elsewhere in the Hebrew Bible. It is, however, a complex symbol. The process of refinement can be unsuccessful (so Jer. 6:29), as when those supposed to be removed (in this case, "the wicked") are not removed. Further, the very logic of refining presumes that something positive will happen, namely, that a residue of worth will emerge (cf. Isa. 1:25–26; Mal. 3:2–4). Some texts that use the image make clear that the process envisioned is not like that of smelting silver (Isa. 48:10), whereas Zech. 13:9 states explicitly that the process is like that of smelting precious metals.

Perhaps the key to understanding the imagery of refining in Zech. 13:9 involves the recognition that refining and testing are used to help define each other. And this juxtaposition is not new. Psalms 17:3; 26:2; and 66:10 place these two verbs together to explain what it means to refine people, as one might refine silver. In all three of these cases, there is no presumption that the individual being refined//tested is to be condemned. On the contrary, in the

---

[42]See Jer. 49:20 and 50:45 for this same idiom of "the little ones of the flock" when directed against national groupings, Edom and Babylon respectively.

[43]The noun *hā'āreṣ* can be translated "earth."

[44]Zechariah 14 also presents a picture of conflict that is located in Syria-Palestine, more particularly, the area directly associated with Jerusalem.

[45]LXX omits the prepositional phrases and in so doing betrays the intent of the author to present limits to the conflict.

first two psalms, the supplicant implores the deity to refine him so as to verify the justice of his cause. The other relevant text in this regard is Jer. 9:7, which also juxtaposes these two verbs: "Behold, I will refine them and test them, for what else can I do, because of my people?" The questions in Jer. 9:9, which elucidate this statement of divine intention, make it plain that Yahweh intends to punish his people. The issue concerning that which will survive the refining process is not addressed. However, one might infer, on the basis of the rhetoric in Psalms, that such language presumes some will survive.

The one-third who are refined result, consistent with Psalms 17, 26, and 66, in something good and precious. Most translations obscure the second instance of personification, which the poet uses to report that which will survive. An individual, who functions as a collective noun to express "my people," will survive. That individual will call on Yahweh's name, at which point Yahweh will respond to the one who has survived the refining process.[46] We are even given the content of that which Yahweh will say to the supplicant, which enables a response from the survivor. Language normally associated with the affirmation of the covenant, "He is my people . . . Yahweh is my God" (cf. Jer. 31:33; Zech. 8:8; Hos. 2:23), constitutes the concluding conversation between Yahweh and the individual who has survived.

The poem provides something of an inclusio, presenting individuals with whom Yahweh interacts both at the beginning and the end of the poem. Yahweh will slay the shepherd, but will ratify a covenantal relationship with the survivor. Through him, whom Yahweh views as symbolizing the people, a new relationship—one may even say a new covenant—is established. Or, using the imagery with which the poem began, the flock has been destroyed, reduced in size, and recreated.

It is difficult to translate this poem into the real world of Persian-period Syro-Palestinian society. The shepherd and the survivor symbolize destruction and renewal; they are not identifiable individuals in the Achaemenid imperial structure. The author apparently foresaw upheavals that would spell trouble for Yahwists. Though however dire their situation might be, the poem points to a situation in which those who call on Yahweh's name can look forward to a renewed relationship with their deity. Compare Zech. 14:9 for further emphasis on the name of Yahweh. Once Yahweh has finished the process of punishing refinement, then the survivors will call on Yahweh's name. The notion of calling on Yahweh is attested in early Persian-period prophetic texts

---

[46]See J. Blenkinsopp's suggestive comments about a Persian-period sect that had as one of its hallmarks special concern for Yahweh's name, as in Isa. 66:5 ("A Jewish Sect of the Persian Period," *CBQ* 52 [1990]: 5–20).

(Isa. 58:9; 65:24; cf. Zeph. 3:9).[47] As a result, the author of this poem and the editor of this prophetic "oracle" have presented both a way to understand what Yahweh is doing and the means to establish that new relationship, namely, to call on his name.

Zechariah 14:1–21

Jerusalem on the day of Yahweh

14:1 Truly, Yahweh's day is imminent,[a]
     when your plunder[b] will be divided in your midst.
2 "I will gather all the nations
     to Jerusalem for the battle.
   The city will be captured,
     the houses will be plundered,
     women will be raped.
   One half of the city will go into exile,
     but the rest of the people will not be cut off from the city."
3 Then Yahweh will go out and fight against those nations,
     as he fights on a day of battle.
4 On that day he will stand with both feet on the Mount of Olives,
     which is situated east of Jerusalem.
   From east to west there will be a very great chasm.
     One half of the mountain will shift to the north,
     the other half to the south,
     so that the Mount of Olives will be split in two.
5 You will flee from the valley of the hills,
     since the valley of the hills will extend to its flank.[c]
   You will flee as you fled from the earthquake
     in the days of Uzziah, king of Judah.
   Yahweh your God[d] will arrive,
     all of his holy ones with him.[e]
6 On that day there will be no light;
     neither cold nor frost.[f]
7 There will be a singular day—
     it will be known only to Yahweh;
   With neither day nor night,
     but with dusk as its light.

---

[47]It is striking that the notion of "calling upon the name of Yahweh" is not well understood. Serving "in the name of Yahweh" is associated with the task of Levites, according to Deut. 18:5, 7.

8   On that day, running water will flow out
               from Jerusalem,
           half to the Eastern Sea,
           half to the Western sea,
           during both summer and winter.

9   On that day,[g]
           Yahweh will become king
               over all the earth;
           Yahweh alone,
               and his name alone.

10   The entire land will become[h] like the Arabah
               from Geba to Rimmon in the south.
           But Jerusalem will rise.[i]
               It will remain in its place,
           From the Benjamin Gate,
               to the place of the Old Gate,
               to the Corner Gate;
           From the Hananel Tower
               to the royal winepresses.

11   They will dwell in it;
               there will be no more destruction;
               Jerusalem will dwell securely.

12   This will be the plague
               with which Yahweh plagues all the peoples
               who fought against Jerusalem:
           Their flesh will decay,
               even while they are standing up;
           their eyes will rot in their eyesockets;
               their tongues will fester in their mouths.

15   Like this plague will be the one that strikes
               horse, donkey, camel, ass;
               every animal that is in those camps.[j]

13   On that day,
           A tremendous panic from Yahweh
               will be (set) against them.
           Each one will attack his comrade,[k]
               his hand raised up against the hand of his comrade;

14   even Judah will fight at[l] Jerusalem.
           The wealth of the surrounding nations
               will be gathered in great quantities—
               gold, silver, garments.

16   All those who had attacked Jerusalem and who
               survived

will come annually
To worship the king, Yahweh of Hosts,
to celebrate the feast of booths.

17 If one of the earth's communities does not come to Jerusalem
to worship the king, Yahweh of Hosts,
they will have no rain.

18 If the community of Egypt does not come up and enter,
then the plague, with which Yahweh plagued the nations
that did not come up to celebrate the feast of booths,
will not occur against them.[m]

19 Such will be the punishment for Egypt,
different from the punishment for all the nations
that did not come up to celebrate the feast of booths.

20 On that day, even the horses' jingling tack
will become holy to Yahweh.
The pots in the temple
will become like basins used at the altar.

21 Moreover, every pot in Jerusalem and in Judah,
will become holy to Yahweh of Hosts.
All those who make sacrifices will come,
and take from among them [the pots],
and boil [the sacrifices] in them.
Moreover, there will no longer be traders
in the temple of Yahweh of Hosts on that day.

a. The initial line is difficult to translate. Elsewhere (Ezek. 30:3; Isa. 2:12), the phrase *yôm lyhwh* can be translated either "Yahweh has a day" or "the day of Yahweh." However, in Zech. 14:1, the verb *bā'* (masc. sing. participle) interrupts this two-word phrase. Hence, the author seems to emphasize that the day of Yahweh is indeed coming or, even more likely, is about to arrive, the so-called *futurum instans,* GKC, 116p. Cf. the phrases in Isa. 13:9, *hinnēh yôm yhwh bā',* and Joel 2:1, *bā' yôm yhwh,* as well as the semantically similar Joel 1:15 and 3:14, *qārôb yôm yhwh.*

b. The term *šělālēk* is ambiguous. It could mean "that which was plundered from someone" or "that which someone has plundered." The noun *šālāl* with a pronominal suffix does allow the latter translation (e.g., Judg. 8:24, 25; Isa. 10:2). However, the noun more frequently has the former meaning (Deut. 20:14; Josh. 8:2; Ezek. 29:19; 2 Chron. 20:25; Esth. 3:13; 8:11). Hence, it is preferable to understand the noun to signify "that which has been plundered from you."

A related problem involves the identification of the referent of the third-person fem. sing. suffix. The most obvious candidate is the city, Jerusalem, which has been the subject of much attention in Zechariah 12–14, and which becomes the focus of attention in chap. 14.

c. These two cola present a number of problems. I read *wěnastem mĕgê' hehārîm* instead of MT *wĕnastem gê' hāray*, with the original preposition *mem* as well as the *mem* as plural morpheme having dropped out by haplography. The versional evidence is complex. V and S agree with MT. The LXX translators understood the verb to be *stm*, "to be stopped up," instead of *nws*, "to flee." The Targum reads the first verb as *stm* and the last two as *nws*. Rudolph translates "valley of Hinnom" (*gê' hinnôm*) instead of "valley of mountains" (*gê' hārîm*). See Otzen, *Deuterosacharja*, 267–68, who follows MT and translates "flee into the valley"; Saebo, *Sacharja 9–14*, 110–15, for a full discussion; and Mitchell, *A Critical and Exegetical Commentary on Haggai and Zechariah*, 345–46, who provides a lucid argument for reading "(the spring) Gihon will be stopped up, the gorge of the mountains will reach to its (Gihon's) side." Given the usage of *stm* elsewhere in the Hebrew Bible, it makes little sense to speak of a valley being stopped up. The diverse ways in which the verbs have been construed depend to a certain extent on the ways in which the nouns have been interpreted, namely, valley of mountains or Gihon.

The text-critical issue really involves a judgment about what the author is describing, whether a spring or valley is being occluded, and from whence people are fleeing. Attention to traditional theophanic language can inform the discussion: mountains shake or are moved, valleys are opened, not shut; and waters flow, and are not stopped (Micah 1:4; Nahum 1:5, 8; Hab. 3:10). Humans cannot stand before such an appearance; they either cower or flee (Zech. 14:5, as translated above). Put another way, a traditio-historical perspective helps resolve a text-critical problem, in this case by sustaining MT.

MT *'āṣal* can be construed either as a place name or as a noun meaning "side" or "flank," here presumably of the Mount of Olives, or even a noun, *'āṣîl*, meaning "far-off places" (Isa. 41:9). I read *'eṣlô*, the final *waw* having been lost by haplography.

d. It seems anomalous to find the author referring to himself, so MT *'ĕlōhay*, "my God." I read *'ĕlōhayik* (the *k* was probably elided by haplography), as do the standard commentaries.

e. Instead of MT *'immāk*, "with you" (second-person masc. sing.), I read *'immô*, "with him," as in virtually all ancient versions.

f. MT *yĕqārôt yĕqippā'ôn*, literally translated, would appear to be "precious ones will congeal." The Qere reading for the second word, *wĕqippā'ôn*, "frost," is attested by A and Origen (Mar.Ant.) as *psychos*. Most LXX manuscripts, e.g., W' B S, read *kai psychē kai pagos*, "and spirit and frost," which is an obvious misreading of the Greek *psychros*, and which does not preserve a Hebrew *Vorlage*. Hence, one properly reconstructs a Hebrew original, *qārût wĕqippā'ôn*.

g. Early in the history of the text, a copyist's mistake resulted in a vertical transposition of *bayyôm hahû'* from the first to the third colon. The original line structure would have read: *wĕhāyāh bayyôm hahû' yihyeh yhwh lĕmelek*. The translation above is based on this reconstruction.

h. MT *yissōb* has the unusual meaning "be changed," so Rudolph, *Sacharja 9–14*, 232. Cf. Otzen, *Deuterosacharja*, 269–70, who notes that the Ugaritic verb *sbb* can have this meaning, and Saebo, *Sacharja 9–14*, 116–22, who solves the problem by making "waters" in v. 8 the subject of the verb in v. 10.

i. MT reads *yĕrûšālāim wĕrā'ămāh*, which makes little sense. This word order is that of a disjunctive clause; cf. Otzen, *Deuterosacharja,* 270, who argues for a change in word order. I construe *wĕrā'ămāh* to be a corrupt form of the verb *rwm,* "to rise"; cf. Rudolph, *Sacharja 9–14,* 233.

j. I agree with Rudolph in thinking that v. 15 originally followed v. 12.

k. I omit *yad* in the first colon as a dittographic expansion based on *yad* in the second colon.

l. Virtually all LXX manuscripts read "in Jerusalem," which is a possible translation of *b.* See commentary for a discussion of the problem.

m. MT reads literally, "there will be no plague against them." LXX and S omit the negative particle *lō'.* See Mitchell, *A Critical and Exegetical Commentary on Haggai and Zechariah,* 355, for a discussion of the syntactic difficulties that occur in vv. 18–19, and also A. van der Woude, "Sacharja 14:18," *ZAW* 97 (1985): 254–56, who proposes reading *wĕlā'ab 'āhû* instead of *wĕlō' bā'āh.*

Any commentary on Zechariah 14 must work with a provisional judgment about the nature of the literature, a judgment that in the first instance involves the question: Is this text essentially one long unit, or is it made up of a number of smaller constitutive sections? Hanson maintains that it is one long composition, an apocalypse, that may be segmented according to elements he thinks are typical of "the conflict myth": threat, 1–2; conflict and victory, 3; theophany and procession, 4–5; shalom, 6–8; manifestation of Yahweh's universal reign, 9–11; covenant curses, 12–15; procession of the nations, 16–19; sacrifice and banquet, 20–21.[48] However, one has the sense that this scheme is an imposition on the relevant verses. For example, the notion of banquet does not do justice to Zech. 14:20–21. Moreover, such an approach does not take into account one important form of textual data, namely, the "on that day" formulae. Since, for example, the *bayyôm hahû'* formulae introduce vv. 6 and 20, each of which, according to Hanson, introduces a thematically distinct section, how is it possible that v. 8, which also begins with such a formula, does not introduce a separate section? An approach that does not take the *bayyôm hahû'* material seriously has difficulty providing a satisfactory answer to the question about the coherence of this chapter.

Zechariah 14 appears similar to Zech. 12:1–13:6, if for no other reason than that the phrase "the day of Yahweh" is so prominent in both sections.[49] Both

---

[48]Hanson, *The Dawn of Apocalyptic,* 372.

[49]See, however, Chary, *Aggée, Zacharie, Malachie,* 209, and Lutz, *Jahwe, Jerusalem und die Völker,* 30–32, for a discussion of the thematic contrasts between chaps. 12 and 14. Lutz's judgment that the traditio-historical underpinnings of the two chapters are distinct appears to have divided overmuch the conflict traditions he postulates. By contrast, D. Jones, "A Fresh Interpretation of Zech. 9–14," understands them to derive from the same tradition. Lacocque, *Zacharie,* 198, views the chapters as parallel.

texts may be divided on the basis of the day of Yahweh formulae.[50] The formulae occur as follows: v. 1, *hinnēh yôm;* v. 4, *bayyôm hahû'* (though not at the beginning of the verse); v. 6, *wĕhāyāh bayyôm hahû';* v. 8, *wĕhāyāh bayyôm hahû';* v. 9, *bayyôm hahû'* (though not at the beginning of the verse); v. 13, *wĕhāyāh bayyôm hahû';* v. 20, *bayyôm hahû'.* If Zech. 12:1–13:6 provides a guide, vv. 6, 8, and 13 would present the only major divisions of the text. However, the disjunctive clause with which v. 12 begins, as well as the change in topic presented in v. 10, marks new vignettes in at least as striking a way as do those elements introduced by *bayyôm hahû'* formulae. Hence, one may say that, despite the prominence of these formulae, chap. 14 seems to be structured by means different from those in its apparent mate, Zech. 12:1–13:6, in the second *maśśā'.* In fact, these sections are quite different.[51] The explicit focus on Jerusalem alone in Zechariah 14, in contrast to the larger concern for Judah in 12:1–13:6, has led some to argue for totally different origins.[52]

What, then, is the structure of Zechariah 14 and what should one use as criteria for determining the structure of the chapter?[53] Complex material such as this requires a complex response, involving form-critical, traditio-historical and literary-critical perspectives.[54] My observations are: first, the formulaic expression *bayyôm hahû'* is important though it works differently than it did in 12:1–13:6. It appears to have been introduced in a secondary fashion to make Zechariah 14 appear like the earlier montage. Second, this material is formulated less as divine utterance and more as prophetic pronouncement or perspec-

---

[50]It is surprising that Saebo, *Sacharja 9–14,* 261, analyzed 12:2–13:6 by using these formulae, but he did not proceed in a similar way when working on chap. 14. Saebo, 285, understands the structure of chap. 14 as follows: A 14:1–5; B 14:6–7; C 14:8–11; D 14:12–19; and E 14:20–21. He is correct in thinking that the rhetoric of the "prophetic speech" is more prominent than that of the "divine speech." Willi-Plein, *Prophetie am Ende,* 35, maintains that the formulae are important, as a *"Gliederungselement."* Nonetheless, she views Zechariah 14 as a literary unity (p. 88).

[51]Hence Stade's judgment, "Deuterosacharja," 36, that Zechariah 14 is a "Doublette" for 12:1–14; 13:1–6 constitutes an overstatement.

[52]So Lutz, *Jahwe, Jerusalem und die Völker.*

[53]Virtually every scholar discerns some segmentation in Zechariah 14. However, few make clear the basis of their judgments, so Rudolph, who discerns the following sections, 1–5, 6–9, 10–11, 12–15, 16–19, 20–21; or Otzen, 1–2, 3–5, 6–11, 12–15, 16–19, 20–21; or Mitchell, 1–5, 6–11, 12–15, 16–21; or Willi-Plein, 1–9, 10–19, 20–21, who depends on the supposed distinction between prose and poetry as well as syntactic judgments (but her assessments, p. 60, which are based on the presence of the *bayyôm hahû'* formulae, run counter to this division).

[54]Willi-Plein, *Prophetie am Ende,* 59–61, emphasizes literary perspectives in developing the notion that Zechariah 14 is divided into three essential parts, vv. 1–9, 10–19, 20–21. The day of Yahweh formulae are not so much formulae introducing originally diverse material but *Leitwörter* used in "a literary unity."

I do not find convincing the judgments of Elliger, *Das Buch der zwölf kleinen Propheten,* 167, Plöger, *Theocracy and Eschatology,* 90, or Sellin, *Das Zwölfprophetenbuch: Nahum-Maleachi,* KAT XII, Leipzig, 578–85, that various redactional strata may be readily identified in this chapter.

tive on Jerusalem and the fate of that place.⁵⁵ Third, the notion of montage remains licit, though the elements and overall rhetoric of the piece are different from the montage in 12:1–13:6. Chapter 14 appears more "literary" than 12:1–13:6, which appeared more "oral"; thus 12:4 "says Yahweh," 13:2 "saying of Yahweh of Hosts." In addition, 12:1–13:6 contains direct human (i.e., nonprophetic) discourse (12:5; 13:3, 5–6), whereas chap. 14 contains none. The "literary" character of Zechariah 14 may be further emphasized by noting the several important ways this chapter seems to allude to earlier texts.⁵⁶

Once these perspectives are integrated, it is possible to maintain that the montage of Zechariah 14 is made up of the following elements, which may be identified, with only two exceptions, on formulaic and thematic grounds: vv. 1–3, *hinnēh yôm*, "battle at Jerusalem"; vv. 4–5, *bayyôm hahû'*, "Yahweh and the Mount of Olives"; vv. 6–7, *wĕhāyāh bayyôm hahû'*, "Yahweh's peculiar day"; v. 8, *wĕhāyāh bayyôm hahû'*, "flowing waters"; v. 9, *bayyôm hahû'*, "Yahweh as sole king"; vv. 10–11, no formula, "Jerusalem and its position"; vv. 12, 15, no formula—though the disjunctive clause functions analogously, "plague"; vv. 13–14, *wĕhāyāh bayyôm hahû'*, "panic"; vv. 16–19, no formula, "pilgrimage, possibility, and punishment"; vv. 20–21, *bayyôm hahû'*, "holiness in Jerusalem." One may describe these sections as units, vignettes, or sayings.⁵⁷

There is a regular, though not inevitable, association between the presence of one of the formulae and a demonstrably separate unit. However, since three units (vv. 10–11; 12, 15; 16–19) are missing formulae and since two of the formulae (vv. 4, 9) occur inside one of the units, it seems licit to suggest that these formulae may have been introduced by an editor to make chap. 14 appear as if it were composed in a fashion similar to 12:1–13:6. Put another way, the formulae in chap. 14 are probably redactional, though different in function from the similar redactional formulae in 12:1–13:6.

The montage of Zechariah 14 is made up of diverse literary elements, but they cohere around a core issue: the status of Jerusalem "on that day." (Only one saying, vv. 6–7, does not include specific mention of Jerusalem.) Some of the elements may well stem from the hand of its collector/creator.

[14:1–3] If the first montage concerning the day of Yahweh (Zech. 12:1–13:6) explores the place of Judah and Jerusalem among the nations, the first element that distinguishes this second montage is a temporal one. What could be discussed as something that would happen becomes something that is about to happen. Although much of what follows in Zechariah 14 focuses the events of

---

⁵⁵So, e.g., Lutz, *Jahwe, Jerusalem und die Völker*, 26.

⁵⁶So Plöger, *Theocracy and Eschatology*, 90–91, though he overemphasizes the importance of Ezekiel as the critical source.

⁵⁷Saebo, too, *Sacharja 9–14*, 282, thinks that the chapter is made up of diverse motifs and traditions. I find it difficult to characterize form-critically each of these vignettes or sayings.

that day spatially within Jerusalem and its immediate environs, the author's first statement involves a claim about the immediacy of Yahweh's intervention.

However, lest anyone anticipate this day in a hopeful way, the author follows up immediately with a temporal clause, in which he provides a vignette of what will happen to Jerusalem. The image of victorious troops dividing up spoil is proleptic, since it must follow the action described in v. 2, namely, the arrival of the conquering troops. One may therefore suggest that in v. 1, the author or collector of "on that day" traditions has taken one very unpleasant element and used it to characterize the whole.[58]

The battle envisioned in vv. 1–3 is more focused in scope than the conflict that lies behind 12:1–13:6 (see 12:2, 6). Whereas Judah was prominent in that earlier section (the word occurs six times in 12:2–7), the word "Judah" appears only once (v. 14 [v. 5 is a Chronistic note]) in Zechariah 14. Instead, Jerusalem is the sole toponym, the referent of the second-person feminine singular suffix on "plunder." Hence, it is a battle against Jerusalem, apparently a version of the Zion tradition, that lies behind these verses and that this author deems as an inherent ingredient of Yahweh's day.

Verse 2 underscores the point that this momentous event is, indeed, Yahweh's day. His is a "proactive" stance rather than a reactive posture. The nations will not simply appear (cf. Zech. 12:3 and other standard exemplars of the Zion tradition, e.g., Ps. 48:4); Yahweh will assemble the nations. This is unusual, but not totally unexpected. The notion of Yahweh as one who might attack Zion is, of course, part of earlier Israelite experience (cf. the thinking that Yahweh was behind the onslaught of the neo-Babylonian forces, Ezek. 9:1). Moreover, the so-called Ariel poem, Isa. 29:1–8, attests to the following sentiment of Yahweh: "I will distress Ariel, and there shall be moaning and lamentation. . . ." There Yahweh, and not the nations, is the enemy. Moreover, according to the concluding verses in that poem, vv. 5–8, the nations as enemies will disappear. Finally, the description of Yahweh as one who might gather the nations to a place in Judah is attested elsewhere, as in Joel 3:2, "I will gather all the nations and bring them down to the valley of Jehoshaphat. . . ." (cf. Ezek. 38:7–9; 39:2).[59] Zechariah 14:1–3 appears to conflate some of these motifs, a combination designed to explore and/or explain Yahweh's relation to Jerusalem and to the nations on his day. The author's perception is that Yahweh will be involved in two different sorts of conflict, though the conflict between Yahweh and Jerusalem is less developed than is the conflict

---

[58]The second part of v. 1 provides an instance of synecdoche, a situation in which the whole is described by one of its parts.

[59]Plöger, *Theocracy and Eschatology,* 90, thinks the first section of Zechariah 14 "could be simply a summary reproduction of what was stated in the last ten chapters of the book of Ezekiel, beginning with the attack of the nations in Ezekiel 38ff."

between Yahweh and the nations. He will bring the nations to Jerusalem for *the* battle and will fight against them. Some from Jerusalem will survive (v. 2), as will some from the nations (v. 16); the notion of a remnant is international.

The identity of the nations is not at issue (unlike, for example, Joel 3:4). They remain an undefined agglomeration, as they typically do in various manifestations of the Zion tradition. What this author does identify is that which the nations will do. However, by using passive verbs the author is able to downplay the importance of the nations; he then highlights the truly important subject, the city and what is happening to it. The author invests three brief lines to highlight the destruction, moving from the physically larger to smaller entities: city–houses–women. The elegant literary construction stands in contrast with the devastating destruction; much will be violated. The book of Lamentations, which reflects the fall of Jerusalem, refers to all three elements, the destruction of the city, presumably its walls (2:8); plundering (1:10) and violation of dwelling places (2:2); women raped (5:11).

The picture of militarily wrought destruction is not one of complete annihilation. Some will be forcibly removed (cf. Lam. 1:3, 5, 18). It is interesting that the Hebrew states, "one half of the city will go into exile," and in so doing emphasizes the urban entity rather than its human population. Also intriguing is the use of fractions to specify what portion will remain. This tack links this day of Yahweh saying with the foregoing section devoted to the sword, shepherd, and flock, which also used the language of fractions (thirds) to articulate the nature of those who will survive. On purely arithmetical grounds, the picture in 14:2 is more sanguine than is that of 13:8–9 since, presumably, one-half will remain in the city and survive.[60]

The most surprising element in this saying involves the timing of Yahweh's move to battle. Earlier in the vignette, we had not been told why Jerusalem was to be attacked. And now we do not know why Yahweh intervenes. Nonetheless, Yahweh steps in and fights with the nations that he has assembled only after Jerusalem has been devastated (the demonstrative pronoun "those" makes it clear that the nations referred to in v. 3 are the same as those mentioned in v. 1). What Yahweh does we are not told; we are only informed that it will be typical of the deity in time of war. The composition does address this issue later, in vv. 12, 15, and 13–14, each of which provide a different perspective on what it is that Yahweh will do to the nations; there will be plague and panic, respectively.

[60]It may be that the use of fractions to depict the status of those who survive provides the warrant for the relative placement of 13:7–9 and 14:1–3. Plöger, *Theocracy and Eschatology,* 93, comments, "The absence of any further announcement by Yahweh, about the position of the surviving remnant . . . is very effective." It is effective because the reader can immediately refer back to the material in 13:7–9 for an answer. Hanson, *The Dawn of Apocalyptic,* 373, prefers to think that the half not cut off represent a distinct social group, a visionary faction.

[4–5] A number of scholars think that vv. 4–5 provide a continuation of the saying begun in the first three verses.[61] Such a view is understandable, since one might expect a description of what Yahweh will do once he has gone out to battle. However, vv. 4–5 neither present a martial scene nor mention the nations. As a result, one may suggest that the author has moved from the world of war to the world of theophany. And that is not the only difference. If according to vv. 1–3 the enemies are inside the city, then according to vv. 4–5 Yahweh is outside the city. The city was the earlier venue; now it has become the Mount of Olives. What enables these two sections to make sense in their current placement is the motif of departure: in the first, people will go into exile; in the second, they will flee from Yahweh's theophany.[62]

Yahweh's appearance on a mountain is a regular feature of theophanic descriptions in the OT (e.g., Sinai; Ex. 19:18). It is rather surprising that such descriptions are not connected with the mountain known as Zion,[63] though theophanic language is used to depict Yahweh's appearance at the temple (Isaiah 6). Mountains themselves are affected by Yahweh's presence: they quake, smoke, and blaze (Ex. 19:18; Nahum 1:5); melt (Ps. 97:5; Micah 1:4; Nahum 1:5); are scattered and sink down (Hab. 3:6; cf. Isa. 40:4); and are removed (Job 9:5). However, the notion of a mountain's splitting (*bq'*) is nowhere else attested. It is striking that the same verb (though in a different conjugation) is used to describe the effect of Yahweh's theophany on valleys, so Micah 1:4, "the valleys will be burst open." Although using traditional vocabulary and notions of theophany, the author has created a new image, a mountain split in two and a mountain not normally associated with Yahweh's theophany.[64] Nonetheless, the notion of Yahweh on this particular mountain probably reflects Ezekiel 43, which spoke of Yahweh's leaving and returning to Jerusalem via this mountain.

This bifurcated massif has a purpose; it provides a way for those who flee (v. 5) to leave the immediate environs of Jerusalem.[65] Those who are in the

[61]See, e.g., Rudolph, *Sacharja 9–14,* 234–35.

[62]For the classic discussion, see J. Jeremias, *Theophanie: Die Geschichte einer alttestamentliche Gattung,* WMANT 10, Neukirchen-Vluyn, 1965. This distinction cannot, of course, be absolute since Yahweh could appear in theophanic fashion when in battle. However, not all theophanies involve war, and such is the case with Zech. 14:4–5.

[63]Psalm 50:2–3 appears to be the sole exception.

[64]Ezekiel 11:23 is not a theophanic depiction.

[65]Cf. Rudolph, *Sacharja 9–14,* 253, who argues that the chasm allows for a *via triumphalis,* or Saebo, *Sacharja 9–14,* 290, who relates the way to Isa. 40:3–5, which provided access to Jerusalem. Zechariah 14:4–5, by contrast, speaks of a road that allows escape from Jerusalem. See Saebo, *Sacharja 9–14,* 291–96; and see Lacocque, *Zacharie 9–14,* 202, for a discussion, based on 2 Kings 23:13, of the notion that the Mount of Olives is present here as part of a polemic against improper worship, in particular the Moloch cult. I find no element in Zech. 14:4–5 that requires this interpretation. I follow Otzen, *Deuterosacharja,* 205, who notes a similar motif in Isa. 2:10, 19.

valleys that surround the city of Jerusalem, the Hinnom and Kidron valleys, which are here described as the valleys of the hills, will be able to flee eastward because the fissure in the Mount of Olives will allow some to flee to the east. The identity of those who flee is not clear. The verbs are constructed with the masculine plural morpheme, which provides a different image than does that of the half-city exiled in v. 2. According to the imagery of this unit, the people flee from Yahweh's theophany, not as the result of military conflict, as would have been the case in v. 2. (For this reason alone, it is inappropriate to think that vv. 4–5 provide a continuous narrative with the foregoing verses.)

Since such a fundamental change in the topography east of Jerusalem would have been difficult to imagine, the author provides a simile. The flight will be like that associated with the earthquake which occurred during the reign of Uzziah. Regrettably, the OT provides no reports about a flight associated with that earthquake. The only other allusion to the earthquake itself occurs in the prologue to Amos, "two years before the earthquake," which must have occurred sometime during the mid-eighth century B.C.E. One may assume that earthquakes caused destruction of buildings and decimation by the ensuing fires, events that would lead to flight from urban areas. More cannot be said.

At the conclusion of this section, the author leaves the world of simile. The final two lines provide a flashback to the events that must have occurred prior to the beginning of v. 4, namely, the arrival of the deity. By dint of its unusual placement, Zech. 14:5c emphasizes that Yahweh will indeed arrive, and with an entourage, "the holy ones." These *qĕdōšîm* are referred to elsewhere in the OT (e.g., Ps. 89:5, 7). They are the minor deities who populate Yahweh's divine council.[66] They are also known as "the sons of God" (Job 1:6; 2:1; Deut. 32:8 [LXX]). Most of these texts place such minor deities in the conciliar setting. However, Deut. 33:2, which may be translated "with him were a multitude of holy ones," presents "the holy ones" as accompanying Yahweh in a theophany.[67] Although few of these texts bear strong military connotations, Deut. 33:3 conveys the image of these holy ones following commands and marching in line. In Zech. 14:5, though they appear in the standard theophanic description, one may anticipate that they might have a military role.[68]

[6–7] The third saying is introduced by the "long" form of the day of Yahweh formula, *wĕhāyāh bayyôm hahû'*, which had appeared in the initial

---

[66]Some have argued that the "holy ones" could be humans (cf. Saebo, *Sacharja 9–14*, 296), citing for example, Isa. 4:3, which does provide an interesting case since it refers to those who are left in Jerusalem. Nonetheless, in the martial setting of Zech. 14:1–5, it is more likely that the *qĕdōšîm* are minor deities.

[67]On Deut. 33:2, see F. Cross and D. Freedman, *Studies in Ancient Yahwistic Poetry*, SBLDS 21, Missoula, Mont., 1975, 99, 105–6.

[68]It seems unlikely that Yahweh and the holy ones arrive via the chasm that had served to allow people to escape; cf. Hanson, *The Dawn of Apocalyptic*, 374.

section of the second *maśśā'* (Zech. 12:3, 9; 13:2, 4) and which appears, as well, three times in Zechariah 14 (vv. 6, 8, 13). However, this long formula does not seem to function in quite the same way as it did in chaps. 12–13, that is, by marking major literary boundaries.

If the first saying derives from predominantly holy-war language and the second from theophanic descriptions, the third seems related to what some scholars have defined as the day of Yahweh traditions.[69] The notion that Yahweh has a special day is attested at least as early as Amos, a day such that he could redefine it as a catastrophic moment (5:18). A full examination of day of Yahweh traditions lies beyond the scope of this commentary, the more so since only one element of those descriptions appears in this saying, namely, the nature of light/dark "on that day." One may infer that prior to the time of Amos the brightness of Yahweh's appearance meant that the day of Yahweh would be a day of light.[70] However, Amos turned this notion on its head by maintaining that the day of Yahweh would be a day characterized by darkness and gloom, a notion that, at least in prophetic literature, became part of the standard expectation for Yahweh's day. Isaiah 13:9–10 states that on that day neither stars, moon, nor sun will provide light. Zephaniah 1:15, though without mentioning the astral sources of light, emphasizes the motif of darkness, "a day of darkness and gloom, a day of clouds and thick darkness." The author of the prophetic text closest in time to the composition of Zech. 14:6 uses both these types of descriptions: he mimes the language of Zephaniah, "a day of darkness and gloom, a day of clouds and thick darkness" (Joel 2:2); he refers to dysfunctional heavenly sources of light: the sun and the moon are darkened, and the stars withdraw their shining (Joel 2:10; 2:31; 3:15; cf. Isa. 60:19).

The first clause of Zech. 14:6 appears to be a concise and fairly colorless way of summarizing the claim that there will be darkness, namely, by stating that there will be no light. When the author adds to the equation the judgment that there will be "neither cold nor frost," the language of negatives impel the reader to ask, what *will* there be?[71] If no light, then no sun; if no cold, then perhaps warmth; but without sun (so the foregoing), it seems that nothing— neither light nor dark—neither warmth nor cold is possible.[72] Such a dialectic

---

[69]Following von Rad, H. Wolff (*Joel and Amos,* Hermeneia, Philadelphia, 1977, 33–34) argues that the day of Yahweh conception derives from holy-war traditions, which have been influenced by theophanic language.

[70]See in this regard Wolff's comments, *Joel and Amos,* 256–57 n. 21, on *nqh.*

[71]By contrast, Saebo, *Sacharja 9–14,* 299, discerns a threatening quality in this verse. Others discern an allusion to the Noachic covenant, e.g., Mason, *The Use of Earlier Biblical Material in Zechariah IX–XIV,* 274.

[72]As with other meteorological phenomena, cold was thought to derive from Yahweh (Job 37:10; Ps. 147:16–17).

serves as the prologue to the author's innovative claim: this day will be unlike any day that has heretofore existed.[73]

Two elements characterize this day: its inconceivability and its peculiar light. The first two lines of v. 7 focus on the former, the last two lines of v. 7 on the latter element. This day will be singular, knowable by only the deity—an odd statement, presumably meaning that only Yahweh could understand this time as a day. That day will be so peculiar that it is inappropriate to characterize it using the terms day and night, which were constituent categories for describing "a day" (Gen. 1:5). To claim that neither "day" nor "night" will exist is to suggest that time and light as they had hitherto been understood would be redefined. Only at the end of v. 7 does the author provide an answer, which also derives from the vocabulary of Genesis 1. There will be a dim twilight that will replace the rotation between light and dark. What was one element, "evening" (*'ereb*) in the daylong cycle, namely, the move from evening to morning (Gen. 1:5 and passim) will become the only form of light, that of dusk. Perhaps this author knew the saying preserved in Isa. 60:19 (cf. Isa. 24:23) that there would no longer be a sun or moon for light; rather, Yahweh would provide light. If such were the case, Zech. 14:7 is spelling out the character of this new light that Yahweh will provide.

The author of these two verses redefines the day of Yahweh tradition on the basis of vocabulary attested in Genesis 1 (day, night, light, dusk, *'eḥād*). In so doing, the author is also redefining the notion of day and, even more, the created order as understood in Genesis 1. The new day will not involve the cycle of darkness and light but will allow for a continuous but dull light. Such a claim strikes at the roots of the "standard" day of Yahweh traditions, which stress the prominence of darkness (e.g., Joel). The author clearly anticipates something new, something (at least to him) unknown. However, he expresses something sanguine since, in his judgment, Yahweh knows and even understands this singular day, presumably since he will have created it just as he had created the earlier form of day.[74]

The montage, which the author or editor is creating, is now moving away from earlier, more typical forms of tradition, for example, the holy-war tradition articulated in vv. 1–3, to greater redefinition of earlier traditions, in this case the day of Yahweh traditions, and even notions of the structure of the cosmos. The radical geographic reconfiguration attested in the second saying is mirrored by an even more radical redefinition of time and light in the third saying. What marks this third saying as unusual in the montage of Zechariah 14 is the absence of a reference to Jerusalem, though the absence of a toponym

---

[73]So similarly, Otzen, *Deuterosacharja*, 205, 268; Willi-Plein, *Prophetie am Ende*, 89.
[74]Mason, *The Books of Haggai, Zechariah, and Malachi*, 127, also discerns a hopeful note.

is consistent with the emphasis on a day of vague light. Particulars, whether place or time, do not belong in this saying. Rather, the author stresses the radicality of that which Yahweh is doing. Not only does it represent a fundamental change in the way Yahweh has structured light and time, it is now conceivable only to Yahweh.

[8] The fourth saying is also introduced by the long form of the formula. It too, like the foregoing sayings, draws on earlier well-known traditions.[75] However, as was the case with the previous saying, this verse does not simply mime earlier manifestations of the tradition but reformats it to suit the demands of this montage.

It is a commonplace to associate this verse with Ezek. 47:1–20; Joel 3:18; and, to a lesser extent, Gen. 2:10–14. All four texts have been construed as exemplars of a tradition involving a freshwater flow from the site of the divine dwelling, which could be symbolized by the divine garden or by the temple.[76] In Joel, a fountain will flow from the temple and will water the valley of acacias.[77] According to Genesis 2, a river will water the garden and then flow from Eden, whereupon it divides into four directions. Its fructifying function is not mentioned once the rivers divide. Ezekiel 47, simply by dint of its length, is more complicated. Water flows toward the east from "below the threshold of the temple." It becomes a great river and moves down to the Arabah and then to the Dead Sea (which could be termed the sea of the Arabah, 2 Kings 14:25), whereupon the sea becomes fresh water, capable of supporting fish. Moreover, the riverbanks will be filled with rich plant life. A hint at the lack of seasonal variation, mentioned in Zechariah 14, is provided by the clause "their leaves will not wither" (Ezek. 47:12).

When set within the context of these four texts, Zechariah is different from Joel and Ezekiel because the latter assume a flow only to the east, and it is different from Genesis because it thinks of two as opposed to four tributaries.[78] Though the tone of Ezekiel 47 suggests an everflowing stream, only Zech. 14:8 stresses the constancy of the flow. The rhetoric of that constancy, using the twofold opposition of summer and winter, may well explain why the binary opposition of east and west were used by this author. Straightforward oppositions, whether points of the compass or seasons, provide the means whereby the author makes his point about the permanence of these living (i.e., running)

---

[75]The riverine flow described in Zech. 14:8 does not function in the same way as does the spring of Zech. 13:1.

[76]Cf. descriptions of El as enthroned at the source of rivers in the Ugaritic texts.

[77]So Wolff, *Joel and Amos,* 83, instead of valley of Shittim.

[78]Cf. Saebo, *Sacharja 9–14,* 300–302, who argues that vv. 8, 10a, 11 were originally related, draw on Ezekiel 47, and express the notion that the entire land would be watered by the streams.

waters that will issue forth from Jerusalem; and interestingly, the temple is not mentioned as the source of the water.[79]

What is significant about this form of the Jerusalem running-water tradition is that the water continues regardless of the season. Unlike the flow of water that might be seasonal and would therefore dry up in the summer, this source will continue. This note of continuity appears consistent with the motif of permanent dusklike light articulated in the previous saying. However, an interpretation that is concerned for consistency will note that since time, that is, day and night, no longer exist, it is difficult to imagine someone's appealing to another sort of time, namely, seasonal regularity.[80] These diverse perspectives on time make it difficult to imagine that Zechariah 14 was composed at one time and by one author. Rather, the notion of a montage, a picture made up of different elements, which the creator deemed appropriate to express a particular theme—in this case, Jerusalem on the day of Yahweh—is a better way to account for the semantic diversity just noted. This saying belongs in the montage because it identifies Jerusalem on that day as a source of permanence and continuity, signified by the flow of water.[81] And, more generally, fertile waters will arise in Jerusalem and fructify far beyond the city's boundary. This notion may bear social and political connotations for those outside Jerusalem.

[9] Again, according to the reconstruction provided in the notes, a saying is introduced with the long form of the "on that day" formula. After that formula, the saying, yet another prophetic utterance, makes two apparently unrelated claims about the status of the deity, namely, that he will be king over all the earth and that he and his name will be one. Are these simply commonplace understandings, and in what sense might they belong together?

The so-called psalms of enthronement (Pss. 93, 96, 97, and 99) include asseverations that Yahweh functions as king: he reigns, or better, "he has become king" (Pss. 93:1; 97:1; 99:1—so REB). These psalms attest to the reality that Zech. 14:9 predicts, namely, that Yahweh will become king. The extent to which such claims involve a festival of enthronement is widely debated. Whether or not the New Year's festival included a liturgy according to which Yahweh was ritually enthroned, Judahites held the conviction that Yahweh was king, even in the second temple period when there was no longer a Davidic king on the throne. Moreover, these same psalms attest to the global character of the deity's rule: "he has established the world, it shall never be moved" (Ps. 93:1); "all the earth" (Ps. 96:1); "let the earth rejoice" (Ps. 97:1);

[79]Hence, there is no warrant to suggest that Zech. 14:8 represents an abbreviated version of Genesis 2. The rhetorical strategies of the two texts are entirely different.

[80]Rudolph, *Sacharja 9–14*, 236.

[81]One might expect that Yahweh as king is responsible for the fertility of the land (Willi-Plein, *Prophetie am Ende*, 89; Hanson, *The Dawn of Apocalyptic*, 377). However, the montage speaks first of fertility, then of kingship.

"let the earth quake" (Ps. 99:1). Hence, the claim of Zech. 14:9, that Yahweh will rule over all the earth, is fully consistent with and an expression of a theologoumenon present in the psalms of enthronement. Moreover, this same notion is present in prophetic texts (e.g., Jer. 3:17) and expresses two motifs present in Zechariah, namely, Yahweh as king, there expressed as "Jerusalem shall be called the throne of the Lord," and "nations shall gather to it," namely, Jerusalem as throne.

The final lines of the saying move to an apparently new topic: the appropriateness of using the notion of *'eḥād,* "one," to describe the deity and his name. Again, it is important to note that the above-mentioned psalms of enthronement refer to the deity's name (Pss. 96:2, 8; 97:12; 99:3). Hence, when attesting the deity's name, this deuteroprophetic author here remains within the universe of discourse appropriate to Yahweh as king. Nonetheless, Zech. 14:9 appears to use the notion of name as a way of speaking about the deity, as also in Lev. 24:11 (*haššēm*). What is unusual, at least in typical enthronement language, is the emphasis on *'eḥād.*[82] The notion of Yahweh being *'eḥād* is, however, preserved in other arenas of OT discourse, the most prominent of which occurs in Deut. 6:4, "Hear, O Israel: Yahweh our God is *yahweh 'eḥād.*" These final two words have proved immensely difficult to interpret. The most compelling translation is: "Our God is Yahweh, Yahweh alone."[83] If, as seems likely, Zech. 14:9 refracts the *šĕma',* the Deuteronomic theologoumenon has apparently been appropriated in a new way, which emphasizes the singularity of the deity as well as the importance of referring to him by reference to name.[84]

Zechariah does not affirm some present reality, as does Deut. 6:4 (Yahweh is one), but instead points to a future reality, namely, what will happen on that day. The appositional predicate enabled the writer to refer to some syntactically prior claim. In Deuteronomy 6 an author claimed that Yahweh was our

---

[82]It may be that *'eḥād* serves as a *Stichwort* (catchword), with reference to Zech. 14:7, where the word is used in quite a different sense.

[83]So S. Dean McBride, Jr., "The Yoke of the Kingdom: An Exposition of Deuteronomy 6:4–5," *Int* 27 (1973): 291–97, who views *'eḥād* as an appositional predicate. Cf. B. Waltke and M. O'Connor, *An Introduction to Biblical Hebrew Syntax,* 1990, 135, "It is hard to say if *'ḥd* can serve as an adjective modifying *yhwh.*" See also J. Janzen, "On the Most Important Word in the Shema (Deuteronomy VI 4–5)," *VT* 37 (1987): 280–300, who focuses on *'eḥād* and claims, contra McBride, that it involves a claim about the "integrity" of Yahweh.

[84]It may be that the author of Zech. 14:9 was drawing on other usages of *'eḥād* as a reference to the deity. For example, Job 31:15 refers clearly to the deity as *'eḥād,* "the One"; Job 23:13 may be construed as stating, "But He is one." The latter text focuses on the consistency of the deity: That which he plans, he will accomplish. Malachi 2:10 refers to the deity as *'ēl 'eḥād,* "one God"; "has not one God created us?" The latter text clearly is involved in a polemic against veneration of deities other than Yahweh, as in Mal. 2:11 (see commentary below). These other usages complicate the picture. But none appear as predicate adjectives, which is apparently the case in Zech. 14:9.

God; in Zech. 14:9 the claim was that Yahweh would be king. In this regard, Zechariah 14 is fundamentally different from all the aforementioned texts that use the term *'eḥād* to refer to the deity. Zechariah 14:9 does not claim that the deity presently is *'eḥād;* rather, that verse projects such a claim into the future. What the *šĕma'* or any of the other texts affirms, Zechariah does not allow for the present. Just as there is now one kind of light or day, there will be a different kind of light or time in the future, so Zech. 14:7. By analogy, the author of Zech. 14:9 seems to claim that Yahweh is not now king but will be in the future.

But what might it mean for an author in Persian-period Judah to say *yahweh 'eḥād?* The answer lies in linking the two claims of this verse, namely, Yahweh as royal and Yahweh as solitary. Yahweh alone will be king over all the earth. No other deity, no Persian emperor, and apparently no Davidic ruler will share in this rule. Yahweh, or the hypostatization "His Name," alone will rule as king of the universe. This theological judgment is consistent with claims about Yahweh's supremacy expressed elsewhere in Zechariah 9–14 (e.g., 9:1–8). And by implication it devalues the role of Yahwistic political leaders, an inference that serves to explain why Judean leaders are not mentioned in Zechariah 14, though they were in Zech. 12:1–13:6.

[10–11] The next two sections (vv. 10–11 and vv. 12, 15) are not introduced by the "on that day" formula. Without that formal marker, one has less obvious warrant for deciding that these verses constitute separate units; hence, the label "vignette" seems especially appropriate. Nonetheless, since the subject matter changes significantly between vv. 9 and 10, and because no element in the entire montage is longer than four verses, it seems reasonable to construe vv. 10–11 and 12, 15 as distinct units, the more so given the syntax with which v. 12 begins (see below).

The sixth saying returns to the topic of geographic dislocation, which had also been addressed in the second saying, vv. 4–5. There the cause of the dislocation was Yahweh's theophany. In vv. 10–11, no direct reference to Yahweh's appearance occurs. Moreover, in this latter saying, the subject is not just Jerusalem's immediate environs, but is instead *kol hā'āreṣ,* the same phrase used in v. 9, and one that serves as a *Stichwort* to link the two sections. However, *'ereṣ* can have different meanings ("the earth" versus "the land of Israel"), and one has the sense that the author is here referring specifically to Syro-Palestinian geography, not something that might include Mesopotamia. Hence, it is appropriate to translate the two phrases differently in the fifth and sixth sayings respectively, earth versus land.

The hallmark of v. 10 is specificity, first the specificity of toponyms and then specificity of sites in Jerusalem, a technique also used in Zechariah 9. As regards the former, the author envisions architectonic activity according to which the land of Syria-Palestine will become like the Arabah. Though the term Arabah is used today to refer to the relatively flat valley between the Dead

Sea and the gulf of Aqabah, in antiquity the term was apparently used to refer to various parts of the Jordan rift valley (e.g., Deut. 3:17).[85] Despite the ambiguity in what might be described by this term, the sense of Zech. 14:10 is clear. Since Arabah normally refers to something that is lower in elevation than the surrounding topography, the author imagines that the entire land, including the Judean hill country, will sink down to correspond to the low elevation of the Arabah.

The author continues in this world of simile by indicating the extent of land that will be so affected: from Geba to Rimmon in the south. These two toponyms are village names. Geba is used in Neh. 11:31 in a similar way, namely, to describe the extent of an area, in this case that belonging to the people of Benjamin, "The people of Benjamin also lived from Geba onward." The village was located approximately six miles northeast of Jerusalem. Rimmon, too, appears in Neh. 11:29, in a list of villages describing where the people of Judah lived, "in En-rimmon."[86] The identification of Rimmon is not certain. If one accepts the equation with En-rimmon, the village would be almost eleven miles north of Beersheba. If one identifies Rimmon with Tel Halif, then the site would be several miles to the northwest of Beersheba.[87] In either case, Rimmon signifies the southern extent and Geba the northern boundary.

These particular toponyms delimit the geographic change to a relatively small territory, slightly larger than the province of Judah during the Persian period, though even this claim is difficult to make because no east-west coordinates are given (east-west was, however, the language of the fourth saying, v. 8). The boundaries of Judah during the Persian period extended further to the north than Geba and not so far south as either putative site for Rimmon. Most of the land would have lain south of Jerusalem. As a result, it is clear that the author was not interested in portraying the exact boundaries of the Judahite province.[88] As befits the world of simile, the north-south coordinates are vague, marked not by cities, but by small villages situated in the Judean hill country. There is, in sum, a contrast between the use of three specific toponyms and the general tone of ambiguity concerning the extent of the territory demarcated.

The diction of toponyms as well as specific urban locations continues in v. 10. One site, the city of Jerusalem, is the primary subject. The contrast between city (Jerusalem) and village (Geba, Rimmon) is consistent with the geological action that the author foresees, namely, the elevation of Jerusalem, which

---

[85]See "Arabah," *IDB*, vol. 1, 177–79.

[86]MT reads *rimmôn negeb* so as to distinguish this Rimmon from a city to the north (Josh. 19:13; 1 Chron. 6:77).

[87]See Rudolph, *Sacharja 9–14*, 237; *HBD*, 872.

[88]On which, see Rudolph, *Sacharja 9–14*, 237.

stands in sharp contrast to the lowering of the Judean hill country. That Jerusalem was understood to be a city of significant, even mythic, elevation is attested in psalmic literature (Ps. 48:2). Moreover, other prophetic texts attest to an expectation that Mount Zion will be elevated over other hills in Judah (Isa. 2:2//Micah 4:1). On the one hand, the author of Zech. 14:10 seems intent on articulating this tradition. On the other hand, the author wants to make a claim about continuity rather like that made in Zech. 12:6, namely, "Jerusalem shall still be inhabited in its place." And, of course, this claim is reaffirmed strongly in v. 11, "they will dwell in it." Awesome though the certain changes might be, things will not be wholly different for those in Jerusalem. Their status will be enhanced, but not changed radically. Jerusalem is, at least in Israel's liturgical language, that which it will become.

The continuity between the new Jerusalem and the old Jerusalem is defined with reference to certain structures, especially as these occur on the perimeter of the city; cf. Jer. 31:38–40, which may provide a different and less traditional picture of restored Jerusalem. The points of reference are: the Benjamin gate, the former gate, the corner gate, the Hananel tower, and the royal winepresses. Before attempting to identify these terms in a specific way, it is appropriate to comment both about the literary effect that the author has achieved by using such language and about the traditional character of these descriptions. As regards the former, the author has created an image of Jerusalem as a walled city, an image that does not, like some descriptions in the OT, focus on Jerusalem as essentially a city that provides the site for a temple. Continuity of city structure, not temple, is the key notion. Compare Zech. 2:5 for quite a different perspective.

A number of the so-called Zion psalms describe Jerusalem using similar language, that of citadels (48:3, 13; 122:7), towers (48:12), ramparts (48:13; 122:7), and gates (87:2; 122:2). The author of Zech. 14:10–11 appropriates standard vocabulary found elsewhere in psalmic descriptions of Jerusalem, namely, that of gate and tower. What is unusual is the identification of specific gates, which more typically occurs in various forms of narrative literature (e.g., Jer. 31:38–41; Neh. 3:1).

Where were these places and how do they function in this text? The first question allows no easy answers.[89] There is general agreement that the corner gate was situated at the northwest corner of the city wall, though strangely that gate is not mentioned in any of the Ezra-Nehemiah narratives. The old gate was probably on the north wall (Neh. 3:6) as was the Tower of Hananel (Neh. 3:1; 12:39; cf. Jer. 31:38). The Benjamin gate, also not mentioned in Ezra-Nehemiah, would—at least according to references to it in Jeremiah (20:2; 37:13; 38:7)—have been situated in the northeastern area of the city wall,

---

[89]See for a brief review of these various sites, *IBD*, vol. 2, 854–56.

though whether in the northern or eastern section of the perimeter is unclear. Despite the apparent ambiguity, all three gates as well the tower would appear to belong to the northern perimeter of the Jerusalem city wall. The only exception is the king's winepresses, which scholars have located (assuming that they provide a reference to the southern extent of the city) in the same general area as the royal gardens in the Valley of Hinnom (Jer. 39:4; Neh. 3:15).[90]

As with Geba and Rimmon, the author has provided an impressionistic description of an area according to its north-south coordinates. However, such similarity of description belies what will happen to the two different areas. The area between Geba and Rimmon will sink, whereas that between the gates and the gardens will be elevated. The specific names provide loci by means of which those who heard or read this oracle could identify that which would be "high ground," the place where Jerusalem's inhabitants would be located. It is, therefore, not surprising that this saying concludes with reference to those who inhabit Jerusalem. The elevation apparently serves to enhance further Jerusalem's security—destruction of the city will be a thing of the past. Moreover, those who live within its boundaries will be able to have confidence in their own security, a claim attested in Jer. 33:16, which depends there on the presence of a new Davidide as well as on the newly named city—"Yahweh is our righteousness."

[12, 15] Since v. 12 begins with a disjunctive clause, one that uses the demonstrative $z'\bar{o}t$ to point to the new topic, that of a plague, it is licit to view this verse, as well as the dislocated v. 15, which explores yet another but related plague as a separate vignette or prophetic saying.[91] Some earlier elements in this montage had expressed the notion that Yahweh would confront the peoples or nations (Zech. 14:3). The montage now returns to that issue, but with attention to the means by which Yahweh would interact with them.[92]

The vocabulary of plague appears rooted in the so-called plague narratives of Exodus, chaps. 7–11, according to which Yahweh afflicted an area in Egypt, and then just the Egyptians. However, language of Yahweh plaguing or slaughtering Israelites (e.g., Num. 14:37; 31:16; 1 Chron. 21:17, 22; 2 Chron. 21:14; Ezek. 24:16) or, much less frequently, non-Israelites (1 Sam. 6:4), appears elsewhere in the OT. By using this diction, the author holds open the possibility that the peoples may not die. The language of plague allowed for death but did not always eventuate in it. This may well be the reason that

---

[90]See, e.g., Mitchell, *A Critical and Exegetical Commentary on Haggai and Zechariah*, 349.

[91]So also Rudolph, *Sacharja 9–14*, 238; Saebo, *Sacharja 9–14*, 306.

[92]This return to an earlier topic has caused some to view this vignette as "intrusive," e.g., Mason, *The Use of Earlier Biblical Material in Zechariah IX–XIV*, 282.

Yahweh plagues his own people; some are chastened, fewer die. Not all those plagued are necessarily slain. However, in battle, when Yahweh or his representative goes out against his foes, the enemy's death is the normal result, so 2 Kings 19:35—and there the word plague is not used.

Even if, however, the notion of plague does not necessarily involve the death of those who suffer, plagues can be horrendous, as in the description in 2 Chron. 21:14–15. It is within this world that Zech. 14:12, 15 fits. The plague described in these two verses will affect animals and humans alike (so also Ex. 11:5) and will involve decay throughout the bodies of those whom it afflicts. (The same Hebrew word, *mqq*, is used in all three lines of the plague description in Zech. 14:12.) Unpleasant as the description is, it does not involve, necessarily, the death of all those who suffer it, whether animal or human.

This seventh saying is graphic. Eyes, mouth, and, more generally, flesh will be subject to suffering. Moreover, the list of animals allows the author to list at least five different species that will suffer this plague: human, horse, donkey, camel, ass. Finally, the author, in an understated way, indicates that the plague will occur in the enemy camp. One almost has the sense that the battle has been fought and that a portion of Jerusalem has been defeated (cf. Zech. 14:2). In any case, the plague does not occur explicitly out on the field of battle. The camp is the primary locus for this destructive affliction.

[13–14] Verses 13–14 are introduced by the long form of the "on that day" formula, which, along with the new mode for conveying Yahweh's action, suggests that v. 13 initiates a new saying, one that draws on so-called holy-war traditions. Yahweh may be the source of panic that is generated by military confrontation (Deut. 7:23; 28:20; 1 Sam. 5:9, 11; Isa. 22:5). Perhaps the most relevant earlier biblical text is 1 Sam. 14:18–20. In this narrative involving the impact of "the ark of God" on Israel's military fortunes, we are told that, when the ark was present and when Saul and his troops went into battle, "every man's sword was against his fellow, and there was very great confusion or panic (*mĕhûmāh*)." The conjunction of these two elements, intratroop combat and panic is also present in Zech. 14:13. This notion of people within an army fighting among themselves constitutes yet another element typical of holy-war depictions in the OT (e.g., Judg. 7:22). Verse 13 makes clear that Yahweh will act, as of old, on behalf of his people in a martial capacity.[93]

Verse 14 offers a tantalizing glimpse of possible intra-Judean strife that might parallel the strife within enemy forces adduced in the previous verse. Zechariah 12:6–7 includes similar language, emphasizing the significance of

---

[93]The language of panic also occurs in covenant curses (e.g., Deut. 28:20), though in both Zech. 14:12, 15 and 14:13–14 the animus is directed against non-Israelites; cf. Hanson, *The Dawn of Apocalyptic*, 383–84.

Judah, not just Jerusalem (see above). Many commentators, who translate *b* in its adversative sense, argue that the first clause of v. 14 is an addition.[94] According to Elliger and Rudolph, a later editor has added a perspective to the text that represents some form of tension between Judah and Jerusalem. However, as both Mitchell and Otzen maintain, to suggest that the text is a gloss may allow for the possibility that Judah will indeed fight against Jerusalem, but it would be a Jerusalem that has already been overwhelmed by enemy troops and, hence, requires liberation.[95] Alternately, one may point to variations within the ancient manuscript evidence, which would allow one to suggest either that Judah will fight at or in Jerusalem.[96] Since both the gloss theory and the LXX readings allow for the possibility that Judah need not fight against Yahwists at Jerusalem, I have elected to translate the preposition *b* with its locative sense, recognizing that this translation involves an interpretive judgment. I adjudge this clause to be integral to the text and consistent with the sentiments expressed in 12:6–7 concerning the symbiosis between Judah and Jerusalem. Judah, namely, the non-Jerusalemite inhabitants of the Judean province, will participate in the conflict at its critical site, that is, the city of Jerusalem. Even if Judah does not fight "against" Jerusalem, this clause does demonstrate that Judah could be viewed as something distinct from Jerusalem, though here the distinction articulates the vast scale of the conflict, not tension between Judah and Jerusalem.

This conflict will eventuate in great riches; yet another traditional element—the despoliation of the nations—used in the creation of this montage. This motif is attested in a variety of contexts, not only those associated with holy war (e.g., Ex. 12:35–36; Isa. 60:4–14; Hag. 2:7–8). As a result, we cannot be certain that the wealth referred to here was understood as present in the enemy camp and therefore immediately available by dint of their defeat. Nonetheless, the defeat attested in this saying is understood to enrich those in Judah and Jerusalem, though specifically where and for whom is left unstated. Such generality suggests the author is recasting traditional material.

[16–19] Like v. 10, which introduces the sixth saying, and like v. 12, which introduces the seventh saying, v. 16 introduces the ninth saying without using the "on that day" formula. One may claim that this is a separate vignette in the

---

[94]See, e.g., Rudolph, *Sacharja 9–14*, 231; Elliger, *Das Buch der zwölf kleinen Propheten*, 168; and, tentatively, Hanson, *The Dawn of Apocalyptic*, 371. The particle with which the clause begins, *wĕgam*, is an abrupt transition.

[95]Mitchell, *A Critical and Exegetical Commentary on Haggai and Zechariah*, 352–53; Otzen, *Deuterosacharja*, 271.

[96]See Otzen, *Deuterosacharja*, 270–71, and Saebo, *Sacharja 9–14*, 123, for a complete discussion. Lacocque, *Zacharie 9–14*, 205, also translates with a locative sense.

montage because of the new topic—that of pilgrimage—and because the syntax—*wĕhāyāh*—allows for a new section.[97] This penultimate saying focuses on a remnant, not of Judeans but of those who had survived defeat by Yahweh and his forces. This remnant is made up of those who had attacked Jerusalem, but who had, perforce, returned to their native lands. Though the notion of their return is not mentioned specifically in the text, it must be presumed; otherwise, a pilgrimage to Jerusalem makes no sense.

The tone is indicative, though—as the rest of the saying shows—it has the force of an imperative. Those who had come to Jerusalem and been defeated are required to reappear there on an annual basis. The first "visit" seems to obligate them to appear regularly, though for a purpose different from their original presence at Jerusalem. Whereas they at first came to do battle, they now must appear for ritual purposes, namely, to venerate the deity who was responsible for their defeat and to celebrate a Yahwistic festival. Travel to do battle has been transformed into an annual pilgrimage.

This charge to undertake a pilgrimage would seem related to the so-called pilgrimage of the nations tradition, as that is expressed in Isa. 2:1–4//Micah 4:1–4; Zech. 8:20–23. However, in these presumably earlier texts, the pilgrimage enables the nations to receive torah and to witness the cessation of military hostilities. There is no specific ritual event mentioned, nor is there reference to calendrical regularity.[98]

In the midst of this general military and "theo-logic," the author provides specificity; Yahweh is to be venerated as king within the context of a specific feast, the feast of *sukkôt*, "booths" or "tabernacles." As for the first category, the montage of Zechariah 14, in the fifth saying (v. 9), had already addressed the notion of Yahweh's becoming king. There the author had emphasized that the sway of Yahweh's rule would be global, which is, of course, consistent with the sentiment expressed in this ninth saying. By contrast, the latter element, the feast of booths, occurs without any forewarning. Why should this particular feast serve as the occasion for the pilgrimage of nations?[99]

First, one must be clear about the feast of booths, and then, about the relation between Yahweh's kingship and that feast. That Israel had three major pilgrimage feasts associated with the annual agricultural cycle is clear (see

---

[97]The appeal to syntax is of secondary importance since the syntax within this saying is not smooth; cf. *wĕhāyāh* in v. 17 and *z'ōt* in v. 19.

[98]Isaiah 66:23 provides the closest analogy, though here the notion is not of an annual festival; see similarly Stade, "Deuterozacharja," 89. Plöger thinks Zech. 14:16–17 constitutes a revision of the banquet motif, attested earlier in Isa. 24:6–8, *Theocracy and Eschatology*, 91; cf. Hanson, *The Dawn of Apocalyptic*, 385.

[99]Mason, *The Use of Earlier Biblical Material in Zechariah IX–XIV*, 285, reports G. Gaide as suggesting that "this one act is intended, by metonymy, to stand for the whole of the religious life."

Ex. 23:16; 34:22). However, in those early lists, the term *sukkôt* (booths or tabernacles) does not occur. Rather, the annual fall harvest festival is called *ḥag hā'āsîp,* "the feast of ingathering." Deuteronomy, however, describes this feast as booths, Deut. 16:13–17. Leviticus (23:39–43; cf. Judg. 21:19) also associates this feast with booths; however, in that book, it is known as "the feast of the Lord," a phrase that would seem to give that celebration preeminent status among the various pilgrimage feasts. A similar tendency may be observed in those texts that refer to this celebration as *"the* festival" (1 Kings 8:2; 2 Chron. 5:3, 7–8; Neh. 8:14; Ezek. 45:23).[100]

Scholars agree that the festival originally involved celebration of the fall harvest and was later "historicized" (Lev. 23:43). However, there are tantalizing hints that more than a celebration of crops was at stake. Mowinckel, among others, has argued that this festival was linked to a celebration of the new year, which, in turn, was an occasion when Yahweh's cosmic kingship was celebrated—even ritually reenacted.[101] This theory regarding a new year's festival has not received general acceptance, though it is difficult to sustain the notion that the major autumn feast was "just" a harvest festival.[102] Even if one rejects the thesis of Mowinckel, Zechariah 14 indicates that *sukkôt* could, for one Israelite writer, involve the elements of pilgrimage, nations or non-Israelites, Yahweh as king, and rain.

Of the various biblical texts that attest to *sukkôt,* the exemplar in Neh. 8:13–18 is probably the closest in time to that of Zechariah. There the hallmark of this festival is the construction of booths in Jerusalem, celebrated by those who had returned from exile (and not simply all Israelite males, so Ex. 34:23). Rather than the expected round of offerings, Nehemiah 8 reports that the essence of the communal gathering was the reading of torah. No mention is made of Yahweh's kingship as an element of the celebration. In fact, the temple itself is not mentioned in Neh. 8:13–18.[103]

For the purposes of this commentary, it is appropriate to focus on the two elements associated with the feast that function prominently in Zechariah 14, the association with Yahweh as king and the notion of pilgrimage. The latter

---

[100]For a general description of the feast and its historical development, see R. de Vaux, *Ancient Israel,* vol. 2: *Religious Institutions,* New York, 1965, 495–502; H.-J. Kraus, *Worship in Israel,* Richmond, 1966, 61–70, who argues for an original "tent" festival; and G. MacRae, "The Meaning and Evolution of the Feast of Tabernacles,' *CBQ* 22 (1960): 251–76.

[101]See the classic statement, S. Mowinckel, *Psalmenstudien II: Das Thronbesteigungsfest Jahwäs und der Ursprung der Eschatologie,* Amsterdam, 1922.

[102]For a recent critique of Mowinckel, see H.-J. Kraus, *Theology of the Psalms,* Minneapolis, 1986, 86–91, which, however, does not suggest why *sukkôt* is *the* feast.

[103]Cf. the assessment of W. Harrelson, "The Celebration of the Feast of Booths according to Zech. 14:16–21," in *Religions in Antiquity: Essays in Memory of Erwin Ramsdell Goodenough,* ed. J. Neusner, Leiden, 1968, 88–96, who focuses on the prominence of covenant renewal in this festival, in this case a covenant that includes all nations.

element, though perhaps not integral to an hypothesized purely agricultural festival, is attested in the oldest OT references, namely, the festival calendars in Exodus 23 and 34. However, in Zechariah 14 the notion of pilgrimage has been transformed. No longer is it an obligation only for Judeans; it has now become incumbent on survivors from among the nations.[104]

The Zechariah text is more a theological program than a concrete proposal. However, lest such a statement suggest that Zechariah 14 is out of touch with the real world, one should compare this sentiment of a multi-ethnic pilgrimage to the sentiment expressed in Nehemiah 8, namely, that only those Judeans who were in exile participated in the feast of booths. Zechariah 14 is presenting quite a different, more inclusive view of what a Yahwistic feast might entail.[105] That it did not develop in such a way is, perhaps, a testimony to the radicality of his rhetoric. Persian-period Yahwists were confronting cultural pluralism and were proposing various ways to address the manner in which those who had not been part of the Israelite heritage might be related to Yahweh.

The former element, the notion of the feast of booths as celebrating Yahweh as king, is not explicitly attested elsewhere in the OT. Rather, here the author has simply employed a well-known liturgical title for Yahweh, namely, "king," which was surely current in Israel as early as the tenth century B.C.E. and, most probably, earlier.[106] One senses that Yahweh as the king in Zech. 14:16–17 is more related to the fifth saying, v. 9, than it is to some postulated connection between a celebration of Yahweh as king and *sukkôt*. In this montage, Yahweh has been depicted in various roles—as creator of theophany, combatant, and now again, as king.

If v. 16 serves as a call to pilgrimage by survivors from the nations, vv. 17–19 challenge those who do not proceed to Jerusalem with a specific threat: absence of rain. There is an intriguing connection between the lack of rain and the festival of *sukkôt*. Though the OT does not attest this link, the section of the Mishnah devoted to this feast, *Sukkah* 4:9–10, reports a libation practice in which both wine and water are dispensed into silver bowls. One may theorize that these two liquids were important in diverse ways: the wine as a symbol of the just-completed harvest (*sukkôt* apparently celebrated both the grain and the grape harvest, Deut. 16:13), and water as a symbol of the soon-to-arrive fall rains.[107] Nonetheless, since *Sukkah* 4:9 indicates that water could be poured into the wine vessel, and wine into the water vessel, one should not press too

---

[104]Given later descriptions of the feast in Mishnah *Sukkah*, there is little reason to think that such a multi-ethnic or international feast ever developed.

[105]This should not be romanticized, since vv. 17–19 allow this inclusiveness to serve as the basis for indictment and punishment of those, e.g., Egypt, who might not participate in the pilgrimage.

[106]On which see, conveniently, Kraus, *Theology of the Psalms,* 26–30.

[107]Cf. MacRae, "The Meaning and Evolution of the Feast of Tabernacles," 273.

strictly the difference between these two liquids. Both symbolize the richness of agricultural fertility.

More importantly, the lack of rain, rather than its presence, is at issue in v. 17. And the threat of drought is a much more universal issue than its putative connection with *sukkôt.* The threat of no rain or drought is found as a treaty curse in Deut. 28:22–24, wherein the issue is lack of obedience to Yahweh's will. And this same issue lies at the heart of Zechariah 14, namely, Yahweh's will that the survivors of the nations appear at Jerusalem. Though the syntax of the final line in v. 17 does not state who will keep the rain from falling, there can be little question that the author and his original audience understood the controlling figure to be "the king, Yahweh of Hosts."

Throughout this montage, its creator has made repeated reference to nations or peoples who would attack Jerusalem or stand in an adversarial status with Yahweh. Zechariah 14:18 identifies a specific nation, Egypt (or more precisely, the community [*mišpāḥāh*] of Egypt). The case of Egypt provides the raison d'être for vv. 18–19, which are concerned to note that if Egypt does not participate in the pilgrimage, then they will suffer a distinctive punishment. The presence of the "if" clause, and not a "when" clause, allows one to maintain that this author held no special animus against Egypt. Rather, the author is concerned to make sure that, of the societies about which he was aware, there was an appropriate punishment. The "plague" of drought would work for any Syro-Palestinian country. But, for a riverine culture, one that depended on the Nile and annual flooding, rather than seasonal rains as is the case in Syria-Palestine, another punishment would be necessary.

Though vv. 18–19 clearly make the case that Egypt will be punished in a manner different from the other countries, the author does not indicate what that plague will be. Why? Perhaps because he does not know. More likely, there was a tradition of many plagues that might be directed against Egypt (Exodus 7–11); and simply to note that there would be a plague against Egypt allowed for manifold possibilities, from the grotesque (frogs) to the lethal (death of the firstborn).[108] By allowing for these options, and by citing none, the author creates an ominous tone. One might think that such rhetoric was designed to gain compliance, by creating fear and anxiety. But there is little reason to envision the author addressing the Egyptians directly—the language is not that of direct discourse. Rather, the saying has more to do with theodicy than it does with polemics. The saying assures those in Judah that whoever does not follow Yahweh's edict will be punished, including the enemy of old, Egypt. As a result, one may view Yahweh's ways as reliable and just.

---

[108]One has the sense that vv. 18–19 are a prolix solution to a problem—how to deal with Egypt. By dint of their specificity, reference to Egypt, and prolixity, one might claim that they have been added to vv. 16–17.

[20–21] The final or tenth saying is like the penultimate one in that it deals with the ritual matters. Moreover, just as vv. 16–19 treated a specific feast, this saying identifies a number of objects: tack, pots, basins. Here, even more than in the last saying, the focus is on *the* holy place, the temple, and the radical holiness that might stem from it. Before attending to this fundamental issue of holiness, it is imperative to be clear about the specific objects mentioned.

Some commentators have begun this process of specification by linking vv. 20–21 to the foregoing ones; in this view, the horses belong to those on the requisite pilgrimage to Jerusalem.[109] Since the formal literary features of this montage make such an approach unlikely, one must ask initially, what sort of horse tack might become holy? Fortunately, one element in the description of Jerusalemite temple practices that Josiah attacked provides help. Second Kings 23:11 reports that Josiah had removed horses from the entrance to the temple. These horses had been dedicated to the sun, presumably to Shamash, the Mesopotamian sun god. In addition, the writer states that he burned the chariots of the sun. Horses could be part of the temple accoutrement. But were they real horses or statuary? Many have presumed the latter.[110] However, the verb used to describe the act with which Josiah dealt with them, *šbt* (hiphil), is also used in 2 Kings 23:5 to describe what he did to priests. He deposed or removed them, he did not have them executed. By analogy, the horses too may have been live animals, which were removed from the temple complex, not slaughtered. (There were, of course, other live animals in and around the temple precinct, i.e., those to be sacrificed.) If live horses were present, they would, no doubt, have been bridled (cf. the tack referred to in Zech. 14:20) in order to enable those responsible to handle them. Nonetheless, even if the horses were statuary and had tack, like the bridles on bronze castings, the basic point would be the same. Something that is not normally construed as holy—horse tack—would become holy on Yahweh's climactic day.

The author makes a similar point in the second part of the verse: normal pots in the temple complex will be as holy as altar basins. Here one enters the complex world of ritual utensils. Both terms, *sîr*, "pot," and *mizrāq*, "basin," refer to metal utensils used in temple ritual. The pot was normally made of bronze and used to collect ashes from the altar (Ex. 27:3; 38:3; 2 Kings 25:14). The basin, though it could belong in a list along with a pot (so Jer. 52:18), was apparently made of gold (1 Kings 7:50; Neh. 7:70; cf. Num. 7:13, where a silver basin is mentioned). Numbers 7:13, 19, 25, et al., provide evidence of one use to which the basin was put, namely, the presentation of a cereal offering (*minḥāh*), and also, apparently, an incense offering. The basin would seem to have been a more holy object, both because it was made of precious

---

[109]See, e.g., Mitchell, *A Critical and Exegetical Commentary on Haggai and Zechariah,* 356.
[110]See, e.g., J. Gray, *I and II Kings,* OTL, Philadelphia, 1977.

metal and because it was used to present offerings.[111] The pot, by comparison, was made of bronze and could be used as a container for the residue of ritual offerings. "On that day," this author avers, these containers will be equally holy, which is the functional meaning of the phrase "like basins used at the altar."

This notion of radical sacrality "on that day" is heightened in v. 21. The author moves beyond those objects normally associated with the temple complex to "every pot in Jerusalem and in Judah." There is no reason to think he is referring only to those pots at ritual sites or only to those pots already devoted to ritual purposes. Rather, as would be consistent with his purposes, he refers, quite simply and literally, to all similar pots throughout Judean territory. Moreover, all who make sacrifices will use these holy receptacles for the purposes of their sacrifice. If one may discern a logic in this verse, it involves the radical increase in the number of people making sacrifices, and the concomitant increased demand for those items used in sacrificial practice. In order to meet this demand, holiness will accrue to all pots of appropriate size so that those who want to perform a sacrifice may do so.[112]

Zechariah 14:21c provides something of an afterthought (see commentary above on the use of "Canaanite" for "trader" in 11:7, 11), one that is, however, consistent with the general tenor of the saying. The temple compound, which was a place of economic transaction, would no longer be such.[113] In the mind of this author, the absence of traders must reflect the radical holiness that would obtain on "the day of the Lord." The author is concerned with creating and preserving the conditions of holiness (cf. Joel 3:17, though there "strangers" might sully Jerusalem, a very different notion from Zech. 14:16-17).

I offer two final comments on the montage of Zechariah 14. First, though I have treated this material as if it were made up of diverse elements, I would reemphasize a point made earlier. The segmentations created by "on that day" formulae divide less diverse material than that which made up 12:1–13:6. Although language of plot is too strong, the text does present a sequence, the flow from disruption to resolution and then to radical holiness, which develops in a programmatic manner. The surface rhetoric of ten distinct sayings may

---

[111]On the different ritual statuses of metals as understood by the notion of "material gradation," see M. Haran, *Temples and Temple-Service in Ancient Israel: An Inquiry into the Character of Cult Phenomena and the Historical Setting of the Priestly School,* Oxford, 1978, 158–59.

[112]It is inappropriate to think of a "universal holiness," Mitchell, *A Critical and Exegetical Commentary on Haggai and Zechariah,* 293; Willi-Plein, *Prophetie am Ende,* 91, or a total abrogation of the distinction between secular and sacred, Mason, *The Books of Haggai, Zechariah, and Malachi,* 133. There will still be "traders," that is to say, nonsacred entities.

[113]Cf. the similar sentiment in Matt. 21:12. More generally, the temple functioned as a treasury; on which see Neh. 10:32–39; 12:44–47.

well belie considerable literature that was created specifically for this montage.[114]

Second, this montage is, despite images of rotting flesh, rape, and destruction, surprisingly favorable to those Yahwists associated with Jerusalem.[115] Of the ten vignettes or sayings, all but the first are decisively favorable.[116] The vivid depiction of devastation, of Yahweh's enemies for the most part, should not prevent us from discerning the author's intent of affirming that Yahweh's day will be, finally, one of weal for Persian-period Yahwists in the province of Judah. For reasons we are now unable to discover, the author thought this "day" was imminent; presumably it was a shared conviction, since no time is spent defending it. What the author does do is create a complex montage of that "day," one that grows out of earlier Israelite traditions but makes the "day" more palatable than it had been in the eyes of his prophetic predecessors or, more concretely, those who knew the story Yahweh's "day" against Jerusalem in 587 B.C.E. Despite those events, this author is able to live out of the earlier convictions according to which Jerusalem will be defended and offer fertility and security to those associated with it and the God who is venerated there.

---

[114]Cf. Saebo, *Sacharja 9–14,* 308, who discerns a complex process of growth, at least three stages, the earliest of which involved day-of-Yahweh traditions. He thinks the process started with traditional prophetic material and moved in a priestly-cultic direction.

[115]Cf. Lacocque, *Zacharie 9–14,* 200, who discerns a dialectical quality, both a positive and negative significance, in Zechariah 14.

[116]Hence I do not agree with Mason, *The Use of Earlier Biblical Material in Zechariah IX–XIV,* 255: "One thing seems clear. Chapter 14 appears to reflect a more pessimistic and hostile attitude to Jerusalem than chapter 12." This judgment obtains only for the first saying in Zechariah 14.

MALACHI
THE THIRD "ORACLE"

Malachi 1:1

Introduction

1:1 An oracle, the word of Yahweh to Israel, through his messenger.[a]

a. Virtually all recent English translations render MT *mal'ākî* as a proper name, "Malachi" (so RSV, NRSV, NASB, NIV, NEB, REB, NAB, GNB, JPS). For a defense of such a construal, see Baldwin, *Haggai, Zechariah, Malachi*, 1972, 211–12; Rudolph, *Haggai-Sacharja 1–8/9–14—Maleachi*, 1976, 247–48; Verhoef, *The Books of Haggai and Malachi*, 154–56; and Glazier-McDonald, *Malachi: The Divine Messenger*, 1987, 27–29. However, a number of scholars have expressed dissatisfaction with such a view, e.g., Mason, *Haggai, Zechariah, Malachi*, 1977, 139, and G. Botterweck, "Jakob habe ich lieb—Esau hasse ich," *BibLeb* 1 (1960): 28–29. R. Veuilleumier, *Aggée, Zacharie, Malachie*, CAT XIc, Neuchâtel, 1981, 223–24, follows LXX and translates "of his messenger," which he deems the original text. LXX reads *en cheiri aggelou autou*, "at/by the hand of his messenger," which apparently presupposes a Hebrew form *mal'ākô*. LXX seems to attest the original form of the superscription. It fits better with the third-person discourse of the booklet's introduction, whereas MT is, in all likelihood, a form influenced by *mal'ākî*, which is found in Mal. 3:1.

At the end of the verse, LXX continues with *thesthe dē epi tas kardias hymōn*, "Lay it, I pray, to heart," a clause that has almost certainly been inserted on the basis of similar language in LXX of Hag. 2:16, 19.

[1:1] As was the case with Zech. 9:1 and 12:1, the word *maśśā'*, "oracle," is followed immediately by the phrase "the word of Yahweh." Next, the aforementioned texts designate a nation: in Zech. 9:1, "against the land of Hadrak," in Zech. 12:1, "concerning Israel." Similarly, Mal. 1:1 names Israel. However, the preposition connecting the oracle to the nation is *'el*, "to," rather than *'al*, "concerning," as it was in Zech. 12:1. If I am correct in understanding Malachi as the third in a series of deuteroprophetic collections, the sequence of prepositions relating these collections to various nations or territories is especially significant: *b*—against a foreign nation (Zech. 9:1), *'al*—concerning Israel (Zech. 12:1), and *'el* to Israel (Mal. 1:1). These introductions make up a sequence rather like that attested in other prophetic books, oracles against nations, oracles against Israel, oracles on behalf of Israel (e.g., the primary sequence in Amos and the Septuagint of Jeremiah). As one moves through the three *maś'ôt*, the discourse has shifted one hundred and eighty degrees, from direct discourse against a foreign nation in Zech. 9:1 to direct affirmation of Israel in Mal. 1:1–5.

The introductory formula in Mal. 1:1 differs from both its predecessors

(Zech. 9:1 and 12:1) in more than just the use of prepositions.[1] Malachi 1:1 includes information about the method by means of which this oracle has been transmitted to Israel. It came *bĕyad mal'ākô,* "through his messenger." We encounter again a personage with the same title as the individual present in the visions of Zechariah 1–8: the divine messenger. However, in Mal. 1:1 the messenger does not stand in dialogue with a human prophet. Instead, the messenger functions as herald of the deity to the nation, or more particularly, to the second temple Judean community, which is here labeled Israel.

The phrase *bĕyad,* "through," is used elsewhere in the prophetic corpus to refer to prophetic intermediation, "through Jeremiah the prophet" (Jer. 50:1), and "through Haggai the prophet" (Hag. 1:1), and "through Isaiah son of Amoz" (Isa. 1:1).[2] As a result, there is prima facie reason to view the messenger here as a human figure. During the early Persian period, another Yahwistic author used the language of "messenger" to refer to prophets (2 Chron. 36:15). The language of *bĕyad,* "through," places this discourse firmly within the ambit of prophetic authority.[3]

With such a superscription, this collection is provided with a different sort of authority than are the initial two *maś'ôt.* The two foregoing collections were anonymous, achieving their "prophetic" authority through the name of Zechariah, the putative author of the earlier prophetic book to which they had been appended. Not so with Malachi, for in this case an unnamed figure is viewed as the vehicle by means of which these speeches had been conveyed and, presumably, preserved. The existence of such an individual explains why a name for him, Malachi, evolved over time and why these verses were attributed to him as a separate prophetic book. However, in their current canonical setting these chapters are related to the world of Zechariah ben Berechiah. For in that corpus there was also a messenger, "the angel of the Lord" (e.g., Zech. 1:1–12).

Perhaps it is enough to claim that the attribution of this collection to "his messenger" represents a move beyond the anonymity of typical deutero-prophetic collections and toward the regular pseudonymity of apocalyptic literature. By including "his messenger" in the booklet's introduction, the author/editor has invested the collection with an authority different from the earlier *maś'sôt,* where the authority is related to the visions of Zechariah I. Here the authority resonates, albeit in an ambiguous way, with the powerful "messenger" depicted in Malachi 3.

---

[1]See also Glazier-McDonald, *Malachi,* 26–27, who emphasizes the differences in the structure and significance of the three formulae. Cf. P. Verhoef, *The Books of Haggai and Zechariah,* 187–92, who devotes considerable attention to the meaning of a *maśśā'* in the formulae.

[2]See similarly, Glazier-McDonald, *Malachi,* 27.

[3]Cf. O. Steck, *Der Abschluss der Prophetie im Alten Testament,* 1991, 133, who thinks the phrase was used to establish continuity with figures at least as far back as Moses.

Malachi 1:2–5

The God who loves and hates

1:2 "I love you,"[a]
   says Yahweh.
   "And yet you say, 'How do you love us?'
   Is not Esau the brother of Jacob?"
   says Yahweh.
   "Although I truly love Jacob,
3   I hate Esau.
   I have made desolate his hills,
   and have given over his inheritance to desert jackals.[b]
4 If Edom says,[c] 'We are broken,
   but we will build again out of the ruins,'
   Thus says Yahweh of Hosts:
   They may build, but I will destroy.
   They will be called 'an evil territory,'
   the people whom Yahweh has cursed forever.
5 Your own eyes will see; you will proclaim,
   'Yahweh is great beyond the borders of Israel.' "

a. See GKC, 106g for a discussion of the *qatal* form used to describe present tense of affections and states of mind; similarly Rudolph, *Maleachi*, 252–53. Cf. Verhoef, *The Books of Haggai and Malachi*, 193.

b. For MT *lĕtannôt*, some have proposed a verb, *nātattî*, i.e., "I have made his inheritance a wilderness." Others have taken that form as a plural construct noun, *lin'ôt*, i.e., "his inheritance to desert dwellings," and in so doing have construed the consonants *lt* as a dittography from the end of the previous word, *naḥălātô*. Most LXX manuscripts read *eis domata erēmou*, "into dwellings of the wilderness." This reading presupposes a Hebrew form *nĕ'ôt*, and is adopted by, among others, REB and JPS. Cf. A. von Bulmerincq, *Der Ausspruch über Edom im Buche Maleachi*, Dorpat, 1906, 10–11.

c. Edom is normally a masculine noun, yet here it is linked to a feminine verb.

[1:2–5] That Yahweh should announce his love for Israel is, perhaps, not unusual (cf. Hos. 11:1, "when Israel was a child, I loved him"). A similar claim may be found in Deut. 7:8, "but it is because Yahweh loves you and is keeping the oath which he swore to your fathers . . . ." The first hallmark of this claim is that Yahweh addresses Israel directly in the second person. At the outset, the discourse involves "you," not the less direct speech about Jacob and Esau.[4]

[4]So similarly, J. Botterweck, "Jakob habe ich lieb—Esau hasse ich: Auslegung von Malachias 1:2–5," *BibLeb* 1 (1960): 35.

Unusual is the direct challenge by an indefinite voice, "How do you love us?" Such a contestive tone might have seemed apt immediately after the defeat of Jerusalem in 587 or during the Babylonian exile, but not during the early part of the fifth century B.C.E.

This challenge to Yahweh's affirmation of his love raises a number of questions, one of which is form-critical. What sort of conversation is going on? More particularly, do vv. 2–5 comprise a particular form of discourse? Here, and elsewhere, the book of Malachi incorporates direct speech and dialogue that is often confrontational. Whether such dialogue entails one specific *Gattung* is the central issue for debate. Since Mal. 1:2–5 really involves three parties in direct speech—Yahweh (1:2a, c, 3, 4b, 5a), Israel (1:2b, 5b), and Edom (1:4a)—it does not seem appropriate to describe the unit as a disputation, which typically presumes that there is an argument between only two parties. This fact, plus the positive affirmation that Yahweh elicits from Israel, constrains one to use a more general formal description than "disputation" to describe this rhetorical unit, which is a diatribe-like construction (see Introduction above).

Israel as a whole appears to respond to this asseveration of love by the deity. The verb, "you say," is second masculine plural in form just as is the pronominal object suffix, "I love *you.*" Conversation occurs between two related partners.

The vocabulary used in this interchange between Yahweh and Israel points directly to the covenant relationship. The term "love" may, of course, refer to deep feelings. However, it may also describe the covenant relationship that existed between Yahweh and Israel, as it does in Deuteronomy.[5] Moreover, this notion expresses aspects of "love" that are peculiar to the covenant idiom, for example, the idea that love may be commanded (Deut. 6:5). Hence, Yahweh's proclamation to Israel not only bears rich emotional connotations but means as well that the covenant between Yahweh and his people remains in force. Therefore, when Israel questions or challenges Yahweh by asking, "How do you love us?" the question could be rephrased, "What demonstrable evidence may be offered to show that Yahweh is acting as if a covenant relationship between the deity and Israel is still in force?"

Yahweh initially responds to Israel's interrogative challenge with another question. (An indicative claim follows but only after the formulaic "saying of Yahweh," which distinguishes a question from the ensuing asseveration.) Moreover, there is a shift in Yahweh's language away from direct discourse—"you"—to third-person reference. Finally, Israel is personified with the name

---

[5]So the classic article by W. Moran, "The Ancient Near Eastern Background of the Love of God in Deuteronomy," *CBQ* 25 (1963): 77–87.

Jacob. The presence of a rhetorical question, "Is not Esau the brother of Jacob?" implies dialogue, albeit increasingly impersonal, between Yahweh and "Jacob."

How does Yahweh choose to prove his love for Israel and so to demonstrate that the covenant is still in force? He begins to discuss international relations by using ancestral kinship language. The relationship between Esau and Jacob, the eponyms for Edom and Israel respectively, provides the takeoff point both for Yahweh's question and answer. Moreover, the rhetorical question elicits the expected answer. If Israel knew one thing about Esau, it is that he was Jacob's brother. Jacob tricked Esau out of his birthright and his proper place in the system of primogeniture. It is one thing for humans—Jacob and Rebekah—to undertake such trickery and deception; it is quite another for the deity to cooperate. Yet it is precisely such cooperation in this turn of kinship relations to which Yahweh commits himself in order to demonstrate his covenant loyalty to Israel.

The divine speech that follows makes an extraordinary claim. The speech in the last line of v. 2 and then in the first line of v. 3 does not provide an answer to the rhetorical question. Rather it designates Yahweh as one who loves and hates, who loves Jacob and hates Esau. This is peculiar. According to Gen. 25:28, Rebekah loved Jacob, but nowhere are we told that Yahweh, or for that matter Isaac, loved Jacob. Moreover, nowhere in the Genesis material do we find the judgment that Yahweh hated Esau—and we are told that Isaac loved Esau (and that, not surprisingly, Esau hated Jacob, Gen. 27:41). Clearly the language of love and hate inheres in the stories involving Jacob and Esau. However, in Malachi's appropriation of this material Yahweh takes on the loving and hating roles. What Rebekah and Jacob had done earlier is now attributed to Yahweh, though, of course, one might say that the oracle in Gen. 25:23 already foreshadows the deity's position on the relationship between Jacob and Esau.

This divine speech, moreover, demonstrates close familiarity with the place of Esau/Edom in Israelite tradition, especially as it is described in Deuteronomy:

> And charge the people as follows, "You are about to pass through the territory of your kindred, the descendants of Esau, who live in Se'ir. They will be afraid of you, so, be very careful not to engage in battle with them, for I will not give you even so much as a foot's length of their land, since I have given Mount Se'ir to Esau as a possession." (Deut. 2:4–5)

Two elements in this text are important for a proper understanding of Mal. 1:2–5. First, Israel is warned to act properly toward "your brethren, the sons of Esau." Second, Yahweh has given the sons of Esau "Mount Se'ir" as a possession.[6] One may presume that Deuteronomy 2 was known to Judahites during the fifth century B.C.E. Hence we are startled to hear that Yahweh hates Edom.[7] To be sure, there is in the postexilic period a pronounced animosity between Edom and Judah. Nevertheless, if covenant loyalty is at stake, it is striking to hear Yahweh announce a position different from that articulated in *the* covenant document, Deuteronomy.

The antagonism that Yahweh avows toward Edom is not expressed in random terms. Rather, the language is directed at the heart of the Edom tradition. Yahweh had given Mount Se'ir to Edom (Deut. 2:4–5). Hence, if Yahweh is going to demonstrate special favor to Judah, what better way to do it than by desolating Edom's hills, which had been Esau's special gift. Moreover, Deut. 2:5 makes it abundantly clear that Yahweh had given Esau-Edom a possession, one that now will be turned into a haunt of jackals. Again, covenant idiom is prominent. Covenant curses may depict in a rather standard way the fate of an inhabited place as a dwelling place of jackals (*tannîm*).[8] Both the discourse about desolation of mountains as well as the transformation of inheritance to a jackal locale grow out of language associated with covenant.

Some scholars have claimed that Yahweh is simply demonstrating preference for Judah over Edom in a way analogous to Deut. 21:15, in which case a man who has two wives loves one and "hates" the other. Clearly, these commentators suggest, the husband does not "hate" the less preferred wife.[9] However, in Malachi 1 the action and attitude of Yahweh toward Edom— violation of a covenant with Edom and invocation of curses—is in no way similar to a husband's treatment of his wife. In Malachi, hate is hate; and it expresses itself in terms of loss of property and covenant curses. Moreover, the rhetoric requires that Yahweh hate Edom virulently in order to demonstrate his unmitigated love toward Israel.

In Mal. 1:4, the basic theme remains the same, but there are some important variations. First, we are now introduced directly to Edom the country rather than continuing with Esau the eponymous ancestor. Second, a new kind of curse language appears. Rather than a straightforward curse, such as that involving a jackal habitat, the poet introduces a futility curse.[10] Although the

---

[6]Cf. Obad. vv. 9, 19, 21 on Mount Esau.

[7]Edom does play a significant role in the oracles against the nations and in later deuteroprophetic literature (Isa. 34:5–17; Isa. 63:1; Ezek. 35:1–15). In Ezek. 35:1–15, the notions of desolation (*šmm*) and loss of inheritance are prominent.

[8]D. Hillers, *Treaty Curses and the Old Testament Prophets*, BibOr 16, Rome, 1964, 53.

[9]For example, G. Botterweck, "Jakob habe ich lieb—Esau hasse ich," 36–37; W. Rudolph, *Haggai—Sacharja 1–8—9–14—Maleachi*, 225.

[10]D. Hillers, *Treaty Curses and the Old Testament Prophets*, 28–29.

Edomites will try to ameliorate their lamentable condition, their action will not come to fruition. In both these instances, the discourse has shifted to straightforward assessment of a country's situation, rather than the earlier and more allusive discourse of animal dwellers and inheritance.

Words are put into the mouths of certain Edomites: "We are broken, but we will build again out of the ruins." However, in order to demonstrate his covenant loyalty to Israel, Yahweh responds to such an assertion by maintaining that, even if the Edomites rebuild, he will destroy. The result is devastating, Edom will be known as "an evil territory."[11] Moreover, Yahweh's speech is introduced by the formula "thus says Yahweh of Hosts," which occurs more than twenty times in this brief booklet.[12] The relative prominence of this formula suggests that, in this author's judgment, new and authentic words from the deity were being addressed to matters of import in the early fifth century B.C.E.

Such negativity directed against Edom raises obvious questions. When was Edom destroyed to such a degree that Yahweh could claim responsibility for its demise? And, with reference to Mal. 1:4, was there a time when Edom attempted a major rebuilding campaign after a defeat?[13] Such questions are difficult to answer, in part because the biblical traditions concerning Esau/Edom are so complex, in part because we possess little extrabiblical information about the history of Edom.[14] Bartlett holds an especially important revisionist view, namely, Edom was not involved in the destruction of Jerusalem.[15] He contends (23), "The only firm piece of evidence suggests that some

---

[11]See Num. 32:33 for this sense of *gĕbûl* and *gĕbûlāh*.

[12]Cf. J. Smith, *Book of Malachi*, 22.

[13]There have been all too many general references to the Nabateans in the commentary literature as well as to Edomites participating in the defeat of Jerusalem as a way of explaining the presumed depth of Edomite-Judahite enmity, e.g., F. Horst, *Die zwölf kleinen Propheten: Nahum bis Maleachi*, HAT 14, Tübingen, 1964, 265; J. Baldwin, *Haggai, Zechariah, Malachi*, 223.

[14]For an analysis of Esau and Edom traditions, see J. Bartlett, "The Brotherhood of Edom," *JSOT* 4 (1977): 2–27; "The Land of Seir and the Brotherhood of Edom," *JTS* 20 (1969): 1–20; and now *Edom and the Edomites*, JSOTSup 77, Sheffield, 1989. Bartlett maintains that Seir and Esau were linked in the earliest traditions, but that Edom was only later connected with that traditiohistorical complex. This later development resulted in part from Edomite western expansion, and in part from Sennacherib's division of Judah, so also H. Ginsberg, "Judah and the Transjordanian States from 734–582 B.C.E.," *Alexander Marx Jubilee Volume*, ed. S. Lieberman, New York, 1950, 347–368. For a general overview of Edomite history as well as Judahite-Edomite interactions, see J. Bartlett, "The Rise and Fall of the Kingdom of Edom," *PEQ* 104 (1972): 26–37; B. Cresson, "The Condemnation of Edom in Post-Exilic Judaism," *The Use of the Old Testament in the New, and Other Essays*, ed. J. Efird, Durham, N.C., 1972, 125–48; and J. Myers, "Edom and Judah in the Sixth-Fifth Centuries B.C.," *Near Eastern Studies in Honor of W. F. Albright*, ed. H. Goedicke, Baltimore, 1971, 377–92. And on Edom in the Persian period, see Bartlett, *Edom and the Edomites*, 163–86.

[15]J. Bartlett, "Edom and the Fall of Jerusalem 587 B.C.," *PEQ* 114 (1982): 13–24.

Judean refugees found sanctuary in Edom." Of critical importance to these discussions is the thesis that Edom was defeated in 552 B.C.E. by Nabonidus in his so-called Arabian campaign.[16] Since Mal. 1:2–3 presupposes a thorough destruction of Edom, it is unlikely that this text could have been written prior to the destruction of Edomite cities, which occurred c.552 B.C.

J. Bartlett has argued convincingly that Edomite society continued after the mid–sixth-century defeat. Rebuilding efforts of a sort presumed by Mal. 1:4 no doubt began sometime in the late sixth century and may have continued into the early fifth century B.C.E. Archaeological evidence of continued Edomite occupation may be found at Buseirah (Bozrah), Tell el-Kheleifeh, and possibly Petra, data which suggest that rebuilding efforts commenced soon after the Edomite monarchy was defeated by the Neo-Babylonians. It is, of course, inappropriate to attempt to date the book of Malachi by such data, but it is clear that at least this pericope may reflect events dating to the late sixth or early fifth century B.C.E.[17]

The historical dynamics between Judah and Edom were, indeed, complex. Malachi 1, however, does not focus on that strident relationship. Moreover, it would be a fundamental mistake to think that a historical reconstruction will serve as an interpretation of the text. Rather, Malachi 1 focuses on Yahweh's willingness to void an earlier grant to Esau/Edom and to act in a way wholly favorable toward Israel. The point of the pericope is that Yahweh will discriminate on behalf of Israel as he had done in the past. Edom is explicitly cursed, and Judah is implicitly blessed.

This sentence upon Edom is not, it must be said, unusual, or for that matter even original. Jeremiah 49:13 attests the notion of Yahweh's eternal curse on Bozrah, a major Edomite city, "For by myself I have sworn, says the Lord, that Bozrah shall become an object of horror and ridicule, a waste and an object of cursing; and all her towns shall be perpetual wastes."

With Mal. 1:5, the author of this oracle leaves the fate of Edom and moves on to address Yahweh's treatment of Israel and the way in which such treatment will be perceived by Israelites. First, a prediction and then a confession are offered. Israel will observe the fate of Edom with its own eyes. What is to happen to Edom will be readily apparent to all Israel. Second, this direct observation will move Israel to speech, though in terms different from those with which Israel and Yahweh began this dialogue. Israel will move from the vocabulary of love and the grammar of interrogation to the affirmation of

---

[16]So J. Lindsay, "The Babylonian Kings and Edom, 609–550 B.C.E.," *PEQ* 108 (1976): 23–37; cf. J. Bartlett's response, "From Edomites to Nabataeans: A Study in Continuity," *PEQ* 111 (1979): 53–66.

[17]Cf. Glazier-McDonald, *Malachi,* 37–41, who argues that Nabatean pressures on Edom may have influenced Mal. 1:2–5.

Yahweh's international power. Israel will confess not only that Yahweh is great but that he is great beyond Judean territory as demonstrated by the decimation and perpetual curse on Edom.

To say that God is great (*yahweh yigdal*) uses traditional language (cf. Pss. 35:27; 40:16; 70:4; 96:4).[18] The same clause, "he is great," also occurs in Micah 5:4, and there it refers to the role of the Davidic king, "for now he shall be great to the ends of the earth." That formulation, too, broaches the same issues as those in Mal. 1:5, namely, the greatness of the king and the demonstration of power in an international mode. However, in Malachi, the language of international context is more specific—reference to the defeat and permanent devastation of Edom. The international veneration of Yahweh is developed in further discourses (e.g., 1:11, 14).

At some point, one is forced to ask whether Yahweh, by demonstrating his hate and vengeance toward Edom, has proved his love for Israel. Had love here signified an emotional relationship, one would have to raise significant questions about the adequacy of such a response. However, since the issue is really that of covenant relationships, the punishment of a foe and the description of such punishment utilizing covenant vocabulary serves to sustain Yahweh's original contention, "I love you," or perhaps better said, "I have remained loyal to you." Yahweh has been able to demonstrate covenant loyalty, "love," by cursing Israel's enemies and by violating his earlier grant of land to Edom. In effect, Mal. 1:2–5 affirms and theologizes the relationship between Jacob and Esau, as that is worked out in the tetrateuchal traditions. Such is Malachi's oracle against a foreign nation and on behalf of his own people, here known as Israel.

Malachi 1:6–2:9

Concerning Aaronid and Levitical priests

1:6   "A son honors his father,[a]
     a servant his master.
   If I am a father,
     where is the honor due?
   If I am a master,
     where is the reverence due me?
   Thus says Yahweh of Hosts to you,

---

[18]I agree with A. von Bulmerincq, *Der Ausspruch über Edom im Buche Maleachi*, 15–16, that such formulations are indicative, not jussive, though I disagree with his claim that this discourse is essentially eschatological and messianic in significance.

    O priests, who despise my name.
You respond,
    'How have we despised your name?'
7   By offering defiled food upon my altar.
But then you say,
    'How have we defiled you?'[b]
When you say,
    'The table of Yahweh may be despised.'
8   When you offer a blind animal for sacrifice—
    and think there is nothing wrong;
When you offer a lame or diseased animal—
    and think there is nothing wrong.
Present such to your governor!
    Will he accept you[c] or act favorably toward you?"
        says Yahweh of Hosts.
9   " 'Now, seek God's favor,
    that he may be gracious to us.'[d]
But if you have done such with your hand,
    will he act favorably toward you?"
        says Yahweh of Hosts.
10   "Would that[e] there were among you
    one who would close the doors,
so that you would not kindle fire
    on my altar in vain.
I take no pleasure in you,"
        says Yahweh of Hosts.
"I will accept no offering
    from your hand.
11   Just as the rising and setting sun,[f]
    so is my name great among the nations.
In every place incense and a pure offering
    are presented to my name,
because my name is great among the nations,"
        says Yahweh of Hosts.
12   "But you profane it when you say,
    'The table of the Lord is defiled.
    Its food may be despised.'[g]
13   You say, 'What a nuisance!'
    But you still ignite it,"
        says Yahweh of Hosts.
"You bring stolen goods,
    the lame, and the diseased.

You bring such an offering!
    Should I accept it from your hand?

14 Cursed is the cheater
    who has a male animal in his flock, and pledges it,
    and yet sacrifices a blemished one to Yahweh.
Truly, I am a great king,"
      says Yahweh of Hosts.
"My name is venerated throughout the nations.

2:1 Now, O priests, this commandment is for you.

2 If you do not listen or lay it to heart,
    to give glory to my holy name,"
      says Yahweh of Hosts,
"then I will let loose the curse against you.
    I will curse your blessings.
In fact, I have already cursed them,[h]
    because you have not laid them to heart.

3 Behold, I am removing your progeny.[i]
I will spread dung over your faces,
    dung which results from your festivals.
You will be carried away from me.[j]

4 Know[k] that I have delivered this commandment to you
    so as to enforce[l] my covenant with Levi,"
      says Yahweh of Hosts.

5 "My covenant was with him,
    and (meant) life and peace.
These I allocated to him and he revered me,
    he venerated[m] my name.

6 True torah[n] was in his mouth,
    perversity could not be found on his lips.
He walked with me peaceably and properly.
    He even turned many away from evil.

7 Indeed, the lips of a priest should preserve knowledge.
    People should seek torah from his mouth
    because he is the messenger of Yahweh of Hosts.

8 But you have left the way.
    You have caused many to fall away from torah.
    You have violated the covenant of Levi,"
      says Yahweh of Hosts.

9 "Hence, I am making you despicable and humiliating you
    before all the people,
Since you have not kept my ways
    and have shown partiality in (matters of) torah."[o]

a. MT reads literally, "a son honors a father."

b. LXX reads "polluted it." Following the principle of *lectio difficilior,* I follow MT.

c. LXX reads "accept it." Again, *lectio difficilior* points to MT as the better reading.

d. Instead of MT *wîḥānēnû,* I read *wîḥānnēnû.*

e. On the rhetorical uses of *mî,* see BDB, 566.

f. Reading *kĕmimmizraḥ* instead of *kî mimmizraḥ.* The author establishes an apt analogy to express the cosmic significance of Yahweh's name. NRSV et al. improperly constrain the image by limiting the analogy to daylight hours.

g. *wĕnîbô* is probably a dittographic expansion based on the first two consonants of the ensuing word, *nibzeh.* After the aforementioned word is excised, the quoted speech has a regular rhythm. Cf. Ehrlich, *Randglossen,* 358, who proposes deleting the entire final clause.

h. Cf. LXX, which presupposes a singular pronominal suffix as opposed to the plural one in MT. The next verb in v. 2 also occurs with a singular suffix.

i. MT reads *gō'ēr,* "rebuke." However, the rest of the verse describes a fate harsher than a rebuke. Moreover, LXX reads *egō aphorizō hymin ton ōmon.* The verb *aphorizō* apparently presupposes the Hebrew form, *gōrēa',* which I translate here as "remove." See the standard commentaries, esp. Verhoef, 240–42; also Glazier-McDonald, *Malachi,* 66–67; and K. Budde, "Zum Text der drei letzten kleinen Propheten," *ZAW* 26 (1906): 22.

j. MT reads literally, "and he will lift you up for or to it." I propose *wĕniśśā'tem,* "you shall be carried away from me." MT, *wĕnāśā' 'etkem 'ēlâw,* represents an incorrect word division and subsequent confusion from the original clause, *wĕniśśā'tem mē'ālay.*

k. See the standard grammars for the use of the converted perfect in the imperative sense.

l. Reading *lĕḥayyôt* instead of MT *liḥĕyôt;* so, e.g., Rudolph, 260.

m. Parsing *niḥat* as a niphal from *ḥtt,* not a piel from *nḥt.* So similarly, Veuilleumier, 239 n. 5., Rudolph, 260 n. 5c.

n. *tôrat 'emet* is a case of hendiadys.

o. Literally, "lifting up faces in the torah."

This complex interweaving of discourse constitutes the longest section in Malachi (eighteen verses).[19] In this second diatribe-like construction, Yahweh speaks with and challenges a more limited audience, the priests, as opposed to all Israel, as was the case in 1:2–5. In 1:6–13, Yahweh prods and the priests

---

[19]These verses have spawned a considerable number of scholarly publications. One monograph is devoted exclusively to these verses, H. Utzschneider, *Künder oder Schreiber? Eine These zum Problem der "Schriftprophetie" auf Grund von Maleachi 1,6–2,9,* BEATAJ 19, Frankfurt, 1989. Utzschneider argues that prophets can undertake their task by writing a text, not (as Gunkel, Koch, et al., argue) only in oral proclamation. Malachi is an example of such a writing or literary prophet. Utzschneider proceeds by addressing the issue of "co-textuality," which involves judgments both about the inner coherence of the pericope and the relationships between this text and other earlier texts.

respond. The speaker alternates at least nine times. But then, in 2:1–9, dialogue ceases. After the curse in 1:14, Yahweh is the sole speaker for the rest of the unit.[20]

This section appears segmented—1:6–11, 12–14; 2:1–3, 4–9 are divisions that may be sustained on grammatical and formulaic grounds. The first two of these sections conclude with an emphasis on the international veneration of Yahweh, as was also the case in the earlier discourse, Mal. 1:5.[21] The last three sections are introduced by direct address, and the middle two by disjunctive syntax.

[1:6] As the diatribe commences, Yahweh cites a proverb that involves appropriate behavior by a son or servant toward his father or master. A quick look at the Decalogue (e.g., Ex. 20:12) reveals that just such behavior is appropriate, namely, the honoring (*kbd*) of one's parents. Numerous proverbs also attest this same notion of the importance of honoring parents (e.g., Prov. 13:1; 19:26). And by inference, servants should adopt a similar attitude (though there is no such claim attested explicitly in the OT). The two-line proverb is presumably cited by way of establishing common ground attested in both Israelite legal and proverbial formulations. Few could disagree with this claim made in Mal. 1:6.

Then Yahweh continues with a series of questions in which he takes the role first of the father and then of the master. The questions are not rhetorical; they demand an answer. But none is provided—at least not immediately. There are, however, implicit answers, though not from those with whom Yahweh is in dialogue. Malachi 1:14 reports that the deity's name is venerated internationally. As a result, one answer to the double-barreled question might be: you are venerated throughout the world (not in Judah?). Malachi 2:5 provides another perspective, namely, that Yahweh had been revered appropriately by certain priests, Levites. However, because of what had happened to the Levites, such veneration was a thing of the past. In sum, there are answers to these questions embedded in the long dialogue. Nonetheless, the individuals responsible for this literature did not juxtapose them directly with the questions. The questions stand without any clear response.

---

[20]It is possible to view 2:1–9 as a word of judgment, so Pfeiffer, who terms it a *Drohrede*, "Die Disputationsworte im Buche Maleachi," 559. However, it is difficult to maintain that this dialogue fits easily the threefold scheme for which Pfeiffer, among others, have argued. Pfeiffer and, most recently, Lescow, "Dialogische Strukturen in den Streitreden des Buches Maleachi," 194–212, have had to argue for numerous additions to an original and shorter (and "purer") form in order to make this case. Cf. M. Fishbane's judgments about the chaotic form of these verses—he views it as a *Mischgattung*, "Form and Reformulation of the Biblical Priestly Blessing," *JAOS* 103 (1983): 119.

[21]The formulaic expressions, "says Yahweh of Hosts," (vv. 8, 9, 10, 11, 13, 14; 2:2, 4, 8) do not appear to mark these major divisions. One almost has the sense that these function not unlike the "on that day" formulae in Zechariah 14.

The final line of Mal. 1:6 includes an indictment against all priests.[22] Yahweh instigates verbal encounter by addressing the priests directly and by characterizing them as those who despise his name. The name of the deity represented the person and honor of a deity. Hence, to despise the name of the deity approximates despising the deity. The charge offers a radical challenge to a priest whose task involves regular veneration of that deity. But why did the author choose to use this circumlocution, namely, despising the deity's name? The answer lies in the primary canonical document that attests the significance of Yahweh's name, Deuteronomy. There Yahweh's name constitutes a theologoumenon bound to a place, the ritual center at Jerusalem (Deut. 12:11, "to the place which the Lord your God will choose to make his name dwell there"; cf. Deut. 16:2, 6). Moreover, these texts (Deut. 12:11 and 16:2a, 6) include admonitions for Israel to offer sacrifices. From the perspective of these admonitions, to despise Yahweh's name means more than simply denigrating the deity in some general way. Despising Yahweh's name involves improper ritual practice at the place where Yahweh has caused his name to dwell. The charge is particularly apt, since it was the priests' responsibility to preside over sacrifices at that place where the name of Yahweh is present, namely, the temple in Jerusalem.

The character of the communication between the deity and the priests is, up to this point, striking. Yahweh had asked two questions and received no responses. Only when they had been indirectly accused does dialogue between Yahweh and the priests develop.

[7] Since this description of the priests strikes at the very heart of their official function, it is not surprising that they respond directly, "How have we despised your name?" The priests' query provokes a charge more specific than that with which the unit began, "By offering defiled food upon my altar." This indictment makes explicit the ritual connotation of the first exchange, namely, that for a priest to despise Yahweh's name is to violate certain ritual practices. But then, we must ask, what is it to offer "defiled food" (*lehem měgō'āl*)? This particular term for defilement or ritual pollution is not to be found in the priestly manuals regarding holiness and impurity. For some reason, the author chose a term which was not part of that refined discourse (cf. the vocabulary in Hag. 2:10–14). Even more significant is the use of this term in literature deriving from the period not long after the second temple had been rebuilt, the period described in Ezra-Nehemiah. Ezra 2 contains a list of those who returned from Babylon to Syria-Palestine under Zerubbabel's leadership. Because their genealogies could not be appropriately verified, they were excluded from the priesthood as defiled (*g'l*). "The governor told them that they were not to partake of the most holy food, until there should be a priest to

---

[22]Cf. Veuilleumier, *Malachie,* CAT XIc, Neuchâtel, 1981, 228.

consult Urim and Thummim" (Ezra 2:63). This final statement is intriguing; the status of these priests did not present an open-and-shut case. The genealogical claims of "the sons of the priests" could not be verified by "the genealogies" and had to await divination by a religious functionary, presumably the high priest.

It is at least conceivable that, with the demise of Zerubbabel, presumably the governor referred to in Ezra 2:63, the preliminary decision about these problematic priests may have been forgotten, the more so if ritual activity at the temple required the services of increasing numbers of priests. Hence, priests with less than clear lineages may have participated in the rituals during the early second temple period.

Nehemiah 13:28–29 suggests the probability of just such a situation. Verse 28 alludes to a priest with an improper lineage whereas v. 29 refers to those who had defiled (*g'l*) the priesthood and the covenant of the priests and Levites.[23] Strikingly, the term "defiled," used in Malachi and in Ezra 2, occurs here as well. Moreover, the issue of a covenant with Levi, which occurs late in this Malachi pericope (Mal. 2:4, 8) occurs in Nehemiah 13 as well. Nehemiah 13 clearly alludes to a time during which the priesthood had been sullied by lineage improprieties. What we learn from this brief examination of Ezra-Nehemiah is that Malachi shares a term for desecration that could be applied to the priesthood. Both Ezra-Nehemiah and Malachi show concern for the ritual purity of the priesthood as well as purported instances in which that purity had been violated.

To the specific charge presented in Mal. 1:7a the priests respond again in a question, "How have we defiled you?" This question sounds odd since it does not fit exactly the previous formulations; the deity had not claimed specifically that he had been defiled. Moreover, it sounds odd to think that a deity could be defiled. For those sorts of reasons, one suspects, LXX revised the text to read "defiled it," namely, the altar. Nonetheless, the principle of *lectio difficilior* should prevent us from adopting that reading. In addition, Isa. 63:3 preserves a use of the word *g'l* in which the term refers to the deity's garments, tainted by the blood of those slain in a cosmic battle. Hence, the question asked by the priests is not nonsensical.

The priests' question receives an immediate answer, first by way of a general statement and then by a detailed list of offenses. In the first instance, Yahweh reverts to vocabulary with which this pericope began, "despising," so that by the end of v. 7 one has the impression that the dialogue is proceeding in circles and going nowhere. The only new element is the term introduced in the final line of the verse, "Yahweh's table." Although this includes new vocabu-

---

[23]On which see J. Blenkinsopp, *Ezra-Nehemiah*, 365–66, who, among others, notes the similarity between the situations reflected in Malachi and Ezra-Nehemiah.

lary, it does not advance the argument beyond where it was in v. 7a, a line that mentions Yahweh's altar. The altar and the table may be understood as functional equivalents (Ezek. 41:22). However, in Solomon's temple the table of Yahweh was different from the altar (1 Kings 7).

Despite the fact that no new charge is presented in Mal. 1:7c, a figure of speech is introduced, namely, hyperbole. No priest would ever say, "The table of Yahweh is despised." And yet, that is precisely the speech that the author has placed on their lips. To what effect? The author apparently thinks the priests act as if they despise Yahweh's table. Hence, he translates their actions into language. They now say what they do. And the effect is striking. It would have jarred anyone who heard it just as it would have jarred someone to see a sick animal offered as a sacrifice. By bringing the activity of the priests to linguistic expression, the author has palpably displayed their disregard for Yahweh and his due.

[8] Verse 8 marks a decisive break from the general accusations and counter-questions. The deity now presents a bill of particulars concerning improper ritual practice. The priests are indicted for offering various improper animal sacrifices, animals that are blind, lame, or sick. Such indictments depend on Israelite norms concerning the character of animals appropriate for sacrifice. These norms were articulated in a number of places, such as Lev. 22:18–25; Deut. 15:19–23. Of these two lists, Mal. 1:8 seems to reflect the norm found in Deuteronomy. Two of the three blemishes, blindness and lameness, are cited in Deut. 15:21 whereas only one, blindness, occurs in Leviticus (Lev. 22:22). Moreover, the noun for blindness in Deuteronomy is identical to the one found in Malachi, whereas the noun in Leviticus is not. These lexical data suggest that the indictment in Malachi depends on the formulations found in Deuteronomy. It is, however, necessary to note that the list in Deuteronomy is couched within a discussion of the firstborn sacrifice and not general animal sacrifice, which is the subject matter of Leviticus 22 and Malachi.

Following these specific indictments, there are clauses which, though difficult to translate, apparently present the sentiment, if not the actual words, of those who offer these improper sacrifices. The priests are charged with claiming "there is nothing wrong" with such sacrifices of a blind, lame, or diseased animal.

After these charges, Yahweh admonishes the priests in a peculiar way: "Present such to your governor!" That clause, by itself, could best be described as ironic discourse. No priest would, presumably, be stupid enough to offer anything second-rate to someone of such importance. What would not work in the "secular" realm should not operate in the "sacred" realm either. It may sound odd to think of offering sacrifices to a civil official. We know, of course, that political officials themselves offered sacrifices, for example, the king in the preexilic period as well as the "prince" according to Ezekiel's polity (Ezek. 46:11–15). But there is no evidence of offerings made to such officials. Hence, the admonition is, perhaps, best understood as a reductio ad absurdum; if a governor would not accept such an offering, how much more will the deity find such an offering offensive?[24]

Mention of the governor (*phh*) raises questions about the context in which this ironic rhetoric arises.[25] Suffice it to say that the presence of this term here does not allow this text to be dated easily. Rather, the noun *phh* does allow us to think about a political entity, which included many Yahwists. It was probably a subprovince of the Persian empire and had a "governor" at its head. This official was almost certainly a native Syro-Palestinian and a Yahwist. For the purposes of commenting on Mal. 1:8, it is inappropriate to say more, since the language is analogical and ironic and does not reflect actual behavior of political obeisance.[26]

One ironic speech deserves another. Verse 1:9a is understandable only as an ironic speech of the priests.[27] The priests say something that sounds pious, but the author thought it signified almost the opposite of that which surface rhetoric conveyed, "Now, seek God's favor that he may be gracious to us." This is deceptive dialogue indeed. After having been charged with improper ritual behavior (1:7c–8), they make no direct response and instead offer liturgical language. Instead of addressing the deity with whom the priests have been in dialogue, the priests turn away and in so doing reject the validity of his charges. Things return to "business as usual."

[9] Verse 9a could be labeled a call to worship, though the phrase, literally, "to seek Yahweh's face," is not a technical priestly expression (cf. 1 Sam. 13:12; 1 Kings 13:6; 2 Chron. 33:12; Ps. 119:58; Dan. 9:13; Zech. 7:2). As the texts just cited attest, to *hlh* or "seek" Yahweh may or may not involve sacrifice.

In spite of the priests' turning away from Yahweh, Yahweh goes on with the "dialogue" in 1:9b. This new step in the exchange between Yahweh and the priests introduces a problematic note. If Yahweh is speaking, why does he refer

---

[24]It is interesting that the author uses a different verb, the hiphil of *qrb*, to describe a presentation to the governor, whereas he had heretofore used *ngš*. This lexical variation should not be absolutized since the hiphil of *qrb* is a technical term for offerings to Yahweh in Ezekiel, P, and Leviticus.

[25]See my discussion of this term and office in *Haggai and Zechariah 1–8*, 24–26; and more recently H. Williamson, "The Governors of Judah under the Persians," *TynBul* 39 (1988): 59–82.

[26]The situation is, of course, different in the Greco-Roman period when sacrifices were presented to civil officials.

[27]So G. Botterweck, "Ideal und Wirklichkeit der Jerusalemer Priester: Auslegung von Mal. 1:6–10; 2:1–9," *BibLeb* 1 (1960): 103.

to himself in the third person?[28] It is likely that what the author has preserved here is a fossilized liturgical usage, reflected in Num. 6:26, in which the priest pronounced a phrase such as "Yahweh has shown favor to you" as part of a standard blessing in the temple service.[29]

Despite the negative tone of this challenge in interrogative form (1:9b), the discussion, in theory, remains open since Yahweh's saying is cast as a question. This openness to future discussion continues in v. 10 with Yahweh—in an aside if not a soliloquy—expressing the hope that someone would force the end of sacrificial rites. What is said specifically about the end of such rites provides a tantalizingly palpable description of second temple ritual practice.

[10] The first line of v. 10 raises two issues: What are the doors to which the deity refers and what priests would be responsible either for closing the doors or for kindling fire? First there is the matter of doors. There were, of course, doors that limited entry to the temple building (1 Sam. 3:15). However, that text does not reckon with the problem of multiple sets of doors. Elsewhere, in a description of Solomon's temple, we are told that the *děbîr* (inner sanctuary or holy of holies) had doors (1 Kings 6:31). In addition the *hêkāl*, or large room of the temple, also was provided with a set of doors (1 Kings 6:33) through which one entered from the *'ûlām*. The description of Solomon's temple provides no information about doors to the temple courtyard. For that, we must turn to descriptions of the Priestly tabernacle, which imply that a gate provided access to the temple courtyard or, later, courtyards.[30] Equally apt are the parallel lines of Ps. 100:4, which, some would argue, date to the postexilic period: "Enter his gates with thanksgiving, and his courts with praise."[31] (One presumes properly that such gates, like city gates, had doors.) In sum, doors limited access to various areas within the temple precinct.

If the doors were those of the gates to the courtyard(s), then they would have controlled access to the so-called high altar, which was located in the temple courtyard. If the doors were those providing access to the *hêkāl*, then they would have controlled access to the incense altar (1 Kings 6:20–21) and table for the bread of presence (1 Kings 7:48). Since animal sacrifice seems to be the

---

[28]LXX reads more easily with a first-person verb.

[29]See M. Fishbane, "Form and Reformulation of the Biblical Priestly Blessing," 115–21, who argues that Mal. 1:6–2:9 constitutes an exegetical reworking of the priestly blessing (Num. 6:23–27) in which the earlier text is recast so as to condemn the priests; thus "the priests' cultic language is desacralized and their actions cursed" (119). Just as the priests will be desecrated (Mal. 2:3), so also their language will be profaned. Since I argue that this text has as one of its salient features strife between Levite and Aaronid, it is appropriate to note that the priestly blessing was only spoken by Aaronids.

[30]See M. Haran, *Temples and Temple Service in Ancient Israel: An Inquiry into the Character of Cult Phenomena and the Historical Setting of the Priestly School*, Oxford, 1978, 184–86, 192–93.

[31]Private communication, James L. Mays.

key issue in this text, one might think that the outermost doors are at stake. However, since the table (Mal. 1:7) and incense (Mal. 1:11) are referred to, activity inside the *hêkāl,* and hence, the doors leading into it, may be implied as well. Since Mal. 1:10 refers explicitly to fire on the altar, it is preferable to think that the doors are those of the outermost gates. A final piece of corroborating evidence, and one which is related to the second question, is provided by Ezra 2:42 and Neh. 11:19, a genealogy of certain Levites known as "gatekeepers," which would presumably refer to the outer gates as well. The doors are probably those of the gates to the temple courtyard and the priests responsible for opening and closing those doors are the Levitical gatekeepers.

Yahweh's response (v. 10) is radical. He would like the courtyard doors closed in order to stop the normal round of ritual activity, what I have elsewhere termed the calendrical or maintenance system of sacrifices. This sentiment is a response to offerings that are being undertaken *ḥinnām,* "in vain." There is, perhaps, no better example than the offering scene embedded in the Cain and Abel narrative. In that episode, Yahweh "looked with favor" on the offering of Abel, but not on Cain's offering. Despite the fact that Cain offered an apparently acceptable sacrifice, it was not accepted, or to use the vocabulary of Mal. 1:10, it was offered "in vain." How much more will the offerings cited in Mal. 1:8—blind, lame, sick—be in vain! As a result, Yahweh will no longer accept as "pleasurable" (*ḥpṣ*) an offering from the priest. At this point in the dialogue, one senses resolution and closure. Interrogation and interaction have given way to a judgment—no more sacrifices will be accepted.

[11] This sense of closure is enhanced by the ensuing formulation, Mal. 1:11. The introductory clause provides the warrant for Yahweh's ability to do just what he had said he would do. Yahweh is, according to v. 11, powerful. In a well-crafted figure of speech, Yahweh announces the extent of his greatness with respect to the rising and setting sun (cf. Ps. 113:3). He then compares this dominion to his name's greatness "among the nations." However, just as the motif of Yahweh's greatness is used for a specific effect in Mal. 1:5, namely, to demonstrate his greatness and loyalty to Israel, so in Mal. 1:11 the author is concerned with a specific issue, proper ritual activity for the veneration of Yahweh. Earlier in this pericope, the author had condemned specific forms of improper ritual practice, namely, the offering of defiled animals, and had pronounced an end to normal ritual activity associated with the Jerusalem temple and its personnel. But, if sacrifice at the temple is to cease, what forms of ritual behavior might continue? Malachi 1:11 addresses this issue.

There is considerable debate about the significance of Mal. 1:11. The syntax is difficult as is the meaning of *muqṭār,* which may be translated incense. But why is there reference to incense and/or a pure offering at this point in the text? At least this may be offered by way of response: incense and offering, in almost meristic fashion, refer to the panoply of Israelite offerings, especially if the incense here alludes to that burned inside the *hêkāl*. M. Haran has argued that "the Old Testament itself assumes that the customary and proper place for the ritual use of incense is the temple alone,"[32] and this despite the fact that there were several different forms of incense offerings (for example, there was a difference between censer/courtyard and altar/*hêkāl* incense). If Haran is correct, Malachi has transformed this notion of the Jerusalem temple as the sole place for ritual practice and opened up geographically the veneration of Yahweh.[33]

The basic purport of Mal. 1:11 seems to be this. Proper ritual outside Jerusalem, even outside Israel, can occur.[34] Whether the author knew about Yahwistic shrines at Elephantine, Leontopolis, Samaria, in the Transjordan, we cannot be sure. But the point is clear, whether or not appropriate ritual occurs in Jerusalem, Yahweh's name will be appropriately venerated in other venues.

[12] After this remarkable claim, Yahweh moves back to the dialogical mode and addresses the priests in a way similar to the manner of vv. 6–8. The manner is, in fact, so similar that one wonders what is in vv. 12–13. The name of Yahweh provides a semantic link between vv. 11 and 12. Yahweh charges that his name, referred to in the form of a pronominal suffix in v. 12, is being profaned by the priests. This situation stands in contrast to the glorification of Yahweh's name "among the nations." However, the resonance with v. 7 is even stronger. Both refer to the table of Yahweh; in v. 7 it is despised, in v. 12 it is polluted. In v. 7, food is defiled, whereas food is despised in v. 12. The author is using the same adjectives, though with different nouns, as if to hammer home the point about a defilement of food and table.

[13] Following this reformulation of the charges in v. 12, the dialogue follows with yet another quotation from the priests, "What a nuisance!" This is initially puzzling, and yet finally seems apt. What is truly a nuisance is, at least

---

[32]Haran, *Temples and Temple Service in Ancient Israel*, 237.

[33]Cf. J. Swetnam, "Malachi 1:11: An Interpretation," *CBQ* 31 (1969) 207–8, who argues that the reference is to synagogue prayer. Given Malachi's use of Deuteronomistic traditions, Swetnam thinks it unlikely that Malachi could allow for the possibility of sacrificial activity apart from the Jerusalem temple.

[34]J. Baldwin, "Malachi 1:11 and the Worship of the Nations in the Old Testament," *TynBul* 23 (1972): 117–24, maintains that the worship is that of the nations, not veneration of Yahweh outside Judah. Cf. Verhoef, *The Books of Haggai and Malachi*, 222–32, for a review of the various positions. Both Baldwin and Verhoef suggest that v. 11 refers not to the current scene but to the eschatological or messianic age; so also M. Rehm, "Das Opfer der Völker nach Mal. 1:11," in *Lex Tua Veritas: Festschrift für Hubert Junker*, ed. H. Gross and F. Mussner, Trier, 1961, 193–208. I agree with Rudolph, *Maleachi*, 263; T. Vriezen, "How to Understand Malachi 1:11," in *Grace upon Grace: Essays in Honor of Lester J. Kuyper*, ed. J. Cook, Grand Rapids, 1975, 126–36, and others that the plain sense of the text involves Malachi's judgment about ritual matters during the early fifth century B.C.E.

to the priests, the bothersome iteration of issues as well as the introduction of international perspectives. Had this quotation occurred after v. 11, the logic of the dialogue would have been much more difficult to understand. Verse 12 is much more nuisancelike, almost redundant, than is the radical claim of v. 11.

This brief statement by the priests (v. 12) provides the occasion for Yahweh's rejoinder, "but you still ignite it." Even after Yahweh has pointed out that the sacrifices were unacceptable and even after he had expressed the desire that the doors to the temple courtyard be closed and sacrifices no more be ignited, the priests persist with such inappropriate activity. As a result, Yahweh renews language of indictment, again echoing language used earlier in the dialogue, namely, that in v. 8. The objects for sacrifice are now characterized as "stolen goods, the lame, and the diseased."[35] Earlier (v. 8) the offerings were "blind, lame, and diseased." Two of the categories remain identical (lame and diseased), but stolen has replaced blind. Is this variation significant? Perhaps. In both vv. 8 and 13, the three improper classes of sacrifice serve as examples of what might be much longer catalogs. However, it is true that an object which has been stolen introduces a note of violence, civil crime, which is not present in the first list.[36] Hence, one may speak of a perceptible intensification of Yahweh's argument.

A more general comment is made hard on the heels of these specific cases: "You bring such an offering" (*minḥâh*). The term *minḥâh* had already appeared in v. 10 in a similar summary statement, "I will accept no offering from your hand." (The use of the term in v. 11 is also generic.) In v. 13, the noun is used in a statement summarizing specific cases of ritual infraction. The matter of nonacceptance is broached in a separate clause. Consistent with the rhetoric of this diatribe-like pericope, Yahweh's claim about nonacceptance occurs in interrogative form and is probably to be viewed as a rhetorical question since no answer is forthcoming, and in view of the fact that one knows the answer should be "no."

This final formulation in v. 13 echoes the indicative statement at the end of v. 10. Both clauses contain the verb *rṣh* and the phrase "from your hand." Both clauses mark the end of units of discourse within the larger pericope (after both clauses new form and content arise). Hence one may speak about two dialogic interchanges, vv. 6–11 and vv. 12–14. The latter repeats and develops the former. Both sections conclude with an international focus, a motif with which the first pericope (1:2–5) also ended.

---

[35]These similarities raise the issue of whether vv. 12–13 are a doublette of earlier texts, or whether both vv. 7–8 and 11–12 derive from an earlier original text. My own provisional judgment is that the author has self-consciously introduced this tone of repetition to suggest that the dialogue is not moving in a productive direction.

[36]See Rudolph, *Maleachi*, 259–60, 264, who argues that *gāzûl* can mean either stolen or taken from among wild animals. However the passive participle is consistently used in the former sense.

[14] Verse 14 intensifies and appears to resolve the issues surrounding the use of animals inappropriate for sacrifice. Curses replace questions. To that extent, the rhetoric in v. 14 is much different from that of the foregoing verses, which were essentially dialogic. A curse ends rather than invites dialogue. A curse is the language of punishment, though *'ārûr,* "cursed be . . . ," does not imply directly what the punishment will be. The topic of improper animal sacrifice remains the same, but the audience has apparently changed (see below).

It is instructive to compare the curse formulation of Mal. 1:14 with the curses in Deut. 27:15–26. In form the curses are similar: *'ārûr* plus noun (27:15) or participle (27:20). Moreover, the first of the curses in the Deuteronomy series is of related subject matter, namely, ritual infraction. Since the book of Deuteronomy is suffused with so-called covenant rhetoric, it is appropriate to view that which is prohibited in the curses as a violation of covenant requirements. Deuteronomy 23:21 and the related material in Leviticus 27, both of which address the issues of an object that has been pledged or vowed to Yahweh, suggest that the issue that has evoked a curse in Mal. 1:14, the breaking of a vow, may be construed as a covenant stipulation.

Given the logic of covenant enforcement, that is, the use of curses, it is appropriate to curse the violation of such a vow. It is precisely such a covenant-based curse that we have in Mal. 1:14. The act cursed in Mal. 1:14 is the substitution of a blemished animal for an (apparently unblemished) male from the flock. This matter is addressed in Lev. 27:9–11:

> If it is an animal such as men offer as an offering to the Lord, all of such that any man gives to the Lord is holy. He shall not substitute anything for it or exchange it, a good for a bad, or a bad for a good; and if he makes any exchange of beast for beast, then both it and that for which it is exchanged shall be holy. And if it is an unclean animal such as is not offered as an offering to the Lord, then the man shall bring the animal before the priest. . . .

Though the vocabulary for the acceptable and unacceptable animal is different in Leviticus from that in Malachi, the fundamental issue remains the same, namely, pledging a good thing and offering an inferior thing.

It has been a commonplace to observe that the object of the curse in Mal. 1:14 is different from the object of the indictments in Mal. 1:6–13. One might have expected the priests still to be addressed; here the one who owns an animal, who has pledged an acceptable animal and yet offers a flawed and therefore unacceptable one, is subject to a curse. Yet the issue is more complicated, since Lev. 27:11–12 demonstrates that the priests determined whether an animal was good or bad: "as you, the priests, value it, so it shall be." Hence, if an improper sacrifice is made, the priests must share in the blame. The curse in Mal. 1:14 affects not only the one who pledged the animal but also the ritual officiant–decision maker. As a result, v. 14 belongs with the foregoing verses; priests are involved here as well.

If Mal. 1:14a is loosely though meaningfully related to the foregoing verses, 1:14b seems to have an even more tenuous connection. Yahweh as great king, one whose name is feared among the nations, does not seem to grow out of the language or logic of vv. 12–14a. Rather, these verses serve to terminate this section, in which certain ritual practices have been indicted, just as a similar formula in v. 11 has concluded an earlier subunit. Moreover, the specific phraseology—Yahweh as great king—strikes a similar note, with another conclusion, that in Mal. 1:5. Finally, the notion of Yahweh's kingship resonates with the so-called enthronement psalms that celebrate Yahweh's kingship over the earth (Pss. 96:10; 97:1; 99:1). Put another way, Mal. 1:14 concludes with an almost psalmic or doxological tone.[37]

[2.1] The presence of a disjunctive clause, introduced by the particle *wĕ'attāh*, indicates that Mal. 2:1 marks a discrete stage in the interchange. Moreover, this section of the diatribe-like discourse begins with vocative, which mirrors the grammar in 1:6. Both verses address *hakkōhănîm*, "O priests!" and, in so doing, emphasize that only a certain sector of Judahites is involved in this dialogue with Yahweh. The phrase "this commandment is for you" raises two discrete questions: What is the command, and is the purpose that of admonition or of judgment? This phrase is not found elsewhere in the Hebrew Bible. However, the occurrences of "this command" in Deuteronomy (e.g., Deut. 27:1) indicate that it can summarize all the discrete stipulations (e.g., Deut. 7:11). In Deuteronomic discourse, "this command" is that which people are called to obey, something that is readily doable (Deut. 30:11). Hence, to hear the phrase "this command" is not to be understood as a negative pronouncement, or as another way of saying, "this judgment is for you."[38] In answer to the former question, it is difficult not to look ahead to the occurrence of "this command" in Mal. 2:4, which relates that phrase to the covenant of Levi. Such a reference to covenant not only helps contextualize the "command," since in that context a command signifies one of the covenant stipulations but also helps us understand the imagery and logic of Mal. 2:2–3. Nonetheless, by itself Mal. 2:1 does not offer an explicit tone of judgment.

[2] Things change in vv. 2–3. Whereas reciprocal dialogue had characterized Mal. 1:6–13, from here to the end of this pericope Yahweh alone speaks and, presumably, to the priests. Verses 2–3 are structured in the form of a judgment oracle. However, what would normally be termed an indictment appears as conditional rhetoric: "if you do not . . ." (cf. Isa. 7:9 for similar rhetoric). The theme involves the veneration of Yahweh's name, which also

---

[37]Cf. the doxologies as marking devices in Amos.
[38]Cf. Glazier-McDonald, *Malachi*, 64–65; Verhoef, *The Books of Haggai and Malachi*, 237–38.

appeared in Mal. 1:11, 14. There, however, the phrase appeared as a conclusion and involved the global veneration of Yahweh. By contrast, Mal. 2:1 turns to Judean veneration of Yahweh's name. It is the priests in and around Jerusalem who are challenged to act appropriately with regard to Yahweh's name.

The tone of responsibility and admonition changes quickly with the language of curse. A commandment disobeyed engenders the covenant's curses (Deut. 28:15–57). This covenant logic informs Mal. 2:2–3. However, unlike the rhetoric of Deuteronomy, which keeps the curses in the future tense, Mal. 2:2 reports that the curses are now in force because "you have not laid them (the blessings that might have been) to heart." That language is too general to be convincing by itself. However, the earlier dialogue, 1:6–14, offered sufficient illustrations that clearly describe what sort of ritual behavior would constitute "not laying something to heart."

Malachi 2:2 refers to "your blessings." What blessing is this? Does it refer to some vague covenant notion, or is something more particular at issue? As will become clear below, I do not think special blessings given to Levites can be the subject of such a curse. Moreover, there is no covenant tradition involving Yahweh and all priests. Perhaps one could suggest that the blessing refers to the blessings that the priests dispense (Num. 6:23–27).[39]

To understand these blessings, one must appeal to the Priestly tradition of a covenant between Yahweh and the Aaronid priests, particularly Phinehas, son of Eleazar, son of Aaron. Numbers 25:12–13 reports a covenant with the Aaronid line, "Behold, I give to him my covenant of peace; and it shall be to him, and to his descendants after him, the covenant of a perpetual priesthood, because he was jealous for his God, and made atonement for the people of Israel."[40] Peace or *shalom* here signifies well-being of various sorts, including material welfare. Moreover, this covenant, like the Davidic covenant, guarantees a grant in perpetuity. Such a covenant was, as Weinfeld has shown, modeled on the covenant of grant.[41] As Weinfeld suggests, Num. 18:8 provides an interpretive key. It speaks generally about the priestly portion, which one may infer is a natural entailment of the covenant of grant, the more so since both Num. 18:8 and 25:13 emphasize the perpetual character of the covenant.[42]

One may therefore think that, by the time of Malachi, Israel knew of a covenant between Yahweh and Aaronid priests. To that extent, anything positive that stems from the covenant relationship may be known as a blessing,

---

[39]So J. Baldwin, *Malachi*, 233.

[40]On Phinehas in postexilic literature, see Ezra 8:2; Sir. 45; 1 Esd. 5:5; 8:29.

[41]M. Weinfeld, "The Covenant of Grant in the Old Testament and in the Ancient Near East," *JAOS* 90 (1970): 201–2.

[42]Numbers 18:8–32 is also important since it distinguishes Levitical from Aaronid prerogatives.

and anything negative that might result from the abrogation of the covenant—here violation of priestly duties—can properly be termed a curse.

It is utterly appropriate that Malachi should speak about Yahweh's cursing the blessings of the priests, since one of the primary blessings of the priests was a portion of certain sacrificial offerings. If the priests were being indicted (Mal. 1:6–14) for allowing improper sacrifices, then the priests suffered the result of second-rate offerings, their portion of lame or sick animals. For Yahweh to curse the priestly blessing has a very particular meaning. Yahweh is simply allowing the priests to receive their portion of second-rate sacrifices. By despising Yahweh, they end up despising themselves.

The author of Malachi has made a radically innovative claim. He has combined Sinaitic treaty ideology, conditionality, blessings and curses, with the covenant of grant in order to explore the significance of the "covenant" between Yahweh and the priests. The notion of cursing and blessing in Mal. 2:2 derives from conditional covenant formulations and has been applied to the tradition of an eternal covenant of peace and salt (Num. 18:19) that signifies a special relationship between Yahweh and the Aaronid line.

[3] With Mal. 2:3, the final condemnation appears in the form of a sentence in a judgment oracle. It strikes at the heart of the priestly covenant to which Malachi has just alluded. For Yahweh to remove priestly progeny is to eviscerate the promise of a perpetual line of Aaronid priests (Num. 25:13). Not only will the priestly house end but the current generation of priests will be defiled. The priests will be defiled by fecal material. The author does not use the generic term for human or animal dung (*gēl, gālāl*) but rather the noun *pereš*, which, with one possible exception (Judg. 3:22), appears in texts that describe ritual behavior (Ex. 29:14; Lev. 4:11; 8:17; 16:27; Num. 19:5). In those contexts, the noun refers to the excrement or intestinal contents from a bull or goat that has been slaughtered for use in animal sacrifice. Interestingly, two of the priestly texts refer to the removal of this material as a part of priestly ordination. In all cases, the dung is to be removed from the temple compound and destroyed, that is, burned.

By way of contrast, the *pereš* in Mal. 2:3 is not removed but applied to the priests' faces. It would appear that this use of dung symbolizes the reversal of the ordination process—it removes those individuals from the status of holy to defiled. The festivals mentioned in v. 3 now effect radical impurity and social disintegration rather than sacral continuity and social integration. As a result, the priests, and not—as one would expect—the dung, will be removed from Yahweh. Here, in the final element of the sentence, the priests now have the status of dung, something that must be removed from the ritual complex. What was holy has now become impure. Ritual logic requires its destruction. No more radical condemnation of the Aaronid line can be imagined.

[4] What comes next has consistently puzzled commentators. One topic

continues on from the foregoing verses, that of covenant. Moreover, the vocabulary of commandment, *miṣwāh,* continues. There is, however, a fundamental difference. The author has turned to a different covenant, that with the Levites, not the one treated between Yahweh and the Aaronids, which had been the subject of the previous verses.[43] That such a covenantal understanding of the relationship between Yahweh and the Levitical priests existed is attested in Jer. 33:19–22, a passage that emphasizes the unconditional character of the Levitical priestly and Davidic covenants.[44]

Perhaps such a reflection about Levi and covenant grows out of Deut. 33:9 (cf. Ex. 32:25–29, in which covenant fidelity of the Levites is stressed). Also important is the distinctiveness of the Levites as a priestly group (Deut. 10:8–9; 18:1), though their distinctiveness is not defined in covenantal terms there. In any case, by the time of the early fifth century B.C.E., each of the priestly houses, Levite or Aaronid, spoke about authenticating covenants.[45] This author has used such covenant language to indict the Aaronids (Mal. 1:7–13); that covenant has been violated. Now, v. 4 expresses the hope that the covenant between Yahweh and Levi may be salvaged. This is, at least, the major thrust of Mal. 2:4.[46]

The author uses two nouns to characterize the Levitical covenant, "life and peace." They are significant both because they are normal ways to express the blessings of a covenant relationship and because they may involve blessing for a community. For there to be shalom in Israel, the entire community had to be involved. The term is inherently relational. Moreover, this covenant is viewed as life-giving, not just for the Levites but for the entire Yahwistic community.

[5] "These I allocated to him" (Mal. 2:5) is enigmatic. The pronoun "these" could refer to the life and peace created by the covenant. This is, however, unlikely, since these benefits would accrue to the entire community and not just to the Levitical priests. Instead, the pronominal suffix probably refers to

---

[43]There were later traditions according to which these two covenants were conflated, as in Neh. 13:29, "covenant of the priesthood and the Levites." S. McKenzie and H. Wallace, "Covenant Themes in Malachi," *CBQ* 45 (1983): 549–63, argue that diverse covenant traditions undergird Malachi. A. Renker, *Die Tora bei Maleachi,* 117–21, discusses the covenant background without clarifying the status of a covenant with Levi. U. Devescovi, "L'alleanza di Jahve con Levi (Mal. 2,1–9)," *BibO* 4 (1962): 205–18, understands this covenant to be rooted in Deuteronomic discourse.

[44]Jeremiah 33:19–22 probably dates to a time in the late sixth century B.C.E.

[45]Cf. A. Renker, *Die Tora bei Maleachi,* 93–97, on the priestly-Levitical distinction. E. Meyers, "Priestly Language in the Book of Malachi," 225–37, speaks of a "twofold role of priesthood," namely teaching and (altar) service. G. Botterweck, "Ideal und Wirklichkeit," 108–09 does not accept a distinction among the priests nor does J. O'Brien, *Priest and Levite in Malachi,* 1991. Cf. A. Gelin, "Message aux prêtres (Malachie 2,1–9)," *BVC* 30 (1959): 14–20.

[46]Contra Veuilleumier, *Malachie,* 235, n. 2.

the stipulations that the covenant entailed. These stipulations were given to stimulate an appropriate "fear," that is, worship or veneration of Yahweh. The word *môrā'* is particularly prominent in Malachi and Deuteronomy[47] and would seem to signify the sort of religious disposition involving wisdom and piety. Levites would seem to have been those fulfilling a role of exemplary lifestyle. With the final bicolon of v. 5, the rhetoric shifts from what Yahweh has done to what sort of response Levi made to Yahweh's covenant. The author claims that they behaved properly. Unlike the Aaronids, who had been indicted for despising Yahweh's name, the Levites venerated Yahweh's name.

[6] Verse 6 continues to affirm that the Levites complied with the covenant, a point also made in Deut. 33:9. Assertions are made not only about good behavior but about good behavior related specifically to the Levitical role. They were supposed to offer judicial decisions and to instruct Israelites regarding their covenant responsibilities.[48] Deuteronomy 33:10 makes it clear that Levites are to provide torah, that is to say, covenant-based instruction.[49] Malachi 2:6 avers that the Levites did, in fact, acquit themselves with distinction. One senses an almost quasi-prophetic role for the Levites in Malachi's depiction.[50] To have "true torah" in one's mouth is strongly reminiscent of the notion of the prophet having Yahweh's word in his mouth (Jer. 1:9; Ezek. 3:3–4).

"Perversity," *'awlāh*, is an appropriate antonym for "true torah." In the context of Job 13:7–8 and Isa. 59:3 it is apt to think of "perversity" as meaning improper behavior, particularly in a judicial context, since Levites were obligated to perform judicial tasks. Hence, Malachi's description of the proper functioning of the Levitical covenant continues to highlight an important role of the Levites as those who articulate Yahweh's will for the community.

The second half of the sixth verse reiterates and develops the nature of Levitical covenant obedience. The use of *hlk* (walk) to describe a person's proper place in a covenant relationship is a hallmark of Deuteronomistic prose.[51] Both "peaceably" and "properly" are apt notions to describe the covenant when it is in force. Moreover, not only do the Levites have a proper relationship with Yahweh, they have helped their fellow Israelites avoid grievous error. Such was their responsibility as communicators of Israel's vital religious traditions.

[7] The rhetoric shifts as the author begins v. 7. Heretofore, the language

---

[47]Deut. 4:34; 11:25; 26:8; 34:12; Mal. 1:6; 2:5; cf. Jer. 32:21 in Deuteronomistic prose.

[48]See A. Renker, *Die Tora bei Maleachi*, 121–22, on the legal and instructional character of torah in Malachi.

[49]Cf. Renker, *Die Torah bei Maleachi*, 101–17, who characterizes torah as instruction.

[50]See similarly E. Meyers, "Priestly Language," 231.

[51]M. Weinfeld, *Deuteronomy and the Deuteronomic School*, Oxford, 1972, 332–34.

had been descriptive, characterizing the Levitical covenant relationship with the deity. Now the language becomes prescriptive, stipulating the responsibilities of Levites, with particular emphasis on the vocal role of the Levite. The vocabulary of lip and mouth is appropriate. The Levite is to articulate knowledge and torah. Resonance with the book of Hosea (Hos. 4:4–6) is pronounced. In both Malachi and Hosea, priests are responsible for knowledge (*da'at*) and the people are affected by the performance or lack thereof by the priests.

Then, having prescribed the role of the Levite, the author offers a phrase to describe him, "the messenger of Yahweh of Hosts." The term *mal'āk* had, of course, been used by earlier Israelite writers to describe a variety of individuals: prophet (Hag. 1:13), angel (Gen. 19:1; 21:17), secular messenger (Judg. 6:35). However, the phrase *mal'āk yahweh* is typically used prior to Hag. 1:13 to refer to a minor deity who does Yahweh's bidding. To use this term of a human, as does Haggai and now Mal. 2:7, is revolutionary, the more so since in Mal. 2:7 an entire group—the Levites—have been so labeled.[52] Just as it is difficult to imagine a more negative picture of the Aaronids than that created in Mal. 2:3, it is difficult to imagine a more positive depiction of the Levites than that offered in Mal. 2:6–7.

[8] Hard on the heels of this positive view of the Levites, the deity turns to address directly the priests who had earlier been indicted. This priest has "left the way," in contradistinction to the Levite who has walked with Yahweh (Mal. 2:6) and "turned many away from evil."[53] Though it is difficult to penetrate the metaphor of "leaving the way," one may presume that it involves errors such as those ritual improprieties indicted earlier in the dialogue. In so doing, these priests have disrupted the covenant between Levi and Yahweh, which had provided beneficial decisions for the community.

[9] The logic of such radical disobedience demands justice and punishment. Although these verses do not comprise a discrete judgment oracle, they do provide, as a final element, a statement of Yahweh's punitive action, that is, what we would expect to conclude a judgment oracle. The judgment, as one would expect on the basis of Mal. 2:2, "I have already cursed them," addresses not some punishment set far off in the future but something happening now. The text could, therefore, explain a present lamentable state of affairs. The terms "despised" and "humiliated" are apt, the more so since the first, *nibzîm*, derives from the root *bzh*, which was used earlier in this pericope (Mal. 1:7,

---

[52]Such wholesale elevated treatment of the Levites also occurs in the early postexilic period within the Chronicler's history, which views the Levitical singers as prophets. To term the Levites as messengers of Yahweh seems similar to the ploy of the Chronicler, namely, to invest Levites with a prophetic-like authority.

[53]In both cases the author has used similar imagery to contrast the situations of these respective priests.

12), at which point the author described the offerings presented by these same priests.[54] To treat the priests as despicable is an apt turning of the tables.

The punishment of the priests was addressed earlier (Mal. 2:2–3), and in a very specific way. The present is already cursed, v. 2b. And this temporal statement probably explains the reason for the imminence of the judgment according to 2:9.

The final portion of v. 9 repeats the rationale for punishment by using the language of v. 7. If I am correct in thinking that the Levites are distinct from other priests, according to Mal. 2:7 the Levite was to provide torah, whereas according to v. 9 non-Levitical priests were issuing biased torah judgments.[55] Although the Levites "walked with me," the priests "have not kept my ways." The author, finishing this section on a decidedly negative note, has ended by focusing on the contrast between good and bad ritual officiants: the Levites who had obeyed, and the priests who had not obeyed, in part by offering improper sacrifices and in part by usurping the Levites' role as providers of torah instruction and judgments for the community.

In sum, Mal. 1:6–2:9 is an extraordinarily complex discourse with a long divine speech at its conclusion. The Aaronid priests are rigorously indicted and judged for at least two reasons: for subverting the work of the Levites and making improper sacrifices. By contrast, the diatribe serves as an apologia for Levites and their place in Judahite society.

Nehemiah 13:29–30 provides a context for understanding these charges. Nehemiah is said to have acted with regard to those who had "defiled the priesthood and the covenant of the priesthood and the Levites." Then "I established the duties of the priests and Levites, each in his work." Not only the language but the themes—defiled priests, an inappropriate mixing of priestly roles—seem related to those of Malachi. What were problems for Malachi were problems for Nehemiah, and Nehemiah claims to have solved them.

Malachi 2:10–16

Religious fidelity

2:10 "Do we not all have one father?
Has not one God created us?

---

[54]The other term, *šĕpālîm*, is sufficiently general, the same form occurs elsewhere only in 2 Sam. 6:22.

[55]For a convenient review of these issues, see A. Cody, *A History of Old Testament Priesthood*, AnBib 35, Rome, 1969.

Why then do we act faithlessly with each other,
so as to profane the covenant of our fathers?

11   Judah has acted faithlessly.[a]
An abomination has been performed
in Israel, in Jerusalem.
Judah has profaned the very holiness of Yahweh.
He loves Asherah;[b]
he has married the daughter of a foreign god.

12   May Yahweh cut off anyone from the tents of Jacob
who does such a thing—[c]involving nakedness and improper
cohabitation;[d]
anyone who presents an offering to Yahweh of Hosts.

13   This also you do:
You cover[e] the altar of Yahweh with tears,
with weeping and groaning.
(Yahweh)[f] no longer accepts the offering,
no longer takes it with pleasure from your hand.

14   But, you ask, 'Why?'
Because Yahweh stands as witness
between you and the wife of your youth,
Toward whom you have acted faithlessly,[g]
even though she is your spouse, your covenantal wife.

15   'Has not (the) One made (us),
his vigorous remnant?
What is the One seeking
but a godly[h] progeny?'
Preserve your vitality!
Let no one[i] act faithlessly with the wife of his youth!

16   Divorce[j] is hateful!"
says Yahweh, God of Israel.
"It is like a garment[k] that covers wrongdoing,"[l]
says Yahweh of Hosts.
"Preserve your vitality!
Do not act faithlessly!"

a. Reading *bāgad* instead of *bāgĕdāh;* the *h* constitutes a dittographic expansion.

b. Revocalizing the consonantal text to read *'ăšērāh 'āhēb,* restoring the *h* of *'ăšērāh,* which was lost by haplography.

c. Note the reordering of the clauses in order to identify the subject of the verb *ya'ăšennāh* with the subject of the participle *maggîš.*

d. I repoint the consonantal text to read *'ōr wĕ'ōnâh,* "nakedness and improper habitation." Apart from the standard commentaries, see B. Hartmann, "Mögen die

Götter Dich behüten und unversehrt bewahren," in *Hebräische Wortforschung: Festschrift zum 80. Geburtstag von Walter Baumgartner*, ed. B. Hartman et al., Leiden, 1967, 104–5; B. Glazier-McDonald, "Malachi 2:12: *'ēr wĕ'ōneh*—Another Look," *JBL* 105 (1986): 295–98. Though I understand the grammar differently from Glazier-McDonald, 296, I agree with her that "both words carry a sexual connotation." Cf. C. Torrey, "'ēr wĕ'ōneh in Malachi 2:12," *JBL* 24 (1905): 176–78. 4QXII[a], which reads *'d w'nh*, postdates the misconstrual of the original text.

e. Reading *tĕkassû*, following the LXX *ekalyptete* and the other Hebrew plural forms (*ta'ăśû, miyyedkem*) in this verse.

f. The Hebrew formulation is impersonal, literally, "there is no more accepting the offering." 4QXII[a] reads *m'wn* instead of MT *m'yn*.

g. 4QXII[a] omits this entire clause.

h. An adjectival use of *'ĕlōhîm*, cf. Gen. 23:6.

i. Cf. LXX V T, which presume *tibgōd*, "you (masc. sing.) shall not . . . ."

j. Reading *kî* as asseverative. *šallaḥ* is correctly parsed as either a piel imperative or infinitive absolute. It is plausible to think the text read originally, *šallēaḥ,* the infinitive absolute. On the various words for divorce, cf. Deut. 24:1, 3; Ezra 10:3; Isa. 50:1; Jer. 3:8.

4QXII[a] provides a significantly divergent reading with a second- person verb (*ky 'm śnth šlḥ*), which Fuller translates "but if you hate (her), send (her) away." (See his nuanced discussion, "Text Critical Problems," 55–56, and as well, D. Jones, "A Note on the LXX of Malachi 2:16, *JBL* 109 [1990]: 683–85.)

k. Following Sellin, *Maleachi*, 601, in positing the form *kĕkassēh* instead of MT *wĕkissāh*. The syntax is irregular and my translation is, therefore, tentative. 4QXII[a] reads *yksw,* a third-person plural form, instead of the MT singular form, which is preferred.

l. *ḥāmās* is often translated "violence." However, this English word, which connotes physical abuse, is inappropriate. See, for example, Gen. 16:5, "May the *ḥāmās* done to me be on you."

In Mal. 2:10–16 the topic changes. In the prior section the author had focused on priestly families and their responsibilities. Now the discourse includes all Israelites, as was the case in 1:1–5. The coordinate subthemes of love and family relationships pervade this pericope as they did the first two sections of Malachi. "Brotherhood" was a key issue in the first pericope, whereas Yahweh's "fatherhood" provides the initial motif in Mal. 2:10–16.

Before exploring the background of the significance of this language, one must note that those speaking occupy a specific rhetorical role, that of progeny conversing among themselves. As a result, there is a juvenile connotation to the questioning and self-judgment. Here again, the author has adopted the strategy of placing words in someone's mouth, which is typical of the diatribe (cf. Mal. 1:12–13, words that no one would have spoken).

After an interchange involving veneration of Asherah as well as other religious improprieties, a scribe has provided commentary (vv. 15b–16) that addresses the topic of divorce.

[2:10] The author's strategies are well chosen. The people speak and, in the interrogative mood, call into question their own behavior. They ask two rhetorical questions and then a "real" one. What is conditional and metaphoric in Mal. 1:6 is now, in Mal. 2:10, made into a stronger claim, namely, that the deity should be understood using paternal imagery. References to the "fatherhood" of God are surprisingly infrequent in the OT. Nonetheless, some proper names reflect this role of the deity—for example, Abi'el (1 Sam. 9:1; 14:51) and Eliab (Num. 16:1; Deut. 11:6)—and indicate that the writer is here using an inherited theological vocabulary.

The language employed in Mal. 2:10 reflects earlier notions of the deity. Deuteronomy 32:6 includes a question similar to that in Malachi, "Is he not your father, who created you, who made you and established you?" There the appellation of Yahweh as father is coupled with the notion of Yahweh as creator. This connection is also attested in Mal. 2:10 in the first two rhetorical questions. And then, in a text written within one hundred years of Malachi's date of composition, this same link occurs, albeit in a highly metaphoric mode: "Yet, O Lord, you are our father, we are the clay and you are the potter. We are all the work of your hand" (Isa. 64:8).[56] The notion of Yahweh as creator does not involve his role as creator of the cosmos. Rather, the language of human relations implied by the word "father" helps keep the focus on Yahweh as creator of Israel, compare Ex. 4:22, "Thus says the Lord, Israel is my firstborn son."

Despite the diverse vocabulary in the first two questions, God as father and God as creator, there is a unifying motif. The word "one" is present in both sentences. This motif, like the other vocabulary, reflects earlier Israelite traditions that speak about Yahweh as one (e.g., Deut. 6:4; cf. Zech. 14:9). The logic of the motif seems to be this: Since Yahweh is one and since he is the father of these children, they too should be one, that is to say, a people who keep covenantal faith with one another and who venerate one deity.

Because Yahweh had created a social unit, Israel, the writer could have the people ask the central—and not rhetorical—question: Why do "we" act in such a way? The term *bgd,* "to act faithlessly or treacherously," presents the driving indictment in this pericope; it occurs in vv. 10, 11, 14, 15, 16. In its first occurrence, the verb is cast in a reflexive form; *bgd* means to act negatively toward one another in the present, which has an effect on one's relationship to past members of the family. Here, language of covenant, as in the previous pericope, becomes specific, namely, "covenant of Levi," "covenant of our fathers."

The two verbs used in this central question carry important connotations. As for *bgd,* Jer. 3:6–10, 20 indicates that the term can refer to marital impropriety,

---

[56]Cf. Isa. 45:11; 63:16; and Jer. 2:27 on the improper veneration of the deity as father.

a situation that can serve analogically to depict an improper relationship between Yahweh and Israel. Or it can refer to the abuse of one's child, as in Ps. 73:15. Perhaps the most interesting use of the term occurs in Ps. 78:57, "they turned away and acted treacherously like their fathers," which raises the intergenerational issue as does Malachi. However, the logic is decidedly different from Mal. 2:10, since the time of the fathers is presumed in 2:10 to be one of obedience, not of apostasy. In all these cases, *bgd* seems particularly appropriate for describing family relationships, which is the formative context for Mal. 2:10.

The word *ḥll*, "profane," is regularly used within the ritual ambit to describe improper performance of sacrifices and other sacral activities. In the piel conjugation, the verb is associated with certain sacral objects, for example, the altar (Ex. 20:25), the land (Jer. 16:18), the name of God (Lev. 19:12). In addition, and consistent with Mal. 2:10, one may "profane" a covenant (Ps. 55:20; cf. Ps. 89:31). Such language of profaning a covenant does not appear in texts normally associated with covenant rhetoric (e.g., Deuteronomy). But the notion of violating a covenant, even a "secular" covenant (Ps. 55:20, "My companion stretched out his hand against his friends, he violated his covenant") is attested in Hebrew discourse. By extension, this language is placed in the deity's mouth (Ps. 89:34, "I will not violate my covenant," which alludes to Yahweh's promises to David).

These references to a secular covenant and to the Davidic covenant raise, in a pointed way, the referent of the phrase in Mal. 1:10, "the covenant of our fathers." To what specific covenant, if any, does the author refer? A number of scholars think immediately of the Sinaitic covenant.[57] Such a claim is, I think, correct, but it is important to note the contexts in which such ways of describing the Sinaitic covenant, as "a covenant made with your fathers," are found: Deut. 4:30–31; 29:24–25; Jer. 34:13–14. The latter two texts, both of which stand in the Deuteronomistic tradition, make it clear that this covenant was the one made between Yahweh and Israel at Sinai. Jeremiah 34:13–14 also refers specifically to Sinaitic covenant stipulations (Ex. 21:2; Deut. 15:12). For this literature, the definitive canonical version of this covenant is represented by Deuteronomy. Finally, as we have already seen, there are many ways, notably the reference to "one God" in this same verse, in which the "oracle" known as Malachi evinces contact with Deuteronomy or the traditions associated with it. Hence, it is appropriate to think about the Deuteronomic notion of covenant as the context for the author's understanding of what the covenant entails and what it might mean to violate the covenant.

---

[57]So, e.g., Rudolph, *Maleachi,* 272; Veuilleumier, *Malachie,* 238 n. 4; cf. Smith, *A Critical and Exegetical Commentary on the Book of Malachi,* ICC, Edinburgh, 1912, 48, "It is not likely that any specific covenant is intended."

Malachi 2:10 raises three questions. None receive explicit response. The first two answers are presumed: yes, yes. But there is no reason proffered for the faithless and profaning forms of behavior that lie behind the third question. One may suggest that it would be premature to offer an answer until more precise charges are brought. These occur in the ensuing verses.

[11] In Mal. 2:11, the speaker changes. Instead of Israel speaking, Judah is spoken about. It is unlikely that we are to think that Yahweh is speaking, since Yahweh is referred to in the third person. Formally, it is best to think of a prophetic speech. The prophet points a finger at Judah and uses the technique of personification to personalize the indictment. By using the word *bgd,* the author joins the present, as already conveyed in v. 10, to the past, which is described in v. 11.

In the second line of v. 11, the author provides a distinctive interpretation of the character of the covenantal violation that was described earlier and is more generally known as "acting faithlessly." We are now told that "an abomination has been performed." This term is prominent in the Deuteronomistic corpus, so much so that Weinfeld includes it in his list of phraseology characteristic of Deuteronomic literature.[58] In that context, the term regularly refers to veneration of deities other than Yahweh (Deut. 7:25, 26; 13:14; 17:4; 18:9; 20:18).[59] To perform an abomination is to perform some non-Yahwistic religious practice, as Deut. 17:3 makes especially clear.

The extent of the abomination in question is made clear by the merismus "in Israel, in Jerusalem." Judah, who had been described earlier in the verse, is now linked to territory as diverse as Israel, the vast empire of David, on one hand, and Jerusalem, one city, on the other. Here the author is again attempting to unite present with past and, simultaneously, to indicate the vast extent of covenant violation. The fact that the author returns to Judah later in this verse indicates that the present community, properly known as Yehud, is in fact the object of prophetic scrutiny.

The specific indictment, the particular abomination, is identified in Mal. 2:11b. The author provides a very specific example of an abomination, namely, an act involving non-Yahwistic worship: Judah has profaned Yahweh by venerating Asherah.[60] The first clause of this charge is straightforward, so long as one recognizes that the ritual language, "holiness," "profaned," predominates.

Who is this Asherah whom Judah is alleged to have loved? There is

---

[58]M. Weinfeld, *Deuteronomy and the Deuteronomic School,* Oxford, 1972, 323.

[59]The term "abomination" is also used this way in the book of Ezekiel.

[60]The phrase *qōdeš yhwh* might refer to the temple (Pss. 63:2; 68:22). However, it need not be so translated, contra RSV; Rudolph, *Maleachi,* 272; and with JPS. The phrase occurs only twice in the Hebrew Bible, here and in Lev. 19:8.

evidence from the Hebrew Bible that Asherah was venerated as a goddess in both Judah (1 Kings 15:9–13) and Israel (1 Kings 18:19). This history of the kingdoms, which was probably available to the writer of Malachi, may explain why both Israel and Judah are included as violators of "the covenant of our fathers."

Asherah was a goddess, known as Athirat, venerated at Ugarit.[61] She was a consort of the high god, El, mother of seventy sons, and designated by the term *qōdĕšāh*.[62] She was often associated with Yam, or sea, though there is ambiguity about whether this was a positive or negative relationship. She served as goddess both of sexual love and war.

The evidence used to create the above description dates to the late Bronze Age. There is, however, an increasing amount of epigraphic evidence to suggest that Asherah was venerated well into the first millennium, and now as part of Yahwistic religion. The inscription discovered at Kuntillet-'Ajrud mentions Yahweh and Asherah, so Naveh's initial translation, "I bless you by Yahweh, our guardian, and by his Asherah."[63] In addition, an inscription discovered at Khirbet el-Qom, and dating to perhaps one century later than the 'Ajrud inscription, also refers to Yahweh and Asherah. One may translate the relevant lines: "I blessed Uryahu to YHWH and from his enemies, O Asherata, save him."[64] In addition, there are numerous biblical references to the veneration of Asherah, many of which occur in the Deuteronomistic history, which itself may be dated to the sixth and fifth centuries.[65]

The chronological thread continues into the sixth century with the association of Asherah with a temple complex at Sidon. Following the analysis of Betlyon, this was a ritual site for the veneration of Asherah and not, as earlier

---

[61]W. Maier, *'Ašerah: Extrabiblical Evidence*, HSM 37, 1986; K. Koch, "Aschera als Himmelskönigin in Jerusalem," *UF* 20 (1988): 96–120; S. Olyan, *Asherah and the Cult of Yahweh in Israel*, SBLMS 34, 1988; M. Smith, "Yahweh and Asherah," *The Early History of God: Yahweh and Other Deities in Ancient Israel*, San Francisco, 1990, 80–103. In these and other works, there is considerable debate about whether Yahwists venerated Asherah the goddess or the asherah as a cult symbol and about whether Asherah was, in the Neo-Assyrian and later periods, linked with the veneration of Ishtar.

[62]This appellation is appropriated ironically in Malachi, namely, Judah has profaned the *qōdeš* of Yahweh.

[63]So the translation of J. Naveh, "Graffiti and Dedications," *BASOR* 235 (1979): 28. This inscription was found at a site in far southern Judah, and may be dated provisionally to the early part of the first millennium, approximately the ninth to eighth centuries B.C.E.

[64]Z. Zevit, "The Khirbet el-Qom Inscription Mentioning a Goddess," *BASOR* 255 (1984): 43. See W. Dever, "Asherah, Consort of Yahweh? New Evidence from Kuntillet 'Ajrud," *BASOR* 255: (1984): 21–37, for an assessment of both the el-Qom and 'Ajrud evidence.

[65]See for a discussion S. Olyan, *Asherah and the Cult of Yahweh in Israel*, who argues that only with the Deuteronomistic history is there a strong polemic against the veneration of Asherah, which was, earlier in Judah and Israel, part of standard Yahwistic practice.

supposed, for Astarte.[66] The case for the veneration of Asherah at Sidon, which depends on an assessment of epigraphic and numismatic materials, is clearest in the late Persian and the Hellenistic periods.

Nonepigraphic, archaeological evidence confirms these judgments based on texts and architectural remains. E. Stern has cataloged and analyzed terra-cotta figurines and noted that at a number of Syro-Palestinian sites, fertility figurines of ancient types continue.[67] There are, to be sure, new forms in the Persian period, most notably pregnant women or women holding children. However, these goddesses, of the so-called Eastern style (for example, those found at Tel Megadim, Beth Shan, and Makmish) clearly stand in continuity with their predecessors in the Iron and Bronze ages. Such figurines corroborate the notion of an important goddess, namely Asherah, continuing into the Persian period.

Robert Oden has argued that Canaanite religion, as it continues in its Phoenician, Punic, and even later forms, is fundamentally conservative.[68] On the basis of Lucian's *De Dea Syria,* and the evidence it presents for the continuing importance of Anat, there is good reason to infer that Asherah, too, remained a fundamental figure in Syro-Palestinian religion. She was venerated throughout the first millennium and hence was a candidate for attack by Malachi, as Mal. 2:11 clearly demonstrates.

To identify the abomination as veneration of Asherah enables a much clearer understanding of the final clause in Mal. 2:11. To venerate Asherah probably involved participation in sexual rituals. Judah, here personified as a male spouse, is described as someone who has joined with the daughter of a foreign god. This phrase vividly refers to Asherah, a foreign goddess.

[12] While verse 11 serves well as an indictment of Judah for violating a fundamental covenant norm, verse 12 follows as the punishing curse. The hiphil jussive verb, *yakrēt,* introduces an impersonal curse formulation, "may x be cut off" (cf. Pss. 12:3; 109:15), and modifies the comprehensive tone of v. 11, namely, (all) Judah. The curse is directed against a specific person, "anyone," and not "everyone," who might abrogate covenant stipulations involving improper worship.

If the curse itself is composed according to standard formulae, the reference to the group from which the miscreant comes is not. The phrase "tents of Jacob" is atypical, occurring only in Mal. 2:12 and in Jer. 30:18. There is good reason to think of Jer. 30:18 as an exilic composition. Moreover, the phrase "tents of Judah" is attested only once, in another postexilic text (Zech. 12:7). It would appear that the phrases "tents of Jacob/Judah" are a postexilic formula-

---

[66]J. Betlyon, "The Cult of 'Asherah/'Elat at Sidon," *JNES* 44 (1985): 53–56.
[67]Stern, *The Material Culture of the Land of the Bible in the Persian Period,* 158–182.
[68]R. Oden, "The Persistence of Canaanite Religion," *BA* 39 (1976): 31–36.

tion, though alluding to earlier language, for example, "to your tents, O Israel," which may be associated with holy war and the premonarchic period.

In the concluding portion of v. 12, the author raises again the nature of the infraction, human behavior that results from the veneration of Asherah. We now learn that the critical issue is multiple religious allegiance, attempting to worship both Yahweh and Asherah. If one has "married" Asherah, then it is inappropriate to present an offering to Yahweh. One should, instead, worship Yahweh alone. Rites involving nakedness and improper cohabitation, or as Glazier-McDonald translates, "the aroused one and the lover," are inappropriate for Yahwism. Here, perhaps in more than any other place, the author of Malachi sounds like a preexilic prophet, echoing the concerns of, especially, northern prophets—Elijah and Hosea, and later Jeremiah (as well as Deuteronomy)—that Yahwism not be contaminated by veneration of other deities.

[13] There can be little doubt that the clause "This also you do" is an editorial comment that connects the originally distinct but thematically related material in Mal. 2:13–15b to 2:10–12.[69] Both texts address religious impropriety, especially as they involve religious practice. Verse 13 itself includes the classical prophetic indictment and sentence. Here, however, the sentence has already been passed.[70]

It is difficult to deny that some form of rite involving crying lies at the heart of the indictment. Some individuals are, literally, weeping at Yahwistic religious sites. To be sure, weeping could have occurred properly within the context of individual lamentation rituals. However, the prophet seems to be arguing against some other religious practice.[71] Ezekiel 8:14 provides the crucial data: "Then he brought me to the entrance of the north gate of the house of the Lord; and behold, there sat women weeping for Tammuz." This text alone demonstrates that certain lacrimatory rites were associated with a deity other than Yahweh and were the subject of prophetic critique. Here, they were related to Tammuz, the dying-rising deity whose activity was often reflected in the annual agricultural cycle. In Mesopotamia, ritual laments were uttered at the end of the growing season.[72] Might similar rites have taken place in Jerusalem one century later, when Malachi was composed? We may answer with a qualified affirmative answer.

The veneration of Ba'al was typologically similar to that of Dumuzi/Tammuz since Ba'al, too, was venerated within the context of the annual

---

[69]Cf. the standard commentaries as well as R. Althann, "Malachy 2,13–14 and UT 125,12–13," *Bib* 58 (1977): 418–21.

[70]See similarly, F. Hvidberg, *Weeping and Laughter in the Old Testament: A Study of Canaanite-Israelite Religion,* Leiden, 1962, 121–22.

[71]On other improper laments, see 1 Kings 14:13 (LXX); Jer. 22:18–19.

[72]See, e.g., A. Falkenstein and W. von Soden, *Sumerische und akkadische Hymnen und Gebete,* Zurich, 1953, 185–87.

religious cycle. So, for example, both El and Anat perform various mourning and lamentation rites after Ba'al has been slain (*CTA* #5). And according to *CTA* #6, Anat weeps and sacrifices as a part of this lamentation process. The venerators of those deities were expected to perform similar rites. This judgment is clearest for Tammuz/Dumuzi: "For Tammuz, the lover of thy youth, thou hast ordained wailing year after year" (*ANET* 84). Hvidberg argues that just "as Anat wept over the dead Ba'al, so all Ba'al's people in Canaan wept over him. In this way she established weeping for Ba'al from year to year, as Ishtar had done it for Tammuz."[73] John Gray argues that the repetition of the details in the so-called Ba'al cycle are best explained as instructions for ritual behavior.[74] We may, therefore, infer that the ritual lamentation alluded to in Mal. 2:13 belonged to improper veneration of a male deity at a Yahwistic shrine, whereas earlier (vv. 10–12) the author had provided a critique of the veneration of a female deity, Asherah.

As a result of such ritual impropriety, Yahweh no longer is willing to accept "the offering." The term *minḥāh,* "offering," is ambiguous. It can refer to a gift or offering that is presented to a human (Gen. 32:13) or to a deity (Gen. 4:4–5). More particularly, within the ritual ambit the term can signify a grain or cereal offering (this is so especially in the Priestly material). Another word used in this verse, *rāṣôn,* "pleasure," can function elsewhere (e.g., Isa. 56:7) to describe the acceptance of burnt offerings and sacrifices as they are accepted on Yahweh's altar. By utilizing the vocabulary of ritual behavior in Mal. 2:13, the author has underscored his point, namely, that Yahwists have engaged in improper ritual practice, lacrimation, which is often associated with the veneration of Ba'al. Therefore, Yahweh no longer accepts sacrifices offered to him at an altar that has been sullied by such acts.

[14] Verse 13 concludes with an asseveration regarding Yahweh's unwillingness to respond in ritual dialogue. However, Mal. 2:14 demonstrates that verbal dialogue is still possible. The author uses the technique of placing words in the mouth of the party being addressed, "why?" which in this case does not constitute a rhetorical question. The interrogative particle offers Yahweh the occasion to develop the argument; and it is a striking development. The rest of the verse should be construed as an explanation of why Yahweh no longer accepts sacrifices. It is an explanation that utilizes the corporate covenantal logic expressed in Mal. 2:10–12. However, the language is personal: "Yahweh stands as witness between you and the wife of your youth." Many interpreters of this verse have gone astray because they have not paid careful attention to the various characters involved. Yahweh is witness concerning the relationship

---

[73]Hvidberg, *Weeping and Laughter in the Old Testament,* 52.

[74]John Gray, *The Legacy of Canaan: The Ras Shamra Texts and Their Relevance to the Old Testament,* VTSup 5, Leiden, 1965, 63. Cf. *TWAT* 1:638–43 (*TDOT* 2:116–20) on *bkh.*

between two parties, "you and the wife of your youth." Clearly "you" is Israel, the male spouse, thus allowing for a female mate. The "wife of your youth" is, I suggest, Yahweh, the deity whom Israel is supposed to venerate; and this in contradistinction to the improper deity, the goddess Asherah, another possible female spouse already identified in Mal. 2:11.[75] Yahweh is here viewed as the spouse of Israel, but this time a female spouse of the male Israel. The gender of the spouses is different from the book of Hosea, in which Yahweh was the male spouse and Israel the female. The reason for the switch in Malachi was the importance of attacking veneration of Asherah, an improper deity of female gender. Given the metaphoric system, Yahweh had to be viewed as the proper female deity.[76]

The verb *bgd*, "to act faithlessly," which occurs in v. 14, is also used to describe Judah's action in v. 11. In that former verse, Judah "acted faithlessly" by loving Asherah. In v. 14, Judah has erred by acting faithlessly toward the spouse, Yahweh. Verses 11 and 14 are two sides of the same coin. To venerate Asherah is to act faithlessly toward the wife of one's youth.

[15a] With the articulation of Yahweh's rationale for no longer accepting Judean offerings, the author concludes this section by asking two more questions. This time, the questions are rhetorical. They elicit a response, though nonverbal, from the hearers and mitigate the strongly negative tone with which this section began (in v. 13). Moreover, these questions create a grammatical inclusio with the questions with which this entire pericope began (v. 10). The inclusio works thematically as well as grammatically, for in both vv. 10 and 15a the theme of creation is present—has not one God created us, has not the One made us? Finally, these questions return to the masculine gender of the earlier verses, "father" in v. 10.

A new issue is, however, broached in the final question, "What is the One seeking but a godly progeny?" The question is rhetorical and the answer "nothing" appears apt. The question provides a transition from the fatherhood of God, v. 10, to that of divine or divinely acceptable offspring. The issue is not progeny. It is on this final and hopeful note that the original pericope concludes, Israel as holy offspring.

Malachi 2:10–15a is replete with flexible family symbolism. Yahweh has moved through the roles of father, female spouse, and, perhaps, mother. Israel has been husband, lover, and child. As the final sentence of this uniquely flexible gender language, the author offers an admonition, "preserve your

---

[75]On gender language for Yahweh, see M. Smith, *The Early History of God,* 97–103.

[76]B. Glazier-McDonald has mounted a similar argument, "Intermarriage, Divorce and the *bat-'ēl nēkār,*" *JBL* 106 (1987): 603–11, which follows up the tentative judgments of Hvidberg. Hvidberg, 123, had stated, "Yahweh is himself very near 'the wife of your youth' with whom Judah had a covenant."

vitality!" which echoes the earlier positive tone since it implies that the people have something vital to preserve.

[15b–16] Things change radically with the interpretation of the original pericope, which begins in the last part of v. 15. Some epigone wrote, "Let no one act faithlessly with the wife of his youth." In so doing, the scribe reuses language that had been created by the original author, though now in third-person masculine singular rather than second-person masculine singular form. What had been language directed toward Judeans, the personified Israel, becomes language directed to individual Israelites. Moreover, the topic changes as well. What had been reflection on improper religious alliances—syncretistic veneration of Asherah—now turns to the issue of divorce in the postexilic Judean community. Such commentary is natural, given the family and spousal imagery in the primary oracular unit.

The new formulation treats explicitly the issue of family integrity, and perhaps endogamy, in postexilic Judah. The language is social. Nonetheless, it is a recasting of earlier rhetoric, using *bgd* and the phrase "preserve your vitality," which concluded the original pericope. These quotations from the earlier text serve as a frame, namely, at the beginning and end of the supplement. However, the core and truly creative part of the interpretive addition may be found in v. 16. The scribe uses a classic prophetic speech formula, "says Yahweh, God of Israel," to buttress his authority. A new issue, divorce, and not simply acting adulterously toward one's spouse, is broached.

The interpreter commences using language appropriated from earlier in the book: the verb *bgd,* "act faithlessly," which occurred in 2:10, 11, 14, and the phrase "wife of your youth" (2:14). However, as v. 16 indicates, the term "wife of your youth" has a new significance. Now the issue is social—marriage and divorce—rather than religious.

Verse 16 begins with a pronouncement: "Divorce is hateful!" This is itself a strong statement, since divorce was a permissible legal act in ancient Israel (Deut. 24:1–4).[77] The key to understanding what this scholiast intends is provided by the simile that follows the formula of divine identification,

---

[77]See S. Schreiner, "Mischehen—Ehebruch—Ehescheidung: Betrachtungen zu Mal 2:10–16," *ZAW* 91 (1979): 207–22, for an innovative analysis of this pericope. Schreiner maintains that Malachi is consistent with Deuteronomistic formulations regarding divorce and presumes a monogamous ideal and contra mixed marriages. Nonetheless, he translates Mal. 2:16a in such a way that it allows for divorce. W. Rudolph, *Maleachi,* 271–75, thinks there are two separate units, vv. 10–12, which address mixed marriages, and vv. 13- 16, which address divorce. In his "Zu Mal. 2:10–16," *ZAW* 83 (1981): 85–90, he argues against Schreiner and reviews other recent studies of this pericope. C. Locher, "Altes und Neues zu Maleachi 2,10–16," *Mélanges Dominique Bar-thélémy: Etudes bibliques offertes à l'occasion de son 60e anniversaire,* ed. P. Easetti et al., OBO 38, Göttingen, 1981, 241–71, attempts to refute Schreiner's text-critical proposal and maintains that one central concern of the text is enabling divorce between Judeans and non-Yahwists.

"divorce is like a garment that covers wrongdoing." For this writer, divorce is judged negatively not because divorce itself is illegal or improper—at least the author does not say this—but because it serves to veil something that is amiss. The terms that this author uses do not allow us to be specific about precisely what is wrong, what is being covered up, unless we read this interpretation within the context of the text that is being interpreted.

In my judgment, the writer is drawing attention to a situation that develops logically out of the impropriety articulated in vv. 13–15. There we heard about Israel as male spouse acting improperly. (Just as the term *ḥms,* "wrongdoing," was used earlier to complain about an improperly developing family and marital situation, so now here the term may describe any improper marital situation involving Yahweh and Israel.) Israel/Judah had ignored Yahweh and gone after another woman, Asherah. Now, the logic articulated by Hosea centuries before weighs in. Divorce between Israel and Yahweh would be one possible outcome, the more so since in Israel the male spouse was usually the one who sued for divorce. Israel might sue to divorce Yahweh in order to respond to Yahweh's charge. However, Mal. 2:16 claims that such a divorce, though legally correct, might mask the impropriety of Israel's ignoring Yahweh. Hence, divorce would not be a viable solution in this situation, if the goal is to maintain the marital unit constituted by Yahweh and Israel. And this appears to be the purport of Mal. 2:16. The scribe insists vigorously that now is not the time for Judah or individual Judeans to sever its or their relations with Yahweh.

Much journal and commentary literature has understood Malachi 2:10–16 to be a negative judgment on human divorce. Such is simply not the case.[78] Rather, as with Hosea or Jeremiah, language about marriage and divorce has been used metaphorically to depict Yahweh's relationship with Israel. In this case, the author uses language of human relationships to comment on the manner in which the improper veneration of another deity, namely, Asherah, constitutes a primary affront to Israel's relationship with Yahweh, the wife of Israel's youth. Although some readers in the Persian period may well have

---

[78]C. C. Torrey made a similar point: "The sin which he is attacking is one of unfaithfulness, of false dealing with Yahweh. . . . To treat these expressions literally, as referring to actual marriage and divorce, involves insuperable difficulties," "The Prophecy of 'Malachi'," *JBL* 17 (1898): 9. So also A. van der Woude, "Malachi's Struggle for a Pure Community: Reflections on Malachi 2:10–16," *Tradition and Re-interpretation in Jewish and Early Christian Literature: Essays in Honour of Jürgen C. H. Lebram,* Leiden, 1986: "More decisive, however, is our conviction that Mal. 2:10–16 does not deal with divorce at all" (66). However, van der Woude thinks marriages between Yahwistic males and foreign women is the main theme. G. Ogden, "The Use of Figurative Language in Malachi 2:10–16," *BT* 39 (1988): 223, maintains "the issue being treated by Malachi is not marriage and divorce practices among the priests, but the failure of the present generation of priests to live by the demands of the priestly code." I disagree that the priests alone are addressed in this text.

heard the admonition, "Divorce is hateful!" to be a directive against divorce in human marriage (especially given Ezra's call for divorce of foreign wives), they, along with many other readers during more recent centuries, would have been guilty of reading a biblical text apart from its original context. The addition in vv. 15b–16 does provide direction to the individual Yahwist, "let no one act faithlessly!" However, the goal of that admonition was not to preserve marriages in Judah but instead to preserve Judah's marriage with Yahweh.

Malachi 2:17–3:5

Theodicy and theophany

2:17 "You have wearied Yahweh with your words.
  But you say, 'How have we wearied him?'ᵃ
When you said,
 'Every one who does evil
  is good in the eyes of Yahweh,
  and in him he delights';
Or (when you said),
 'Where is the god of justice?'

3:1 Behold, I am sending my messenger,
  he will prepare the way before me.
The lord whom you are seeking
  will come suddenly to his temple.
The covenant messenger in whom you delight,
  he is indeed coming,"
   says Yahweh of hosts.

2 "But who could survive the day of his coming?
  Who could stand when he appears?
For he is like a refiner's fire,
  like cleansing soap.ᵇ

3 He will sit, smelting and purifying silver,
  and he will purify the sons of Levi.
He will refine them as he does silver and gold,
  so that they might become officiants of proper offerings to Yahweh,

4 and so that the offering of Judah and Jerusalem will be pleasing to
   Yahweh
  as in days of old, as in former years."

5 "Then I will approach you for judgment
  I will be a swift witness

against the sorcerers and the adulterers
against those who swear falsely,[c]
against those who oppress the wage earner,[d] widow, and orphan,
against those who abuse the sojourner.[e]
They have not feared me,"
    says Yahweh of Hosts.

a. I read *hôgā'nuhû* instead of MT *hôgā'nû*. S V and many LXX manuscripts include the third-person masc. sing. pronoun.

b. An interesting case can be made for interpreting *bōrît měkabběsîm* as a substance used in the refining process, in which case the language of smelting would be the sole and controlling image in Mal. 3:1b-4. See Glazier-McDonald, *Malachi*, 147–48. One might therefore translate, "like smelter's alkali." Perhaps there is a double entendre.

c. LXX reads "who swear falsely by my name," which is a reading influenced by the identical phrase in Zech. 5:4. Hence, contra D. Freedman, "An Unnoted Support for a Variant to the MT of Mal 3:5," *JBL* 98 (1979): 405–6, MT is to be preferred.

d. Omit *šĕkar* as a dittography.

e. The phrase *ûmaṭṭê gēr* is probably to be reconstructed as *ûbĕmaṭṭê gēr*, the *b* having dropped out as a result of the word's having three labial consonants (*w,b,m*) in a row.

These verses do not appear to cohere. Why is the appearance of the messenger a suitable response to the questions about theodicy? What sort of transition occurs between vv. 4 and 5? There are no satisfactory answers. As a result, I will treat Mal. 2:17–3:1a, 5 as the original oracle, which focuses on the issue of theodicy, and 3:1b–4 as an interpretation, which highlights the impact of Yahweh's theophany on ritual behavior—a concern addressed elsewhere in the dialogues.

[2:17] Malachi 2:17 begins with a very brief claim that some group has wearied Yahweh with its words. The charge is so brief that it demands elucidation and response. Moreover, the charge is particularly apt, coming as it does beyond the book's halfway point. The people have already been speaking (Mal. 1:2, 6–7, 13; 2:14). Now Yahweh is tired of hearing them, even though the charge elicits further conversation.[79]

In this pericope, however, two particular utterances, and not simply all the accumulated speeches of the folk, provide the reason for Yahweh's weariness. The people made a statement and asked a question. Both seem to challenge the notions of justice that undergird much in standard Israelite wisdom, priestly, and prophetic rhetoric.

Of these two quotations, the second is, in both form and content, less radical

---

[79]Cf. the similar language in Isa. 43:24, "you have burdened me with your sins."

a challenge to the Israelite notions of theodicy than is the first one. Hence, the ordering of these quotations allows for the dialogical moves in a way it would not have done if the order were reversed. The question, "Where is the god of justice?" presents no obvious negative connotations. Such a plea might well occur in a psalm of lament; compare Ps. 89:49, "Lord, where is thy steadfast love of old . . . " or Ps. 22:1, "My God, My God, why have you forsaken me?" Moreover, to speak of a god of justice is to invite the sort of postexilic rhetoric preserved elsewhere in the prophetic corpus:[80]

> Therefore the Lord waits to be gracious to you;
>   therefore he will rise up to show mercy to you;
> For the Lord is a God of justice;
>   blessed are all those who wait for him. (Isa. 30:18)

To speak of a "God of justice" and to ask about the presence of the deity is, therefore, not unusual. If this question had occurred alone, we might be able to interpret it in this straightforward fashion.

However, such an interpretation is not possible because of the remarkable speech that precedes it. The tone of the speech is hyperbolic, as is clear from its reference to everyone who does evil. Moreover, the content of the speech runs contrary to the standard notions of theophany in Yahwism. This speech, like the questions that follow, echo formulations elsewhere in the Hebrew Bible. In this case, the linguistic resonances are with Deuteronomy:

> For whoever does these things is abhorrent to the Lord. (Deut. 18:12)
> For all who do such things, all who act dishonestly, are abhorrent to the Lord your God. (Deut. 25:16)

The similarities between the statement in Mal. 2:17 and those in Deuteronomy are so striking that they cannot be accidental. The author of Mal. 2:17 appears to have taken these formulae and turned them inside out. Instead of the expected, "for whoever does evil is an abomination to the Lord," we read, "everyone who does evil is good in the eyes of Yahweh." The transformation from *tôʿēbāh* (abomination) to *ṭôb* (good) is enhanced by assonance. And the purport of the transformation is to characterize Yahweh as perverse, as one who approves evil rather than good.

In most of the other quotations, the people ask questions (Mal. 1:2, 6, 7; 2:14). In the sole other noninterrogative formulation, namely, Mal. 1:13, the sentiment is negative: "what a nuisance." As with Mal. 2:17, it is difficult to imagine anyone actually saying such a thing—a rhetorical tactic characteristic

---

[80]On Isa. 30:18 as a postexilic text, see B. Childs, *Isaiah and the Assyrian Crisis*, SBT 3, London, 1967, 63.

of a diatribe. However, the claim about nuisance is in no way as radical a challenge to Yahwistic orthodoxies as is the long speech in v. 17. It is this radical affront to Yahweh's capacities as a just God that prompts the rejoinder in Malachi 3. One might well ask why the less severe of the two quotations comes first. The answer is simple. The question allows the deity (or author) to provide a response. In answer to the question of the deity's whereabouts as a just God, the author says: "The lord whom you are seeking will come suddenly."

Malachi 3:1–5 is complex, if for no other reason than that it is so difficult to determine the number of characters involved. There are references to "my messenger," "me," *hā'ādôn* (the lord/Lord), and the covenant messenger. In order to resolve the complexity presented by these characters, one must first recognize that these five verses are the product of a complex process of growth.[81] There is first-person discourse in Mal. 3:1a, 5 and second-person discourse in 3:1b–4. Malachi 3:1a, 5 have as their hallmark the explication of two roles, that of the messenger, who will appear before Yahweh comes, and that of Yahweh himself, when he appears as judge. These verses address the claims of the people in Mal. 2:17. In contrast, Mal. 3:1b–4 provides new information about only one character—the messenger—and what he must do.

[3:1a, 5] The deity begins this response by indirection, "I am sending my messenger."[82] This language echoes that of Isa. 40:3, a text in which a member of the divine council is summoned to prepare the way for Yahweh. Moreover, both Isa. 6:1–8 and 1 Kings 22 indicate that Israelites thought it possible for a human intermediary, namely, a prophet, to function in the divine assembly.

Once the way has been prepared, Yahweh will be able to approach Israel and enact the role of judge. However, unlike Isa. 40:1–11, the deity will not appear to comfort Israel. Rather, he will "draw near for judgment." In so doing,

---

[81]See similarly, Mason, 152; B. Malchow, "The Messenger of the Covenant in Mal. 3:1," *JBL* 103 (1984): 255; and A. van der Woude, "Der Engel des Bundes: Bemerkungen zu Maleachi 3:1c und seinem Kontext," *Die Botschaft und die Boten: Festschrift für H. W. Wolff zum 70. Geburtstag,* ed. J. Jeremias and L. Perlitt, Neukirchen-Vluyn, 1981, 290–92, and his review of scholarship; A. Renker, "Wer sind die drei Persönlichkeiten von Mal. 3,1?" *Die Tora bei Maleachi,* 90–93. Cf. Rudolph, *Maleachi,* 279, who thinks vv. 3–4 are secondary; Wallis, "Wesen und Struktur der Botschaft Maleachis," *Das ferne und nahe Wort: Festschrift Leonhard Rost zur Vollendung seines 70. Lebensjahres am 30. November gewidmet,* ed. F. Maas, Berlin, 1967, 232–36; Verhoef, *The Books of Haggai and Malachi,* 283, Glazier-McDonald, *Malachi,* 129, 149.

[82]For recent analysis of this verse, see esp. B. Malchow, "The Messenger of the Covenant in Mal. 3:1," *JBL* 103 (1984): 252–55, who argues that the messenger of the covenant is a priestly figure, one with an afterlife in expectations of a messiah from the tribe of Levi; and B. Glazier-McDonald, in *Malachi,* 1987, 128–35, and *"Mal'āk habbĕrît:* the Messenger of the Covenant in Mal. 3:1," *HAR* 11 (1987): 93–104, who thinks "the covenant messenger" and "the Lord" both refer to Yahweh.

the answer to the question, "Where is the god of justice?" will be given. In theophany, Yahweh will respond to concerns for theodicy.

However, there is an even more striking resonance with earlier biblical traditions. Malachi 3:1 echoes Ex. 23:20, "Behold, I send my messenger before you to guard your way."[83] The author of Mal. 3:1 has incorporated this motif of a messenger who will appear before Yahweh himself arrives. The figure is surely a prophetic one, since it was common in the postexilic period to think about prophets as messengers (e.g., 2 Chron. 36:15–16).

We are told nothing other than that the task of this prophetic messenger is to "prepare the way," a notion that is articulated in the book's epilogue (Mal. 4:5–6). There, identified as Elijah, he is to reconcile the fathers to the sons. Moreover, if one uses Ex. 23:20–22 as an interpretive backdrop, "my messenger" is supposed to enable the people to do something. In both Exodus 23 and Mal. 3:1b, 5, that "something" is obeying the stipulations of the covenant. Hence, the later interpretation of "my messenger" as "the covenant messenger" (3:1b) is an altogether natural one, as is the specification of the messenger as Elijah (4:5).

When the messenger has done his preparatory work, the deity can appear in a judicial role. As with Zech. 5:3, so also with Mal. 3:5 one has the impression that the author alludes to Decalogue-like formulations for at least some of the issues that Yahweh will address, namely, "against the adulterer, against those who swear falsely."[84] However, there are more infractions, which fall outside the boundary of the Decalogue. These non-Decalogue-attested topics—sorcerers, those who oppress wage earners, widows and orphans, those who abuse sojourners—are all addressed in Deuteronomy. Sorcery is condemned in Deut. 18:10. Concern for the wage earner, the sojourner, the widow and orphan are all attested in Deut. 24:14–17. Put another way, all the infractions cited in Mal. 3:5 are infractions against the stipulations of covenant as understood in the book of Deuteronomy. The final charge, "They have not feared me," functions as a summation concerning those who commit these various infractions.[85] And it too is characteristic of Deuteronomic rhetoric.[86] The list of those who act improperly is a broad one, encompassing both the secular and the sacred, though with predominant interest in the former, as befits the challenge to Yahweh's justice expressed in Mal. 2:17.

With this affirmation that Yahweh will punish various sorts of wrongdoers, Yahweh answers, decisively and directly, the two utterances that raised the

---

[83]See Petersen, *Late Israelite Prophecy*, 42–43.

[84]The vocabulary for lack of truthfulness is different here than it is in the Decalogue. In Malachi the idiom is *nišbā' laššāqer*, "swear falsely" whereas in the Decalogue (Ex. 20:7; Deut. 5:11) the key word is *šāw'*, "false." See textual note c to Mal. 3:5.

[85]Though, as Mal. 3:16–4:3 indicates, there are indeed some who do fear Yahweh.

[86]Weinfeld, *Deuteronomy and the Deuteronomic School*, 332, 335.

issue of theodicy. The god about whom they asked will soon appear. Yahweh does not take delight in various evildoers; he judges them.

[3:1b–4] Into this tightly constructed reflection on theophany and theodicy, another author has added commentary that expands on the notion of messenger. This author proclaims the imminent arrival of some character who will purify the sons of Levi and, in so doing, correct problems in ritual performance. Rather than the swift justice of 3:1a, 5, we now hear about a process like that of refining metal or, apparently, cleaning fabric (see above, note b). It is best explained with similes. This process of purification will eventuate in the presentation of proper offerings—an issue addressed earlier in the book (1:6–2:9), and hence, an issue that inheres in both primary and secondary material in Malachi. The fire is not one of destruction, but one of purification (cf. Ezek. 22:19–21; Zeph. 1:18).

The author recognizes that some fundamental transformation, like that of ore to precious metal, or like that of dirty to clean fabric, has become necessary.[87] Moreover, Levites are to suffer this change. The change, is, however, not total, as the similes themselves suggest. Silver is present in the ore, sometimes even visible, and is there as precious metal. The same fabric is there, whether dirty or clean. And Levites are the same Levites, not a future generation, not a different priestly group. The text concludes with reference to an earlier time, when Judean offerings were proper. The hoped-for future reflects an earlier satisfactory time, one involving, presumably, Levites active in Jerusalem. This commentator is, therefore, not a utopian but a realist, one who could imagine a proper prior moment and one who could imagine Levites acting properly in the ritual ambit.

The ambiguity in this material involves the identity of the lord and covenant messenger, who will do the act of refining.[88] Van der Woude is surely correct in arguing that the covenant alluded to involves reference to the covenant community and not simply a reference to the Sinai covenant.[89] Is he a minor deity or a prophetic figure as was the messenger in Mal. 3:1a? Is he the major deity, namely, Yahweh? We cannot be certain. If one accepts the latter option, the notion of *mal'āk* has changed from member to head of divine council, a change wrought by the author of Mal. 3:1b-4. If, however, one accepts the former, as seems more likely, then the prophetic messenger has been endowed

---

[87]A. Robinson, "God, the Refiner of Silver," *CBQ* 11 (1949): 188–89, maintains that silver is especially prominent here because in Israel's earliest experience it was more valuable than gold and because it was more difficult to refine than gold.

[88]One could argue that the covenant messenger and the lord are two different characters. However, the strong elements of parallelism between the two lines militate against such a claim.

[89]Van der Woude, "Der Engel des Bundes," 297. However, unlike van der Woude, I do not think that the author has in mind a particular protective angelic intermediary.

with the same sorts of powerful abilities that Elijah received according to Mal. 3:23–24 [4:5–6].

This commentary on the earlier, original text has a more "eschatological" tone, though it continues to treat matters of ritual concern. All this will happen soon, suddenly; and the effects will appear in the ritual world. The presence of the word "swift" (*mĕmahēr*) in the original pericope (v. 5), and the presence of the word "suddenly" (*pit'ōm*) in the commentary (v. 1b) demonstrate a common link, which is enhanced by the sense of movement by both messenger (3:1a) and the deity (3:1b, 5). Both these primary and secondary texts expect imminent action by the deity.

I have argued above that the "title" for this book probably derives from the use of the word *mal'āk* in Mal. 3:1. Why would a prophetic tradent have composed such a title? I suggest that, because of the content of this pericope, the use of "my messenger" in the title emphasized the imminence of Yahweh's arrival. If a booklet could be attributed to Yahweh's messenger, then, because such a messenger was to prepare the way for Yahweh's sudden appearance, one could reasonably view Yahweh as an about-to-appear swift witness. The title of the third *maśśā'* is itself an eschatological interpretation of material that seems less eschatological than that in the first two "oracles."

Malachi 3:6–12

Tithes, curses, and blessings

3:6 "Truly, I am Yahweh;
 I have not changed.
 Moreover, you are the children of Jacob;[a]
 you have not been destroyed.
7 From the days of your fathers,
 you have turned aside from my statutes,
 you have not observed them.
 Return to me and I will return to you!"
     says Yahweh of Hosts.[b]
 "But you say, 'How should we return?'
8 Should a human deceive God?
 Nonetheless, you are deceiving me.
 But you respond, 'How have we deceived you?'
 With the tithe and tithe tax.
9 You are now being afflicted with a curse,[c]
 and yet you still deceive me—
 the entire community!

10 Bring the full tithe to the storehouse
  so that there may be fresh food in my house!
Test me in this way!"
    says Yahweh of Hosts.
"I swear that I shall surely open up for you the windows of the heavens.
  I shall pour out upon you a totally sufficient blessing.
11 I will rebuke the devourer.
  He will not destroy the produce of your land.
The vines of your fields will no longer be unfruitful,"
    says Yahweh of Hosts.
12 "All the nations will deem you fortunate
  because you will become a pleasurable land,"
    says Yahweh of Hosts.

a. Cf. NRSV, "For I the Lord do not change; therefore you, O children of Jacob, have not perished." See J. Miklik, "Textkritische und exegetische Bemerkungen zu Mal. 3, 6," *BZ* 17 (1925–26): 225–37; N. Waldman, "Some Notes on Malachi 3:6; 3:13; and Psalm 42:11," *JBL* 93 (1974): 543–45; Rudolph, *Maleachi*, 1976, 281–82; Verhoef, *The Books of Haggai and Malachi*, 1987, 299–300; Glazier-McDonald, *Malachi*, 175–80. The first two lines exhibit several forms of parallelism, especially that of word order: particles, independent personal pronouns, proper names, verbs.

b. 4QXII[c] reads *yahweh elohim.*

c. 4QXII[a] apparently reads *wmr'ym 'tm r'ym,* which may lie behind LXX *kai apoblepontes hymeis apoblepete* (and you do indeed gaze away from me). MT is preferable as the more difficult reading.

Dialogue continues. After an initial proclamation, indictment, and admonition, there is a reciprocating movement between the people and Yahweh. The author refers to various problems, especially the lack of proper tithing practices, and agricultural difficulties. In analysis similar to that in Haggai (e.g., Hag. 1:7–11), the writer links proper human activity toward the deity with agricultural yield. Despite mention of the temple (v. 10), ritual matters as such (i.e., the sacrificial system) do not appear to be the subject of the discussion.

[3:6] The unit begins with observations by the deity about his constancy. Yahweh himself is unchanging, and the people have not been annihilated, as they well might have been. The characterization of the people as "the children of Jacob" underlines this theme of continuity; that is to say, this group may trace its ancestry to an ancestor who lived long ago. Despite slavery in Egypt, various military defeats, and exile in Mesopotamia, they still exist as an identifiable social, political (though now dependent), and religious entity. Yahweh could have wiped them out, but he has not acted in this way. He has consistently acted to preserve these "children of Jacob."

The first lines seem to reflect the logic and vocabulary of the first speech in the book. There too Jacob served not only as the means whereby Israel could be characterized but also as the way in which Israel could be viewed as someone whom Yahweh had favored. In that instance, Yahweh favored Jacob over Esau. Now, Yahweh avows that the people of Israel, as the children of Jacob, have not been destroyed, a clear demonstration of Yahweh's constancy toward Israel.

[7] If v. 6 alludes to Mal. 1:2–5, v. 7 picks up the theme and language present in Zech. 1:2–6.[90] The intertextual fabric is woven not only within this final *maśśā'* but between it and other biblical literature (cf. Ps. 78:8). Both texts refer to an earlier period, which is defined as that of "your fathers." And there is, in both, the rhetoric of mutual return, Israel to Yahweh—Yahweh to Israel. Moreover, both texts refer to Yahweh's (or "my") statutes (Zech. 1:6; Mal. 3:7). Despite these similarities, there are important differences. Zechariah refers to the time *of* the fathers, whereas Malachi refers to the time *from* the fathers. Zechariah admonishes the people, but receives no response; whereas Malachi admonishes and then receives a question from the audience "How should we return?" It is not clear that "my statutes" are the same in each text—in Zechariah they seem to refer to the judgment—the covenant curses— foreseen by the prophets; whereas in Malachi they seem to be covenant stipulations. Malachi, therefore, presents no simple echo of Zech. 1:2–6. The primary difference between these two pericopes is that Zechariah focuses on a moment in the past, whereas Malachi speaks of continuity with the past, Yahweh's consistency and Israel's disobedience.

[8–10a] The deity responds to the people's question with another one, "Should a human deceive God?" The deity does not directly answer their question nor does he wait for an answer. The deity's question is surely best construed as a rhetorical one with an expected negative answer. In its implicit form, the question serves as the basis for the deity's ensuing comment: "You are deceiving me." As the dialogue continues, "the children of Jacob" respond to that statement of Yahweh, and again in interrogative form. It is the last time that we will hear the voice of the people in this pericope.

In this, and at other points in these dialogues, it is clear that the continued interchange between these two parties is more than a simple statement, challenge, and response, as earlier form-critical judgments suggested. Continuing discussion or dialogue, and not a highly structured three-part discourse, is at work.[91]

Just as there was a general verbal encounter before the specific topic of

---

[90]Cf. Glazier-McDonald, *Malachi,* 183–87, who identifies a Deuteronomistic concept of repentance as the background for this verse.

[91]Again, Lescow, "Dialogische Strukturen," 198–200, recognizes some of this complexity, but deems it to result from accretions to the text.

polluted food had been addressed in Mal. 1:7, so here, tithe and offering only appear in the second part of v. 8, in Yahweh's response to the people's question. In v. 9, Yahweh continues to answer the question by indicating that the whole community is culpable and that a curse, which remains undefined, is now in force. (Verse 11, by implication, suggests that the curse involved a lack of agricultural productivity.)

To the question "How have we deceived you?" Yahweh ultimately provides a definitive admonition, "Bring the full tithe to the storehouse." Here, in pragmatic language, the issue is made very specific by dint of its reference to the tithe. As a result, one must understand something about tithing practices in ancient Israel. Unfortunately, this topic involves considerable complexity. The notion of a 10 percent tax or levy is attested for both temple and royalty (1 Sam. 8:15, 17). As regards the former, a number of pentateuchal texts, Lev. 27:30–33; Num. 18:21–32; Deut. 14:22–29, address the tithe. Leviticus 27:30 and 32, like Mal. 3:10, speak of the "full" tithe, which involves both agricultural goods, the flock as well as the harvest. However, Leviticus 27 does not indicate what the disposition of the tithe is to be. Numbers 18:21–32, by contrast, stipulates that the tithe is to be given for the support of the Levites—as their inheritance—and it too refers to the "entire" tithe. The Levites may consume this food in their homes, but they are required to provide one-tenth of that given to them as an offering (*tĕrûmāh*) to Yahweh. (The noun for this one-tenth of a tithe offering is the same as the one I have translated "tithe tax" in Mal. 3:8). Deuteronomy 14:22–29 discusses the tithe from several different angles, but focuses on two primary issues—the place where the tithe is to be offered and what is to be done with it. The tithe is to be taken to "the place which Yahweh chooses, to set his name there," namely, the temple. When there, the person who offers the tithe is to spend it on some comestible, whether food or drink. A connection of the tithe to Levites is mentioned, but is vague (Deut. 14:27). As with the other pentateuchal texts, Deuteronomy refers to the notion of the "entire" tithe (14:28). The third-year provision (14:28–29) appears to have the Levite in mind and is obviously a tithe different from the annual one, since the third-year tithe is to be held in the local towns and used by the Levites, widows, orphans, and resident aliens.

The most important nonpentateuchal references to the tithe occur in the book of Nehemiah. These illumine even more the admonition in Mal. 3:10:

> We obligate ourselves . . . to bring to the Levites the tithes from our ground, for it is the Levites who collect the tithes in all our rural towns. And the priest, the son of Aaron, shall be with the Levites, when the Levites receive the tithes; and the Levites shall bring up the tithe of tithes to the house of our God, to the chambers, to the storehouse. For the people of Israel and the sons of Levi shall bring the contribution of grain, wine, and oil to the chambers, where are the

vessels of the sanctuary, and the priests that minister, and the gatekeepers and the singers. We will not neglect the house of our God. (Neh. 10:35, 37–40; cf. Neh. 12:44; 13:5)

However, in Nehemiah's report, 13:10–12, we learn that these tithes had not regularly been collected, with the result that Levites and singers had to leave Jerusalem in order to make a livelihood (though how a Levite could own a field is difficult to comprehend).[92] Nehemiah's question, "Why is the house of God forsaken?" fits precisely with the discourse in Mal. 3:6–12. One may infer that in the early Persian period, Judahites were not practicing the tithe in an appropriate way.

This commentary does not provide the occasion for a detailed reconstruction of the tithe in ancient Israel.[93] However, it seems clear that Numbers 18 and Nehemiah 10 are concerned with the form of tithing referred to in Mal. 3, namely, the general tithe and the tithe of the tithe or tithe tax. All three texts may reasonably be dated to the Persian period and all speak of two tithes. Malachi 3:8, when referring to tithe and *tĕrûmāh*, is referring not to tithes and general offerings but to general tithes, which were collected in regional storehouses, and the tithe tax, which was sent to the temple in Jerusalem.

When Mal. 3:8 may be understood in this way, we are in a position to comprehend the two coordinate clauses of Mal. 3:10. The full or general tithe brought to the Levites was subject to a 10 percent levy. And it is this 10 percent tax which serves to provision Yahweh's house. Without the full tithe coming in, the *tĕrûmāh*, or tithe of tithe, will not exist or will be insufficient. Hence, the admonition in v. 10 is to the entire community (see Neh. 10:39, which refers to "the people of Israel and the sons of Levi" as those who will bring in the produce; cf. 13:12–13).

Malachi 3:10a stipulates not only that the tithe should be paid but that it is to be presented at a specific place, *bêt hā'ôṣār*, "storehouse" (cf. Neh. 10:39 [38]; 12:44; 13:4), *hallĕšākôt*, "the chambers." Nehemiah 13:12 refers to *lā'ôṣārôt*, "the storehouses," to which "all Judah" brought the tithe. These chambers were in Jerusalem, probably part of the temple complex, whereas the storehouses were out in the province. The people brought the general tithe to the storehouse(s), whereas Levitical priests brought the tithe tax to the chambers in Jerusalem.[94]

---

[92]See Blenkinsopp, *Ezra-Nehemiah*, 318, and Haran, *Temples and Temple Service in Ancient Israel*, 109, on Levites and the tithe.

[93]See conveniently R. North, "*'eśer*," *TWAT*, 6:434–38, who attempts a historical reconstruction of Israelite tithing practices.

[94]For a brief discussion of the *liškāh*, see M. Haran, *Temples and Temple Service in Ancient Israel*, 1978, 24 n. 20, 193. Weinfeld, *Deuteronomy and the Deuteronomic School*, 357, judges them to be "basically non-cultic."

The concluding segment of this first portion of the pericope provides the rationale for such tithing practice: "fresh food for my house." The author could have written, "fresh food for the temple." The formulation here is both personal, "my house," and vivid. The noun *ṭerep* is used to describe that which a wild animal kills and eats, for example, a lion devouring its kill (Num. 23:24; Ezek. 19:3; cf. Ps. 111:5; Prov. 31:15 for more general usage). Such usage requires a translation such as "fresh food." Foodstuffs were necessary to supply the sacrifices and to provision the priests (and the two could overlap; cf. Ezek. 44:29 and the diet of Levites). This pericope does not allow us to know the purpose that the fresh food would serve.

[**10b–12**] With the specific problem of general tithe and temple tithe addressed, Yahweh can continue in a new admonitory vein. Hence, this section is not so much formally as thematically distinct. First, the community is challenged to "test" Yahweh, to verify the constancy asserted in Mal. 3:6. This is unusual language. We know of instances in which Yahweh tests individuals (e.g., Pss. 26:2; 66:10); but only Mal. 3:10, 15 and Ps. 95:9 refer to a human's testing Yahweh. Psalm 95 construes the Meribah/Massah incident as an occasion in which humans tested Yahweh. There (see below) the notion of a human's testing the deity is decidedly negative. Malachi 3:15, in which the people argue against theodicy by observing that those who "test" the deity escape, is also improper testing. However, Mal. 3:10 presents a different picture, one in which Israel is challenged to offer tithes in order to require Yahweh to provide the bounty promised in Mal. 3:10b–12. The people are truly offered an unusual opportunity, the sole occasion when it might be possible properly to test Yahweh. This initial challenge concludes with a formula, "says Yahweh of Hosts," which also serves to conclude vv. 11 and 12.

The extraordinary character of this just-completed admonition is underlined by Yahweh's making an oath, the content of which continues through the end of v. 11. Yahweh swears that he will act in certain ways, if the proper tithe is offered. Although the promises might appear to constitute a new topic; namely, that which engenders as well as provides evidence of agricultural fertility, they appear implicitly in the dialogue before v. 10b. Tithes were normally paid in agricultural commodities, hence the standard phrase "grain, wine, and oil" (Neh. 10:39; 13:5, 12). Hence, for Yahweh to promise agricultural bounty is to retain the imagery of that from which the tithe is paid.

Malachi 3:10 not only promises rain but also underlines Yahweh's role as author of fertility, which, in turn, provides warrant for viewing the tithe as something due the deity. The poet, without using straightforward language for rain, appeals to commonly known features of the ancient Near Eastern cosmology; namely, the heavenly vault above which there is water, which may fall down through openings known as windows (cf. Gen. 7:11). Moreover, the vocabulary "pour out" is apt for water, even though the word choice is more conceptual ("blessing") than literal ("rain").

Verse 11 moves to a different aspect of agricultural life, something that might destroy the crops once they had begun to grow. The Hebrew participle *'ōkēl* has often been translated, one might better say interpreted, "locust." However, other creatures devour (flies, Ps. 78:45; worms, Deut. 28:39). Hence, though the author might have had the locust in mind, it seems better to translate with the more general term "the devourer." In using the more general term, as the poet had already done in v. 10, he has offered a more encompassing mantle of protection than if he had just cited one insect. (If he had, he would have used the vocabulary of Joel 1:4.)

The following two lines, which commence with parallel word order (negative particle, verb, preposition with pronominal suffix), stipulate that which will be preserved, again in quite general terms. "The produce of your land" and "the vines of your fields" are important in this oracle and in this general way because they provide the commodities from which the tithe will be taken. Such produce and vines yield the "grain, wine, and oil" mentioned above. However, the effect of such fertility will not only enable the tithe to be paid bountifully. The author avows that all the nations, a classic instance of hyperbole, will recognize Israel's good fortune as a pleasant land, so characterized by agricultural fertility. Yet this hyperbole emphasizes a motif important elsewhere in the book, the place of God's people among the nations.

It is difficult to read Mal. 3:10b–12 and not recognize the covenant ethos exemplified in Deuteronomy. Disobedience eventuates in curses (Mal. 3:9). And obedience results in blessings. In particular, the covenant blessings articulated in Deut. 28:10–12 refer to Yahweh's providing rain from the heavens, to abundant harvest, and to recognition by "all the peoples of the earth." The author of Mal. 3:10–12 has appropriated such covenant language and traditions to serve the cause of the tithe in Persian-period Judah. But such bounty will now result from a testing of the deity, rather than from straightforward covenant obedience.

This pericope is not addressed solely to the priests. The motif "all," vv. 9, 10, and 12, emphasizes that the total community is responsible for presenting the tithe. The people grow the crops and present the tithe to the Levites. But it is "the children of Jacob" who have been promised such marvelous bounty, and they are the people who will benefit from the round of sacrifices that have been properly provisioned.

Malachi 3:13–21 [3:13–18; 4:1–3 E]

Those who fear Yahweh's name

3:13 "Your words concerning me have been harsh,"[a]
　　　says Yahweh of Hosts.[b]
　　"Yet you say, 'What have we spoken against you?'

14　You have said, 'It is useless to serve God.
　　　What profit is there if we observe his requirements,
　　　if we walk piously before Yahweh of Hosts?

15　Hence, we call the presumptuous fortunate;
　　　even evildoers are established.
　　　They test Yahweh and then escape.' "

16　Then[c] those who fear Yahweh spoke among themselves;[d]
　　　Yahweh listened carefully and heard them.
　　Then a scroll memorializing those who fear Yahweh, those who ponder
　　　his name,
　　　was written in his presence.

17　"They shall be mine,"
　　　says Yahweh of Hosts,
　　　"a special possession for the day which I am creating.
　　I will act favorably toward them,
　　　just as a man acts favorably toward his son who serves him.

18　You shall again be able to distinguish
　　　between the righteous and the wicked,
　　Between the one who serves God
　　　and the one who does not.

19[4:1] For indeed, the day is coming,
　　　burning like an oven!
　　All those who are presumptuous and those who do evil
　　　will be stubble.
　　The coming day will consume them,"
　　　says Yahweh of Hosts,
　　　"And will leave remaining neither root nor branch.

20[2] But for you who fear my name,
　　　a sun of righteousness will shine,
　　　with healing in its wings.
　　You will go out, leaping about
　　　like calves[e] from a stall.

21[3] You will crush the wicked; they shall truly be
　　　like ashes under the soles of your feet,

on the day that I am making,"
says Yahweh of Hosts.

a. On the phrase *ḥāzĕqû ʿālay,* cf. N. Waldman, "Some Notes on Malachi 3:6; 3:13; and Psalm 42:11," 545–48, who translates, "Your words have been too much for me."

b. Restoring *ṣĕbāʾôt* on the basis both of a number of LXX manuscripts and the consistency with which that formula occurs in both this and the foregoing pericope.

c. LXX reads *tauta,* which would require the translation "thus" or "these things." The difference between MT and LXX is profound. If one follows MT, as I do, there are two groups, those quoted in vv. 13–15 and those who fear Yahweh and are addressed for the remainder of the pericope. If one follows LXX, those who fear Yahweh are those who have spoken that which is quoted in vv. 13–15.

d. 4QXII[a] reads the preposition *ʾl* instead of MT *ʾt.*

e. 4QXII[a] reads the singular *ʿgl.*

This final diatribe-like discourse is decidedly different from all those that have preceded it. The first two verses strike the reader as similar in form to the foregoing dialogues, with an opening comment by the deity and a questioning response by those addressed. However, the expected response of the deity to the people as a whole does not occur. In its place, the author introduces a new group, "those who fear Yahweh." They too speak, as did those quoted earlier; but we are not privy to what they say. Instead, the author simply tells us that Yahweh pays attention to what they say, and in a way that signals the acceptability of their conversations. Moreover, he speaks to them offering something very much like an oracle of salvation (3:17–21 [3:17–18; 4:1–3]).

One senses that the inability of these diatribes to effect significant change in the verbal behavior of Judean Yahwists makes this final pericope so different. Dialogue between the deity and "the sons of Jacob" has not proven productive. That which is said about Yahweh (3:14–15) could have been placed in the fourth unit, so Mal. 2:17. Put another way, Yahweh's speech in Mal. 3:1–5 appears to have had little effect upon those with whom he was in dialogue. As a result, the pursuit of such discourse now seems fruitless. Hence the audience for Yahweh's speech narrows to those who fear him. This final diatribe in the book of Malachi demonstrates the fundamental problematics of conversation between Yahweh and all Israel, even though the epilogue appears to attend again to "all Israel" (Mal. 4:4).

[3:13–15] The position of this dialogue as the final one in the book gives a special poignancy to the initial charge. There is now an accumulation of words to which the deity might be referring. Although the dialogue itself provides one set of words that the deity might construe as harsh (vv. 14–15), we may also infer that the author allows the reader to subsume all that which has been said by the "sons of Jacob" throughout the book as that which Yahweh construes as harsh. Hence this dialogue means something different in its position at the end of the book than it would have meant at the beginning.

The people's question repeats the adversative preposition '*al* with which Yahweh announced his initial charge. Hence, at this point the dialogue appears to be direct and engaged. That impression continues in v. 14. The deity quotes words that are harsh, that challenge certain traditional notions of what an individual might expect were he or she to obey the covenant stipulations. The rhetoric of the people includes both indicative and interrogative language—a charge that it is useless to serve the deity and a question as to what benefit would ensue were one to serve the deity. The question is surely rhetorical, presuming a negative answer. Verse 15 provides not so much an answer to the question as it does the response of those who view themselves as pious—they view the presumptuous in a certain way, as "fortunate," "established." Moreover, Yahweh treats them in a similar way, allowing them to escape unscathed when they test him.

Malachi 3:14–15 is a quotation that sets the context for all that follows. As in Proverbs, there is a bifurcated world in which there are the evil and the righteous, the wise and the fool. On the one side there are those who serve God, who observe his requirements, who walk piously, who are not presumptuous, who adjudge people, who are not evildoers, who do not test Yahweh. On the other hand, there are those who do not serve God, who do not observe his requirements, who do not walk piously, who are presumptuous, who are adjudged, who are evildoers, and who test Yahweh and escape. We are not told that the former group suffers, does not escape, or is not established. Rather, we may infer that this former group is upset that the latter group prospers ("is established," "escapes"). Instead of social alienation, there is jealousy and theological discontent. The issue, again, is theodicy (cf. 2:17–3:5 and many psalms [11; 12; 14; 54]).

But there is more than just a theological problem—there is a problem within the community. Who is it that one can identify as properly religious? What is the correct mode of behavior for a Yahwist? What external marks, especially as regards social standing and economic prosperity, might one identify as signs of Yahweh's blessing? These are reasonable questions, given the sorts of weal anticipated for righteous behavior in both the book of Proverbs and the book of Deuteronomy. Malachi 3:14–15 quotes the sons of Jacob as claiming that there is no correlation between serving God and well-being. The fortunes of the evildoers falsifies any such relation. (See the commentary on 3:6–12 for the notion of testing God.)

[3:16–18] The particle '*āz* marks a significant boundary in the text. It is a strong temporal statement, which denotes a break not only in the dialogue of vv. 13–15 but also in the dialogue overall. For the remainder of Malachi, including both the end of this pericope and the epilogue, either Yahweh speaks to the people, or the people speak among themselves, but the people never again speak to Yahweh. That mode of discourse is abandoned. Human conversation and divine admonition replace divine-human dialogue.

A new entity, "the Yahweh-fearers" are introduced in v. 16. How they fit into the bifurcation of the previous verses is not altogether clear, since the phrases used to characterize them (fear Yahweh, ponder his name) are not used in vv. 14–15. Moreover, we can only guess at what they might have said among themselves. All we can infer is that their words must have been acceptable to Yahweh, since after he hears what they say, they are memorialized in a scroll. The problem identified in vv. 14–15 is solved in theory, at least Yahweh knows who are true Yahwists. Moreover, there is a place—wherever the names have been written—where one could find out who it is that exemplifies truly proper behavior.

The notion of those who fear Yahweh is not idiosyncratic to this text. Psalm 15:4 refers to "those who fear the Lord" as those who are to be honored by the one who shall be present at the temple. Those who fear the Lord are admonished to praise Yahweh according to Ps. 22:23. But Pss. 115:11–13; 118:4; and 135:19–20 link the fearing of Yahweh with certain identifiable priestly houses, as in 135:20, "O house of Levi, bless the Lord! You that fear the Lord, bless the Lord!" Whether or not it is appropriate to think that those speaking among themselves are priests, either Levites alone or Levites and Aaronids, one must affirm that "the fearers" are part of those who were in dialogue earlier. To be sure, a distinct group is now overheard by Yahweh, but they are part of all Israel; they too have been part of the dialogue out of which this third "oracle" has been constructed. They are distinct and identifiable only to and by Yahweh and by their existence as a group in conversation.

The ability to identify these "fearers" is enhanced by the apparent inscription of their names in a scroll. But what is this book or scroll?[95] The only hint provided by v. 16 is that it was written before him, which probably means in the divine council. However, the ensuing verse provides the key. On "the day," Yahweh will construe these "fearers" as a special possession. This book will allow him (and them) to identify those who belong as his treasure. Without the book, it would not be clear—as it was not in Mal. 3:15—who the fearers might be. This scroll addresses a problem that had arisen in the dialogue and serves to remind Yahweh about the identity of those who feared him and who venerated

---

[95]Esther 6:1 uses the same phrase, *sēper zikkārôn* (NRSV translates it there "book of records"). The extent to which the book in Mal. 3:16 is identical or related to the so-called heavenly books (Ps. 69:28) or the book of life (Isa. 4:3) is much debated; cf. Ex. 32:32–33; Ezek. 13:9. See B. Glazier-McDonald, *Malachi*, 220–21; cf. J. Botterweck, "Die Sonne der Gerechtigkeit am Tage Jahwes: Auslegung von Mal 3,13–21," *BibLeb* 1 (1960): 256–57, who speaks of "one heavenly book."

his name. Moreover, the book's function on "the day" will be to enable the "fearers" to make the sorts of distinctions between the righteous and the wicked that had heretofore been impossible to make. The language of bifurcation (righteous, serves God—versus wicked, does not serve God) in v. 18 echoes the similar distinctions in vv. 14–15. But now, because of this book, both God and at least some Yahwists, namely, the "fearers," will be able to distinguish between the good and the bad within the Judean community.

According to v. 18, the "fearers" will be able to determine who the righteous are. This claim allows one to infer that those who are righteous form a larger group than that of the fearers, who are presumably "righteous" as well. But they—the "fearers"—are the ones called upon to make distinctions, to label someone as righteous or not. Such labeling is characteristic of the priestly role, determining eligibility for entry into the temple precinct, a role that may have been undertaken by the Levitical gatekeepers. This component of the text, when coupled with the relation of "fearers" to priests, suggests even more strongly that the "fearers" may be Levitical priests.[96]

The working out of the significance of the book is presented in 3:17–24 [3:17–18; 4:1–3] and from the perspective of day-of-Yahweh traditions. The noun "day" (*yôm*) occurs in 3:17, 19, 21 [3:17; 4:1, 3] and links this discourse with other OT texts that refer to Yahweh's special time as a "day."[97] What we learn first is that there will be a few people who belong to Yahweh in some special way. These "fearers" will be Yahweh's special possession or treasure.[98]

Malachi 3:17b notes the way in which Yahweh will act toward this special group, though with a remarkably general verb. Since the verb (*ḥml*) does not indicate precisely what Yahweh will do for these people, a simile is required. Yahweh will act toward his special possession as does a father toward his son who *serves* him.[99] This simile is odd. Another possible, more traditional simile might have read "toward his son." In that example, an expression of paternal love would have been at work. However, the notion of a son "serving" his father obviates that interpretation. Not only must the individual be a son, that

[96]See P. Hanson, *The People Called: The Growth of Community in the Bible,* San Francisco, 1986, 284: " 'Those who fear the Lord' in these psalms seems to designate a group entitled to a place of honor in the worship life of the people equivalent to that of the priestly house. . . ." J. Blenkinsopp, "A Jewish Sect of the Persian Period," *CBQ* 52 (1990): 5–20, identifies these "fearers" as "a pietist and prophetic-eschatological group" that is also attested in Isa. 65:13–16; 66:1–5.

[97]Cf. the many references to Yahweh's day in the second "oracle" and in other prophetic texts, e.g., Zeph. 3:11–13.

[98]See M. Greenberg, "Hebrew *Sĕgullāh:* Akkadian *Sikiltu,*" *JAOS* 71 (1951): 172–74 for a discussion of this Hebrew word. I agree with Glazier-McDonald, *Malachi,* 224, that the term here does not refer to all Israel, as it does in Ex. 19:5 and elsewhere, but only to a portion of Yahwists, in this case probably priests.

[99]Though the vocabulary of father and son occurs in Mal. 1:6, the issue is different.

individual must "serve" his father. Only then will the father act favorably toward the son. The imagery is something other than "normal" paternal affection.[100] One senses that the peculiar character of this rhetoric depends on the problem that it is addressing, namely, Mal. 3:14, which states that serving God provides no reward. Verse 17 denies this charge, but promises reward only for those who "fear Yahweh."

[3:19–21 (4:1–3E)] The final three verses are introduced by a disjunctive clause that highlights the immediacy and prominence of "the day" as well as sets off these verses as a distinct section in the pericope.[101] "The day" is important in this final pericope. However, the author is not interested in exploring the "the day of Yahweh" as does the author of the second "oracle" (Zechariah 12–14). Instead, the author of Mal. 3:13–21 [3:13–18; 4:1–3] is interested primarily in how certain humans, characterized as the evil or wicked versus the "fearers" or righteous, will fare and function at that momentous time. Dichotomous language for humans continues, as it had in vv. 14–15, 18.

The section commences with attention to both the imminence and the flammatory character of that day. The author uses a simile—the image of an oven—to characterize the intense heat, a motif that unites these three verses. Unlike the fire for smelting (cf. Mal. 3:2–3), this oven, which presumably refers to the earthenware oven used for cooking, produces a kind of heat that this author construes as essentially destructive. On that day, the evil ones will be burned as stubble is burned. Then, in yet another image, extremities of vegetable growth, root or branch, will be burned (cf. Isa. 6:13). The author anticipates that the wicked will be destroyed totally.

Here too, the imagery provides an answer to the problem raised in the dialogue. According to Mal. 3:15, evildoers do not suffer; Mal. 3:19 [4:1] counters with imagery of their conflagration (the same word for evil occurs in both verses). The author refers to those who will suffer this fate in third-person terms, "all those who" and "them." They are not in dialogue with the deity, nor are they addressed directly. The difference between third-person and second-person grammar underscores the dichotomy between the good and the evil.

In contrast to the way 3:19 [4:1E] refers to the presumptuous ones, the next two verses address a group with second-person plural grammar, "you." These are the "fearers" of his name (cf. the similar description in 3:16). Their fate on that day is linked with an object often associated with heat, the sun. However,

---

[100]Cf. J. Greenfield, "Two Biblical Passages in the Light of Their Near Eastern Background—Ezekiel 16:30 and Malachi 3:17," *EI* 19 (1982): 56–60, who maintains that there is a standard ancient Near Eastern practice in which parents offer preferential treatment for the son who "serves" them.

[101]English translations signal this break with the beginning of a new chapter, Malachi 4, a division that dates to a period at least as early as the LXX. This segmentation of the text breaks the integrity of the pericope.

unlike the oven (v. 1), the sun may also illumine a scene and induce certain forms of behavior. However, the poet does much more than refer to the general power of the sun. The language is both conceptual and graphic: "a sun of righteousness . . . with healing in its wings." How may the sun be related to righteousness and what does it mean to speak of a winged sun? Fortunately, it is possible to proffer answers for both these questions. First, Othmar Keel has collected abundant examples of a winged sun disk in the artifactual remains of both ancient Mesopotamia and Egypt.[102] Throughout the ancient Near East, the upper tier of the universe could be represented by a circle or disk, which has wings on either side. The disk surely symbolizes the sun, and the wings symbolize the heavenly vault or sky, or possibly the rays of the sun. The wings signify not so much the movement of the sun through the sky but rather the sheltering presence of the firmament, which held back the heavenly ocean. Moreover, the winged sun disk could serve as an icon for the Mesopotamian god associated with the sun, Shamash. This last connection helps answer the second question, which involves the significance of "righteousness."[103] Shamash served as the god associated with the principles of law, namely, the distributive principle of justice and the principle of beneficence, "righteousness" (in Akkadian, *mešarum* and *kittum* respectively).[104] Hence, it is altogether proper to think of the sun as signifying righteousness (the more so since this "sun of righteousness" is to shine on the righteous, v. 18).

These notions were not foreign to Israel. There is mounting evidence that Yahweh was venerated using solar imagery in ancient Israel, particularly with the rise of monarchy.[105] The notion of the sun shining may symbolize the effect of the deity functioning as ruler. Compare the analogical description of the human king in 2 Sam. 23:3–4: "One who rules over people justly, ruling in the fear of God, he shines on them . . . . " (It is striking that in both 2 Sam. 23:4 and in Mal. 3:13–21 [3:13–18; 4:1–3] "fear" is prominent.) The accompanying notion of health is emblematic of the well-being associated with a king ruling properly; compare Isa. 58:8, another late prophetic text that links light, health, and righteousness.

The poet picks out one element of this promise for elucidation, namely, that of health. F. Vattioni has argued, on the basis of month names preserved in Phoenician inscriptions, that the sun god is to be associated with healing.[106] As

---

[102]O. Keel, *The Symbolism of the Biblical World: Ancient Near Eastern Iconography and the Book of Psalms*, New York, 1978, 27–30.

[103]See similarly, F. Vattioni, "Malachia 3,20 e l'origine della giustizia in Oriente," *RBiblt* 6 (1958): 353–60; Botterweck, "Die Sonne der Gerechtigkeit am Tage Jahwes," 259.

[104]See S. Paul, *Studies in the Book of the Covenant in the Light of Cuneiform and Biblical Law*, VTSup 18, Leiden, 1970, 5–7.

[105]So M. Smith, *The Early History of God: Yahweh and Other Deities in Ancient Israel*, 115–21.

[106]F. Vattioni, "Mal. 3,20 e un mese del calendario fenicio," *Bib* 40 (1959): 1012–15.

a result, one should think that the phrase "with health in its wings" reflects standard understandings of the sun god. The image of the "fearers," who benefit from such health, is then athleticized and explored with a simile. In a truly creative move, the author expresses health with fertility imagery. They shall go "leaping about" into the full light of the sun, just as does a calf from its stall (cf. Jer. 46:21). The vehicle of the simile, imagery drawn from animal husbandry, is apt for a discussion of fertility; thus the young male animal is itself a sign of its parents' fecundity.[107]

Does the author remain with this simile in 3:21 [4:3], or does the imagery revert to that of humans? There is no obvious answer. Either an animal or a human could crush (*'ss*) something, though the nominal form *'āsîs*, "wine," appears to refer to wine that has resulted from grapes crushed by humans. "The soles of your feet" can refer either to a human, Deut. 2:5, or to an animal, Ezek. 1:7—a calf. However, there is strong parallelism, both in sound and in grammar, between the lines: "you will go out leaping" and "you will crush the wicked" (in Hebrew, *wîṣā'tem ûpištem // wĕ'assôtem rĕšā'îm*), forms of parallelism that allow one to infer that the simile does not continue; the line "you will go out leaping" precedes the simile. The "fearers" will crush the wicked since the latter will be like ashes lying on the ground upon which the people are running about (so v. 1). The simile does not convey an image of combat or conflict. The "fearers" step on the residue from the fiery destruction of the wicked, who have already been destroyed.

This final discussion in Malachi stands somewhere between the negative conclusion to the first "oracle" and the positive conclusion to the second "oracle." Malachi 3:1–21 [3:1–18; 4:1–3] proffers good news to the righteous and news of destruction to the wicked. One does not, however, on the basis of either the entire book or the imagery of Mal. 3:16, have the impression that the final scroll has been written. Moreover, the testimony of Mal. 3:14–15 indicates that it is difficult indeed to know who are the righteous and who are the wicked. Finally, since so much of the book has occurred in diatribe-like form, one senses that the rhetoric of Malachi is not that of announcing a decision but rather of calling people to ponder that which has been said, both by the deity and by some Judean Yahwists.

---

[107]The reference to stall may also enhance the notion of fertility if, as some claim, animals were tied in stalls when they were fed, e.g., Glazier-McDonald, *Malachi*, 241.

Malachi 3:22–24 [4:4–6E]

Epilogue

3:22[4:4] "Remember the torah of my servant Moses,
      that which I commanded him
    at Horeb for all Israel—
        statutes and judgments!
23[5] Truly, I am sending to you
    Eliyah[a] the prophet
  before the great and fearful
    day of Yahweh arrives.
24[6] He will reconcile fathers to sons
    and sons to their fathers.[b]
  Otherwise I would come[c]
    and strike the earth with a curse."[d]

a. I use this spelling to signify that here (and in 2 Kings 1:3, 4, 8, 12) the name of that prophet is spelled *'ēliyyāh* instead of *'ēliyyāhû,* as it is in all other instances, e.g., 1 Kings 17:1. The difference involves an abbreviation of the divine name, *yāhû* to *yāh,* and may be viewed simply as a variant spelling.

b. Literally, "he will turn hearts of fathers to sons and hearts of sons to their fathers."

c. The syntax allows various translations; cf. NRSV "so that I will not come and strike the land with a curse"; JPS "so that, when I come, I do not strike the whole land with utter destruction"; and REB "lest I come and put the land under a ban to destroy it." The key issue involves the translation of *pen,* traditionally "lest," which I take to introduce a contrary-to-fact clause, so B. Waltke and M. O'Connor, *An Introduction to Biblical Hebrew Syntax* (Winona Lake, Ind., 1990), section 31.6.1., on "the use of the unmarked prefix conjugation with irreal modal nuances" and *pen* as a negative telic particle.

d. LXX has a different word order. Verse 22 [4] occurs after vv. 23–24 [5–6], which, given LXX's translation of MT's v. 24b [6b], offers a gentler ending to the book.

These verses do not constitute another diatribe. The opening imperative verb demonstrates that the poetic world is one of admonitory discourse (and divine declaration, 3:23 [4:5]). The first question that these verses raise is that of coherence. Are there two sayings (v. 21 [3] and vv. 23–24 [5–6]) or one (vv. 21–24 [3–6])? Despite the reconfiguration of these verses in the LXX, I find no compelling reason to view them as something other than a single, monitory and explanatory epilogue to the series of dialogues that have made up the book.[108] Though the mood of the verbs is different, with them an author has created a careful tapestry that both challenges and provides a hopeful perspective to the readers of the foregoing literature. It is tapestry woven out of diverse threads from Malachi (1:6), from other prophetic books (e.g., Joel 2:31), from prophetic traditions in the former prophets (i.e., Elijah), and from the pentateuch (v. 4 and its allusions to "statutes and judgments"). Whether the author is the same as the one responsible for either the primary or secondary material in the dialogues is impossible to determine.[109] However, indecision on this issue need not preclude attention to the significance of this epilogue (see below on the specific character of these verses as an epilogue).

[3:22 (4:4E)] The author challenges his audience to "remember the torah of my servant Moses."[110] What would it mean to do that, or more specifically: what does it mean to remember torah, and what is this torah? We are aided in answering these questions when we recognize that much of the language in this verse may also be found in Deuteronomy or the Deuteronomistic history.[111] The phrase, "the torah of Moses" (Josh. 8:31, and then later in Neh. 8:1), Moses as Yahweh's servant (Deut. 34:5; Josh. 1:2), the vocabulary of statutes and judgments (e.g., Deut. 4:5), reference to Yahweh's will as torah (Deut. 17:19), reference to the mountain as Horeb (Deut. 1:2), reference to "all Israel" (Deut. 1:1)—all these characterize the book of Deuteronomy (or the Deuteronomistic history).

However, not all the rhetoric echoes that of Deuteronomy. "Remember" in Deuteronomy does not mean remember and do, as it apparently does in Mal. 3:22 [4:4].[112] Rather, in Deuteronomy the verb means to recollect some earlier act of Yahweh (Deut. 7:18; 9:7, 27; 25:17). But in Malachi, Israel is called to recollect the torah. The granting of torah to Israel has, in the eyes of the author, become analogous to the other mighty acts of Yahweh. Moreover, and this is a creative move on the prophet's part, remembering torah involves something more concrete than recollecting earlier deeds. Torah includes "statutes and judgments," which require obedience not simply recitation. The author of these

[108]Cf. Rudolph, *Maleachi,* 289–90; Coggins, *Haggai, Zechariah, Malachi,* 78–80; Smith, *Micah-Malachi,* 340, who understand these to comprise two different additions.

[109]The most compelling argument for a different author is that v. 23 [4:5] attempts to specify the identity of the messenger identified in Mal. 3:1.

[110]On the fourteen occurrences of this phrase, see A. Renker, *Die Tora bei Maleachi,* 98–101, and the literature cited there. Many of the fifth-century B.C.E. references to torah of Moses specify that it is a written document, so 2 Chron. 23:18; Ezra 3:2; Neh. 8:1. Renker thinks Mal. 3:22 [4:4] is related to the *Schema der Beweisführung.*

[111]This argument has been made by numerous scholars, e.g., Mason, *The Books of Haggai, Zechariah, and Malachi,* 159; cf. A. van der Woude, *Haggai-Maleachi,* De Prediking van het Oude Testament, Nijkerk, 1982, 157–58, who maintains it is Chronistic.

[112]Contra Mason, *The Books of Haggai, Zechariah, and Malachi,* 159.

verses has redefined the notion of remembering, as it was exemplified in the torah, to include that of compliance with the covenant statutes.[113]

There are even more creative ploys at work in this initial verse of the epilogue. Malachi 3:22 [4:4] embodies a claim that torah is still valid, that something like the covenant between Yahweh and Israel expressed in the book of Deuteronomy remains in force. No new covenant needs to be created, nor does an old one need to be renewed. Yahweh's covenant with Israel remains a conditional covenant, which can either be obeyed or disobeyed. The defeat of Jerusalem in 587 B.C.E., when read as the invocation of the covenant curses, did not spell the end of the covenant relationship between Yahweh and his people. As a result, the people can be called to remember (and obey) the discrete statutes of the covenant.

Moreover, Moses is viewed by this author as the one who received torah from Yahweh. In emphasizing this role of Moses, the author at the same time deemphasizes another role of Moses, namely, that of prophet.[114] This author is interested in Moses, not as paradigmatic prophet (Deut. 18; 34:10–12) but as torah recipient.[115] It is this role that enables the author to link the last "oracle" to the beginning of the canon, the torah. To meet the challenges addressed in the discussions that make up this third oracle, the author maintains that one must "remember" torah, which can signify the earliest part of the canon.

[3:23–24 (4:5–6)] There is no direct syntactic link between vv. 22 and 23 [4–5]. The particle *hinnēh* introduces a new form of discourse, participle followed by converted perfect verb ("he will reconcile"). The author emphasizes the contrast between what Yahweh is about to do for Judean Yahwists, namely, send Eliyah, and what he might have done, namely, blast the land with a curse.

---

[113]Contra S. Sperling, "Rethinking Covenant in Late Biblical Books," *Bib* 70 (1989): 50–73, who maintains that covenant formulations in postexilic literature, including Mal. 3:22 [4:4], involve the notion of an unconditional covenant. Cf. D. McCarthy, "Covenant in Narratives from Late OT Times," *The Quest for the Kingdom of God: Studies in Honor of George E. Mendenhall*, Winona Lake, Ind., 1983, 92, who makes a similar judgment based on even later material.

One must recognize the prominence of this so-called Deuteronomic language in Ezra-Nehemiah. Nehemiah 1:7–9 speaks of "statutes and judgments"; Neh. 8:1 refers to "the book of the torah of Moses." McCarthy's articulation of "covenant renewal" in Ezra-Nehemiah suggests that an unconditional covenant did not inhere in that literature; see "Covenant and Law in Chronicles-Nehemiah," *CBQ* 44 (1982): 32–35.

[114]This ploy is doubly important since it opens the opportunity for another prophet, Elijah, to fill the role of "the prophet," Mal. 3:23 [4:5]. The interplay between Moses and Elijah in these verses suggests strongly that they stem from one hand.

[115]Contra Glazier-McDonald, *Malachi*, 265–67; Blenkinsopp, *Prophecy and Canon*, 183 n. 79. D. Clark argues that Mal. 3:23–24 [4:5–6] is "a counterpart" to Deut. 34:10–12, "Elijah as Eschatological High Priest: An Examination of the Elijah Tradition in Mal. 3:23–24" (Ph.D. diss., University of Notre Dame, 1975).

Moreover, the first clause of 3:23 [4:5] echoes that of 3:1, "Truly I am sending . . . ," and the individual who wrote it seems interested in identifying the messenger.[116] In so doing, he has placed the messenger language within the eschatological scenario, namely, the expectation that a prophet will presage the theophany of Yahweh.

This divine speech builds on the expectation that prophecy in some form will return before Yahweh acts decisively on his day.[117] Apart from Mal. 3:23–24 [4:5–6], this expectation is expressed elsewhere in Ezek. 39:29 and Joel 2:28. Some early Persian-period authors deemed prophecy to be a thing of the past or to be polemicized (e.g., Zech. 13:2–6). But they anticipated a renaissance of prophetic intermediation.

The choice of Elijah to personify this expectation is readily understandable. That prophet had not died but had been taken into the heavenly realm (2 Kings 2:11). He was therefore available to return in a way that neither Moses nor other prophets were.[118] Moreover, as Childs has argued, there are a number of key relationships between Elijah and the situation addressed by Malachi.

> Like Malachi, Elijah addressed 'all Israel' (I Kings 18.20). The people of Israel were severely fragmented by indecision of faith (18.21). A curse had fallen on the land (18.1//Mal. 3.24, EVV 4.6). Elijah challenged all Israel to respond to God by forcing a decision between the right and the wrong (//Mal. 3.18). He did it by means of the right offering (//Mal. 3.3) and a fire which fell from heaven (//Mal. 3.3,19).[119]

Unlike most other prophets, Elijah had been successful. Through his instrumentality, Israel had turned to Yahweh and away from Ba'al. As a result, the writer of Mal. 3:23–24 [4:5–6] is sanguine that Elijah might again act to enable reconciliation, just as he is sanguine that (some of?) the people will respond positively to the appearance of Elijah as had Israelites a half millennium earlier.

Malachi 3:23 [4:5] also provides a temporal context for the appearance of

---

[116]So, e.g., O. Eissfeldt, *The Old Testament: An Introduction,* Blackwell, 1965, 442, "Mal. 3:23–24, however, are intended to make precise the proclamation of 3:1, of a heavenly messenger who is to precede Yahweh when he appears for judgment, and to correct this by indicating that Elijah is this messenger."

[117]See D. Petersen, *Late Israelite Prophecy,* 14–17.

[118]If Moses was *the* prophet from the perspective of Deut. 18:15, Elijah is *the* prophet for Mal. 3:23 [4:5]. This judgment does not involve a devaluation of Moses, but rather a recognition in the Persian period that Moses was increasingly associated with a distinct and nonprophetic body of literature, namely, the torah or pentateuch.

[119]B. Childs, *Introduction to the Old Testament as Scripture,* 495–96.

"the prophet."[120] We are not told how soon Eliyah will arrive, but we do know that he will come before the *yôm yahweh*. The author creates this clause using language extant in another prophetic book, Joel 2:31 (and Joel 2:11).[121] There, in a text that attests to the return of prophecy before Yahweh's day, an early Persian-period author claims that certain meteorological phenomena will presage that day. In Malachi, Elijah appears, substituting the sun turning to darkness and the moon to blood. Why? The person who composed the epilogue is anxious to address the question, raised in Mal. 3:2, of who will be able to survive *the* day and by what means. Malachi 3:24 [4:6] provides an answer, namely, that fathers and sons, reconciled through the agency of Elijah, will be able to survive the terrible day of Yahweh.

It is not altogether clear what sort of problem provides the figurative backdrop for Mal. 3:24 [4:6].[122] What might lack of reconciliation between fathers and sons mean? Several things may be said. First, mutual behavior using family language, "sons, daughters, fathers," also appears in Joel 2:28— they prophesy.[123] Reflection about Israel's covenant traditions provides the best answer. A curse could, according to normative covenant traditions (e.g., Ex. 20:5–6), extend over several generations. If one links this understanding to Israel's experience in the late sixth and early fifth centuries B.C.E., namely, of living a disrupted existence because of the "sins" of the fathers, one can imagine that the issue involves nothing less than Judean Yahwists' relationship to their ancestors (see also Pss. 78 and 106). The question of continuity with earlier Yahwists had been raised earlier in this "book."[124] Now, the author reports that it will be possible for the fathers to be related in a positive way with their sons through the actions of Elijah.[125] Without the integrity between generations, Israel would not be Israel. The covenant community extends both among people at one time and among people over time. In Mal. 4:6, the author worries about this latter feature of the sons of Jacob.

---

[120]As noted above, Elijah is "the" prophet, which is an even stronger claim than that he is a "type-prophet," the latter of which is maintained by R. Mason, *Preaching the Tradition: Homily and Hermeneutics after the Exile,* Cambridge, 1990, 137.

[121]Though arguments for sharing or dependence are often complex, since this epilogue presumes the existence of the minor prophets, it is altogether likely that the author of Mal. 3:22–24 [4:4–6] knew and used language in the book of Joel.

[122]One should reject historicizing interpretations, e.g., that fathers and sons might have been alienated when younger Judeans adopted Greek customs in the Hellenistic period.

[123]I have argued elsewhere that this text serves as the conceptual backdrop for Mal. 3:22–24 [4:4–6]; see my *Late Israelite Prophecy,* 44.

[124]See P. Verhoef, *The Books of Haggai and Malachi,* 342, on the comparable text, Isa. 63:16, "Abraham does not know us and Israel does not acknowledge us."

[125]It is not clear how Mal. 3:17 relates to this verse, though both use the vocabulary of father and son.

Malachi 4:6 concludes with a contrary-to-fact clause, which describes what might happen if Yahweh were not to send Elijah. Yahweh would send a curse against the earth.[126] The expectation of a worldwide, not just a Judean, catastrophe inheres in late prophetic material (e.g., Isa. 24:1; Joel 2:30). The scope of Yahweh's punishment for disobeying the "statutes and judgments" would involve covenant curses of cosmic scope. The concluding tone is, however, "contrary to that fact," as is Zech. 14:11. In the second "oracle," the author maintains that there will be no curse on Jerusalem. In Malachi, that promissory note extends to the cosmos. Here it is linked to the activity of Elijah, whereas in Zechariah 14 we are presented with no comment about how the absence of curse will be achieved. Yahweh will send Elijah to enable Judean Yahwists, who have followed the covenant dictates, to achieve some sort of reconciliation with their normative religious traditions and to survive Yahweh's moment of truth.

I maintained earlier that Mal. 3:22–24 [4:4–6] is an epilogue. But to what is it an epilogue? There are numerous possible responses: it is an epilogue to the book of Malachi, to the three "oracles," to the so-called Book of the Twelve or minor prophets, to "the prophets," to "the prophets" and "the torah," or to the entire Hebrew Bible? Though there is no easy answer, I offer three observations.[127]

First, this passage is not a summary of Malachi. It does not simply put that book in perspective, though it does diminish, as opposed to the introductory title (Mal. 1:1), the sense of immediacy one finds within some of the individual diatribes. Rather, the epilogue interprets some of the language in the dialogues; it is a making specific of the general expectation in Mal. 3:1. Hence, it is difficult to think that these three verses were composed by the same person who wrote the primary material in the dialogues.

Second, this passage knits the third "oracle" into the prior fabric of the Hebrew Bible. If Mal. 3:22 [4:4] establishes a canonical link between the third oracle and the pentateuch, vv. 23–24 [4:5–6] integrate the third oracle with the former prophets and the latter prophets. The former connection is established by allusion, the latter by quotation. Verses 22–24 [4:4–6] serve to integrate the third oracle into the first two portions of the canon.

Moreover, this canonical integration has a purpose. In a time when the various books were being stylized into larger collections, the author of Mal. 3:22–24 [4:4–6] does not argue that one section is superior to another but that

---

[126]Some prefer to translate "land," meaning Judah, e.g., Glazier-McDonald, *Malachi*, 258–59.

[127]For example, Rudolph, *Maleachi*, 291, argues that they serve as a conclusion to "the prophets," i.e., the major and minor prophets. Coggins thinks of them as a conclusion to the minor prophets, *Haggai, Zechariah, Malachi*, 84.

they were to be read together. As one confronts the problems articulated in the Malachi diatribes, which are themselves situated in the canonical context of the book of the twelve, one must yet remain loyal to torah and recognize what Yahweh is doing through the instrumentality of the former prophets. The past, as exemplified in Moses the torah figure and Elijah "the prophet," instructs the reader about behavior appropriate for the present and informs the reader about what to anticipate in the future.[128]

Third, an assessment of this passage is enhanced by comparing it to the epilogues of other prophetic books.[129] In fact, there are few epilogues in prophetic literature. I would argue that the only real candidates are Hos. 14:10 [9]and Hab. 3:19b. The latter is really a dedication of the sort one normally finds in Psalms. When that is admitted, the only two epilogues in the latter prophets occur at the end of the first and last books of the twelve minor prophets.

Hosea 14:10 [9] is similar in two ways to Mal. 3:22–24 [4:4–6], though their respective content is different. The Hosean epilogue relates both to the book itself and to another section of the canon. As Mays argues, the book's epilogue adumbrates "stumbling," which is an important theme in Hosea 14.[130] Moreover, Hos. 14:10 picks up vocabulary used earlier (e.g., *pš'* in (7:13; 8:1).[131] And there are resonances with another section of the canon, the writings (Ps. 107:43), and more particularly, the wisdom literature (Prov. 10:29; 24:16; Eccl. 8:1). Just as Mal. 3:22–24 [4:4–6] establishes connections with the torah and the former prophets, Hos. 14:10 [9] provides a linkage with the third section of the canon.[132] The two epilogues work together to relate the book of the XII to the other sections of the canon. One may argue that these two epilogues act as a canonical envelope, which encloses the minor prophets. They not only mark off but also integrate the minor prophets with the rest of the canon.

---

[128]See similarly B. Childs, "The Canonical Shape of the Prophetic Literature," *Int* 32 (1978): 46–55, though he argues for two appendices and not one epilogue. "The canonical effect of the first appendix to Malachi testifies that the law and the prophets are not to be heard as rivals but as an essential unity within the one divine purpose. The effect of the second appendix (3:23–24) [4:5–6] is to balance the memory of the past with the anticipation of the future."

[129]None of the three major prophetic books has what might reasonably be called an epilogue.

[130]J. Mays, *Hosea,* OTL, Philadelphia, 1969, 190.

[131]H. W. Wolff, *Hosea,* Hermeneia, Philadelphia, 1974, 239.

[132]One has the sense that, at the time the epilogues for Hosea and Malachi were composed, the canon was already being stylized if not divided up into a tripartite structure. Moreover, as I have argued above, ancient authority figures were being associated with one or another part of the canon, e.g., Moses with torah, as is evident in Mal. 3:22–24 [4:4–6].